Understanding Karmic Complexes

Evolutionary Astrology and Regression Therapy

Patricia L. Walsh

The Wessex Astrologer

Published in 2009 by
The Wessex Astrologer Ltd
4A Woodside Road
Bournemouth
BH5 2AZ
England

www.wessexastrologer.com

ISBN 9781902405438

A catalogue record of this book is available at The British Library

Cover design by Dave at Creative Byte, Poole, Dorset

Printed and bound in the UK by Cambrian Printers, Aberystwyth

All charts used and astrological calculations generated using Solar Fire Gold.

Contents

About the Cover

The photographer, Kimberley Flowers, named one version of this photo 'Blue Moon Lily Unfolding'.[1] The flower is of the Datura Genus and is known by other common names such as Jimson Weed, Moonflower, Moon Lily, Hell's Bells, Devil's Weed, Devil's Cucumber, Devil's Trumpet and the flip side – Angel's Trumpet. The different parts of the Datura plant have both poisonous and hallucinogenic properties - in other words, it can act as a devil who destroys you or as the angel who leads you to higher realms. Interestingly, in India this plant was once considered sacred to Shiva and Kali, who represent the paradoxes of simultaneous creation and destruction. In many indigenous traditions of South and North America it was the Datura who aided the shaman in journeying. Don Juan of the Castaneda books initiates his apprentice through the use of this sacred plant. The Datura plant is said to induce a 'true trance' state, unlike other hallucinogens that blur the lines of reality, Datura causes one to be totally unable to distinguish 'reality' from 'fantasy' which leads to the question… what is reality anyway?

Its presence on the cover of this book is appropriate, as a metaphor for the way we arrive on this planet – 'trailing clouds of glory' along with bucket loads of s**t. Our karmic condition can either imprison us in a hellish nightmare of endless repetition, which is poisonous to the soul, or serve to initiate us in blazing new evolutionary trails. The ultimate shamanic journey is not in-between the worlds, but here, in this life. The soul has journeyed here, to enter this dreamlike realm we call reality, to discover new depths of its own being. The 'medicine' of the Datura must be approached with healthy respect for its danger, much like our own deep processes. But the beauty of its gentle, spiral unfolding, reminds us that grace is ever-present and abundant…. despite our fears.

---

1. Cover photograph by kind permission of Kimberley Flowers of Kimayame Photography http://www.kimayamephotography.com

Acknowledgements

This book is dedicated to my Father
John Patrick Walsh
who joined our ancestors on the other side
the month before this book went to press.

There were two things my father consistently told me, "I am proud of you" and "Whatever you put your mind to you will accomplish it". Regardless of what I was dreaming up as my life's direction while growing up, from shoveling manure at horse farms to managing rock bands, my Dad's faith in me never failed. Because of him, there is a glowing ember of self-confidence deep in my core, that admittedly does brighten and dim, but never goes out. Through his graciousness, my father helped to create a 'blueprint' in my psyche of an archetypal 'wise and mentoring father'. This gift not only healed parts of my past karmas, but allowed me to be open in this life to receive guidance from other 'Fathers', which leads me to... Jeffrey Wolf Green and Roger Woolger. The process of writing this book triggered many of my own past karmas of persecution because of books I wrote or beliefs I spoke out about. The karmic scars of persecution stayed with me and caused me to fear 'coming out' and 'being seen'. Both Jeffrey and Roger helped me in their own way to heal those scars and learn to reclaim my voice and authentic self.

Thank you, Jeffrey, for making Evolutionary Astrology your life's work. Your passion for what you do, and unfailing desire to serve God/dess is reflected in the many lives that you have touched, including my own. I am personally grateful to you for your encouragement and support for this work. Long before I saw myself as a teacher or writer, you pointed me in that direction, with a certainty as if my own soul was speaking to me.

Roger, you have been a teacher/mentor, healer and 'soul brother' to me. From my first major regression where I 'got my tongue back' to teaching workshops with you, more than anyone else, you always encouraged my potential. In fact, it was your lighthearted comment ("Gee you have enough material there for a book"), while looking at all the case studies I had sprawled across the table, when preparing for a lecture, which set this book into motion. Your pioneering work has not only transformed thousands of individual lives, but has created a map that can be followed into a new psychology of the soul. It is my deepest hope that this book, serves as a signpost on this map, pointing people to the potential for deep soul healing that exists for all of us.

Special thanks to Moira Brown, who I consider my personal 'Shamanka', not because you do not belong to the world, but because when you work with me in sessions, it is as if only you and I exist. Your graciousness of spirit is only matched by the depth of your humility. Beside all of the soul crises you helped lay to rest, you taught me how to 'listen' with my whole being, and without that I would never be able to midwife healing for anyone else. For those who don't know you, your healing gifts and wisdom can't be summed up in a few short words, so readers please visit www.praesepeansessionwork.com/ or www.moirabrown.com

My humble gratitude goes to all the clients and students, for their courage to walk through the 'scary' places of their psyches, and allow me to be their guide. I hope this book with some of your personal stories included, has created a tribute to your indomitable spirits.

Special thanks to Margaret at The Wessex Astrologer. Working with you has been a pleasure and you have been a caring midwife for the birth of this baby.

Thanks to my friends, cheerleaders and various 'tribe' members who also encouraged and supported me in myriad ways: Rose Marcus, Kristen Fontana, Victoria Ramos, Maria Sullivan, Kim-Marie and LeRoy Weimer, Jinny Rodrigo, Tracey Savo, Lynn Bourbeau, Stephanie Clement, Deva Green, Muriel McMahon, Lisa Abend, Pam Strugar, Steve Wolfson, Charlie Edgarton, Patty Hall, Kim Burgess, Laura Nalbandian, Steve Wolfgram, Casandra Akins, Steven and Jodie Forrest, Harriet Oomen, Rainer Offen, Imsara, Nicole Williams, Deborah Ervin, Eva and Lawrence, Carol Beck and Hugh Colmer, and Kitty Kennard.

Thank you to my family and finally... Lawrence Kaczmarek (my Brother in Law) who did nothing for this book but wanted to be mentioned anyway.

Foreword by Jeffrey Wolf Green

Author of

Pluto: The Evolutionary Journey of the Soul
Pluto in Relationship
Uranus: Freedom from the known
Measuring the Night (Vol. 1 and 2, with Steven Forrest)

> "A child is born on the day and at that hour when the celestial rays are in mathematical harmony with his or her individual karma. The individual's horoscope is a challenging portrait revealing the unalterable past, and its probable results. But the natal chart can be rightly interpreted only by men or women of wisdom: these are few."

This is a statement by the great Indian Guru and teacher Sri Yukestwar who was the teacher and Guru of the great Paramahansa Yogananda. Yukestwar was himself an astrologer of galactic dimensions in his own life. The very origins of what we now call Evolutionary Astrology comes from this Soul. And it is with this type of astrology that we can truly and accurately symbolize and map the evolutionary development and progression of each Soul on Earth.

The root cause of evolution in any Soul is DESIRE. It is this simple yet profound truth that was the very basis of Buddha's enlightenment as he sat underneath the famous Bodhi Tree contemplating the nature of and the causes for, sorrow, pain, and suffering. Within each Soul there are two almost coequal desires. One desire is to separate from all that appears to be the totality of Creation, including the Creator Itself. The other desire is to unite with the totality of the Creation, including the Creator Itself.

The evolution of each Soul is determined by the interaction of these dual desires for it is these desires themselves that determine what the life experiences are. Evolutionary Astrology is a symbolic system that allows the astrologer to determine what the desire nature has been and is in each Soul. It is a system that is provable to anyone who takes the time to deeply study it, and to apply it. It requires no belief system at all. It only requires that one validate one's life experience.

For example we can have whatever separating desires that we have: the new career post, a desire for wealth, the new lover, and so on. And we may in fact have the ability to actualize those desires. And when we do we can certainly have a sense of satisfaction. Yet this sense of satisfaction is soon replaced by the sense of dissatisfaction: the sense of something more. It is this sense of dissatisfaction that echoes or mirrors the desire to return to the Source of Creation itself in which the ultimate satisfaction occurs.

All Souls on Earth know and experience this natural law and truth. It does not require beliefs. It is simply a validation of that which is. The Soul can be understood to be an immutable consciousness or energy: that which cannot be destroyed. The Soul is pure energy just as our emotions and feelings are. We cannot open the body up and find emotions or feelings, yet most of us would agree that we do indeed have them. For those who doubt that a Soul even exists there are simple ways to know that in fact that we all have Souls. For example, how many of us have awoken from a deep sleep and when we first wake up we don't know who we are, or where we are. We might actually find ourselves inwardly asking in such moments, 'who am I', and 'where am I'? The 'I' here implies a current life ego that is the very basis, in any life, of our sense of individual identity: I am so and so, and I am here, the current place that I am living. So ask yourself in those moments in which you first awaken and ask those questions: 'who am I, and where am I'? Who at that moment is doing the asking? It is the timeless Soul within all of us. And, yes, it is that timeless Soul within all of us that has its own unique identity and individuality that is the basis or cause of the ego centric structures that it manifests from life to life in order to accomplish its ongoing evolutionary intentions.

Physics has proved that energy can never be destroyed, it can only change form. Thus, the Soul can never be destroyed, it can only change forms. The forms that it changes into, manifest as specific identities from life to life. And the determinant in those identities from life to life is, again, desire. The nature of the energy of desire is to act: to act upon the desire(s) them self. As the Soul manifests various identities in and through time it collects a vast amount of memories that are rooted in each one of the distinct lives that it has lived. The storehouse of various memories from lives that have preceded the present, influence the behavior of the life being currently lived. These past life memories are stored in what the Jungian psychologist calls the individuated unconscious. In Freudian terms these memories correlate to the sub-conscious. Roughly eighty percent of our current life behavior is directly influenced or conditioned by these past life memories.

As an example, one of the clients I had many years ago had a son who refused to take a shower until he was thirteen years old. From the point of view of the current life there was simply no way of understanding why this was so. No amount of talking to him could get him to shower. Looking into the boy's past lifetimes, using the lens of Evolutionary Astrology, it became clear that the last lifetime that this boy had lived during World War II, he had been a Jew in Hitler's Germany, and had been rounded up with his family and taken to one of the concentration camps. With his mother he was forced into one of those buildings where they were told that they could take a shower. But, of course, instead of shower water only the poison gas rained down upon them and they died. Thus, the trauma of this memory resided within him as he was born into the current life. And it is this memory rooted in his individuated unconscious that created the fear of taking a shower in the current life.

It may be asked of course as to why that particular kind of life happened in the first place. And the answer in all cases, for any of us, is rooted, again, in our desire nature. Desires are acted upon. And those desires create reactions to themselves. Every action has a proportionate reaction. This is the natural law that many call Karma. In this boy's case, the life that preceded the one in which he ended up in the concentration camps as a Jew, was a life in which he had desired social position, power and wealth and subsequently was born into a family that was of royalty. So he was born into the Spanish royalty during the last inquisition in Spain. The existing Church of that time was rounding up all the Jews that lived in Spain and persecuting them without mercy, submitting many to unspeakable tortures in order to extract confessions not only about themselves, but who they could also turn in. The Soul within the boy felt deep inner guilt based on his participation in this. And it was that guilt that created a desire or need within his Soul to atone for that guilt. The atonement thus linked with guilt then became the basis or cause of then being born into a Jewish family in Germany at the time of Hitler, which led directly to the concentration camps and his own death.

The point here is that all Souls on Earth have had many, many prior lives in which all of them in total correlate to memories that reside in the individuated unconscious. As such, they influence or condition our current life behavior in ways that most of us have no idea is happening. And the reason that most of us do not have this understanding is because of the nature of consensus societies that we are born into that do not have any understanding of this natural fact. As a result the citizens of such societies are not taught about these natural laws and facts. And because of this when any of us manifests psychological 'problems' that create 'abnormal' behavior the typical psychological approach to dealing with this through consensus societies is called 'behavioral modification'. Behavioral modification is aimed simply at retraining the individual to act 'normally' as prescribed by the consensus of the society that he or she is born into. It does not identify the reasons for the apparent 'abnormal' behavior at all, as with the boy who refused to take a shower until he was around thirteen years of age.

To have a healing or true understanding of any behavior is to understand the causes for that behavior. The essential value of Evolutionary Astrology is that it can precisely identify the root causes for any behavior or psychological orientation to phenomenal reality. And it can do so because it is a system that is rooted in Natural Law in which it is understood that the determinant that sets in motion the evolution of all Souls is desire itself. Evolutionary Astrology can precisely identify the types of desires that any Soul has, or has had, and how these desires are the essential causes for the overall reality that the Soul creates from life to life. It provides a perspective about our lives that tells us the WHY of anything, and does not allow for the consciousness of victimization whatsoever. We are all responsible for that which we have created from life to life because of the nature of our own desires. Evolutionary Astrology is the astrology for SOUL WORKERS because it is the stuff of the Soul itself.

Patricia Walsh's book is rooted and based in this system of Evolutionary Astrology. Her understanding of it is deep. This is so because of her extensive work in past life regressions. Because of this work she has had Souls report some of their past life stories and then linked these experiences to the karmic dynamics in the chart as described by Evolutionary Astrology. In so doing she has created a 'proving' of Evolutionary Astrology itself because these 'stories' do in fact reflect the archetypal nature of the symbols of Evolutionary Astrology.

In this way Patricia has created an invaluable work on behalf of Evolutionary Astrology generally, and to all students of this work specifically. Patricia Walsh is indeed one of those few men or women of wisdom who can accurately interpret the natal chart of each Soul.

I cannot more highly recommend this work to any serious student who endeavors to understand the true beauty of what Evolutionary Astrology is. And that is to be a true SOUL WORKER who desires to help any Soul understand their own unique, individual, evolutionary journey that ultimately takes them back from where they began: God.

Foreword by Roger Woolger PhD

Author of

Other Lives, Other Selves
Healing Your Past Lives
The Goddess Within

In the 30 years or so that I have investigated the phenomenon of past life memory and worked on developing a practical method to heal the soul's inherited wounds (today called Deep Memory Process), I have naturally searched in the literature of astrology for validation and confirmation of my findings. But there is hardly a book written by an astrologer on past lives that I haven't found disappointing. Even the few astrologers who claimed to practice regression to past lives with their clients, for me, had little of substance to offer, since, for the most part, they had no practical awareness of the deeper issues of psychotherapy.

Patricia Walsh's monumental and unique contribution to an authentic astrologically based psychotherapy of the soul is the book I personally have been waiting for. This ground-breaking book must surely be welcomed by all practicing astrologers, whether or not they use regression therapy or believe in reincarnation. The fact that Patricia has recorded several thousand cases of regression therapy (over 50 of them included in this book) and matched them meticulously with the charts of each of these clients must surely count as a double breakthrough: for one thing, it is an entirely original contribution to the literature and research into reincarnation and past lives and on the other it adds a major new dimension to the astrological interpretation of the soul's karmic inheritance. To be sure, like all innovators, Patricia's work builds on previous research and theory – in psychotherapy she is deeply influenced by Deep Memory Process; in astrology by the Evolutionary Astrology of Jeffrey Green – but it is her brilliant synthesis that breaks such fertile new ground.

Most of all we should be grateful to Patricia for advancing and helping re-build a lost science, what I can only call the science of the Soul. It is worth sketching the history of how this science got lost , because it will help place this radical new work in the context it deserves. Modern science, with the exception of a few visionary quantum physicists like Fritjof Capra, Amit Goswami and Fred Wolf, has more or less painted itself into a corner with its unrelenting determination to reduce everything to material or neurological explanations. To paraphrase Jung we could say that modern science has "lost its soul" by banishing the metaphysical or spiritual dimension and pouring ignorant contempt on religion – the English writer Richard Dawkins is a sad example of this. But I believe that research like Patricia's, and the learning and wisdom she brings to it, are signs that herald a new renaissance of the ancient science of the Soul and its true relationship to the Cosmos.

Such a science of the Soul has always existed in the East, in the yoga teachings of Patanjali for example, or in the alchemical energy practices of Chinese Taoism, but it has gotten lost or driven underground in the west. We know how the early Roman Church, for various reasons, suppressed teachings and probably burned texts regarding reincarnation and the progress (or regress) of the soul through various lifetimes. Such teachings were almost universal among the Mystery Schools of the ancient world and among many so-called 'Gnostic' sects. The philosopher and initiate Plutarch, who became a priest at Delphi, wrote:

> We know that the soul is indestructible and should think of its experience as like that of a bird in a cage. If it has been kept in a body for a long time and become tamed to this life as a result of all sorts of involvements and long habituation, it will alight back to a body again after birth and will never stop becoming entangled in the passions and chances of this world.

Many surviving Gnostic writings, whose origins are hotly debated by scholars, show striking similarities to Buddhist and Hindu teachings about the soul's journey after death, no doubt because of many centuries of contact between Eastern and Western cultures following the conquests of Alexander the Great. (It is known, for example, that Buddhists taught in Alexandria and that yogis reached Athens, where they were dubbed the 'gymnophysicists').

But perhaps the most luminous synthesis of all these doctrines is to be found in the 2nd century collection of texts known as the *Corpus Hermeticum*, said to have been transmitted from the ancient Egyptian sage Hermes Trismegistos or Thoth. The teachings enshrined in the *Hermetica* provide an amazingly lucid metaphysical underpinning to astrology and the alchemical arts and above all the mystery of the soul's ascent through the planetary spheres to the Empyreum, the divine realm of pure light (the *Dharmakaya* of Mahayana Buddhism, the *Tao*, the *Al Haq* of Sufism). According to the famous Hermetic Law of Correspondences, "as above, so below," these spheres symbolize the external hierarchy of the subtle world and exactly mirror the inner degrees through which the initiate must pass on the way to enlightenment. This mirroring of the macrocosm and the microcosm is first found written in Plato's *Timeaus*, but is obviously much more ancient.

Before the third century C.E., pagan and early Christian beliefs exist side by side in the Roman Empire. But when the emperor Constantine adopted Christianity as the religion of the state, the Gnostics and the Mystery schools came under persecution and reincarnation came to be seen as a heresy. It is finally excised from Roman Church thinking in 553, when the teachings of Origen about the preexistence of the soul are anathematized by the emperor Justinian. After this, it disappears from Church history for nearly a thousand years, briefly entering Europe as part of the teachings of the Cathars, the late Gnostic group that flourished in Northern Italy and Southern France in the 12th and 13th centuries. Considered a threat to orthodoxy, the Cathars are brutally extirpated by the Church in the notorious Albigensian Crusade, which spawns the early Inquisition founded by Saint Dominic.

In the East, reincarnation survives, buried within Hermetic and Platonic teachings that are secretly preserved by certain monastic orders during the hegemony of the Orthodox Church in Byzantium. These teachings, along with hundreds of lost manuscripts, come west again in the 15th century when Cosimo de Medici acquires a collection for his famous Academy in Florence, modeled on Plato's own. This priceless library of ancient texts – among them, famously, the lost books of Plato – lays the intellectual and spiritual foundations of the Renaissance.

But the fearful years of the 16th and 17th centuries, the Wars of Religion in Europe, force many of the Hermetic teachings underground once more. They are carefully disguised in the opaque symbolism of alchemy and in Rosicrucian allegories that only initiates can penetrate; one such initiate, who surely knows of reincarnation and a great deal more, is Shakespeare. (Others are the painters Durer, Botticelli, and da Vinci, the poet Edward Spenser, and the English magus Dr John Dee.)

From the Renaissance on, with the rise of rationalism and early science, the psyche of the West begins to split. More and more, rationalist philosophers attack anything spiritual as superstition. In the 18th century, John Locke proclaims that the mind is a *tabula rasa*, a blank slate, at birth. Building on this dogma the burgeoning 'science' of psychology will eventually decide to throw out any idea of psychic inheritance, inborn memories or traits, thus breaking with three thousand years of wisdom gleaned from the ancient philosophy of the Soul. (Perhaps it's no coincidence that this doctrine appeared just as all of Europe and its land-grabbing settlers were trying to disown flagrant acts of colonial aggression, genocide, and the horrors of slavery. With events like these to remember, collective memory could prove embarrassing!)

But side by side with the growth of scientific rationalism, whose achievements within its own domain should never be underestimated, we see the appearance of the great Enlightenment explorers of the soul – Swedenborg, Mesmer, Goethe, Schelling – followed by the "visionary company" of the Romantic movement, as Harold Bloom has called them: Blake, Coleridge, Shelley, Keats, and Wordsworth. A generation after Locke's *tabula rasa*, Wordsworth pens one of the great affirmations of the soul's "eternal return":

> Our birth is but a sleep and a forgetting;
> The soul that rises with us, our life's star,
> Hath had elsewhere its setting
> And cometh from afar;
> Not in entire forgetfulness,
> And not in utter nakedness,
> But trailing clouds of glory do we come
> From God, who is our home…

In fact, it is this 'alternative' (actually, Neoplatonic) philosophy of the soul, declared by the Romantic poets all over Europe and later taken up by the Transcendentalists in New England, that lays the groundwork for the study of the deeper soul that 19th-century philosophers begin to call the unconscious. And this whole rich tradition, fired by Nietzsche's dismantling of the Christian psyche and Schopenhauer's sense of a divine Will (imported from the Hindu Upanishads), leads us straight to Freud, Jung, and the psychoanalytic movement: the closest thing the modern world has seen to an authentic science of the soul.

At various points in its increasingly conservative history, mainstream psychology, with a zeal worthy of the early Church casting out heretics, has thrown out the soul, thrown out spiritual and psychic experiences, and even come close to throwing out the personal testimony of subjective experience – all with that deadly Behaviorist movement that is still stifling research today.

To this day, Freudian psychoanalysis is heretical at most universities; Jung is taught only at more radical institutions. Yet we don't have to look far to see that the idea of the unconscious mind as the repository of the soul's experience is still very much alive. Thanks to Thomas Moore's bestseller *Care of the Soul*, inspired in part by his great mentor James Hillman, we can now talk more openly about the soul. And thanks to transpersonal psychology, with its appreciation of "altered states of consciousness" (Charles Tart); the manifest benefits of meditation; the "spectrum of consciousness" behind our spiritual evolution (Ken Wilbur); the soul's memories before birth (Stanislav Grof); the psychic journeys of the shaman (Michael Harner); and the healing power of imagery (Joan Borysenko), we can seriously boast a growing science that is neither narrow nor dogmatic.

Astrology has always been able to provide an uncannily accurate map of the inner dynamics of the soul and its manifold psychic configurations and transformations. But with its fundamental emphasis on the mystical imprint of the planetary positions at the moment of birth, astrology implicitly rejects the *tabula rasa* doctrine that has become engrained in post-Enlightenment philosophical and scientific thinking. Freud, who otherwise had deep insight into the human soul, was so brainwashed by this doctrine he could not look deeper or beyond childhood for the imprints of human conflict and anguish.

For all the purported love of truth and research that scientists are supposed to subscribe to, many are caught in dogmas and *a priori* assumptions every bit as rigid as those of the Church Fathers. Typical arguments I often hear are "we know that reincarnation is impossible so there is obviously no need to research it!" or "it is not worth employing regression therapy because reincarnation has not been proven" – to this one I retort, "But we practice dream therapy even though no one has ever photographed a dream, empirically proving dreams exist" (maybe they are just fantasies!)

I doubt that this book will be read by persons with such closed minds. Actually what Patricia is summarizing here is casuistic research of a specific and unusual kind; she can demonstrate 1. What astrology would predict with such-and-such a Pluto and Lunar nodes configuration and produce a case to match it, and 2. She can take a case blind and predict, with great accuracy, what astrological configuration the client will have. I have seen her do both of these personally in workshops. When you have read a few of her cases, you will be astonished by the accuracy of this model.

Finally I must add that although this book is targeted primarily for astrologers I am personally deeply gratified by the excellent job Patricia has done in presenting the huge range and depth of what can be accomplished by Deep Memory Process as a therapy and how successful it is at bringing new levels of healing and personal transformation. I am surely no astrologer, but I do know that the major keyword for Pluto is transformation and in this sense it is entirely appropriate that this therapeutic marriage of Jeffrey Green's brilliant astrological vision and my form of regression therapy, Deep Memory Process, should have been created by Patricia's work.

It was philosopher Alfred Kozybski who famously said "the map is not the territory". Though he was not thinking of astrological charts (in Spanish and Portuguese a chart is called a 'mappa') his dictum could be applied as a challenge to astrologers who read this book. Many an astrologer, in my experience, is content to offer interpretations and homilies derived from a chart but rarely to delve into it at an experiential level. Patricia here offers an unprecedented model of how the map can genuinely lead us into the territory and prepare us for what we meet when we are there. Her many cases illuminate how the rich symbolic language of the chart gives bounteous clues as to the therapeutic strategies needed, the dynamic of the opposites to be played out (this is profoundly Jungian) and the many subtle karmic learnings to be assimilated once the territory has been traversed. None of this can happen from a simple reading of the map. But once the therapeutic journey has been made, the map appears in a newer and more nuanced light. The soul is now learning, in Jung's way of putting it, to think symbolically as it threads its pathway towards individuation.

Patricia's rich and deeply researched book will provoke all kinds of reactions and echoes in your own experience as you read it. You will recognize many people you know. Her cases are vivid living stories, not abstract portraits or impersonal summaries. She has brought the stories of the soul to life, because in using the psychodramatic play and counterplay of Deep Memory Process, the chart has become the script for the transformational theater of healing. The Greek God of Theater was Dionysus, the only god in the Greek pantheon who dies and is re-born. Some say he is the western equivalent of Siva, the Indian luminary of death and re-birth. So it is no surprise that psychodrama, as refurbished in Deep Memory Process, should re-discover a rich and fruitful compatibility with the most dramatic of all the astrological principles, Pluto. I personally look forward to more and more commerce between astrology and regression therapy.

Patricia has shown us how fruitful this union can be in this remarkable book.

Introduction

My work with past lives began in 1995, as I was working with hands-on energy healing techniques. I found that images from other times and places would pop into my mind as I worked on an individual. With practice, I learned to stay with these images and follow them, like watching a movie. Often, not only the circumstances of the story would unfold, but more importantly the emotions and thoughts of the past life character I was watching. These glimpses into the past often would mirror the client's present life experience. When I shared these 'stories' with my clients they often provided a deeper view into why certain issues existed presently. I learned much about the nature of the soul, how it carries wounding from life to life, and the process of 'soul retrieval' through working in this way. Around the same time I came upon *Pluto: The Evolutionary Journey of the Soul* and started using astrological charts as a part of every healing session. It was then that I noticed the similarities between 'past life stories' and the karmic symbols in the chart as described by Evolutionary Astrology (EA). Later I was fortunate to study with Jeffrey Wolf Green and graduated from the last school he taught personally and have been learning and using EA ever since.

Around the same time, I met Roger Woolger PhD and completed several years of training in his method known as Deep Memory Process (DMP). Dr Woolger, a Jungian, stumbled onto past lives through his personal process and work with clients. He wrote a seminal book in 1987, *Other Lives, Other Selves*, which birthed his unique approach to regression therapy and made him a pioneer in the field. The process of DMP is a comprehensive form of present and past life regression work that blends Jungian thought, spiritual psychology, shamanic healing and self-experiential forms of psychological approaches such as Gestalt, Psychodrama, Reichien body work and more. After finishing my training, Roger and I jointly developed a form of working with ancestral and other earthbound spirits and started teaching together. I also became the chief trainer for the Deep Memory Process, US training program, and continue to teach and work with Roger.

Now that I was doing regression work, my own subjective views were further removed from the process and the similarities between Evolutionary

Astrology and people's own past life recall continued to fascinate me so I kept records of all my sessions for my own learning purposes. Since I was still teaching, I continued to gather past life stories and charts from students and participants of our workshops. After several years of doing this, a friend pointed out to me that this material should be shared, so others could learn from it also. This book is the result of seven years of research and several thousand case studies.

While many of you are not working with your clients with regression therapy, I hope to demonstrate to you how these past life experiences live in the chart, in you and in your clients. By seeing the exact 'language' that the psyche is using, you gain the ability, especially in counseling, to speak directly to those subconscious patterns in a way that the client can deeply absorb what is being said. The language of the soul is one of images, imagination, symbols, and metaphors expressed in myth and story. Learning to tell the stories (the Soul Dramas), or to have a discussion of the core karmic themes and the possibility of growth beyond them with your clients can be a way to awaken an unconscious inner character, previously stuck in the past, to a new potentiality.

All the cases presented in this book are from regression work and not 'psychic investigation'. Because this has been the basis of much of my work with clients I have been able to peer as a guide and an observer into the deep inner life of the soul as it reincarnates from life to life. Regression work also adds to the dimensions of the astrological archetypes that can be understood from the past life perspective. For example, using one of the symbols in a chart that represents past life history – the south node (SN) – if a man has a SN in Scorpio and finds out that he was a banker in a past life and is a banker in the present life, this is interesting but what does it really tell us? This is a circumstantial layer of the archetype. If the man relives the past life as a banker, maybe we find out that there was a depression and he lost everything. In that past life he never recovered emotionally from the shock. Now we can understand a different dimension of how that Scorpio SN is acting in his psyche today. He may be a banker now because the fear of loss (Scorpio) is so great it becomes a compulsion for him to continue to acquire more and more resources (especially other people's resources – Scorpio). The subconscious fear of loss from this past life may be driving him at this point in his current life. The compulsion isn't really evolution, it is a repetition of the past dynamics fueled by an unresolved wound in the psyche. The polarity point of the Taurus north node (NN) indicates one of the areas where evolution is intended – inner self reliance and a rebirth of trust in the natural abundance of life. The types of issues that arise in past life regressions to be healed are also the exact dynamics that Evolutionary Astrology aims to describe:

- To understand the past security patterns, emotional and mental imprints that have conditioned the consciousness previous to this life.
- To point the way to the path of evolution beyond these.

In the following sections I have introduced principles that permeate the chapters on the archetypes. This book is not written in a 'cook book' style. It will become apparent that the understanding of previous lives is not such a simple matter as a few keywords or thoughts relating to one or two symbols in the chart. Rather, this book is written like a journey through the archetypes, from the depths to the heights of each, and is meant to be read in that way, sequentially from Aries to Pisces. Once the elements of the karmic axis in a chart are understood, all the related archetypes in this book can be read in relation to a single chart and synthesized to give a whole picture.

At the beginning of each chapter there is a list of keywords presented which serves as a guide to spark your own associations. At the end of the book in the Appendix is a list of facets of the archetypes in their natural state, paired with a brief recounting of how that characteristic has shown up in various past life recalls. These lists can serve as a tool to prompt your own associations, for any chart you are working with.

Past Life Astrological Archetypal Themes

> "...the journey through the planetary houses boils down to becoming conscious of the good and bad qualities in our character, and the apotheosis means no more than maximum freedom of will".
>
> Carl Jung

For the purposes of this book, the term archetype is intended to mean a universally experienced limit of potential manifestation of human consciousness. Several writers, for example Liz Greene, have described archetypes as "universal energy patterns". The archetypes then can be likened to an artist's palate that the soul uses to paint its experiences. For example, let's look at one color on that palate: red. Within the spectrum of the color red, there are many shades along with many applications and ways to use it. Further, red can be mixed with blue or any other color. No two artists will use red in exactly the same way. Thus no two souls will use the exact combination or expression of archetypes in the same way. Each life is a completely individual interpretation of a potential of expression. The color red has a limitation in its use and expression but within those limits it has a broad potentiality. Thus the twelve signs of the zodiac, or the astrological archetypes, become twelve divisions of potential human conscious expression.

One size does not fit all; we are individuals in our outer appearance as much as our inner world. This is starkly represented in the birth chart, where many individuals may be born on the same day, in the same town, at the same (or near same) time, and still be quite different from each other. Astrologers who have studied twins and their charts point out that even if the ascendant or Moon has not changed sign, the twins may be radically different from each other. Taken from the karmic perspective this makes absolute sense. Each soul has had a unique journey through many lives, during which the individual has been conditioned by a variety of unique experiences and retains 'memory' of this. The type of actual cognitive memory varies, but past life conditioning, just like childhood conditioning from the current life, remains even when the memory of the actual events does not.

When we look at the archetype of each sign, we see it has a broad range of potentiality. For a microcosmic to macrocosmic example, one astrologer can look at Saturn/tenth house/Capricorn as a way of discerning career and social standing; another could look it as the father and another as the structure of consciousness itself. Because the spectrum of meaning within each archetype is so broad, the slice that is presented here relates to how those archetypes emerge during past life stories. But what is interesting to note is that even within a single slice, each past life story will contain a range of expression of each archetype that is relevant to personal karmic history.

For example let's use a Capricorn south node. In one past life a person may find themselves as the son of a politician, living in a time of oppression. His experience causes him to be depressive, because tradition dictates he must follow in his father's footsteps. All these factors, from the mundane to the psychological and circumstantial, are very Capricornian and arise spontaneously during regression in exactly that way.

Each archetype has a natural expression, or one might say a 'divine intention', and there are myriad ways for individuals to express that archetype. When an archetype is a part of the karmic axis, representing the past, a main aspect of its expression in the individual psyche is one of woundedness. Not all past lives are traumatic, but the ones that are problematic in our current lives were. There are also gifts that are present in the archetypes that represent our past, but mainly these have been smoothly integrated, so we use them well and often without much attention. Someone may be born with an inborn talent, or a propensity to excel in different areas of expression. Natural tendencies that come easily to us are also our inheritance from past lives and can also be explored in past life work and through astrology. But it's the tooth with the cavity that causes us to go to the dentist, just as it's the places of pain and dis-ease that cause us to seek therapy or counseling. As astrological counselors we can use the chart to illuminate these trouble spots, not with a sense of doom – this is not why we incarnate with wounds – but with the knowing that healing and evolving beyond their limitations is the divine intention. This is what the opening quotation from Jung refers to; we have within us the capacity to elevate any quality of our character. Through the transformation of the negative, we reach new frontiers of individual expression of free will. In Evolutionary Astrology it is said that to evolve from any natal planetary position to its polarity point is to move from Karma to Dharma, which is, at its apex, personal will aligned with divine will.

What is Evolutionary Astrology?

> Suspiciendo despicio – "By looking up I see downward".
>
> Tycho Brahe

Alchemy and Astrology were at one point inseparable, the main Hermetic principle being 'as above, so below'; if it is in the heavens it is in us. In alchemy the understanding of the concept 'as above so below', includes also the linking of the inner and outer worlds. Much more than the material process of turning lead into gold, alchemy is a path of the transformation of consciousness from its baser matter to a more refined substance: it is a spiritual path.

From the Middle Ages to today, in various forms astrology has bridged the mechanistic movement of the spheres with the psycho/spiritual dimensions of human consciousness. Late 19th and early 20th century writers such as Alan Leo, Madame Blavatsky and Alice Bailey, pioneered today's transpersonal use of astrology by elucidating more esoteric concepts, while serving to seed new awareness and ignite deeper thinkers in astrology. Unfortunately, much of the material was too esoteric for most people to apply on an individual basis or in day to day life. Later, astrologer Dane Rudhyar took a more psychological approach that expanded upon the symbols of astrology as they related to the human psyche. He founded what has been called Humanistic Astrology, which effectively wrestled away the power of fate and destiny from the stars and put it squarely on the shoulders of the individual. This reflected a leap in what collective human consciousness was ready to accept – the idea that perhaps life and its events are not solely fated and beyond our control, but that we have some responsibility in the creation of events in our life. Several other astrologers who also have contributed to the psycho/spiritual approach include Liz Greene, Isabel Hickey, and Alan Oken, to name a few. We might look at the discovery of the outer planets beyond Saturn, also called the transpersonal planets, as less a feat of science or astronomy, and more as a synchronistic event that points to the progressive growth of collective consciousness.

Initially, it was a popular misconception in astrology that these outer/transpersonal planets did not have any effect in the individual's life. That because they were so slow moving they had only a generational or collective influence. This view did not take into account the intimate way in which the microcosm reflects the macrocosm. The collective is evident in the personal psyche and vice versa. Carl Jung, who delved deeply into the psyche, charted the understanding of the 'collective unconscious', and often used astrology in his diagnosis with clients; the language of the psyche being for him archetypal, metaphoric and symbolic. In fact Jung, who wrote much about synchronicity and alchemy, was 'synchronistically' probing the depth of the psyche during the time of Pluto's actual discovery (1930). Depth psychology is part of the Scorpio (Pluto) archetype. It makes sense that as psychology has progressed, astrology has needed to birth new paradigms that embrace the totality of human consciousness and the reality of the soul.

Evolutionary Astrology (EA) as developed and taught by Jeffrey Wolf Green is a system that has at its core an astrological view of the life of the soul and its expression through many lives. The Plutonian based paradigm of Evolutionary Astrology was introduced by Jeffrey Wolf Green in his book *Pluto: The Evolutionary Journey of the Soul* in 1985 and expanded upon in *Pluto Volume II: The Soul's Evolution Through Relationships* (1997). Jeffrey's writing and continued teaching not only give us a deeper understanding of Pluto as a symbol for the soul and the dynamics of evolution, but also set a new pace for the growth of transpersonal astrology.

Evolutionary Astrology, through its emphasis on Pluto and the nodes as symbols for the soul and its evolutionary journey, has developed specific methodologies that represent a departure from traditional astrology. First, the twelve archetypes are understood in a new light that is actually quite old; that of Natural Law. Collectively, it seems humanity has progressively become estranged from its place and connection with natural law. EA re-describes the archetypes from the natural perspective and also takes into account the soul's imprinting through its many lives as a result of individual experiences and choices, along with the collective accumulated effect of unnatural conditioning. With the understanding that there is a natural expression of each archetype the next step is to explore the places the soul has become estranged from that, and how it is seeking to realign itself.

The Karmic Axis

As a bottom line to this paradigm, the karmic axis is examined first as the baseline of understanding the individual. This axis is comprised of the placements (by house and sign) of Pluto and the nodes of the Moon, plus their rulers and aspects to them all. Pluto in EA is understood to work in concert with the nodes of the Moon to describe the karmic complexes a person is born with. Pluto is like the drummer in the band that sets the beat, while the south node (SN) of the Moon is like the bass player and the north node (NN) the lead singer. The drum beat of Pluto is the accumulated intention that lies behind the previous actions and present conditions. You might not notice the drummer so much; usually he prefers it that way (think Scorpio). But the drummer sets the pace for the whole song, and you'll be tapping your foot right along without even noticing. It's almost compulsory, as Pluto reflects the deeper meaning and the 'why' of any single or series of past life experience(s) and continues the rhythm into the current life. Understanding Pluto's meaning in the chart is like peering into the psychology of the soul, beyond the present or past life personalities. The bass player follows along with the drummer, but gives the beat notes. He has a scale he can play on. The south node of the Moon shows how the intention of Pluto has expressed itself in a variety of past life experiences. Circumstances have changed, lifetime to lifetime, but imprints are retained emotionally and mentally and they condition future experiences – this is the beat they share. Both Pluto and the nodes carry these past life memories and imprints.

In bands the lead singer is usually the one in the spotlight the most, he often get the most attention, has the most notoriety and is frequently known as the leader. The NN shows the leading edge of evolutionary potential. However, the NN can't perform well if the rest of the band doesn't. He represents the potential to bring forth what is within, and can only do so when everyone works well together.

The combined elements of the karmic axis tell the stories of past history and current life intentions for healing and evolution. I have found from facilitating numerous past life stories that in actuality, simplistic models – for example, just using the south node to describe the totality of the past life experience of the soul, at least as it is represented in the current life – are not inclusive of the range of the soul's experience. Our present life psyche is more complex than one symbol can represent, so why would we think it was not the case in past lives as well? This is also the exact point made by Evolutionary Astrology. What I've learned from comparing past life experiences to the chart is that in each lifetime the soul works on several karmic themes simultaneously. This is reflected by the various elements that make up the karmic axis. In some charts the karmic axis is not that complex, involving only a few aspects, but in other charts the combined aspects to Pluto, the nodes and their rulers may involve most of the planets in the chart. This may lead some astrologers to conclude that all the planets in the chart have a past life relevance. What I have found is that all the past life stories that arise in therapy will be contained within the archetypes of the karmic axis. This is true for both simple and more complex charts; it is not necessary to look beyond the karmic axis for the past life content. Taking into account all the archetypes represented by the houses, signs, planets and aspects that are involved in the karmic axis broadens the possibilities of what the past life experiences have been, and what influences lie behind the present life incarnation. It may seem like a daunting task at first to try to synthesize all that information, but once the archetypes are understood from the past life perspective one finds it easier to discern patterns and issues. Following are the basic steps of chart analysis:

Step One – Pluto

In this system the chart analysis starts with Pluto by sign and then house. Pluto as a symbol for the soul and the force of evolution that it is subject to shows what the soul has chosen to develop in past lives and the primary psychology that lies behind the ego structure and personality. Essential reading for understanding Pluto in this context is *Pluto: The Evolutionary Journey of the Soul* by Jeff Wolf Green.

Pluto is a slow moving planet and its passage through each sign denotes generations of individuals that incarnate together with a similar basic soul orientation. For example, someone from the Pluto in Leo generation has a radically different basic soul orientation than one from the Pluto in Virgo generation.

Leo is an archetype of fullness of self while Virgo represents a deflation of self (humility). The Pluto in Leo soul comes into this life with a sense of self already developed and a natural urge for creative self expression. It was largely the Pluto in Leo generation, in their youth in the 1960s, who coined such terms as "Do your own thing", "If it feels good do it" and "Free Love". The core desire of this soul structure is unhindered creative self expression. Virgo is an archetype of improvement and purification. The Pluto in Virgo generation, unlike Pluto in Leo, never feels ready or good enough; there is always one more thing to improve upon before they feel perfect. Leo feels 'comfortable in its own skin', while Virgo picks at its own scabs. The soul that has been developing through the Virgo archetype at a core level will not share in Leo's grand sense of personal creative power, but most likely will work diligently behind the scenes improving upon (and cleaning up the messes) of what the previous generation brought forth into the world. Past life stories from these different generations reflect their different paths of evolution.

The house position modifies the generalized understanding and makes it more personalized. A Pluto in Leo in the first house will have had many past lives of striking out in new directions for the purpose of creative expression. In the earlier stages of this soul's development it may have been excessively narcissistic and known no limits in its desire for power to meet its objectives, and the earlier past lives will reflect this orientation. If the soul has 'been around the block a few times' it may have attempted to balance its distant past of abuses of power, but may still feel hampered in self-expression because of subconscious memories of this. Having gone to an extreme, the soul may conclude "I'll never do that again", which can cause caution at a soul level, yet the desire and drive for creative self expression is still burning deeply within. A complication exists then at the soul level about self expression yet the cause is different than a Pluto in Leo in the second house, who will have experienced more insular and isolated lives. The desire for self expression is still there yet the individual may have kept their gifts and talents more to themselves in the past (or situations may have forced them to). As a result of these insular lives, they may have become 'possessive' of their talents. The accumulated fear from these lives would be that putting one's gifts out in the world is dangerous and threatening to one's very survival. So like the first house Pluto, they may also feel a conflict around openly expressing their talents and gifts yet the cause, and therefore the resolution, is very different for each.

From these two examples it easy to see how only the house position modifies and colors the past life experience. Just by interpreting Pluto's sign and house, very deep levels of a person's psyche can be revealed.

Step Two – The Nodes of the Moon

The South Node (SN) represents how the core desires of the soul (Pluto) have been acted upon in past lives, while the North Node (NN) points the way to growth and a new future. Combined with the understanding of Pluto the SN shows 'how' things have happened in the past and Pluto shows 'why'. The SN is like a natural pause at the end of a long sentence. It is a culminating symbol that concludes the previous 'statement' and makes it clear that a new sentence, paragraph or even chapter is meant to begin. The 'conclusions' that are inherent in the SN include previous life thoughts, feelings and unquestioned assumptions. Painful experiences in life can cause us to draw conclusions mentally and emotionally that color our future experiences. For example a woman whose husband is unfaithful may feel devastated when she finds out. Because of the pain of this betrayal, she may draw a conscious or unconscious conclusion, "Men can't be trusted". This will certainly affect and color the way she behaves in relationships in the future. Emotionally she will be carrying unresolved wounds to her ability to trust into the future. This current life event may actually be a replay of past lives, for example we could put her SN in Scorpio in the seventh house. This would show that she has had many lives with a similar theme, loss, betrayal, abandonment in relationships.

Adding that she might have a Pluto in Virgo in the sixth house, we could see that her accumulated underlying psychology may be one of inferiority. Because of past wounds in relationships she has deeply and subconsciously internalized a belief that, "There must be something wrong with me". She simply doesn't feel that whatever she does is good enough – she feels intrinsically flawed and she struggles constantly with self doubt. She has already come into this life with the subconscious script which sets the stage for relationships to 'prove' her underlying thesis that she is imperfect and doesn't really deserve love.

Because this underlying attitude is part of her karmic inheritance, she is meant to continue to heal it, simply because it isn't the truth. With this karmic signature, we could imagine that in one of her past lives she was a young woman forced into an arranged marriage (Scorpio/seventh house) where she was treated like a possession. Maybe her husband had some wealth or prestige and he ran around and did whatever he wanted but when he came home she was expected to service him (Pluto in Virgo). In such a powerless role (Scorpio) maybe she tried to keep her sense of self intact by honing her feminine charms (seventh house) such as seduction (Scorpio). But regardless of how much she made herself attractive to her husband, she still couldn't keep him faithful and her sense of personal power was damaged.

The SN in Scorpio in the seventh also holds the ability to transform the way she is in relationship. The NN in Taurus in the first house is whispering to her, "You know you can survive on your own, trust yourself and your instincts". It doesn't mean she is not meant to be in relationship, but she needs to heal enough to know that her needs and self esteem should be intact so she can have an equal relationship with someone else.

The ruler of the SN (by sign and house and aspects) is an extension of the SN and adds further details about the past life experiences. This is similar to the way that, in traditional astrology, the ruler of the Ascendant or Sun sign adds details to the way a person manifests its qualities.

Step Three – The Polarity Point of Pluto and the position of the North Node

As the name Evolutionary Astrology implies, the soul continues to reincarnate seeking healing and growth beyond the repeated patterns it has already developed. These repeated patterns become habitual and are often deeply buried in the subconscious. We are meant to evolve beyond our limiting patterns. Our life experience is a combination of both replays of the past and potential growth beyond it. This tension exists within us with every life choice we make or don't make. The opposite point of Pluto (180 degrees), called the Polarity Point (PP) shows the direction for evolution. This is also true of the South Node which has the North Node as its polarity point. After assessing Pluto's natal meaning, a look at the polarity point, by sign and house, will show a primary area of growth for the soul in this lifetime. If the polarity point is tenanted by a planet it means that individual has already worked to develop some of its qualities, and what the experience has been, is colored by which planet it is. If a planet opposes Pluto (is in the polarity point) the past life experience with both the PP and the planet may not have been healthy or positive.

For example, a typical understanding of the first house Pluto is that the person needs to move away from being a loner (first house) and into relatedness (seventh house). One client with a Pluto in Leo in the first house had both the Moon and Venus in Aquarius opposed to it. This person did not come into this life avoiding relationships but sought them out almost compulsively (Pluto-Venus) and they were always complicated. His karmic issues with relationships would come to the forefront each time he met another lover and his frustration was not about having a relationship, but how to be in a relationship in a healthy way. This is in contrast to another client also with a Pluto in Leo in the first house with no planets in opposition who told me, "I'm used to being alone and I don't even want to have a relationship although I feel I should". In the first case the client needed to transform the way he was participating in relationships and in the second case the client needed to discover relationship was even a possibility.

The polarity point of Pluto and the chart position of the north node often feel like unfamiliar territory simply because they are! Even when a familiarity with the PP is indicated, evolving beyond the old pattern can feel like breaking the rules. For example many of my Pluto in Libra or seventh house Pluto clients will exclaim, “I can’t do that, that would be selfish”, when they are presented with the idea that their personal needs might be as important to fulfill as their partner’s needs are. The unconscious ‘rules’ say, “Partnership matters more than the self” and striking out beyond that can feel wrong and terrifying. But because the polarity point is the archetype of Aries, it is exactly what they are meant to do.

Often in past life work when a wounded aspect of Pluto or the south node is resolved, an instantaneous awareness of the possibility of the polarity point spontaneously makes itself known. The same energy that was stuck in limitation, once it is released, brings the equal amount of energy for growth to the present life. This often happens in one session and it is delightful to see that, as soon as we delve into our fears and limitations and work them through, life and evolution conspires with our highest good to align us to our soul’s purpose. This is the meaning of moving from the karma of the natal placement to the dharma (soul purpose) of the polarity point.

Step Four – Exceptions to the Rules

Planets Squaring the Nodal Axis

A unique point of Evolutionary Astrology is that the basic principles of the SN and NN can be modified by aspects. The most dramatic modification is easily illustrated when the nodes are squared by a planet or planets. This aspect draws the squaring planet into the karmic axis. The tension inherent in this T-square, when it involves the nodal axis, implies that the soul’s usual struggle between the SN and NN opposition must be amplified by the presence of a third pull, causing a tense triangle of forces seeking equal integration. What has happened in the soul’s history is that none of these forces have been fully integrated, and so the tension continues. Not only are the archetypes of the SN and the squaring planet(s) a part of the karmic history but so is the NN. The reasons for the inability to integrate these factors are different in every case. Mainly there is a simple division, resistance to evolution, or extenuating circumstances, seemingly beyond the control of the individual, that prevented embracing and integrating the archetypes represented in a healthy way.

For any of these reasons, the squaring planet is referred to as a Skipped Step. It represents an aspect of the soul’s growth that has been missed and thus becomes a highly focused point of tension in the current life so it can be worked on. The archetypes represented by the squaring planet (planet, sign and house) are areas where the soul has a 'hang up' and will be prominent in the person's current life. If one has a sexual hang up, for example, there are two basic ways that manifests. Either a person is in 'overdrive' in some way around their sexuality, such as being compulsively promiscuous, or they may be puritanically repressed. Either scenario represents an unhealthy relationship with the issue of sexuality.

In the cases that constitute my research, there are a disproportionately higher amount of cases that have squares to the nodes. In other words, it seems that people with these squares must feel the karmic quandary more keenly in their psyche, and they are the ones who seek out past life therapy more often. As a result many of the cases in this book have these aspects, and the clients' stories demonstrate the impact and resolution.

Planets Conjunct the Nodes

When planets conjunct the SN they also become a part of the past life experience. The archetype of the planet strongly colors the past. For example an Aries SN with no planets is very different than one with Saturn conjunct it. There are three possibilities of meaning when planets conjunct the SN.

1) The person is reliving conditions of that planet from the past and it represents a karmic condition that is still being worked through.

2) The planet is in a state of fruition and brings a special gift or reward from the past.

3) A combination of both possibilities. This is the most common, which is also the way that the SN acts for most people – there are issues to be resolved and gifts or rewards that come through easily.

When a planet conjuncts the SN it is naturally opposed to the NN. This implies (especially in the instance of #1 and #3) that something from the past opposes the progress in the future. Until it is resolved, healed and brought to conscious completion it, like the SN, represents an unconscious pull, back into past patterns.

When a planet conjuncts the NN it supports the ability to manifest the NN's potential. It also opposes the SN and that planet often shows up in past life stories as an external opposing factor to the NN's intention, but the person often has integrated the planet's qualities enough to have overcome such adversity. Quite frequently there are gifts and abilities represented by that planet that can be accessed in the current life. A planet conjuncting the NN indicates that the archetype has already been worked with in the past so there is a familiarity with it, and this is similar to a planet opposing Pluto.

When Pluto conjuncts the NN it also shows that the archetypes of the NN have already been worked upon in the past. The polarity point of Pluto does not apply. The person is meant to continue working on the qualities of Pluto and the NN. The SN in this instance is not canceled out, it also acts as a symbol for past life experiences along with the NN.

There are over fifty cases in this book and many of the principles of EA and the modifications to the normal understanding of the nodal axis are clearly demonstrated by the clients' own past life stories. In the many case studies in this book, all the archetypes represented by the karmic axis are not always equally emphasized in a single past life story. One or a few aspects of the Pluto placement or the node pattern can become more emphasized in one past life story than in another from the same individual. This becomes even more evident when a series of past lives are known, and several cases in this book include more than one past life to illustrate this point. Each past life story can be looked at like an act in a greater epic drama: that of the experience of the soul. Yet each past life will correlate to the archetypes represented by the karmic axis, with Pluto and the SN becoming the bottom line reference point, as they show also the accumulated past life issues and patterns. It is also important to keep in mind that the current life interpretation of other planets that become involved in the karmic axis by aspect or as rulers is not mitigated. Rather, these planets have a past life dimension of meaning and a current life one as well. Just as one can look at a planet and its aspects in a chart from the medical astrology perspective and use the same planet for another meaning, a Mars conjunct the SN has a past life meaning as well as its other meanings in the natal chart.

Past Life Wounds – Present Life Problems

Past life issues that carry into the current life are often thought of as being the result of karma. The Western notion of karma can sometimes be simplistic in this regard, implying that if something bad happens to you it is because you did the same thing to someone else in the past. This idea of karma as a sort of Old Testament 'eye for an eye' justice is not the whole picture.

The wounds and unhealed traumas that we have experienced in past lives contribute greatly to our current life experience and constitute a large part of our karma. To understand how past life wounds impact us in the present, we need to look at how trauma affects the psyche in the current life.

A traumatic event is any overwhelming experience (physical, emotional, mental or spiritual) that has caused an inability in the psyche to integrate it fully and continue in the same manner as before the traumatic event was experienced. Thus trauma leaves a lasting and damaging impression that manifests as a combination of symptoms, including but not limited to chronic dissociation, anxiety, phobias, fears, hyper vigilance, inhibitions, paranoia, neurosis, avoidance, armoring or rigidity, suppression of emotions, emotional or physical numbness, mental confusion and compulsions. In psychological language combinations of these symptoms are classified as post traumatic stress disorder/syndrome (PTSD or PTSS). Dr Peter Levine, author of *Waking the Tiger: Healing Trauma*, explains that PTSD symptoms are caused by a "frozen residue of energy" that was not discharged or resolved when the person was threatened.

The natural 'fight or flight' response is activated when an individual is faced with a threat. If the person is overwhelmed or defeated (they can't fight or escape) the natural response becomes a frozen impulse – an action that was never completed. The potential to develop PTSD varies from person to person, but when it does take hold the physiology changes as does the psychological state. People with PTSD cannot integrate the memory of the trauma properly. Psychologically unable to integrate the trauma in conscious terms, a part of the psyche becomes 'split-off' and stays, in essence, frozen in time. This is what shamans have described for ages as 'soul loss' or 'soul fragmentation.' This part of the psyche separates from the ego structure and remains that way. When these soul fragments are encountered in past or present life regression or through inner journeying, they seem to have a life of their own. The fragments appear to be the same age they were when they split off. Often they don't have an awareness that life has moved on, or if they are aware of the present day personality, they are reluctant to be a part of it. The difference between conscious and subconscious memories is a matter of the perception of chronological time. The conscious mind perceives time as changing, moving from the past through the present, to the future. To the subconscious mind, memories (especially traumatic ones) retained there, are happening in the now.

An example of this comes from a client who was abused repeatedly as a young child. Her first soul fragment to emerge was a four-year-old self. This soul fragment (the part of her that dissociated) was found to be hiding in a corner of Grandma's old kitchen. This was where that piece of her went away (into a happy, warm and safe space) when her father started abusing her at four years old. This little girl self was unaware that there was an adult self now. All she was aware of was how nice and safe Grandma's kitchen was. Because she was too young and small to fight off or escape her father, the inability to complete the 'fight or flight' response caused her to fragment. After some work the child fragment did reintegrate with the present day adult self of the client. When that fragment came back, she brought with her the ability to remember safety and to experience nurturing, thus returning new potential energy to be used in the present.

Sometimes when the soul fragments, the conscious memory of the traumatic event goes away with it or becomes buried with the split-off part. This inability to remember a trauma is commonly called a repressed/ suppressed memory. Split-off parts of the psyche do not always leave the energy field of the person to 'go off' somewhere. They also can be buried deep in the interior world of the psyche, making them inaccessible to the conscious mind.

In essence a trauma is a scar that won't seem to heal. This scar then becomes a weak or vulnerable spot in the psyche, seeming to attract to it similar experiences over and over. Traumatized people find themselves re-enacting the whole trauma or aspects of it without conscious awareness that they are doing so. This often happens on anniversaries of events or can be a chronic recreation, such as an abused woman who continually, subconsciously, chooses abusive partners. This is what Freud described as 'Repetition Compulsion'. Freud initially theorized that this is the psyche's attempt to heal. By recreating the event, symbolically or in actuality, the psyche is attempting to gain mastery and completion. This idea of 'Repetition Compulsion' that applies to a trauma experienced during a single lifetime also makes sense in a longer timeline – over the many lives of the soul. It would seem that the soul over the course of many lifetimes attempts to heal by recreating in essence or in actuality, traumas experienced in its past. This also needs to be understood in the context of karma.

Eastern traditions that have reincarnation and karma central to their belief system teach about an aspect of karma called Samskara. Karma literally means actions, and many of those actions come from the deep impressions of habit that are called samskaras. Samskara then is intrinsically tied into the laws of karma that govern the cycle of rebirth. Keeping in mind the nature of traumatic imprints and how they cause continual recreation of the original traumatic event, one can also look at samskaras as trauma imprints re-manifested from life to life. It is the essence of karma to bring forth the actions of the past to the present. The inability to complete even the simple action of 'fight or flight' as a result of trauma in past lives is also carried into the present as the soul continues to create from its own wounded place in an ongoing effort to heal. Because of this, the reality is that most of us are born already with some degree of PTSD. Sri Swami Chidananda states that "Each Samskara has inherent in it the capacity to once again recreate that very experience which originally caused it". Our past life physical, emotional and mental bodies are not wiped clean in-between lives, but continue to recreate themselves in each incarnation through the subtle bodies. This transmission of past physical, emotional and mental wounds constitute a large part of what we are meant to heal in our present lives.

Beside the repetitive nature of trauma, the thoughts, feelings and attitudes we have formed also dictate how our future is created from the present and past. It would seem that the circumstances of past lives are less important to the soul than the attitudes we have formed because of them. These are the imprints we carry, that are in need of change and healing. What is true for the individual is also true for the collective. Thus the adage, History repeats itself! In fact, look back at history and look at the present. Most of the recorded history of humanity has been one of dominance and war, violence, suppression and exploitation of the weak – you were either the victim or the perpetrator or both. Man's inhumanity to man has known no bounds, especially in the last few thousand years. If we take reincarnation literally, then by just looking at history we know that each of us carries these imprints as unresolved traumas. It is a part of our collective and individual psychic inheritance that we are here to heal.

The Dynamics of Past Life Therapy

The healing of samskaras and imprints is the aim of Past Life Therapy (PLT). To understand the cases presented in this book, it is necessary to outline the stages of this healing process as it happens through the process of Past Life Therapy (PLT).

Our past life selves are not only characters in past dramas, but they also live within us today as sub-personalities. We feel their emotions, manifest their talents, think their thoughts, are limited by their fears and perpetuate their quandaries. We often act this out without consciously knowing we are doing so, simply because we are unaware they exist within us. The most problematic past lives for us today are the ones that have unresolved trauma or 'unfinished business'. In PLT these problematic inner characters are brought to the forefront of consciousness and worked with to bring resolution and healing to their complexes, so that they cease to affect the current life.

Usually during a regression session one past life story is worked with. This is not always the case, because resonant stories with a similar theme may also arise in the course of one session, and almost certainly do in successive sessions. In past life work it seems that 'clusters' of similar past lives emerge from the soul's history. They are connected by the same theme yet each may reflect a different facet or aspect. For example, a man may find himself a slave in a past life, where the theme or personal imprint is one of hopelessness. If we are exploring the personal theme of hopelessness, several past life stories may arise that carry different aspects of how this was imprinted. The circumstances may change through lifetimes in which hopelessness became a part of each life. In one life it may be because of slavery, in another life it may be because of feeling trapped in an arranged, loveless marriage where he felt like a slave; or in another instance he may be a hardworking farmer and sole provider of a large family or community and blight comes that kills the crops. In the slave scenario, he may die with the idea that 'there's no way out', and quite literally this may be true; in the marriage he may simply feel trapped and may commit suicide out of depression. The farmer may come to the end of that life feeling that "no matter what I do, the odds are against me, it's hopeless". All these different lives will be connected and recalled by an exploration of what is called the core theme. These core themes are present in our current life and are noticed by examining recurring patterns of behavior. This is one way that karmic imprints and samskaras reveal themselves in our current lives.

A few simple questions will open the door to streams of past life imprints. Just finish the sentence "I always…" or "I never…" One could answer, "I always have to do it all alone" or "I never have enough money". Sometimes we even make casual comments when describing our feelings that are loaded with past life imagery, such as, "I feel like a slave"; "My hands are tied"; "I've been stabbed in the back"; "There's no way out". These repetitive themes, that we take as actual truth and that shape our reality, are most likely core themes that past life characters are still unresolved with. They are changeable, but they are also so darn familiar, that one can't even conceive that it might be possible to change them. Astrologically, the karmic axis points to the core themes because we are already born with them.

Stage One

Inducing Past Life Memories

The first stage of PLT is the induction of the past life memory. This is the method used to recall the past life. Following is a brief outline of some of the methods:

Exploration of Current Life Themes – This is like doing a Google search by typing in keywords and pulling up relevant content. In PLT, thoughts and emotions at the center of any particular complex are uncovered and then used to follow backwards through time to find relevant present and past life formative experiences. This happens through an interview process with a client, when discussing issues or doing a review of different areas of their life such as the history of their relationships, upbringing or work. This also serves to identify core themes together before starting regression work.

Dream Fragments and Imagery – Past life memories can arise within the dream state and often this imagery is fragmentary, but a particularly charged scene in a dream can be explored for past life content. An example of this could be a dream of being chased by wolves. Exploration of this may lead to a literal past life where that happened or it may be a metaphoric image that leads to a different past life memory of being a child in the forest running from invaders.

Fear/Phobias – Present life fears, such as those that seem to not be connected with any current life cause. When these fears are explored they are often found to have their root in past life traumatic deaths. Fear of water or heights for example, is often caused by past life drowning or death by falling.

Womb Regression – Going back to the womb can happen during regression either by direction or spontaneously. Quite frequently while in this state of memory past life content arises. This is discussed in depth in the Cancer archetype.

Spontaneous Memory or Imagery – People, places and charged events in one's life can often 'shake to the surface' deeper associative past life memories. This can happen spontaneously, and the amount of detail recalled in such an event varies from person to person. Some people recall the whole past life, some only fragments of it. When a client comes to therapy with such memories, these can be explored in PLT to go deeper into the story.

Body/Somatic Memory – The mind is not located in the brain but permeates our entire being, including the body. The principle at play is that our current life bodies are recreated from a subtle energy body that is a part of the soul's memory. 'Cellular Memory' is the term often used to describe subconscious body imprints. Thus a chronic neck pain may come from a past life hanging or beheading that has been traumatically imprinted and carried into the current life body. Exploration of current life somatic pains, repeated injuries to a part of the body, illnesses, deformities or even birth marks may reveal past life content. This is discussed in the Taurus chapter.

Guided Imagery – This is a directive process that allows a past life memory to arise spontaneously, where a scene is set in the imagination intending to lead to a past life. This could be the suggestion of imagining crossing a bridge and coming into a past life scene, or walking down a hallway with many closed doors and choosing one, opening it and walking into a past life scene. There are myriad variations of the initial imagery used to get to the past life. This is the induction that most people think of when they think of past life work. It is most commonly used in hypnotherapy and used less frequently in the style of regression that I work with.

All of these methods and combinations of each are used in the cases in this book. No matter how the past life memory was accessed or who performed the regression, the stories still relate to the karmic axis within the birth chart.

Stage Two

Reliving the Past Life

Because we find imprints and samskaras at the heart of our core themes, the emotions and thoughts of the past life character must be explored in depth to reveal what is being carried from life to life. In the form of regression therapy that I teach and practice (Deep Memory Process) it is essential to relive the past life as fully as possible during the session. There are many reasons why this is a part of the therapy, but there are two main points to be made. First, trauma causes freezing and dissociation. Second, one needs to uncover the depth of the past life character's experience to actually heal it. Regarding the first point, reliving the past life helps in the 'unfreezing process.' In essence, unfreezing wakes up that soul fragment that may still be stuck or split off from the whole psyche. Reliving acts as a way to revive this 'dead' aspect of the soul. Recalling a past life story from the perspective of an observer instead of being fully in the story suggests that a dissociated part of the psyche is having the memory. A dissociated memory is not an accurate account because, that part of the psyche split off as soon as things got difficult. In present life traumatic recall, people often report watching themselves from 'above' or 'off to the side' while the traumatic event is happening. The dissociated part of the psyche can remember the details through observation from the sidelines, but the memory will often not include the emotions, thoughts, and imprints that were present in the body, where the actual event was taking place, simply because that part was not present while the trauma was happening. The second point follows the first one closely. As a therapist in past life work, it is essential to know the inner life of the past life self to affect change and healing.

Stage Three

Death and the Afterlife

Every past life we have had ended in death. Each death is a decisive transition stage for the soul. In therapy, this is where the most crucial part of the healing begins – finishing the unfinished business. Since we know that consciousness survives death, it is possible to follow it in PLT through the death process into the afterlife. Deep Memory Process work in this area is based loosely on the Tibetan Buddhist understanding of the Bardos. Throughout this book I use the terms bardo, spirit world, and afterlife to mean the same thing. The bardo is a transitional state; the term is most commonly used for the state after death and before reincarnation although in the Buddhist view all states of existence are bardo states. The bardo of dying is the transitional plane between life and death, when the elements of the body are breaking down. Traditionally a Lama or priest would read the *Bardo Thotrol* or *Thodol* (*The Tibetan Book of the Dead*) to the dying or recently deceased person. It tells them not to fear death, and explains to them the experiences they will have on the other side so that they can safely navigate through these planes. It warns that once awareness is no longer in a body it will continue to create a reality in the afterlife. The person is urged to turn from the living, to die with peace of mind and heart so that they do not go further into the lower bardos, and attachments are not recreated and experienced as reality on the other side.

The Tibetans describe the light that is perceived immediately after death, and say we must recognize this light as our own true 'Buddha' nature to merge with it. But they also warn there are other lights, one is the light of your own individuated mind. If you fail to see through the illusions and merge with the true light, you will journey further into the lower bardos which eventually lead to rebirth. Many souls obviously do not achieve this recognition upon dying. They bathe temporarily in the light, or miss it altogether, and the weight of the unresolved issues causes them to wander confused, getting lost in the lower bardos where 'karmic gravity' pulls them back into incarnation. Yes, that's why we are all here! Some confusion as to what the afterlife of the soul is like exists today because of the information that is gathered from Near Death Experiences. Many NDE cases document going into a supernal light (although some do describe hellish states as well), meeting loved ones or higher beings, and then being directed or feeling pulled back into their body on the earth plane. Because this is not a full death experience, it is possibly only this first stage of the bardo that is temporarily encountered. This can lead to the misconception that we all go 'to the light' after death and remain there. With NDE, the death process and entry into the bardos can be like visiting a place as opposed to moving there permanently. When you visit somewhere it can be fresh and exciting, you may think, "Gee, this would be a great place to live". When you finally move to that place a different reality sets in. There may be difficulties and complications that arise that were never experienced when just visiting there.

In working with many cases over the years it is apparent to me that it is only a part of the soul that remains in the lower bardos. I think of these parts of the soul as 'split-off psychological complexes' frozen in time. This is the fragmenting effect that trauma has on the psyche. In shamanic terms this is a soul fragment that is split off and stuck in a kind of tape loop, replaying its worries, fears, and unresolved complexes. It is not the entire energy of the soul, but is an earthbound fragment. Thus, a dying thought of "I can't leave them" may play over and over immediately after death at such an increased rate that it fixes the attention of the newly departed soul on the earth plane, causing it to miss its opportunity to fully ascend to higher planes. Such a dying thought can take over the awareness of the departing consciousness, causing it to remain partially earthbound, obsessively focused on its single objective. Consciousness not anchored in physical matter creates reality faster than the speed of light. Songyol Rimpoche writes in the *Tibetan Book of Living and Dying* that once awareness or mind is free of the body at death, it vibrates hundreds of times faster. Thus thought manifests instantly in the bardo, much like it does in our dream states. We create our reality in the afterlife instantaneously.

Buddhism and other traditions such as Hinduism teach that one of the main objectives of life is to be able to die well, thus to achieve eternal freedom from the earth plane or cycle of rebirth. Traditions that have a place for reincarnation in their beliefs all have similar teachings – it is of utmost importance to the evolutionary well being of the soul to die as consciously and untroubled as possible. They explain that the intensity and weight of unfinished desires, emotions, and thoughts in life slow and even retard the soul's progress after death, like taking too much baggage with you on a long journey. Thus they teach that by limiting desires and purifying thoughts and emotions during life, the afterlife passage to higher planes will be easier to complete. It also is taught that meditation on, or invocation of the divine, or a divine being at the moment of death, as a continuation of a lifelong spiritual practice, will also result in clear passage through the bardos. Unfortunately, uttering "Oh My God" at that last moment doesn't seem to work.

Anyone who works in the style of PLT that follows the consciousness into the afterlife will report that many do not perceive the light after death. They are still caught in their emotions and dying thoughts, they are still looking for their loved ones, or they are still angry at the ones who killed them. There are so many variations of the kinds of imprints held at death. That is why in PLT, the state of mind and emotions at death are most important to capture and bring to consciousness because these lead to the lost parts of the soul. A main principle of the bardos is that recognition and liberation are instantaneous. In other words, we only need to see beyond the illusion to be liberated from it. This is useful to know when working with past life characters that are stuck after death. Often the work that happens in the bardo involves getting the soul to give up its obsessive thoughts and leave its complexes behind. You will see in the case studies the different kinds of resolution that happen in these bardo states. They can include the healing of physical traumas carried in the subtle body, reunion with lost loved ones, dialogue with perpetrators, seeking forgiveness from those one has hurt, the finishing of unfinished desires/impulses, or just having a good old catharsis. The reworking of all these imprints in the bardo allows this part of the soul to complete its unfinished business and more fully ascend to higher planes.

Stage Four

Overview, Integration and Review

Once resolution happens in the lower bardos, it is as if the consciousness becomes lighter. It is possible then to ascend to the higher bardos and this often happens spontaneously. These realms are more like the natural domain of spirit that is unfettered by earthly existence. This is the original light the Tibetans describe that consists of unconditional love and grace. Wise beings and images of the divine are often met here. It is a place of clear, pure supernal light where overview of the past life happens, where inspired connections to current life people and places are made, or whole patterns of past lives and the reason for them are revealed, often spontaneously and without direction. It is the place of higher view. Communication here is often direct and intuitive without words. Questions are answered by higher beings concerning the meaning and lessons of the life that was just re-experienced. Often new current life directions and potentials are pointed out. The soul fragment that is resurrected and brought to this plane is often overjoyed to finally come to this place of peace. The experiences that happen here cannot be contained by words. Often I leave my clients in silence to have their own experiences there, but in my many years of working as a guide, the moment still brings tears to my eyes. The energy of the room changes palpably. Every time a client reaches this state during a session, I feel gifted to glimpse this realm of pure divine being along with them, temporarily to bask in it and to witness its direct grace.

After bringing the client fully back into present day consciousness, we work together to recap how this experience fits into the current life context. Often further insight happens this way, but in the following hours and days after a session, clients often report that the insights occur like dominos falling into one another, as they go about their day to day business. After time, the changes that have occurred as a result of the session also become more noticeable, so in some of the cases in this book, the afterthoughts of clients are included.

The stages that occur in regression illuminate much about the psychology of the soul. Even though a lifetime may be in the distant past, it can be very present in the current life psyche. These circumstances from the past shape who we are today – this is the crux of Evolutionary Astrology. The past and the future are tied together by the present, and the choices we make now affect both. Self knowledge of where we have been, and resolution of any limitations from the past, allows us greater freedom in the present and subsequently the future. Hopefully the journey through the archetypes in this book will assist you in deepening your understanding of the past and creating a brighter future for yourself and those you come in contact with.

1

Aries/Mars and the First House

"The ONE, hidden by void,
felt the generation of heat, came into being
as Desire, first seed of Mind..."

Rig Veda

Keywords

Cardinal/Yang//Fire
Separation/anxiety of separation
Initiative
Anger/Rage
Initiation
Desires and Desire nature
Expression of will
Identity
Super human
Freedom
Zarathustra
Independence
Special destiny
War
Narcissism
Loner
Self interest
Self
Roman soldier
Warrior
Violence
Pioneer
Sexual Instinct
Manifestation
Impatience
Sexual Violence
Anger at Limitations
Intolerance for weakness
Destroyer
Instinct
Paranoia
Confrontation
Impulse
Primal
Pushing the limits
Spontaneous enthusiasm
Competition

The Natural Archetype

Aries as the first sign of the zodiac wheel is a primary, youthful energy. It is associated with the springtime and the beginnings of life. Aries as Yang/Male energy moves outwards and emerges out of the Pisces archetype which is the end of the zodiac wheel. Pisces is the cosmic ocean where life arises from and eventually returns to. Dane Rudhyar attributes 'the-will-to-be-manifest' as a part of the Aries archetype and describes the Sabian symbol of the first degree of Aries as "A woman has arisen from the ocean; a seal embraces her". The individual emerges from the collective and realizes 'self' for the first time. Without movement away from the source, there would be no individuality or diversity. The core urge within Aries is to become a separate, distinct being.

Aries can be likened to the 'terrible twos' that any parent is familiar with. In fact using this stage of childhood as a lens to look at some of the natural qualities of Aries is quite appropriate, as it coincides with the first Mars return.

As the child nears the age of two it bewilders the parents who perhaps just a few months earlier found him/her to be quite compliant and attentive to every word they said, but now, he/she stops listening. The child's impulse is purely self motivated. It is what I want (desire) and I want it now! Being a toddler, the child now has a new sense of mobility, and wants to explore and discover new things; there is an essential need for freedom. This newly found sense of independence tolerates no limitations. The child is fully open to new experience and can be bold and daring in going about it, taking risks beyond what had been normal up to this point.

Here the child is making the first separation from the parents and is willfully developing a sense of self. This developmental stage is characterized by the child forcefully expressing its will, "MINE" and "NO!" become the child's favorite words. This sense of self is instinctual and not premeditated. It is created by aggressive assertion of self and at this stage that point is made by angry outbursts. The child is discovering itself through confrontation and opposition. The anger in the terrible twos arises from impatience, and a frustration or intolerance of limitations. Again, because all of this is happening instinctually, we can understand that the anger can arise as a way to create an immediate boundary. In this case it is a boundary of 'I' and 'Me' in opposition to 'You'. As the microcosm reflects the macrocosm, the stages of our life mirror the larger process of evolution and growth.

Mars and its relationship to Pluto is central to the foundational principles of Evolutionary Astrology (EA). Before Pluto's discovery Mars ruled both Aries and Scorpio, and this shows us different aspects of Mars. Mars as the ancient ruler of Scorpio is where personal will eventually meets a higher will. Pluto in EA correlates to the soul and the force of evolution that it is subject to. Pluto as a symbol for the soul inherently reflects the desire nature that is at the core of every soul. There exist within two primary desires, one to separate from the source and one to return. Mars as ruler of Aries, with its outward yang energy represents unbridled personal will. The will is directed outward towards fulfillment of whatever is desired. The divine intention here is to separate, to become distinct and have a unique identity. As this relates to the desire nature, Aries/Mars is the personal will to act upon desires. But separation from the source and fulfillment of personal desires is not meant to be everlasting, at one point the wheel turns and it becomes necessary to forge a path of return. This happens slowly over the course of many lifetimes and is what evolution is about.

Throughout time all spiritual paths have intended to point a way back to the source. But the personal desire must be ignited to pursue such a path. It takes many lifetimes for this desire to awaken within and many more to complete the path of return. Mars as the lower octave of Pluto shows the struggle that happens when the personal will to remain separate clashes with the soul's will to return to the source. Evolution nonetheless is a natural cycle, and is reflected symbolically, through the zodiac wheel as a progression of consciousness. In Aries, to separate from the source and become a distinct being is where the soul dies, and the small egocentric self reigns, but the cycle turns in the upper half of the chart at the cusp of Libra, as consciousness expands to include ever increasing circles of awareness of the world outside of the self. The polarity point to Aries is Libra, and that is where 'the other' is met. The challenge, and often the battle between oneself and others, is a turning point for soul consciousness to awaken and begin to eclipse the 'small self'.

Mars' relationship to Scorpio as its ancient ruler continues this awakening, as the battles that happen here challenge one to merge more deeply with others, and also to penetrate to the core of oneself, to find the soul within. Soul consciousness is 'birthed' by personal trials and effort in Scorpio and this is the true esoteric meaning of the death and rebirth cycles this sign is known for – the 'small self' – dies, so the 'greater self' can be born. In Scorpio the personal will combines with the soul's and eventually divine will is realized. Within Scorpio desire is purified, intentions and motives are examined, resulting in transformation. This is why most Eastern traditions, being aligned closely with the evolution of the soul, teach about the purification of desires so that divine reality is realized. The Hindu practice called 'Neti, Neti', 'Not this, Not This', is a mantra that is meant to evolve consciousness to the point of its true identity (one with the divine).

The repeating of 'not this' as thoughts, sensations, desires arise... is meant to eliminate anything that separates the individual consciousness from the all encompassing divine within.

This is like the parable of the prodigal son, who leaves the father's house and becomes mired in all the pleasures and stimulations of life. He wanders far and wide, squanders his father's fortune and eventually desires to return home. He is welcomed home lavishly by the father, who then says to the jealous brother who stayed home, "My son, you are always with me, and everything I have is yours. But we had to celebrate and be glad, because this brother of yours was dead and is alive again; he was lost and is now found" (Luke 15:11-32). On an esoteric level this parable can be seen to reflect the exact intention of creation that is reflected in the zodiac wheel; leaving the father's house (Involution, Incarnation); the adventures on the journey (many past lives) and then, satiated, returning home (Evolution). Like the prodigal son, the soul must first experience its separating desires and eventually exhaust them, before turning back home. Mars is the force that allows one to accomplish either intention.

Aries in Past Life Experiences

The Aries archetype is a part of the karmic axis when:

Pluto is in Aries or the first house or
The South Node is in Aries or the first house or
The ruler of the South Node is in Aries or the first house or
Mars aspects Pluto, the nodal axis or rulers of the nodes.

Identity

Because identity is at the core of this archetype, individuals with strong Aries often have a sense of rightness and purpose about their individuality and the will and courage to manifest it. In past lives, issues surrounding 'identity' come to the forefront. Having such a strong sense of self can leave one feeling lonely or singled out as 'special' by others. In times past, being the 'chosen one' was often not that much fun. Typical scenarios include being identified as special, chosen for some great work or destiny and being cultivated to fulfill that role.

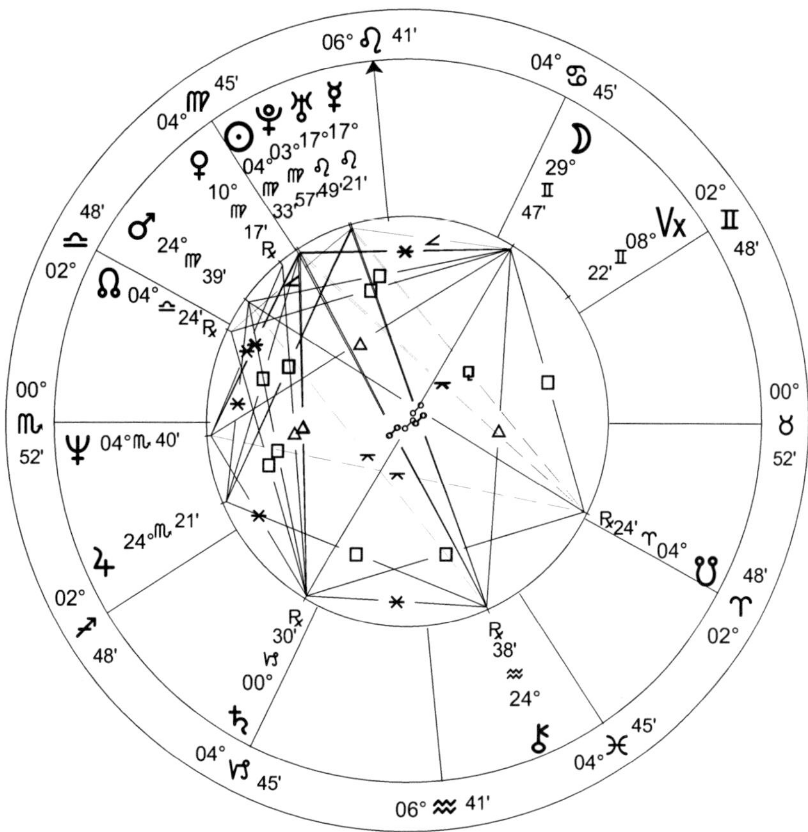

Chart A (Porphyry houses)

Chart A

One client with an Aries SN in the sixth house was chosen in a past life as a young child to be an escort to the Pharaoh in his afterlife. Because she was only eight or so at the time, she had no idea what this meant, but felt very proud of her 'special destiny.' She was taken from her home, but that was not painful to her because she was overcome with excitement at what this new adventure was going to bring. She was taken to a palace and adorned with jewels and fine clothes, all the time being told what a special honor she was chosen for. She stayed there for few months, being adored and pampered, and loving every moment of all the attention, which was quite a contrast from her humble roots (Pluto and ruler of the SN in Virgo). One day she was told that finally she was going to meet the Pharaoh; she was adorned and given a liquid drug to drink (Neptune inconjunct SN). Feeling woozy and quite relaxed, she was laid into a sarcophagus and sealed in. She remained there for some time singing to herself, imagining what this meeting was going to be like. When she tired of this, she called out to the others and to the Pharaoh. She didn't get any response and eventually panic set in. Inevitably, she died of suffocation in terror and with the deep imprint that being special or having a destiny is deadly. In her current life she had a deep need to be noticed, with a subconscious fear of the same. Psychologically she feared limitations and commitments of any sort (Saturn square the nodes, Pluto is also in the tenth) including relationships (Aries/Libra). Physically, the fear of limitation manifested as actual claustrophobia. After working with this past life, the client was able to reclaim her essential need for freedom, yet not have it compulsively control her life.

When one has experienced a sense of a destiny that is unfulfilled, or it turned out to be not what was expected, the subconscious self will still be seeking a completion. There can be an over attachment to the 'special' identity, which stops one from participating in the ongoing process of self-discovery that is the healthy and unhindered expression of Aries. The natural square from Capricorn can cause a fear that tries to solidify this natural process and fixate on one identity. The natural square from Cancer adds the element of emotional security tied into a fixed image of oneself. But as Aries marches on, despite Cancer and Capricorn's urgings, often an 'identity crisis' is the result. In past lives, if one was unable to fully form their identity or became overly attached to it, much of the current life energy may go into protecting even the slightest sense of self, even if it is not deeply felt. Constantly arguing to have one's 'own way' can be a substitute for an authentic sense of being. Or because one may subconsciously fear losing their individuality, they may have an overly narcissistic orientation in relationship to others or may avoid involvement altogether.

Destiny and Mission

The imprint of the loneliness associated with being special often shows up in past lives spent as a leader or a person consumed with a mission (another version of a special destiny). In one past life, a young man with Mars conjunct a Gemini SN was a courier/messenger delivering war time commands in an ancient culture. He believed fervently in his mission and took great care and pride in his ability to evade capture through his physical agility and intelligence (Mars/athletics and Gemini/cleverness). The Mars conjunction to the SN signified this Gemini energy in overdrive. In that past life it seemed that he experienced an addiction (what we would call 'runner's high' today), so much so that it was all consuming. Aries/Mars also rules adrenals/adrenaline. As he grew older, it became physically impossible to continue with this mission, yet he refused to acknowledge his own ageing body (both Mars and Gemini contain elements of the Puer – the eternal youth). When out on a mission he was ambushed and killed. He died angry that his body failed him and that he had to face the fact that he was not eternally young or invincible (Mars/Gemini). In his current life, his main complaint was that he couldn't stay still long enough to accomplish anything of value. He felt he was always in 'overdrive' and described himself as having ADD (attention deficit disorder). Mars conjunct his Gemini SN added fuel to the diverse interests of Gemini not allowing him to focus on one goal – his Sagittarian NN. Once this past life self realized it was not invincible and was able to put to rest the 'need for speed' (Mars) he was able to embrace the qualities of his NN by maintaining a broad yet more focused approach to life.

Other 'mission' stories include being unable to complete what one set out for. Commonly one was too young or was ill equipped for the mission. Past life soldiers, crusaders and young initiates who failed their mission or died as a result of it can experience a present life fear of starting things. Another common scenario is the pioneer, either actual or someone who was ahead of his or her time in some way. Many pioneers set off on their own and never made it to their 'manifest destiny', being ambushed along the way or dying of illness or hardships. Additionally, people who 'pioneer' in other ways by being ahead of their time often suffer imprints of being persecuted or misunderstood. Those who blaze trails often have had to 'go it alone'. People who have had such lives can find solace in actualizing their Libra NN potential. Finding not only love partnerships but creative or even intellectual partners that they can share their inspiration with, will broaden their ability to affect the 'world at large'. But more importantly such partnerships, if approached openly, will soothe their lonely hearts.

Initiations

Initiation is a frequent theme in Aries involving either initiating action or actual initiations. Failed or thwarted initiations can leave people with the feeling that they constantly need to prove themselves in their current life, especially if they died mid-process in a past life. Anxiety can lie behind much of what they do in the current life, pushing them to achieve, to accomplish more and more, without being able to take comfort in what they have done already. There may also be extreme anxiety at the prospect of any test or competition, or a complete avoidance of such circumstances.

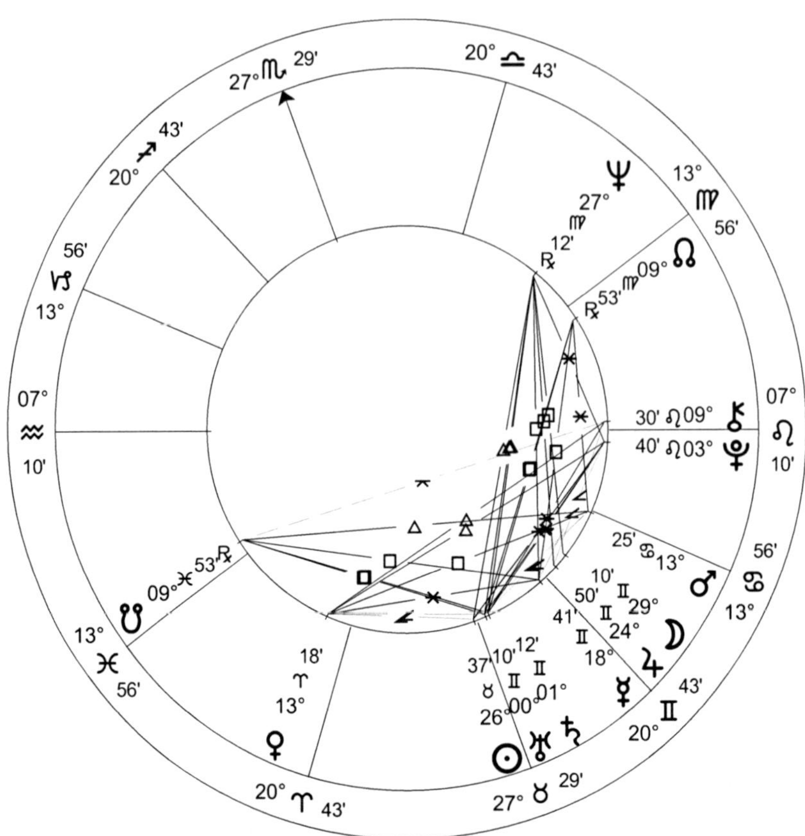

Chart B (Porphyry houses)

Chart B

A client with a Pisces SN in the first house (Aries' natural house) was a young man in desert culture. He was given a message to deliver (ruler of SN is squared by three planets in Gemini), but with unclear directions (Pisces). He set off, regardless, feeling quite proud that he was chosen and full of confidence (first house and Pluto in Leo) but because of his youth, lack of clear guidance and experience, he got lost (Pisces) and ended up dying. This past life character died with the imprint that he failed, and in the after-life was merciless towards himself that despite his youth and unclear directions he should have been able to accomplish the task (ruler of SN in Virgo also Pluto in the sixth house – not good enough).

This imprint played out in another past life that reflected the aspects of pushing the limits and going too far - too fast. In that lifetime he was a young boy who set off on an initiation-into-manhood journey with another boy. This time the elders gave them clear instruction, they were to arrive at a particular location as fast as possible (Gemini planets square ruler of SN, and the first house SN – speed), complete several tasks, and bring back proof of each. They were told that the journey had to take place solely by land, but this young boy, filled with the spirit of competition, ended up arguing with his reluctant partner on the journey, convincing him through sheer force of will that they must take to the river in order to beat the other boys (Aries/first house).

Prior to this journey, the boy had felt quite unnoticed (Pisces) in his tribe and was seizing this opportunity to prove himself and gain recognition. They took to the river in a makeshift boat which ended up capsizing and drowning them both (Pisces). In the afterlife the boy met with the elders again in spirit form, and the first thing they said to him was, "You should have listened to us!" The past life directly reflects some of the lessons of this client's current life, indicated by the seventh house NN polarity point. Being open to others is a general way to look at the learning for Aries/first house moving towards Libra/seventh house, which includes taking other's needs into consideration and being open to listen and really hear other people.

Instinct

Aries is associated with instinct in that there isn't much that is premeditated when Mars is involved; impulsive, immediate action is the natural expression of this archetype. The primal energy of Mars also relates to the basic animal instinct and when it has been wounded in the past it results in an alienation from an essential part of oneself.

A woman with Mars conjunct her Scorpio SN in the sixth house had a past life as a primitive woman. Her role or service (sixth house) was to find food sources for her community. She had a name in the tribe which pointed to this natural ability which roughly translated as 'she whose feet know where to go'. She would instinctually (Mars) follow her feet to find game, the primary natural resource (Scorpio) of the time. One particularly hard winter she didn't get the instinctive message about where to go. This resulted in all the people falling into sickness and starvation and eventually they all froze to death. She died with a huge sense of guilt (Pluto/Virgo and SN in the sixth house). In her current life she is a natural intuitive, and her intuition is based quite deeply in her instinctual nature. In order for her to bring this gift out fully in her current life as a healer (her nodes are on the sixth/twelfth house axis), she has had to heal many layers of fears, doubts and wounding relating to this ability.

Competition and Impatience

Predator and Prey is another theme that falls into the Aries/Mars realm. It is not uncommon for individuals with this archetype in the karmic axis to recall very primitive past lives, when to hunt or be hunted was the main theme. Gladiator lives (Mars/Aries is also associated with the Roman Empire) can also carry this kind of theme. It is either you or the lion and most of the time the lion wins. The raw energy of competition is clear in nature and is necessary to maintain life. Animals and humans all compete for resources and the right to mate. Well harnessed Aries/Mars energy is the edge one has over any competitor. Because Aries precedes Taurus (survival) in the natural zodiac, this edge is needed to survive. One man with Mars square the nodal axis of SN Taurus/NN Scorpio went back to a primitive life in which he and an older male sibling were in constant competition for food. In a particularly violent confrontation he smashed this brother's head in, killing him and feeling no remorse about it. To this client's dismay, he realized that this past life was the root cause of an extreme current life sibling rivalry, as the one he had killed was his brother again. This one past life was the beginning of a long karmic history between the two of them, each repeatedly vowing vengeance and switching roles as victim and persecutor through many lifetimes. Mars/Aries when combined with Scorpio is particularly potent in this regard, and can reflect this type of imprint, causing one to be locked in battle with someone over eons. 'Evening out the score' takes on a different meaning when seen in Venus' light. The learning in the Libra polarity is not only about inclusiveness and sharing but also equality.

Sun sign Aries people are often described as impatient, itching to go, and unable to tolerate any limitations in the pursuit of what they want. I have many clients with Aries/Mars in the karmic axis who died prematurely in past lives because of sudden, rash or careless action. Their stories contain elements of not listening to sound advice, disregarding warnings of danger, and even tempting danger with an attitude of extreme willfulness. Lives cut short by premature death form another theme in Aries past lives. The residue left from this type of experience can include always feeling rushed for time, a fear or paranoia of dying at young age, inability to complete things, living recklessly, tempting death or deciding "What's the use?" because subconsciously one feels the end is just around the corner.

Anger and Rage

Anger is often the first energy expressed when one's boundaries are threatened or violated. Healthy anger helps one to maintain their sense of 'self' (Aries). When we feel our life is in danger, our biology immediately reacts by releasing adrenalin (adrenals are ruled by Mars) into the system, activating the fight or flight response. Simultaneously, the immediate emotional reaction is often anger, which motivates the entire psyche to respond to the threat. When a person consciously attempts to override this natural reaction "I mustn't be angry", or is forced to because of circumstances, a complex with anger at its core can form.

The deeper in the subconscious the complex is buried, the more degenerated and debilitating may be the imprint. Likewise, the deeper the trauma from the past, the more buried it may be. As part of the Aries archetype, anger is often deeply buried and suppressed because societal conditioning commonly disallows its expression (especially for women) or the anger was part of the fight or flight response which did not serve to protect one from danger. Repressed or thwarted anger can turn into seething rage, and as an energy it demands expression. Denial or suppression of it will not make it go away.

A person's unexpressed rage from a past life can carry into the current life in a plethora of ways. It may be somatic, meaning stored in the body (migraines and tight muscles are common); it may be just in a general tendency to be combative, driving others away and not allowing that person to connect in meaningful ways; or there may be unexpected outbursts that seem to take over at the slightest trigger. In the current life, these symptoms reflect deeper causes, and the more removed from consciousness they are, the more the archetype takes on negative qualities. Ultimately though, the evolutionary intention indicated by the Libra NN includes healing of these symptoms to bring the person into balance and harmony with themselves and with others. Healing is found within the problem by delving into the rage instead of keeping the same defense of suppression. Energy is freed to allow for not only healing but also movement to a higher octave of the same energy. The same rage that drives people away, when healed and restored to its natural stasis in the psyche, becomes the outward moving energy of Mars that allows one to say "YES" to life and be open to others (Libra). Thus the wounded expression of anger is no longer compulsive, and new potentials emerge.

One client with a Sun in Aries in the twelfth house square the nodal axis of Leo SN/Aquarius NN had difficulties with the open expression of anger. Because the Sun is the ruler of the SN and squares the axis, its sign of Aries combined with the twelfth house archetype of Pisces, contributed to the past life source of her issue. The combination of the Aries/Pisces archetypes, are often described as manifesting as a passive/aggressive complex. In her past life it became clear how such a complex formed. She was a hungry young boy who was caught for stealing some food from a medieval marketplace. Without any trial or time to integrate his captivity he was ruthlessly dragged away, chained to a wall in a dungeon and left to hang there alone. He struggled furiously to escape, screaming, pulling until he exhausted himself and collapsed. This alternating cycle of fury (Aries) and collapse (twelfth house) went on as he fluctuated between rage/fury and hopelessness and grief. The erosion (twelfth house) of his will (Aries) happened progressively over time as he starved to death and eventually died. Even though he had expressed his rage, this past life self was deeply wounded, as for all his fight, it got him nowhere. This young boy's life was cut short (common in the Aries archetype) and all his unspent youth and vigor was shut down. This also had contributed to a current life issue of feeling energetically depleted. Once the young boy was able to break free from the past life dungeon and reclaim his freedom, new healthy energy returned to the client's current life allowing her to express her natural anger and will more freely.

Will and Power

Friedrich Nietzsche, best known for *Thus Spoke Zarathustra,* expounded upon a theory that the will for power is greater than even the will to survive. Mars, in its most primate expression, can manifest as a raw, will-to-power, creating a 'god-like' complex.

In the positive expression of being 'god-like', the individual has embraced and integrated the Libra polarity and becomes a co-creator with the divine. Personal will is consciously linked with divine will. The separate self has realized its interconnectedness and harmoniously acts in cooperation. In a distorted or evolving form of this ideal, personal will solely for one's own gain becomes a narcissistic complex, or even worse a 'Zarathustra' complex – being 'god-like.' Several clients with Pluto in Leo in the first house had past lives as 'god-like' kings or rulers. This carried over in the current life as a larger-than-life sense of self and purpose (delusions of grandeur) that was not reflected in their current life circumstances. Yet the urge to strive for rulership was still there, causing a profound inability to connect with others or themselves in a natural, meaningful way.

Pushing the limits of the 'god-like' experience can result in intoxication with power that can urge the person to assume power over life and death itself. This is one way that violence and destruction become a part of the Aries archetype. Like Shiva who dances both the dance of creation and destruction, inherent within life is death. In order for anything to live, something must die, so the paradox found in this first sign of zodiac, is that the very force of creation carries destruction inherent in it. Sigmund Freud identified conflicting urges in the psyche, which he called Eros/Libido and Thanatos/Destrudo – that are constantly at war with each other. Eros/Libido is the instinct towards life and creation, Thanatos/Destrudo is the death instinct and the urge of destruction.

The destrudo urge arises out of fear: we project outward whatever we fear or are unable to integrate in ourselves and often fight it 'out there'. Intrinsically, Aries/Mars does not seek integration as it is an outward moving energy; this dynamic makes it easy for others to become the enemy that needs to be destroyed. For the most part the thanatos/destrudo urges lie deep in the shadow of our psyche, not acted upon consciously and not without checks and balances, hiding behind the veneer of civility. Unfortunately, anything that is repressed comes out distorted or twisted in some way, in the individual and the collective. When our life force is blocked or wounded in any way, it flows to the lower aspects. Perhaps this was Jung's reflection when he stated, "An unconscious Eros always expresses itself as will to power". To see thanatos/destrudo unchecked one must look into the world of the psychopath or in one of Mars' favorite haunts – the battlefield.

The Wounds of the Warrior

> "However much soldiers regret killing, once it is finished, however much they spend their lives trying to cope with the experience, the act itself, fueled by fear, excitement, the pull of the crowd, and the god-like exhilaration of destroying is often thrilling."
>
> Chris Hedges – *War is a Force That Gives Us Meaning*[1]

War is a collective illness that plays out the shadow side of any society. The natural square between Aries and Capricorn seems to point to the fact that war and politics feed off each other's dysfunction. One of the sickest aspects of a war-like society is that war is considered normal: Saturn/Capricorn, this is reality and the ends justify the means. Furthermore, society can hide in Saturn's well defined boundary of normalcy; but to the individual who is in the war zone, this reality can be quite a different picture.

Soldier and warrior past lives are predominate in both Aries/Mars and Capricorn/Saturn signatures. Because of the frequency in which warrior/soldier past lives show up in these archetypes, and the fact that war colors much of human history, the past life imprints of war need to be explored in depth.

Capricorn/Saturn signatures are more often career soldiers, those who are climbing the military ladder of promotion; patriots; and those who have followed in the father's or ancestor's footsteps. The sense of duty/responsibility and honor plays a major role for this type of soldier. Equally, this signature reflects the repressive nature of Saturn and can be found in the past lives of those who are brutalized themselves or were conscripted/drafted into service. The Aries/Mars signature carries with it more the wound of the sheer violence of war (destrudo) and the madness of killing. As the opening quote says "the act itself, fueled by fear, excitement, the pull of the crowd, and the god-like exhilaration of destroying is often thrilling", the Mars warrior can easily find himself swept up in the thrill and power of killing. In both signatures I have seen the brute, or the grunt who just kills without remorse or any question of why.

We must keep in mind that the face of war has changed. Since World War I, war has become more systemized and mechanized, cold and calculated – actually much more Saturn-like. We live in the age of the 'Military

---

1. Hedges, Chris, *War is a Force that Gives us Meaning*, Public Affairs, NY, NY, 2002.

Industrial Complex' – the business of war. During their time, the gods of war Ares and Mars inspired a different kind of battle – one of individual heroism, hand to hand combat, swords, and knives. The range of the arrow and the catapult were the furthest distance participants could stand outside the bloodshed (Mars associated with both weaponry and blood). Since past life experiences come from all periods of history and the range of different types of wars fought, from ancient territorial/tribal battles to holy wars and even recent wars, it is important to understand the context in which the soldier was fighting. The experience of the 'divinely' inspired crusader can be very different than the soldier killed in Vietnam.

Regardless, there is a commonality of wounds from such lives: shut down, loss of humanity, isolation, shock, disillusionment, guilt, horror, continued cycles of violence and rage to name a few. We only need to look at any present day soldier who has seen battle to understand the depth of trauma to the soul that happens. The term PTSD (Post Traumatic Stress Disorder) is used to describe these lingering psychological wounds that haunt present day soldiers who return from war. When one has seen battle or been a victim of it in past lives, it is highly possible that these PTSD symptoms are carried forward into the current life.

To begin with, archetypally, the warrior/soldier often leaves behind a family or lover/wife. Those left behind symbolically represent the disowned anima (his own inner feminine) that he must disconnect from in order to conquer the world. War is also often waged to conquer a people and/or their territory. Many of my clients with Aries/Mars and also Saturn/Capricorn in the karmic axis had past lives where they were caught up in the drive to conquer as leaders or soldiers. Soldiers cannot ride into battle with their hearts on their sleeve. It is much better to leave those things at home. This is one of the first wounds, the disconnection from personal feelings. The feeling nature can become compartmentalized, locked away from the total psyche. It may only be safe to feel in certain circumstances, or it may not be safe to feel at all. A famous painting by Rubens and Brueghel entitled *The Return from War: Venus disarms Mars* shows Mars being held and transfixed in Venus' gaze while his sword, shield and helmet are removed. Looking at this painting, you can imagine that Mars not only erotically desires Venus, but through her also wants to heal and reclaim his own disowned anima. Sadly though, in the painting, as a comment on our collective obsession with war, the forge of Vulcan in the background continues to create weapons.

Showing that love and peace can only disarm Mars for a short time, before his Eros is projected back into the battle, making war an erotic act. Venus, or the Libra polarity, offers a return to the heart and feeling nature, that must happen at some point in anyone's incarnational history who has lost their humanity in war.

Dying in the midst of battle, in a state of hyper-arousal and fear, 'kill or be killed' is imprinted upon the psyche with such force that the raw impact can take many, many lifetimes to heal. A soldier/warrior who dies with such a fresh imprint can carry a general sense of paranoia into future lives. The person may fear any energy moving towards them as the enemy. That energy can be represented by people, events, or just opportunities that life presents. Further, dying in the midst of battle leaves a huge unfinished impulse (in this case kill or defend oneself), which can be the cause of a formation of a complex. Defeat in the Aries consciousness is not necessarily registered as lingering defeat (as in the Capricorn consciousness) but is more commonly carried into the current life as suppressed rage. The slightest trigger can set off that rage and can start a new a cycle of violence in the current life. Even if the violence is not acted upon physically, the person psychologically is caught in the dynamic of feeling "the world is not a safe place" or "life is a battle" and thus reality responds.

Most men who go into battle are in the prime of their youth, the springtime of their lives. Having life cut off prematurely in the past can lead to a pervasive sense of there not being enough time in the present life. This manifests as a race against time, and can even play out in the bedroom (Mars being sexual libido) as premature ejaculation. Mentioned earlier, Mars/Aries signatures in the nodal axis can often indicate a violent and/or premature death. Such sudden deaths can affect the soul profoundly. When our past life selves don't know they are dead, their unfinished urges can overtake our consciousness with a force not unlike being possessed. One stunned past life warrior was living inside a client, giving him a sense of invincibility. This warrior died so suddenly on the battlefield he never realized he was dead. A fragment of this client's soul was still strutting-his-stuff outside of some castle, where he had been storming the walls when he died. Because this past life self was still trying to conquer the castle, this client also lived continuously on the offensive causing confrontation in all his endeavors and was bewildered as to how this repeatedly happened. His past life sense of invincibility caused him in the present to push boundaries and limits with no thought of his own frailty. Many times in his life he said, he was stunned when he was rebuked or wounded, as it never occurred to him that he was vulnerable. The Libra polarity is the essence of vulnerability, as Venus desires to embrace all of life with heart wide open.

Warriors can come to rely only on themselves. Ultimately, when the fighting begins, their survival depends mainly upon their own instincts. This is another way the loner becomes a part of the Aries archetype. Especially if death as a part of a platoon was the result, one can die with the feeling that others cannot be relied upon. Such past life conditioning makes it difficult to be inclusive and open to others. Confrontation has been conditioned to be a way of life. Most of the time the person is quite unaware of the tendency to attract confrontational situations. Via the polarity point of Libra/Venus, the evolutionary intention is open to a new level of relatedness with the world and with others.

Aries/Mars past life signatures can also form a sort of consciousness that comes into life with what I call the 'volume turned up to 100'. As mentioned earlier, society 'normalizes' war, making it just another day in the history of humanity. Past lives of violence and terror can create a sense of normalized violence in the present. "Oh, ho hum, it's just another life of hacking off heads, raping and pillaging". This destrudo urge can also lie at the root of any thrill seeking behavior that constantly pushes limits. It can be acted out in skydiving and bungee jumping, or in extreme forms of sadistic sex or even self-mutilation. One client with an Aries SN and Pluto in the eighth house had a past life experience as a woman passionately having sex with her lover. Her lover was strangling her during sex, heightening her ecstasy, the passion was out of control and he accidently killed her. She died before she completed her orgasm, which caused a variety of present life sexual complications.

Aries is the first of the angular/cardinal signs in the natural chart (Cancer, Libra and Capricorn are the others). Angular energy is about initiating change. When a SN or Pluto is in an angular sign or house it indicates a new cycle of evolution is occurring in the current life. Many people with this placement can feel that they are at the end of long karmic cycles – they finally have exhausted particular themes. In the life of the soul this is not always an easy process. It appears that souls choose to 'experiment' with certain themes and then have successive lifetimes that progressively go through every possible experience with that theme.

The following case shows the long, arduous process of how a soul comes to the end of a cycle. The series of lifetimes shows the evolution of the soldier/warrior and some of the basic wounds and the resolution of the cycle of a typical Aries/first house/Mars theme – Violence and the Warrior. This chart also illustrates both types of the soldier/warrior as the SN is in Capricorn and Pluto is in the first house, which blends the archetypes of Aries and Capricorn.

Chart C

Some of this client's earliest past life memories are of battle scenes, many of those that arose spontaneously in his life without him actively seeking them out. One of his first complete regressions into such memories was as a barbarian living a life of complete violence and plunder. He had vivid recalls of rape of women, taking over villages and hacking people to death with

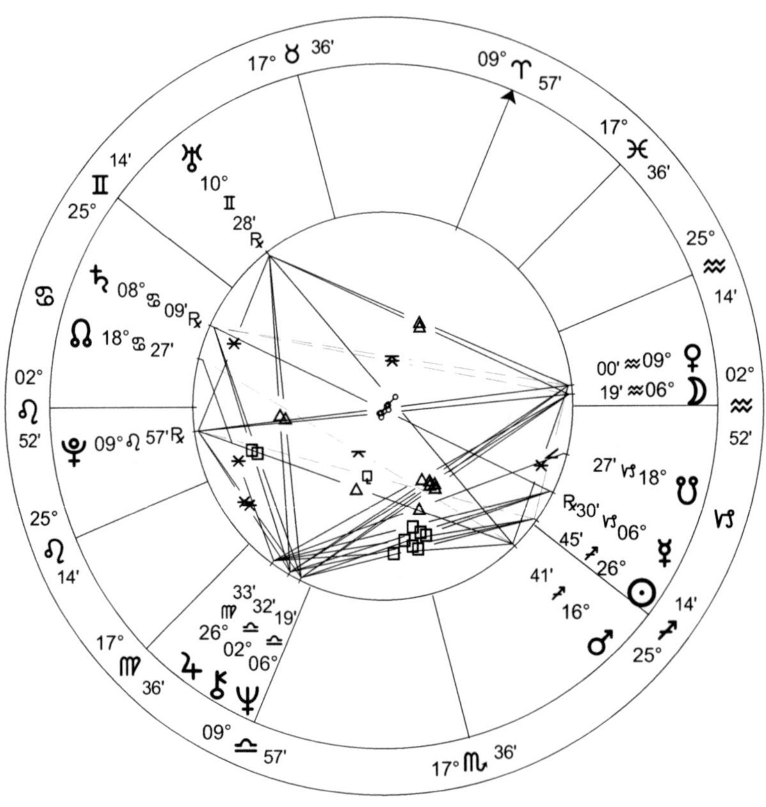

Chart C (Porphyry houses)

swords and battle axes (Aries/Mars rules swords and knives). Furthermore, he was completely in character and had no remorse, and admitted to feeling intoxicated with the power of killing (destrudo in action). If we put this into a linear context we might assume this was an early past life in his incarnational history. The Pluto in Leo in the first house combined with the Capricorn SN created a 'what I want I take' mentality and the brute authority to do so.

In a later regression he had the memory of a life as a Roman soldier (Aries/Mars associated with the Roman Empire), trudging through the desert. His Pluto in the first house with the south node in Capricorn in the sixth, was now expressed as soldiering as a way of life (career). But he had also witnessed the brutality of the Roman Empire and how they tortured or killed their own soldiers and centurions if they failed in their job of killing. It was a life of drudgery living under the oppression (Capricorn) of the Roman Empire. In this life he died violently but not in battle, he was killed by a lion (Pluto is in Leo) while going out to pee in the bush.

He had several other warrior/soldier lives in between these, a few of them are lifetimes spent at sea in battle (ruler of the SN is in Cancer in the twelfth).

Next he found himself as a mercenary soldier. His 'career' continued as he was hired by the papal army, which was assembled to destroy a group of people that had been deemed heretical. Now he was working under the authority (Capricorn) of the church. Christianity is correlated with the Virgo/Pisces, sixth/twelfth house axis, which is his nodal axis. He had been born into a peasant family and his father was an authoritative abuser (SN in Capricorn).

The army advanced upon the 'heretics' and he found himself participating in the most brutal forms of killing he had ever seen. He relived, with horror, that amidst the orgy of violence (first house Pluto), he cut the arms off of a woman he had just raped (Pluto in the first house acting like a Pluto/Mars aspect). In his current life he met this woman and married her, Venus and the Moon in the seventh house are both opposed his Pluto – he had to work out some of this karma through relationship. The polarity point to Pluto is also the seventh house. At this point in the past life he admitted he was swimming in blood and dizzy with the sickness of it all. Unlike his earlier brutal lives, he was nauseated, and completely crushed with the weight of the guilt of killing, and he threw himself off a cliff. The SN in

Capricorn and also in the sixth house correlates to guilt causing a feeling of absolute futility/hopelessness, with suicide perceived as the only way out. The fall failed to kill him and he lay there broken and crippled. Some of the surviving 'heretics' actually came to rescue him and although he was partially crippled they nursed him back to health. He stayed with them, learning to respect them and their ways and three years later they were again, the victims of another onslaught. He was burned alive with them in another wave of persecution.

In retrospect, he claims that this was the rock bottom of all of his soldier lives... the seeds for the turning point have now been sown. This final story is his actual last life before his current one. Here we see the end of the cycle happening in his last life and his current life as a combination of culmination and initiation, in a new stage of evolution.

He was the son of a well-to-do landowner in Bavaria, Germany in the 1880s. He described his father as distant and cold like the previous past life (Capricorn SN). His father sent him to military school where he trained to become a lower echelon military officer (Capricorn SN). World War I started and he was sent to the front lines commanding a small unit. Now instead of himself doing the killing he was ordering others to do so. Regardless, he was wounded by a shell and was sent back home, having lost his leg below the knee. He was now crippled (Capricorn SN and Chiron squaring ruler of the SN, Saturn) as he was in his previous life. He ended up getting a supervisory job at a munitions plant, overseeing the shipment of needed arms for the war (first house Pluto – weaponry).

He started to get disillusioned with the war (Neptune squares ruler of his SN – Saturn), knowing the amount of destruction the arms he is sending out will do. His view now is that the war is not an honorable war it is simply mass slaughter (warrior honor codes and honor in battle belong both to the Aries and Capricorn archetype). Further to this, the ruler of Pluto's sign is the Sun in Sagittarius and also the ruler of his SN, Saturn, is squared by Neptune both pointing to idealism. He left this post and started another business with a friend. Economically, Germany was in deep depression at the time. The disillusionment now was about his father's class and the military class that he came from, who were currently running the country. He was seething with hatred and rage (Pluto in the first), and along with his friend joined the Communist party (Capricorn – politics). The Communist party at the time was to the left of the official party and was outlawed. The Nazi party (the Brown Shirts) was on the rise politically to the right. He met regularly in secret with his communist friends but one night several Nazis burst in and took them captive. He and his friends were brought to a work camp. Separated from them at the camp he lived as slave labor and was slowly starving to death. He was also periodically dragged into interrogation about his fellow Communists and over a period of weeks he was tortured to death. He died with an enormous sense of guilt because he was not sure if under torture he betrayed any of his comrades or not. Fortunately, after death he met again with his comrades and found out that he did not betray them. But he was still seething with hatred for the Nazis in the afterlife, and eventually as he met the souls of the torturers, he confronted them. During this cathartic process suddenly he had an epiphany. He was stunned with the sudden realization that they are he and he is them. That they were simply rivals: two sides of the same coin. Had circumstances been different, and he and his party had been in power, he felt they would just as easily have ordered the incarceration, killing and torture of their political rivals.

A high light-filled entity spontaneously appeared to him; he identified this being as Jesus. He was shown a panorama of what he described as the last two thousand years of his participation in the karma of violence and war, which caused him to sob saying, "it is endless". This spiritual being gently told him, "It is over, you are finished with that". He sobbed more with this realization, feeling deep in his soul the truth of that statement. He stayed with this 'knowing' for some time in this state, letting thousands of years of guilt, violence, anger and abuse wash away in his tears.

He realized that this is why in his current life he chose to be a pacifist, renouncing ever taking up arms. Even when he was small he refused to join the Boy Scouts (seeing them as a pseudo-military group). He also knew that he met this inner warrior earlier in his life, when he was a school boy. He jumped on a boy who angered him, and it took four others to pull him off. He was shaken then by the power of the deadly rage unleashed in him and vowed not to let it take over him again. Had he not met these inner characters therapeutically in the later course of his life, they would have remained suppressed and unhealed, most likely taking over his actions at the slightest trigger and when he least expected it. Without conscious work and healing he would simply have continued the violent cycles of rage.

In reviewing these lives and others, he came to understand that the whole cycle of warriorship was created because he rejected his own disempowered inner feminine. In one earlier lifetime where he was brutalized as a young girl of 12, he emphatically stated at death that he never wanted to be a female again, "I won't get hurt again". His soul then created many male lives, which in a patriarchal society often meant being a warrior or soldier. Once he set on this path he had to bring it to completion, which is the cycle just described, to come to his present life where his nodes on the Cancer/Capricorn axis are pointing the way for him to balance out his own anima and animus. He has also gravitated in his current life spiritual path to reunite with the Goddess and 'de-condition' from past involvement with such patriarchal systems. He joked that, "I have finally earned the right to be a woman in my next life" (Cancer/Capricorn axis – gender switching). This is also reflected by Pluto in the first house opposing Venus conjunct Moon in Aquarius. The warrior, who detaches (Aquarius) from his feeling and emotional nature, needs to regain it to come back to wholeness. After much of his own personal work he is now also a healer for others (sixth/twelfth house axis).

2

Taurus/Venus and the Second House

"The senses don't just make sense of life ... they tear reality apart into vibrant morsels and reassemble them into a meaningful pattern".

Diane Ackerman, *A Natural History of the Senses*.

Keywords

Fixed/Yin/Earth	Self Sufficiency/ Security	Stubborn
Survival	Isolated	Hoarding
Fertility	Withdrawal	The Body
Procreation	Stagnation	Pleasure
Preservation	Feeling	Cautious
The Senses	Personal worth/Value	Literal
Self as Resource	Urges	Materialist
Inner resources	Self Esteem	Possessions
Values	Patience	Landowner
Beauty	Give up	Farmer
Prostitution	Suppress emotions	Carpenter
Poverty	Shut Down	Shepherd
Starvation		

The Natural Archetype

Following Aries and Mars, we meet Venus in her inner form as the ruler of Taurus. Aries represents the raw thrust of life force. In Taurus, that force grounds in form and takes root to spread and become bountiful. The lush green of spring after winter displays earth's amazing ability to regenerate itself. This is truly the meaning of self-sustenance and is where Taurus gets its association with the ability to self-sustain and survive. The spring time of the year – observing the 'greening' of the earth – allows one to free associate with certain qualities of the Taurus archetype: fertility, abundance, Mother Earth, perseverance, stamina, beauty, gentleness, procreation, and sensual pleasure, to name a few.

Venus rules both Taurus (Yin – inner) and Libra (Yang – outer). Both Venus and Mars are associated with Eros, but this is a different sort of Eros that Venus as ruler of Taurus promises: an ever abundant taste of sweetness that can gently call the soul back to remember the goodness of life. Unlike the Libra/Venus where Eros is easily projected outward onto the 'other', Taurus/Venus is Eros bubbling up from inside, drawing us deeper into relationship with ourselves.

The act of procreation is a survival function. Taurus is about our own personal self preservation (survival) which is then reflected in the larger order of nature as the ongoing preservation of the species, urging each individual to procreate. In Taurus, sex becomes pleasurable, as do all the ways to fulfill the body's basic needs. The senses of the body are stimulated and pleasured, and fulfillment of the basic need to survive is ensured. Similarly, the taste buds send signals of delight, and the aroma and texture of our favorite foods pleasure us, while the body receives sustenance.

Through the senses life is also given color, texture, quality and depth. In Taurus, things that appease the senses are given meaning and we in turn value them. They act as a passage to our inner world, taking in what appears to be separate and making it intimately our own internal experience. Senses also act in a way to draw us deeper into our earthly experience, rooting us in our physicality. Moon planting charts indicate that the Taurus Moon is the time to plant root crops. Following Aries, the seeds have been sown; the impulse 'to become' is already integrated. Now the seed takes root as it develops its own ability to grow and draw what it needs from its environment.

Taurus as the first earth sign is not only associated with Mother Earth but also the home base for our consciousness while on earth – the Body. The first relationship we discover with our self is through our body. When we are still infants we are amazed by our own toes, explore our fingers and delight in our senses and body functions. Our sensual discovery is unhindered by moral overlays or inhibitions. If it feels good – do it, is the rule. What a pleasure it would be if we could grow into adulthood with our sensuality fully intact. Instead, what often happens as we grow is that we need to reunite with our bodies, and discover ourselves anew, as physical beings.

In modern forms of somatic psychology, we see that the body has a language or consciousness unique unto itself. This body consciousness is basic and literal, unconditioned by the complexities of conscious thinking (spoken language and rational thought arise in the next archetype, Gemini). Just as it is possible to communicate to another through body language, our own bodies are speaking volumes to us.

I have noticed that many skilled body workers have strong Taurus/Venus/second house signatures in their charts. Finely attuned Taurus consciousness 'gets' the body and knows how to work with its subtle energies. Whole systems of psychology, such as Body Psychotherapy and Somatic Psychology, have developed in recent years. These integrative therapies contained within Psycho-Somatic psychology reflect a balance of the Taurus/Scorpio axis (psychology being in the realm of the Scorpio archetype). Many people drawn to work in such fields have a pronounced Taurus/Scorpio or second/eighth house axis in their charts.

Physical sensation is the most primary means the body has to let you know what it needs. Furthermore, the body has a memory and store of information that is not readily available to the conscious mind. This is most pronounced in instances where trauma has caused a split between body and mind, as the body can retrieve and manifest memories that the mind has no awareness of (somatic memory). In some forms of shamanism, consciousness is divided into three worlds that correlate in psychological understanding as the subconscious, conscious and super conscious mind. The etheric body, which is the energetic template for the physical body, is correlated with the subconscious mind.

Somatic memory is stored in the etheric body, just as it is in the other subtle bodies, not only from the current life but past lives as well. The type of memory this body carries is basic and literal. Reasoning is not part of the process. The thought, "He is such a pain in my butt", if repeated enough, is manifested through the etheric body into the physical as an actual pain in the butt. Emotions also somaticize; for example feelings of being burdened or overwhelmed can result in weight or pain on/in the shoulders, causing a stooping posture, or if chronic, curvature of the spine. One can also be born with physical deformities or illnesses that have their root in past lives but are carried into the current life through the etheric body. The etheric body correlates to Taurus as the blueprint for not only the body, but also the feeling nature.

No unified theory exists about what is the difference between feeling and emotion. In fact there is not even a consensus about what the core human emotions are. What is clear is that even though feeling and emotion are often used interchangeably in common language, technically feeling relates more to sensory experience and emotion more to the reaction and expression of what has been sensed. For the purpose of this astrological exploration, I place the feeling nature – the sentient ability to be affected – in Taurus, followed by Gemini – which includes the mental classification of input and reaction to any experience. This leads to Cancer – the actual emotional response. Common sense then dictates that the ability to feel precedes the ability to emote. In past life observations, the person with Taurus accented in their karmic axis often has very deep somaticized emotional memory and it is only through direct work with the body that the emotion surfaces. Since the sensitivity of the feeling nature includes the receptivity to feel emotion, if it is numbed by trauma, the emotions are never expressed and because of this become deeply somaticized.

Taurus in Past Life Experiences

The Taurus archetype is a part of the karmic axis when:

Pluto is in Taurus or the second house or
The South Node is in Taurus or the second house or
The ruler of the South Node is in Taurus or the second house or
Venus aspects Pluto, the nodal axis or rulers of the nodes.

'Shut Down' to Survive

Damage to the feeling layer of the self can result in an imprint I call "shut down to survive". Shutting down the feelings or emotions, in the face of overwhelming circumstances as a means to survive, is prominent in Taurus. All forms of trauma in all the archetypes cause a degree of shut down, and in Taurus this has often been experienced as a means of basic survival. This 'shut down to survive' is perhaps one of the most subtle yet pervasive forms of trauma in this archetype, as it stops the person in the current life from tapping into their emotional and feeling core. In the Taurus archetype, just as a plant reaches down with its roots into the rich earth for sustenance, the soul of each person needs the well of healthy emotion to draw from to sustain and feed its growth. When this rootedness in the self has been severed and/or suppressed because of the imprint of a conflict between feeling and survival, emotions in the present life can be chronically suppressed or numbed because they are perceived to be life threatening.

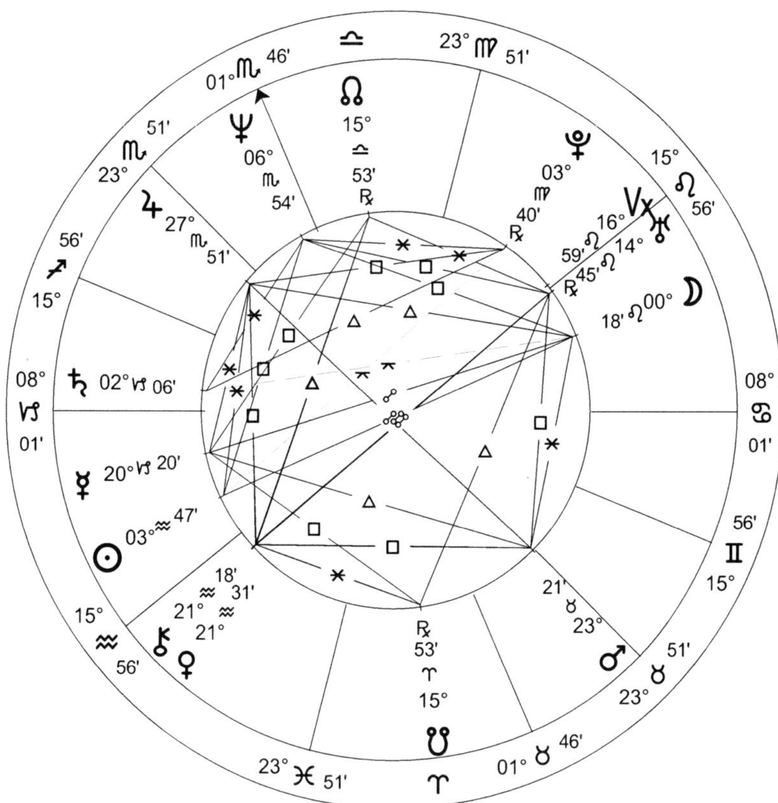

Chart A (Porphyry houses)

Chart A

Two stories from the same client illustrate how the 'shut down to survive' imprint happens in past lives and the effect it has on the current life. The main astrological signature in this chart is the ruler of the SN in Taurus in the fourth house, squared by Venus conjunct Chiron in Aquarius in the second. His SN is in Aries in the third. He commented about a year after these sessions that healing the trauma in these two stories became the foundation for him to begin to allow himself to fully feel his emotions and his deep authentic self.

He regressed back to being a young boy twin in an Eskimo tribe (tribal – Aquarius, and twin – SN in third). One day he and his twin were some distance from the village when wolves attacked. He ran to hide behind a rock and watched desperately as his twin was dragged off. He was torn for what seems like an eternity between the desire to scream and yell and his own survival. He wanted to save his twin, but knew if he shouted out, he would draw attention to himself and probably also be killed (Aries SN – instinct at odds with ruler of SN, Mars in Taurus – survival). After the death of his twin, he went into shock (Aquarius) and complete shut down and lived the rest of that life as if on automatic pilot. Because of the shock to his feeling and emotional nature, he became dulled and numb. Commenting on that, the client said, "For the rest of my life, it was as if I could sit at a hole in the ice for hours, almost catatonic, waiting for the seals to come". In this way, the patience that Taurus is associated with was for him a reaction to shock, (ruler of the SN Mars in Taurus, square Venus conjunct Chiron in Aquarius in the second house).

It took the client a month to let emotions come – the 'slow to react' side of Taurus. Finally, he felt waves of grief over the loss of his twin, whom he had felt deeply as a part of himself. Through his grieving process, his instinct (Aries and Mars) and his feeling and emotional nature (ruler of SN in the fourth house of emotion squaring Venus in the second house of feeling) were reunited.

In the second story, the client found himself as a Bedouin (again in a tribe). There was an attack from a warring tribe. He was able to slip away and hide behind a camel. When he came out, he found his people slaughtered, including his wife and child. He went into shock again and he wandered into the desert. He had a deep internal conflict raging within himself, as he slowly dehydrated to death.

Even through the shock or because of it, his instinct to survive took over as he went along as if on automatic pilot again. In this story he held back his tears intentionally because he needed to conserve water to survive. This semi conscious urge left a deep imprint and colored his dying thoughts with the lasting impression, "If I cry, I will die". The imprint of this story acted like a post hypnotic command, very basic and very Taurus, and was carried over via the etheric body to this lifetime.

Like his previous past life, his ability to actually feel, cry or grieve was wounded again. During work with this past life, his tears flowed more spontaneously and freely. By rediscovering his own innate sensitivity and the deeply buried emotions he was healing the wounded aspects of Venus and acting upon the Venusian level of the evolutionary intention indicated in his chart. His Aries SN has Libra as the polarity and his eighth house Pluto has the second house as an area of growth.

I had noticed from many regressions with clients that past life soldiers and warriors have had an archetypal experience arise spontaneously. In the afterlife they wanted only to find a spot of greenness and lay down in the grass. Since it happened frequently with past life Roman soldiers in particular, I thought it was a part of the past cultural belief system, a memory of the Elysian Fields – the Greco-Roman paradise of the afterlife. But other soldiers, after death, also longed for their place in the grass.

One client with the Scorpio SN in the first house (warrior) had a horrible past life as a Russian soldier who was pushed to the extremes of violence. In the afterlife, he only wanted to go to a stream to wash the blood away and then lay down in the soft grass. As he lay there, I suggested that a healing spirit might come to help him, and he described a green nature spirit who appeared instantly in feminine form. He sobbed as this spirit came and gently held him, offering him healing and restoration. She eventually returned to him his heart (his Venusian feeling nature). Representing his Taurus NN in the seventh house, she told him that in this life, through his restored heart, he could be gentle and accept that his heart will lead him where conquest can't. The feeling nature that is numbed by trauma yearns for the sensual, moist feminine energy to seep into every pore and restore wholeness.

When the feeling nature is restored it allows the Scorpio polarity point to be manifested. Taurus may prefer isolation as way of insulating itself from bonding, but Scorpio demands that intimacy be part of evolutionary experience. When one is in right relationship with oneself (Taurus) the experience of true intimacy with another becomes possible.

Limitations and Growth

It seems logical that a sign that is associated with rootedness is not very mobile or movable. Because the qualities of Venus are internalized in Taurus, the propensity is towards isolation. This can also be expressed literally in the Taurus archetype as past lives spent living away from society in isolation. The cumulative perspective gained from such lives can be very limited. In just the last few hundred years the amount of information we take in daily has grown exponentially and can equal an entire single past life's worth. If one lived many simple or isolated lives removed from the influence of the world-at-large it may be necessary, for evolution, to start to expand one's world view. The polarity point or the area of evolution for Taurus is Scorpio – to transform limitations by merging with something greater than the known self, moving beyond whatever limits ongoing growth. The limitations can also be the very nature of the things that are precious to Taurus, what it values either externally or internally, such as possessions, talent etc. These very things may not be limiting in and of themselves, but how they are constellated in the individual consciousness and the importance they have in self value is what is crucial. For one person a car is simply a mode of transport, while to another it is way to get ahead with girls, compete with others etc.

How we respond to the potential to transform limitations is related to how the universe will deliver these messages. If resistance is strong, then the person will experience what I call the 'cosmic 2 x 4' upside the head; the event will be confrontational and cataclysmic in nature. To the person who feels the car is an extension of the very self, its importance is out of proportion with reality, causing a limitation. In fact it is most likely a compensation for an inner sense of worthlessness. Since having an intrinsic sense of worth is part of the empowered Taurus archetype, the car will most likely have to be removed at some point for growth to occur. The Scorpio polarity of loss will be experienced, with the intention to fulfill the soul's desire for evolution (Pluto).

Poverty Consciousness

This internal side of Venus is how we relate to ourselves and thus become aware of what our own needs are. Venus shows what meaning or value we give to those things that are integral to our survival (possessions), and what internal resources we can draw from within ourselves (self worth). Before we have identified how others can fulfill our needs (Libra Venus), we find in Taurus our ability to fulfill our own needs (self-sufficiency). Because of the natural inconjunct between Taurus and Libra, and the different aspects of Venus these signs represent, our relationships often become the place we seek fulfillment of our needs in lieu of looking within ourselves. In the Maslow model of the hierarchy of needs, Taurus represents the base of the triangle, our basic needs for safety, food, clothing and shelter. Taking Maslow's view, gratification of basic needs provides a healthy state of consciousness that allows us to evolve to higher needs. Blocking gratification or an inability to fulfill basic needs can make us sick and dysfunctional. Then the Scorpio polarity swings into action, causing fixation and compulsion.

In the Taurus archetype, one could have lived close to the land as a farmer or shepherd, as a way to fulfill these basic needs. These simple lives, entwined with the cycles of nature to provide for survival, are common in Taurus. But the agrarian and pastoral lifestyle is tenuous and can quickly be devastated by invasion or failure of crops. Loss of land and possessions in past lives can leave the current life personality unable to feel its own ability to survive and flourish. This following case shows the impact of this type of past life experience.

Chart B

The most pervasive issue was this client's lack of money and his feelings of inadequacy in providing for himself. He had an active 'poverty consciousness' that was limiting any advancement in his life. He felt that an inner unconscious saboteur was at work thwarting any progress he was trying to make. This type of conflicted psychology points directly to the unresolved wounds of past life character clashing with the current life intentions. In Taurus, self-sufficiency and survival are often deeply intertwined with the core sense of worth. Even though the person feels deserving in the present life, sometimes subconsciously the effects from a past life of destitution or loss undermines current life efforts, causing one to live a hand to mouth type of existence. The nodal axis has a double signature of the archetype of Taurus, as his Taurus SN is in the second house. The exception is that his nodal axis is squared by Mars in Capricorn in the eleventh house. Because of the square to the nodes, this makes the archetypes of Taurus/second house, Scorpio/eighth house and Mars in Capricorn/eleventh house, all part of his soul's past life experiences.

In this past life he was a young man living a simple pastoral life (Taurus) with his parents and siblings, tending sheep. It was an ancient land and he identified himself as being a part of a Jewish tribe (SN ruler Venus is in Aquarius in the eleventh – tribal). He met a woman and married. His brothers encouraged him to move to the city where he could use his intellect (Aquarius) more. Once he arrived in the city with his new wife, he started to feel he didn't fit in because everyone seemed so different (Aquarius). It was a city that had been occupied by the Romans (Mars) for some time. At first life was good, he started a business brokering and trading sheep from

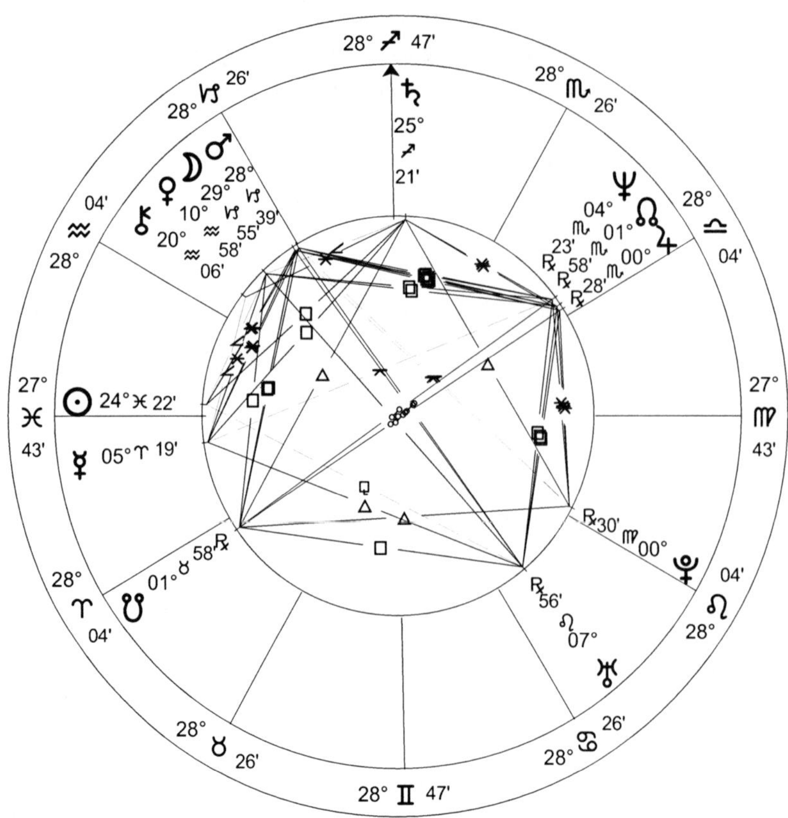

Chart B (Porphyry houses)

the countryside, and selling them for slaughter in the city. So far his pastoral connections and roots were working well for him. He was able to provide a good life for his wife and now young daughter.

The Romans started to become more oppressive (Capricorn) and demanded more taxes and began to seize possessions. He was concerned about his family and his community and found a few other like-minded people (Aquarius) who were speaking out against the injustices and rebelling against the status quo (Aquarius/Mars square the nodes from the 11th). The Romans came and took a large portion of his business, and his rage built to the point of explosion (Mars square nodes), yet he repressed it (Mars in Capricorn) because speaking out openly meant certain death.

After a bit of time people started to fall ill, and it seemed the water supply had become polluted. His wife became ill and he watched while she died, feeling totally helpless, (tainted resources – Scorpio/Taurus). Now his rage was mixed with deep grief, and he found himself ranting (Mars) in front of a crowd.

Later that night the Romans came and took him away. They tortured him and then disemboweled him. He held in his rage during the torture with the sheer force of his Mars in Capricorn and Scorpio will, saying, "I won't scream I won't make a sound, I won't let them get me". The stubbornness that Taurus is famous for. After the death his first feeling was, "I won. (Mars) They didn't get to me". Then futility (Capricorn) started to emerge, "It wasn't worth dying for".

He hung around as an earthbound spirit, still angry and wanting revenge (Scorpio and Mars). Eventually he faced his persecutors in the spirit world. They seemed less powerful there, yet it was still important that he and his people felt a sense of completion by taking back their land (Taurus) from these invaders. Further healing work allowed him to finally let out the screams he held in when he was tortured (Taurus rules the throat). After that, his energy flowed more freely and he became softer. The session ended with him and his people feeling complete as they were able to re-inhabit the land they loved, albeit not on the earth plane, but in the spirit world.

A few months later, on the phone he told me, "I'm in the car with my partner and we are in the process of buying a piece of land". His ability to reconnect with the abundance of his Taurus SN, and avail himself of his resources (Scorpio) is a beautiful illustration of one layer of a balancing and healing of his nodal axis.

Self-Sufficiency and Worth

One of the strengths of the Taurus archetype is to discover within oneself the capacity for self sufficiency. Often when self-sufficiency has been part of the soul's past life experience via the Taurus archetype, individuals come into life with that principle overemphasized or wounded in some way.

A client with the SN in Taurus in the ninth house told a story of having been orphaned and raised by grandparents. One day he came back to his house to find his grandparents had perished in a fire. He learned by being orphaned to become self-sufficient, living in a cabin in the woods. Isolated, he found he could satisfy himself with simple pleasures (Taurus). One day while he was enjoying a meal (very Taurus), men burst into the cabin, dragged him outside, tied him to a post, and castrated him; leaving him there to die. They did this because of his differing religious beliefs (ninth house). In the afterlife he learned, much to his surprise, that the meaning of that life was to learn self-sufficiency, albeit the hard way!

How we make our way in the world and provide for ourselves either strengthens or undermines our feelings of self-worth. Imprints from lives where the means to survive was destructive to the sense of self worth carry from life to life as "I don't deserve to be who I really am", "I have nothing to offer", and/or "I am worthless". A general sense of stuckness can pervade the entire personality. For example, a client with a second house/Taurus karmic signature was a juggler in a freak show in a past life. Although he was a talented juggler, he was popular with the crowds because he had a physical deformity and not because of his talent. This misplaced popularity left an imprint of anger and hopelessness in his current life about expressing his gifts. Because he was de-valued, he was unable to find his own value within himself.

In past lives during patriarchal times, financial and sexual independence was rare for women; they were often treated as possessions or had to resort to prostitution as a means of financial independence. This wounded aspect of Venus excludes her from participating fully in society as an equal. Lives of poverty or prostitution (using the self or body as a resource via the Scorpio polarity) can leave one feeling worthless. Prostitution lives also can carry many layers of damage to the soul, affecting not only one's sense of worth, but sexual pleasure as well. One of the common defenses of any type of sexual abuse is to numb the genitals. As a means to survive, what the psyche may register as daily rape, a prostitute can develop emotional and mental shut down as well as physical. This type of shut down carries from life to life and can result in an inability to feel sexual pleasure or reach orgasm. Psychologically, the subconscious fear of being used may carry over into the present life also causing avoidance and shut down. Conversely, one can come into life as highly promiscuous (Scorpio polarity – compulsion), which can be in compensation for the numbness.

Present life males can have the same subconscious attitudes from past lives as females as much as women do because the degradation of women has been a prevalent collective theme for ages. In the current life, this is also a reason why a man would devalue his own anima (his inner feminine), which then extends to the way he relates to women. A woman can also devalue her feminine and over emphasize her animus (her inner masculine) as in today's society 'playing a man's game' in the business world is the norm. A woman with the archetype of Taurus squaring her nodes stated that from the age of thirteen she had the distinct memory of not wanting to be a woman because she was felt that they had no real power in the world.

Possessions

A displaced sense of personal value, projected onto possessions is common in the Taurus archetype. If in the past life those possessions were lost, self-esteem may have been lost also. This loss can carry over in the present life as hoarding, the inability to let go of anything that is owned, as one feels that personal survival depends upon those possessions. The past life wounds from loss of possessions can carry over into the present life as a pervasive fear of losing them again or giving up and not ever trying to acquire anything.

Chart C

A client experienced uncontrollable weeping spells when she considered selling her house. She couldn't sleep at night and felt paralyzed by fear, but could not understand why. In fact, consciously she wanted to move, but another part of her was subconsciously reacting with abject fear. When discussing selling her home, tears welled up in her eyes and she said, "They're taking it all away. It's unique and is never going to happen again".

The significant signature in her karmic axis for this past life includes the two planets in Scorpio in the second house squaring the nodal axis (Venus and Jupiter are also part of this chain of planets but are out of orb of the square). The Scorpio planets are also opposed by Saturn in Taurus in the eighth. The nodes are Leo SN in the eleventh and Aquarius NN in the fifth. Thus the Sun, ruler of the Leo SN, also squares the nodes. Neptune in Sagittarius also squares the nodes and conjuncts the Sun.

Her comment about the house being unique seemed to point to a fear that she could not create (Leo) something new and unique (eleventh house) again. The first phrase, "They're taking it all away", pointed directly to the ruler of SN in Scorpio (loss) in the second house (possessions). The second house itself is ruled by Scorpio, also pointing further to loss and betrayal of some sort (Sun squaring the nodal axis).

In her past life story, she was a black woman who was poor but self sufficient (second house planets including the ruler of SN in the second,

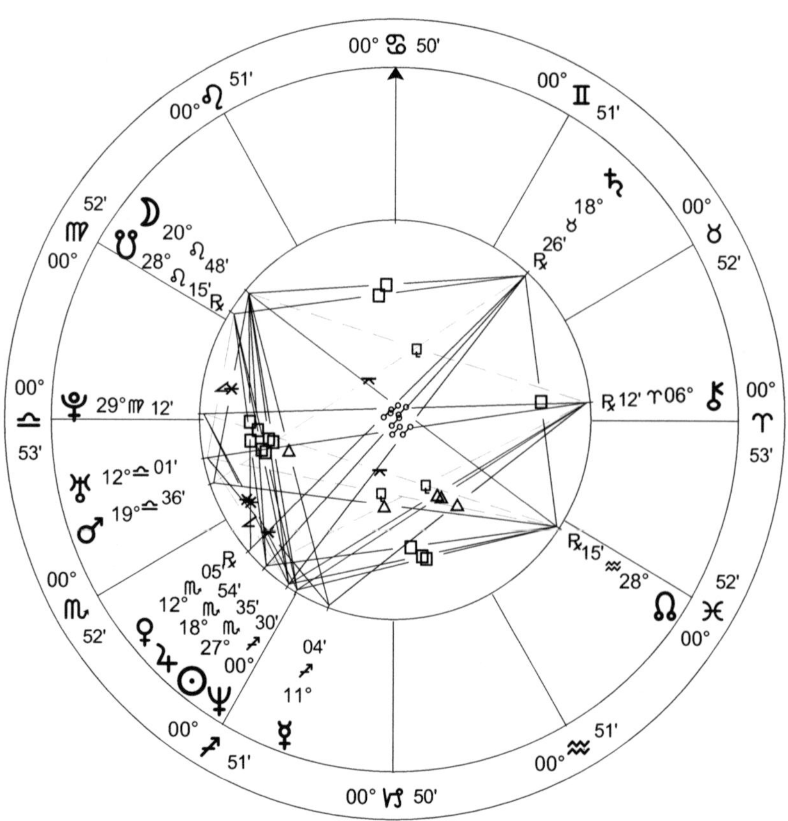

Chart C (Porphyry houses)

square the nodes and Saturn in Taurus in the eighth in opposition). She had a small house of which she was proud (Leo) and a young son who she was raising alone. A white man with whom she had some brief business interaction with came to her home one day with other men. They burst into her home as she opened the door and raped her in front of her son (loss of self, Sun and Neptune square the nodes).

She went into shock (Aquarius/eleventh house) and subsequent complete emotional shutdown. She lived the rest of her life this way; her home, which she was once very proud of, fell into decay and her son grew up to live on his own. She died bitter and alone (Saturn). In the afterlife, she sat on a bench and stubbornly refused to go anywhere (second house and also the fixed nature of the T-square). She said, "What's the use? I give up"

(Taurus, second house, also the Neptune square the nodes and conjunct the Sun). The loss of freedom is also indicated by Neptune in Sagittarius square nodes.

Even in tragedy, the humor of spirit can come through. She said during the afterlife work of that past life character, "This is funny! My realtor is here in the spirit world! She is pulling me off the bench!" (What a Taurus/Scorpio archetype)! This image of the realtor encouraged her to get on with it. With the realtor's encouragement, other spirit helpers arrived to assist her and she eventually found forgiveness for her attackers, was reunited with her son and received healing from spirit guides. She then went back to the old house in spirit form and cleaned it up, reclaiming it for herself. As a result, shortly thereafter she did sell her house easily, and indeed her realtor was instrumental in helping her. Reclaiming the house, for this past life character, equaled regaining her sense of self worth.

Chart D

This client had done regression work for over twenty years. She is quoted here as she recounted the common themes of many of her past lives to me.

The south node in Taurus in the second house gives her a double Taurus signature. Taurus is not highly emphasized anywhere else in her chart, yet her stories are all very Taurean. Because the nodes are squared by Uranus, both Scorpio and Taurus become part of the past life experience as do the squaring planets.

"Many lives of poverty, of being alone and isolated"

The main memory of one of these past lives is as a very poor, older woman who doesn't have anything. She says, "I lived a simple life; I grew my own food". Her husband had died a while before and she lived most of her life alone. People from the town felt she was weird and avoided her, "I felt I was different in some way, I couldn't fit in, so it suited me fine they left me alone even though I was lonely".

In this brief story a few of the aspects of the archetype of Taurus are clear. The natural self-containment of the Taurus archetype often becomes isolation in past lives. In this chart the issue of isolation is further compounded by the fact that the nodes are squared by Uranus and Chiron in Aquarius. This resonance is represented by her being viewed as weird and feeling outcast and alienated (Uranus/Aquarius).

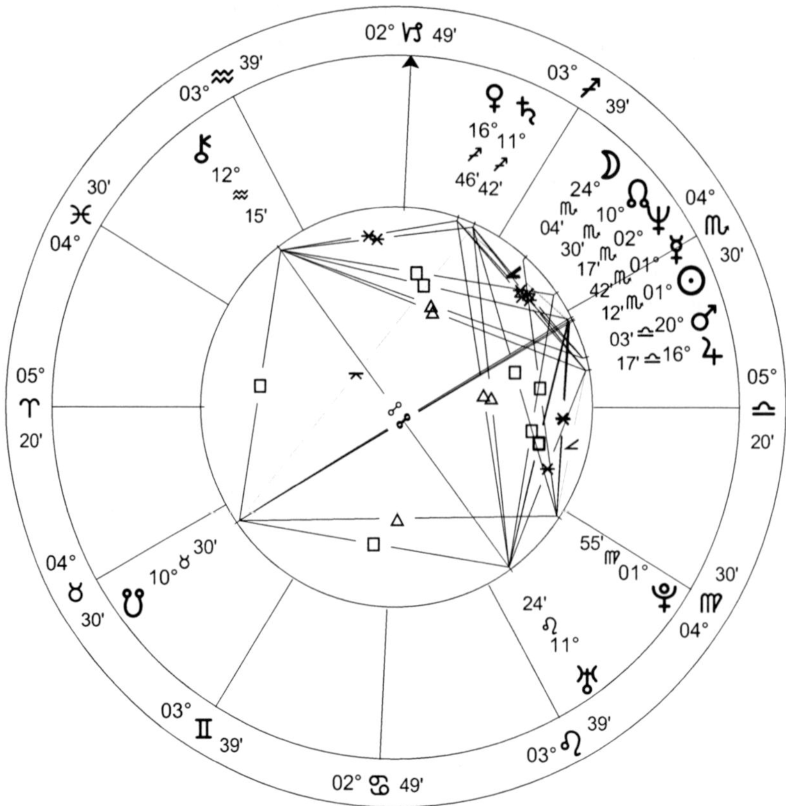

Chart D (Porphyry houses)

In another of her poverty lives she was a small child who she said was like "the matchstick girl without the matchsticks"; "I remembered being always cold, hungry and dirty". She was an orphan whose main goal in life was "to be able to survive long enough to be able to work in some kind of servitude, like a scullery maid or house servant", (survival of Taurus and Pluto in Virgo – servitude). "It was a simple goal but one I desperately wanted", a simple (Taurus) goal (ruler of SN in Sagittarius in the ninth). She is aware that she had a chronic rash on her arms and body which made her repulsive to others and they avoided her, (again the alienation, outcast theme). She said it was very painful as she was just a small child and wanted someone to hold her but no one would come near. She died very young of what she identified as a plague with influenza-type symptoms. (Neptune is in Scorpio opposing her SN).

"Many throat wounds" (Taurus ruling the throat)

In one of these lives she was a young child captured by pirate-type men who slit her throat after using her sexually (orally) and threw her overboard.

And in another she was a destitute Asian child living in a very muddy, dirty place who died by choking on a piece of scrounged food.

In another she was a very young child who died in a mudslide by choking on mud caught in her throat.

In almost all these past lives we see an emphasis on her ability to survive amidst emotional difficulties (survival – Taurus). This is often a highlighted theme in the Taurus archetype. Other correlations are that wounded-child past lives most often occur within the Cancer and Leo archetypes. Here her Pluto is in the fifth house and also squares the Moon. The result of such poverty-stricken past lives left her with the subconscious imprint of 'not being good enough' (Pluto in Virgo) and feeling unlovable (Pluto in the fifth). Wounds to the giving and receiving of love are also common in the Leo/fifth house archetype as it relates to past lives, (Uranus is also in Leo in the fifth squaring the nodal axis). Further, the ruler of the SN (Venus) is conjunct Saturn. Repressive and oppressive past lives with deprivation are possibilities in the Capricorn/Saturn archetype.

In another of her past lives the emphasis on survival and the stubbornness of Taurus in that regard is highly emphasized. This past life experience is also an example of how the body can remember, as the entire past life memory surfaced through body sensations with few mental pictures. In the first recall of the past life she was aware that she was cold and confused. Slowly she started to feel as if she had been drugged and was nauseous. As this past life person, she wanted to stand but as she tried, she then felt intense pain in her back and was aware that she had been shot there and fell to the ground. At this point she became aware that she was a man, who had been shot, drugged and possibly poisoned (Neptune in Scorpio opposing SN, Scorpio NN). He was quite convinced that this was not happening to him, he kept trying to squirm or crawl away saying, "I can get through this; I will survive (Taurus); I have utter faith I will not die", (Neptune and Sagittarius – faith); "Why did I eat that poison? I should have known they were out to get me; I was betrayed, I trusted them", (Neptune in Scorpio, Scorpio NN – betrayal). The attackers did not give up and they bound him hand and foot, dragged him through the snow and threw him into a freezing body of water, leaving him to die. Even as he started to freeze, it took a long time for him to die (common in the Taurus archetype) and he still tried convincing himself (Sagittarius) that he would survive (Taurus). He struggled until the end, even succeeding in getting one hand free from his bonds, but at that point he slipped under the ice and everything went dark.

My client realized after the regression that the point where the bullet entered her back corresponded to several present life moles that she had removed but, stubbornly they had grown back. A prominent past life researcher Dr. Ian Stevenson researching children's spontaneous past life memories, found that current day birth markings on the body such as moles can often relate to past life wounds, particularly fatal ones.[1] In this case, also because of the strong Taurus signature, it illustrates further the embodying (somaticizing) of wounds from past lives that are carried life to life in the etheric body and recreated in the physical body. The stubbornness of her mole in the current life (no matter how it was removed it was going to grow back) echoes the exact energy of this 'Taurean' past life character.

Furthermore, after this past life character died, as a spirit he still didn't want to leave his body. This is also quite common within the Taurus archetype as the attachment and identification with the physical nature and body can be quite strong. Further information about this past life revealed that he was a natural born psychic counselor and seer (Neptune in Scorpio) who became a priest (ruler of SN in Sagittarius in the ninth) in an esoteric order. Associations with past life esoteric societies are correlated most frequently to the archetypes of Scorpio (secrecy), Pisces (mysticism) and Aquarius (fringe groups). The client said an underlying attitude during the entire past life ordeal was that "I had total faith that I was connected with something universal, something magical, I had utter faith I would not die". The ruler of the SN in Sagittarius here blends the survival of Taurus and faith of Sagittarius. Of course this isn't what happened, and another aspect of Neptune and Sagittarius were revealed in her past life death imprints – disillusionment and questioning of faith, which was worked with further in the session. The betrayal by others (the ones who caused this death) are represented by Neptune in Scorpio opposing her SN, and the Scorpio NN.

---

1. Stevenson, I. (1987), *Children Who Remember Previous Lives*, Charlottesville: University Press of Virginia.
   Also, Stevenson, I (1993), Journal of Scientific Exploration, Vol. 7, No.4, pp 403-410, 1993. Copyright © 1993, Society for Scientific Exploration.

In her current life she said that the theme of survival was prevalent in that she had several health crises that brought her to death's door and back again. While it is apparent that we all died in our past lives in one way or another, this doesn't mean that the struggle between life and death is prevalent in our consciousness as an imprint needing to be healed. In this chart, the pronounced Scorpio/Taurus axis, and her past life experiences show that indeed life and death is an issue for this soul.

In other past lives she had the experience of seeking and having wealth and power but was driven by a tremendous fear in those lives of losing it all, and also went to quite manipulative ends to get it (also thematic with Taurus/Scorpio).

In one such life she was a priest (Sagittarius) who only wanted sex and power (Scorpio). As this priest, he had a male lover who was the son of a prominent politician (an interesting take on the union of church and state – Saturn conjunct ruler of SN in Sagittarius). Their relationship was solely usury (Scorpio/Taurus) each taking advantage of the other and their position to push matters of church or state. The relationship degraded into a love-hate dynamic, each staying in it for their own selfish means, yet fearing the other would expose them and destroy their power (Scorpio). Eventually the priest won, under the guise of seduction and reconciliation, he beckoned the young man to him, promising a night of uninhibited passion (Scorpio). The client described herself at this point in that past life as wholly ruthless and unfeeling (Saturn conjunct ruler of SN). During the evening together he murdered the young man by slipping him poison (Scorpio). It was a tactical (Saturn) victory for the priest, but hollow, as he was so consumed by his lust for power that he could not even feel the pleasure of winning (Taurus/Scorpio). He lived on, but the client describes his consciousness at the point of death as totally non-feeling, bitter and shut down (Saturn and Taurus).

Put into the context of her current life she was born into a poor but not destitute family, but she said as long as she could remember she was convinced she was not going to remain poor. "That was not going to be my lot in life". She had this attitude long before she had the conscious recall of her past lives, so it would seem her soul's urge to experience the healing of those wounded aspects of the Taurus archetype (from her past lives) was already inherent in her consciousness. This inborn attitude also shows some of the strengths that she learned from these past lives of the combined archetypes of Taurus/Sagittarius: the self reliance and stubborn determination of Taurus and optimism of Sagittarius. She found as she started doing inner work on herself, that she did have a subconscious fear of poverty, of there not being enough and losing what she did have despite her conscious thinking. This was the voice, fears and experiences of her inner past life selves. She also said that these fears were closely tied into a fear of "not being able to work, and not being of useful service" (Pluto in Virgo). At times in her life poor health caused her to be unable to work and sustain herself and she had felt immensely guilty (Virgo and Saturn).

Through her work on herself she did heal these subconscious fears and manifested abundance and better health in her life. She also had to learn to identify her own unique talents from deep within (Pluto in the fifth and the Uranus/Aquarius aspects to the nodes, and the SN in Taurus). She did do stage performance at one point in her life (Leo). But to get to that point she also had to overcome her fears of "not being good enough or feeling deserving" (Virgo and Taurus – self worth), especially as it related to her bringing her talents out into the world. Trust in her own intuition and innate spirituality was identified as another theme she had to work on in this lifetime. To this end she currently is working as a therapist and psychic/intuitive counselor through which she says her main interest "is to help others accept their own selves, find self love and their inherent worth". This is a lovely expression of the effect of the healing of her Taurus SN wounds, leading her to the NN in Scorpio in the eighth house, conjunct Neptune and the NN's ruler, Pluto in Virgo (in service to others).

3

Gemini/Mercury and the Third House

"When once the Primal Simplicity diversified, Different names appeared".

Lao Tzu *Tao Teh Ching*

Keywords

Mutable/Yang/Air	Ideas	Instability
Communication	Cynic	Immediate
Learning/Teaching	Opinion	Environment
Writing	Short-term memory	Classification
Speaking	Impermanent	Ever changing
Thinking/left brain	The Fool	Teacher
Information	Curiosity	Scribe
Messenger	Fluctuating viewpoint	Short journeys
Duality	Rationalization	Storyteller
Scattered	Siblings/Twins	Trader/Merchant
Superficial	Relatives	Trickster
Logic	Intellectual doubt	Liar/Lies
Literal	Paradox	Thief

The Natural Archetype

The energy of Gemini bursts forth out of the consolidation that occurred in Taurus and echoing Aries' 'take no prisoners' attitude, charges into the realm of what can be known. In Gemini, consciousness eagerly explores its surroundings with curiosity, seeking variety and diversity. I recently worked with a client who found the first image that arose for him in our session, was that of a man in a library looking for a book. He described in his inner imagery, that the walls were covered in shelves of many enticing books. Usually in regression, the person goes immediately into a past life image, but I recognized this image as not an actual memory but a metaphor. As his subconscious was searching for what past life memory to bring up to work on, it offered this image of this man in a library who was saying, "I know it's here, but which one?" He labored in the library for some time, finding it difficult to decide on just one book. This client has Mercury in Gemini; Uranus and Sun in Cancer all in the third house square his nodal axis of Aries/Libra. So much to know, so many books… so little time! And hard to choose!

Gemini as a yang, mutable air sign, thrives on change and the impermanent. It shares with the polarity sign, Sagittarius, the energy of restless seeking that is a characteristic of the mental nature. Gemini represents the left hemisphere of the brain that gives one the ability to order existence logically. The linear process that connects one piece of information to another is the foundation of rational thought.

Gemini and Virgo share Mercury as a ruler. Gemini best exemplifies the outer form of Mercury while Virgo the inner. The duality of Mercury is one of his characteristics and is easily recognized in Gemini whose symbol is the twins. Mercury's energy in Gemini is divisive; it breaks down reality into opposites making distinctions apparent. Once distinction is arrived at, classification and ordering and naming can be accomplished. The mental process in Gemini is about gathering bits of information to form an understandable picture of the world and then to communicate that in a variety of ways to others. Mercury's energy in Virgo draws the scattered pieces into itself in the act of inner integration. The mental process in Virgo is about the application and practical use of information, using critical thinking to arrival at an analysis of data. Building upon distinction, Virgo adds the quality of discernment.

Mercury as a substance appears materially to be both a liquid and a solid, again implying duality. In its outer form (Gemini), the duality and paradox is apparent. In Virgo, Mercury becomes the potential to release the spirit hidden in form, which is represented by Virgo as the pregnant virgin. The child gestating within is the 'Son of God', or the part of our consciousness that knows its divine nature. Mercury, as an archetype, paradoxically (as Mercury would like it), contains both separation and the unification of opposites. This is most apparent in the study of Hermeticism, of which alchemy is a major component. Hermes is the Greek equivalent of the Roman god Mercury. In one interpretation, Hermes was combined with the

Egyptian god Thoth, to become Hermes Trismegistus (thrice great) who was the source of the teachings that would become the body of Hermeticism.

Hermes in this Trismegistus aspect is unlike other Hellenistic gods and is more akin to the Hindu concept of an avatar, which is a divine incarnation that becomes fully human and comes to teach and uplift humanity. His goal as the founder of Hermeticism was to impart wisdom that would illuminate humanity's intellect. One path to this goal is described in the process of alchemy as a spiritual practice. At the core of this work is the teaching on the nature of duality, the human and the divine, and the process of merging and reconciling the two. This leads to one meaning of the synthesis of the Gemini/Sagittarius polarity with Virgo as the mediator. Gemini as the one who gathers and imparts knowledge also reigns over duality, showing that knowledge outside of oneself is limited in nature. When it is internalized through Virgo, knowledge becomes more refined. In Virgo it is tested through personal experience and practical application, and through that process discernment is arrived at.

What then is extracted and remains is wisdom (Sagittarius). This also alludes to the alchemical process. The symbol of the centaur of Sagittarius is also often associated with duality as he is half horse and half man. But in the spiritual context, the centaur is actually the fusion of the divine and humanity, through the animal or natural world. Again we have the theme of merging what seems to be opposite. Sagittarius as the polarity to Gemini is the ability to synthesize all of the various viewpoints, facts and sources of knowledge into one cohesive philosophy or cosmology. Gemini collects – Sagittarius synthesizes.

The spoken and written word and how we have used different forms of communication in past lives is highlighted in the Gemini archetype. As an air sign the natural impulse is to circulate and disseminate. Mercury and his Greek counterpart Hermes are both known as messengers of the gods. In past lives when Mercury/Gemini or the third house are a part of the karmic axis, being a messenger or having something to say of importance is often a central theme.

Gemini in Past Life Experiences

The Gemini archetype is a part of the karmic axis when:

Pluto is in Gemini or the third house or
The South Node is in Gemini or the third house or
The ruler of the South Node is in Gemini or the third house or
Mercury aspects Pluto, the nodal axis or rulers of the nodes.

Communication and the Messenger

My Gemini cases are full of stories about being the one trying to deliver a message and the consequences and difficulties in doing so. The last case presented in this chapter shows several variations of this theme. Sometimes these stories have to do with being persecuted for speaking one's truth (especially when Sagittarius/Jupiter and the ninth house or Virgo/sixth house are also involved in the karmic axis). Lives where one was outcast or judged as a heretic are quite common with these combined archetypes. When Uranus and Aquarius are combined with Gemini archetypes one also could have been ahead of their time because of their message, and either was celebrated, outcast or executed because of their genius. In other past lives, the person with the Gemini energy is often trying to deliver an urgent message, such as news of a coming attack, a disaster about to happen, and often they are not heard or are ridiculed because of what they are trying to say. In these lives one often dies with immense frustration or hopelessness because they were unable to get the message across. This urgency can carry into the current life as 'Gemini on overdrive', where one simply always has to have something to say and be heard. Some other scenarios include being a source of gossip and getting oneself or others into trouble because of it, or having been the target of gossip. Sometimes past lives contain the lighter side of Gemini's communicative skills as a storyteller or traveling bard.

I have also found that various types of vows from religious ones to those made in the form of a promise to another, are often a feature in Gemini-type past lives. Quite often vows that are made in the past can bind us through many lifetimes. This following case shows the power of words spoken in the past.

Chart A

In this chart, the real gravity of the karma formed in his past lives is contained in the archetypes of the Libra SN in the twelfth and Pluto in Leo in the tenth house. The nodes are squared by Jupiter in Capricorn and Mercury in

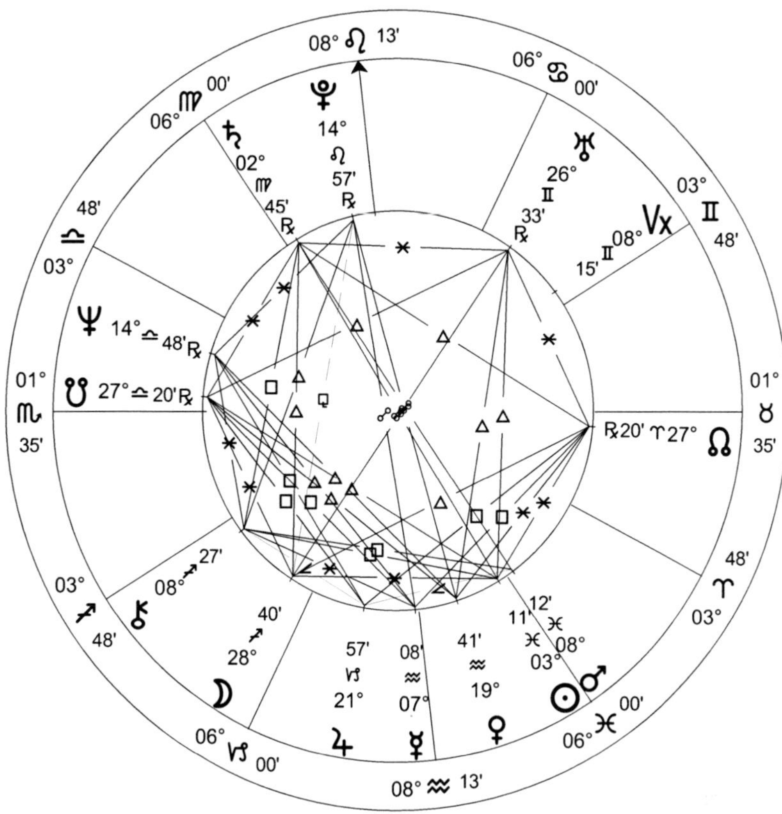

Chart A (Porphyry houses)

Aquarius in the third house and this is where the Gemini archetype starts to blend into his past life experiences. Also, Pluto is opposed by Mercury in the third and Uranus is in Gemini in the eighth house trine the SN and its ruler. Since his SN is in Libra one can imagine that his past lives may feature interdependence in relationship. With it being in the twelfth house, sacrifice and unclear boundaries also add to the mix, laying the foundation for a past life co-dependent nature. This is discussed in length in the Libra chapter where this case would also fit nicely, but since the nature of how these two individuals became entwined with each other has to do with vows from the past, it is also very illustrative of the dynamics of this aspect of Gemini.

This man is in a current marriage that both parties have tried to end for several years. It is not an abusive or horrible relationship, but the feeling has been for both of them that it is time to move on, yet neither has been able to do so. He especially had felt bound in a way that he could not explain; the past lives connected with his current life wife explained why.

He was a young man about twenty years old married to a woman who was giving birth to their first child. He anxiously awaited the arrival of the baby as the women were tending to his wife in the birthing room. When he was allowed to go in he saw his beautiful baby girl and his wife and was filled with gratitude and love. Unfortunately the events turned quickly into tragedy as his wife started to bleed profusely. Despite the efforts of her attendants who were unable to stop the bleeding, as he held her tightly in his arms she bled to death. During this process she said to him, "Don't let me go" and his response was "On all I consider holy, my word is my vow; I will never let you go". She died with him holding her, and he stayed that way for several hours, refusing to let her go. His family members and those helping with the birth eventually had to pry her from his arms. With Pluto in the tenth and Jupiter in Capricorn, his honor and integrity combined with calling upon the power of his beliefs through his word (third house and Mercury opposite Pluto) solidified a lasting bond between them. It was a classic case of 'my word is my vow'.

In another lifetime he was a Native American man who found a young lost or abandoned white girl in the forest. Taking her back with him to his tribe, he asked the elders what to do about this situation. They told him that he had saved her life and now he was responsible for her. He did raise her in that life as his own child and they shared a special bond.

In the present life, the mix of deep connection intertwined with a sense of responsibility and the vow colored the way they were able to relate to each other. In the afterlife of the story, as the man and his wife, he did not choose to rework the vow with her. Instead he said he now had the realization that he could let her go, with consciousness, if he chose to. The Gemini part of him was satiated enough to know that now he could make 'an informed decision'. The valuable lesson to take away from this case is that vows from the past do bind us, but are able to be reworked just as any other karmic condition may be. Other past life vows that often lie behind current sexual and financial issues are religious vows of poverty and celibacy. Words spoken in the past may have been appropriate then, but just like other residue from the past, may not be appropriate in the present.

Duality and Double Lives

The energy of duality is central to Gemini. This shows up in various ways in past lives. Having actually been a twin is not uncommon, but more frequently there is a sense of duality that is played out in scenarios such as 'living a double life' or 'living a lie'. This following story continues from the previous chart (Chart A) and is a different expression of the meaning of the Gemini signatures in his chart.

In this past life he was a young man sent to military school by his father. It was his father's and family tradition and it was expected for him to follow this (Capricorn/tenth house – fourth house – conditioning and following expectations – Libra). He unwaveringly followed this duty and became first a soldier then an officer. The opposition to Pluto from the Aquarius planets manifested as he went on in his military career and started to rebel against the system. First, he had concealed even from himself that he was actually gay, (the Cancer/Capricorn, fourth/tenth house axis is associated with gender roles and issues). He was essentially living a lie (Gemini) by fooling himself. Eventually he did take a lover who was also in the military. Both of them were fairly high ranking and did not want to risk their careers (tenth house). They of course did not reveal their relationship to anyone and continued to live this split existence. Inwardly he felt a sense of liberation (Aquarius/Uranus) by the fact that he had come to terms with being gay, and this set in motion a desire to follow that feeling further. He and his lover had access to classified secrets (Uranus in Gemini in the eighth house – secret information) and in an act of subversive rebellion (also Uranus in Scorpio) they started to sell some information to the enemy. Spying and related activities are associated with both the Gemini and Scorpio archetypes. They eventually got caught and were tried and sentenced to the firing squad for treason. Both of them died keeping the secret of their relationship, and he personally felt both grief and shame about this in his final moments.

In his chart we can see that Jupiter in Capricorn squaring the nodes becomes a focal point in this past life story. Most of the energy of the story is contained within the archetypes of Jupiter, Capricorn and the third house. He felt unable to openly live his truth (Jupiter) and had to hide because of the system and his conformity to it (Capricorn), thus living a dual existence (third house/Gemini). His Pluto being in the tenth house shows that in this lifetime he is meant to 'de-condition' from anything that suppresses his creative self-actualization (Leo). The polarity point is in Aquarius in the fourth house so he is meant to build his own sense of emotional security through acknowledging and living that which makes him unique and different.

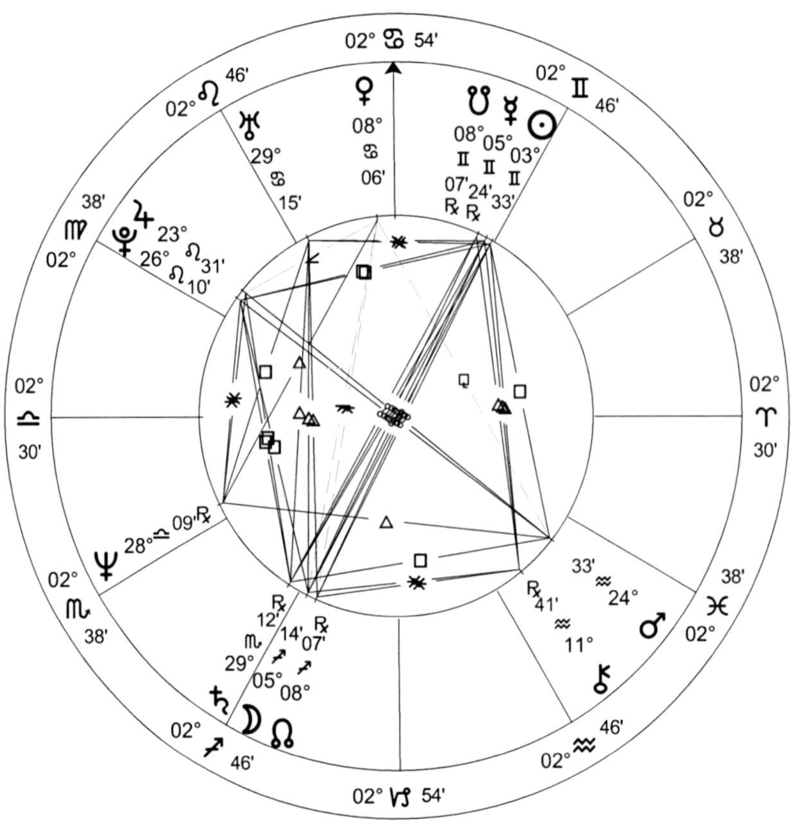

Chart B (Porphyry houses)

Chart B

This case shows various aspects of the duality of Gemini as both a messenger and living in two worlds. This chart also has the nature of paradox in it, as the Gemini SN is in the ninth house and the Sagittarius NN is in the third. The ruler of the SN, Mercury, is also in the ninth conjunct the SN. The nodes are not directly squared within a ten degree orb, but Mercury is conjunct the Sun which is squared and also conjuncts the SN. This brings both the archetypes of Gemini and Sagittarius strongly into his past life experiences.

In one past life he was an academic explorer (Mars square the ruler of SN – also ninth house of long journeys and Gemini/Sagittarius – learning) who stayed for some time with a tribal people (Pluto in the eleventh – Mars in Aquarius). He was an observer at first (eleventh house), coming from a completely different culture (Gemini in the ninth, Pluto in the eleventh – being different) but started to relate to this tribe's ways, forming a connection with them. When it came time for him to leave he felt split (Gemini) as on one hand a deeper part of him had opened up through his contact with these people and their natural ways (ninth house) yet he had a family and an academic career at home (Saturn conjunct NN and opposing SN). Before he was forced to make up his mind, a war broke out in the area and his traveling companions would not delay the return any longer so he left with them. When he arrived back home he was unable to relate at all to what had been his way of life. Having come from feeling like a 'stranger in a strange land', he was now a 'stranger in a familiar land'. This caused a deep sense of alienation (Aquarius/eleventh house, ninth house) and he tried teaching (Gemini/Sagittarius) what he had learned about these people as a way to maintain the connection with them. Unfortunately, he found few in the academic community that wanted to hear what he had learned about these 'savages' and no one in his personal life that cared.

Another fact became clear at this point in the story that we had not known before; the object of his academic exploration was supposed to be about flora and fauna and not 'savages'. While he also had much to report on botanical topics, it was not what had fired his passion from the journey. Here we can see the clash of Gemini, gathering information and knowledge with Sagittarius' need to get to a deeper meaning of things (Jupiter also conjuncts Pluto in the eleventh). He had experienced the natural world, in a deep and profoundly moving way, through its people and now had no outlet for what he had learned and experienced. His personal life meaning had changed radically (Jupiter eleventh house and Gemini/Sagittarius with Aquarius aspects) and he found it increasingly more difficult to merge the two disparate worlds. He lived the rest of his life with the conflict unresolved, progressively becoming more and more alienated from those around him and also within himself.

In his current life he described himself as a "black man born into a white man's world". He felt equally estranged from both cultures since birth. He was currently studying shamanism, yet worked in an Ivy League university, not as an academic (he probably had enough of that from his past life), but in administration. He felt equally estranged from himself and it would seem he carried this dilemma into his current life from the past. It is clear from his chart that his path in this life is to tap into his deeper wisdom, what is true for him, and communicate that in some form. He is meant to speak his truth and bring together these two worlds, first in the inner world, then in the outer world.

The Trickster plays an honored role in various traditions and mythologies. Mercury and Hermes as the trickster are known to be the ones who cross archetypal boundaries. Hermes, who conveyed messages between the worlds of the gods and humans, was also the only god, outside of Hades and Persephone, who could cross safely back and forth into the underworld. Because of this, he also had the role of psychopomp, leading the souls of the dead to the underworld. Another face of the trickster (he has many) uses whatever means at his disposal, usually trickery and mischief, to reveal a greater truth or to expand awareness. This trickster's mission is to get everyone to think outside of the box. In this way the Trickster is an archetype that symbolizes the integrated Gemini/Sagittarius polarity and it is exactly this power that the previous client needed to access within himself. In fact, shortly after this session he had a dream where he was in tribal shamanic clothing but was at a banquet surrounded by his white collegial peers. Of course he was feeling odd and that he didn't quite belong there. He had a medicine bag around his neck and someone came up from behind him and stole it. We talked about the meaning of the dream, and I reminded him that the trickster is often a thief and that he should look into this archetype, as it seemed to me the trickster is a spiritual ally for him to learn from. Both aspects of the trickster, as a liaison or bridge between the worlds and as a messenger, carry a meaning for his karmic axis.

As both these cases show, with Gemini as a part of the karmic axis there is often an essential truth that the person needs to come to, either about their situation or themselves, in their current life. Sometimes this manifests as having created a mental view and picture of oneself that is not in synch with the authentic self. This is especially true when one has worn 'two faces' for whatever reason in past lives. Mercury is a generator of ideas, and we often believe the idea of something more than the truth of what is, which is why advertising (Mercury ruled) is so successful. We can also fall into an easy trap of thinking that the idea of something is the real thing. In the world of revolving ideas one can also start to believe that if they have simply thought about something they have actually become it and integrated it. We can literally 'trick' ourselves into believing lies. The polarity of Sagittarius challenges the individual to continue to seek for the truth about all situations but mostly about oneself. It also, along with Virgo, shows the need to digest and assimilate ideas, and in doing that, an idea of who one truly is can emerge.

Impulse, Immediacy and Reactions

"I think therefore I am" is a fitting aphorism for Gemini's need to know. Gemini's propensity to question everything and its natural inquisitiveness can show up in past lives as literally having been a victim of an interrogation or inquisition or as having been an inquisitor themselves. When this has been a past life experience, the person in the current life may feel a dreadful fear of making a mistake, being wrong or feeling they always have to have the answer. This is in part how the idea of Gemini as a know-it-all can become a part of the archetype. Past lives where mistakes were damaging or fatal to one's self or others, also feed this complex. One client with Jupiter in Gemini in the eighth house square a Pisces SN/Virgo NN, had a short past life as young man who was an apprentice in alchemical studies, (both Scorpio/eighth house and Gemini/Virgo have an association with the knowledge and practices of alchemy).

As he was overseeing less advanced students in this practice perform an experiment, he was frustrated with their early attempts. He exclaimed, "They are so stupid, they are doing it wrong". He rushed over and grabbed a vessel of liquid from one of the students as he proclaimed, "I'll show you how to do this, I can do it better". His rashness caused the vessel to spill the liquid all over his hands (Gemini rules the hands). It contained a caustic chemical which burned his hands and was also poisonous (eighth house). He died shortly thereafter regretting his condescension and impulsiveness, and died saying, "I made a terrible mistake, I was so stupid". Since Gemini is also associated with humor, it was fitting that when he got into the spirit world the guides told him that he was not supposed to die at that time, and that he really had made a mistake. Fortunately from his perspective in the spirit world he was able to laugh about that, and promised to do better in this life and in the future. Death by accident, often through one's own 'stupidity' is common in the Gemini archetype.

The lady in the case history at the end of this chapter, with a Gemini SN in the first house with Mars conjunct, had a past life as a woman who was walking along a busy road. She was very involved in having an inner conversation with herself (Gemini – mental chatter) was not paying attention and stepped in front of a wagon and was killed! Another client with a Taurus SN in the third house and its ruler Venus conjunct Mercury in Virgo, had a past life as a rather simple man (Taurus) who killed himself by accident when he was cleaning his gun. He also died screaming at himself, "I was so stupid. How could I make such a stupid mistake?" When he went into his afterlife he continued to be critical of himself (Virgo) and was stuck going over and over the details (Virgo) of his last moments, so that he could figure out what he did wrong. He spent a lot of time analyzing how he was cleaning his gun until finally the spirit guides, exasperated with him, chimed in to tell him to get over it, let it go and move on.

The mercurial nature of Gemini gives it the ability to respond to stimuli from the environment. In fact Gemini thrives on this ability to react. But 'reactive-ness' can also be at the core of aimless wandering or even just going in circles. Learning about how to consider action, before simply reacting, is a part of Gemini's lesson that is learned from Sagittarius.

Chart C

This client came into a session as she was in a time of transition and had fears about her future and what path to choose. She felt that she had too many people in her life offering her advice and she felt divided (Gemini) and torn (Libra). She also was trying to decide if she should pursue a further degree, but was in a relationship that if she decided to commit to would cause her to move. Doing this would necessitate considering even further options. She simply felt she was spinning in one place without the ability to move forward.

This is not an unusual issue for a Gemini SN moving to a Sagittarius NN. This chart already shows a propensity to be open to others and their ideas as Pluto is in the third in Libra. The SN is in Gemini in the eleventh and also adds to this. In her case she was 'Gemini-overloaded' with too many revolving viewpoints and too much information to process. As we explored her fears, she went back into a past life memory as an orphan boy (Pluto is squared by Saturn in Cancer in the twelfth) who was about nine years old and was under the care of nuns who ran an orphanage. The

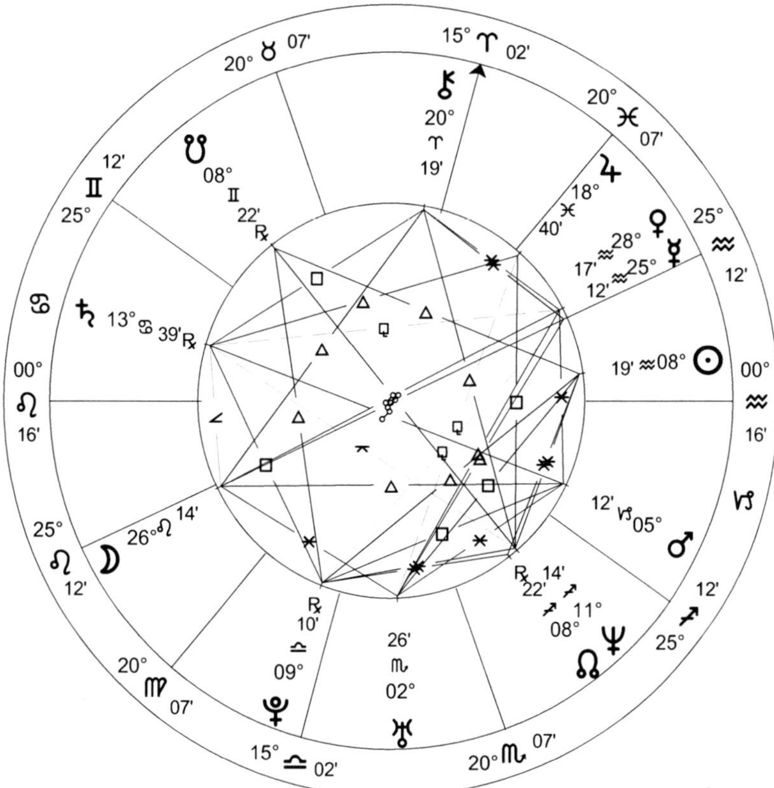

Chart C (Porphyry houses)

treatment was not horrible but it also wasn't exciting enough for the restless spirits of young boys and several of them decided to run away. Running away is also associated with Gemini/Sagittarius as is Neptune – escapism, which conjuncts her NN opposing the SN. Several of them left the orphanage one night with some supplies. As they wandered through towns and villages their supplies started to run low and the older boys decided that they needed to start stealing so that they could eat (Gemini SN – Mercury conjunct Venus in the eighth – thievery to survive).

At first he did not want do this, as he had been taught that stealing was wrong, but the older boys teased him and because he wanted to belong and not be an outsider (eleventh house/Aquarius) eventually he caved in. Because of this lifestyle, the young boys were constantly on the move, not able to stay in one place for too long (Gemini SN). After a while of doing this, he started to enjoy it and since he was smaller than the others he could slip in and out of tight spaces easily and quickly (Gemini). Because of this, he became rather good at thievery, and was often chosen to be the first one to be slipped into a window or hoisted over a wall to get at the goods. At one time while he was sneaking into a house, while the other boys waited outside, he slipped and fell into some furniture creating a huge crash, which woke the occupants. Unable to get away quickly enough, he was caught by the owner of the house. Angry, the owner held the boy and dragged him outside to take him into town to the authorities. The young boy struggled during the trip and succeeded in getting away (again, the slippery nature of Gemini and Neptune).

When he went back to the place that he and the other boys had recently been hiding out, he found they were not there. It seemed they had all taken off in fear of getting caught (there is no honor among thieves). He was crushed by this, feeling abandoned all over again (Saturn in Cancer square Pluto) and he lay there grieving. He waited for days but they never returned and eventually he came to terms with the fact that he had to move on to survive (Gemini and ruler of SN in the eighth). He continued with his petty thievery and eventually came across some older, more serious nefarious characters (ruler of SN in the eighth). They were like a medieval mafia. They put him to work, using him to run errands and small thieving jobs. He did not feel camaraderie with these men like he had before with his peers (Aquarius) and this caused him to feel sad. Regardless, they gave him a means to get by and a place to live, so he decided that was enough. As he worked more with this group of men, he became more privy to their secrets and plans and overheard some of their conversations (Gemini SN ruler in the eighth also Pluto in the third).

Since he had now become a bit inflated with a borrowed (Gemini) sense of importance, he bragged about some plans to some local boys. This led to an important man within the circle getting caught. The other men suspected him as the leak and interrogated him, which he unsuccessfully tried to lie his way through (Gemini – ruler in the eighth and Pluto in the third). Being exposed as the leak and a liar, the other men put him in a sack and threw him off a cliff. He died with the thoughts, "I made bad choices", Libra, Gemini and Scorpio all associated with choosing and choices. "I should have stayed with the nuns and finished my education so I could have made something of myself. Why did I listen to them and not what I wanted?"

Learning and teaching are also themes that are central to both the Gemini and Sagittarius axis. When Gemini is a part of the karmic axis in past lives one may have had difficulty, or may have been blocked/restricted externally from learning.

As we worked through the different layers of imprints carried from that life, it came to light that this young boy did at one time have ideas and plans for his own future. When he was at the orphanage the nuns had a 'business' baking, and he occasionally went with them to the market to sell these goods. These trips gave him the ability to see and meet merchants, which excited him and he had hoped to grow up, travel and become "just like them" (Gemini/Sag). But his feelings of loneliness and abandonment caused him to listen to these other boys which set him on an alternate path that became deadly. Gemini is also associated with mimicry, and we can see that this young boy was clearly forming his ideas of himself by what he felt he was able to copy. Libra also has this tendency. The higher guides came to counsel this young boy towards the end of our work and spoke to the present day client as well.

"Trust your own knowing" they said, echoing her Sagittarius NN. "You don't have to fear making the wrong choice anymore as long as you listen to and follow your own truth". We can see from her chart that the polarity point of Pluto, being Aries and the ninth house, also brings in the lesson of fearlessly going for one's own goals. We worked further on getting her in touch with feeling her internal compass and the clarity of her own inner truth. After clearing this lifetime of crossed purposes she was able to start to set her own life course based on her own inner direction.

Another archetype that is associated with the trickster and Gemini is the Fool. Aside from clowning around, the Fool represents a carefree attitude that is ready to hit the road, in a moment's notice, without much thought of the direction that is being taken. The fool is also related to Pisces as his naiveté is what allows him to blissfully step off the cliff, with absolute trust. The mutable signs are about the ability to change, to be adaptable and flexible. In the previous story, these natural qualities made the young boy open to peer pressure and in the chart we can see there is a significant emphasis on the fixed modality that is relevant to her current life. Perhaps it is time for her to start manifesting those ideas?

The mutable quality of Gemini can be behind other past lives that were spent living as a drifter or a vagrant, like a leaf on the wind (also relevant to the Sagittarius archetype – the nomad). This underscores the tendency towards reaction versus considered action. When these types of lives have been experienced, in the current life it is understandable that finding a life direction may be hard. When a person lives or has lived constantly in reaction to circumstances and life, they can develop a defeatist or victim complex about knowing and going for what they want and may not be able to form a clear picture of their future. The key with the Sagittarius polarity is to embrace the ability to set goals. Gemini is about the present moment, the immediate environment, while Sagittarius is about the future and long term goals.

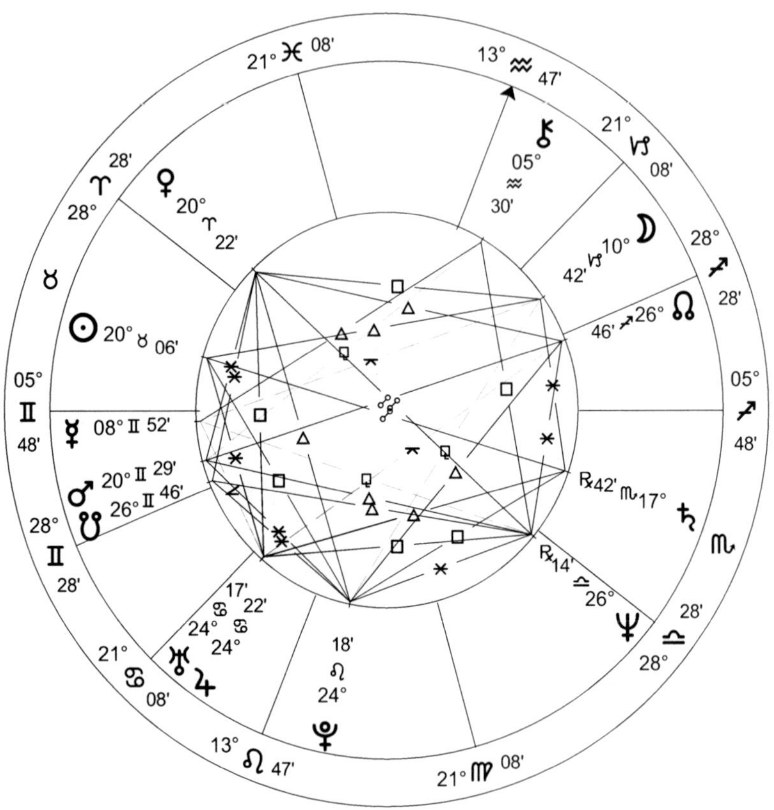

Chart D (Porphyry houses)

Chart D

It had been said that if you want to observe a planet or sign in action, look to someone who has it in their first house as you will see a very immediate, direct and pure expression. This final case has not only a Gemini SN in the first, but its ruler, Mercury as well, which is also conjunct the ascendant. Mars also conjuncts the SN, bringing the energy of Gemini to the forefront even more. This woman has done a lot of regression work which allows us to see many different stories and expressions of how the archetype has conditioned and expressed itself in her past lives. The past lives that I did not have in my files, I asked her to report on, so the quotes are hers.

I asked her first to summarize her past life themes.

"Many lives of being my own thinker, not doing things the normal way".
"Getting in trouble for opening my mouth, or not being able to when I really needed to".
"Not listening to good advice".
"Being the messenger but not being heard, or getting in trouble for what I had to say".
"Being falsely accused".
"Many lives of violence".
"Being a warrior, killed in battle in many different forms".

Just from these statements we can see Gemini and Mars/first house working in unison in the past. Since her Pluto is in the fourth house in Leo there are other themes as well that had to do with family, loss of children and being abandoned.

"Being left as a single mother".
"Being abandoned or loosing my children and family".
"Tedious lives of poverty and servitude". (Sun in Taurus, oppose Saturn in sixth square Pluto).
"Getting in trouble because of pregnancy".
"Lives of hard childhood, abuse and traumas in childhood".

A main current and past life issue had to do with the Gemini theme of communication, in many different forms.

In one past life she was a Geisha in training, living in an environment that was closed off from the outside world (Pluto is squared by a Taurus Sun in the twelfth). But she had not been born in that environment and had knowledge of the outside world and her own ideas when she entered her schooling and training (Gemini). She spoke out openly and freely about her beliefs, which was inappropriate and she was executed by having her head chopped off with a sword (Gemini in the first house/Mars conjunct – ruling the head and swords). Her dying thoughts were, "I didn't do anything wrong" and "I was just letting them know there was something more".

From this story we can see the theme of expansiveness of knowledge and the desire to disseminate what is known. The theme of having her head cut off for speaking out was repeated in several lives. This left a dual imprint of the urge to continue to speak out and the fear of doing so in her current life.

Along similar lines, in another life she was a male courier in France, during the revolution. This man lived alone in a small village and because of the nature of his work was traveling frequently (Gemini). He was a natural loner (Mars/first house) and had no real intimate connections with anyone. At one time as he was returning to his own town, he rode in through surrounding villages and saw they were ablaze. He knew that this destruction was heading for his town. He galloped ahead of the destruction, through villages banging on doors, bursting into an inn and screaming at the people to get out now. He was waving his sword frantically, and this obviously scared the people so they did not take what he was saying seriously, thinking him quite mad. This infuriated him (Mars/first house), as he screamed at them, "You're all so stupid, don't you hear what I'm saying? Move or die you idiots". This was also an unusual behavior for him, as he was not that interested in other people and their lives. Because he was coming out of his reclusive shell (Pluto in the fourth/Taurus Sun square) and was trying to help but was not being heard, this frustrated him further. His anger, anxiety and frustration worked him into a frenzy (Mars/Gemini) and he continued to ride on screaming at people. During this, in the surrounding chaos, someone came up behind him and stabbed him; he didn't see it coming and it proved to be a fatal wound. His survival instinct was strong (Taurus Sun square Pluto and Mars in the first) as he staggered back to his own home in great pain but refusing to die. He struggled for a long time but eventually died from blood loss, despondent and alone. His dying thoughts were, "No one wants to listen so why bother, just leave me alone". The client later commented about this life, "I learned from that life that my exuberance scares people; If I want to be heard I have to quiet down".

This brings in elements of the first house/seventh house polarity lessons of the client's karmic axis. Aries moving towards Libra implies that opening to others and listening to them is essential to learning relatedness. As in her case also, this past life character was a loner, who hadn't learned how to relate, or maybe even have certain social skills (Libra/seventh house). As this related to her Gemini lessons moving towards the Sagittarius polarity, it means that she has had to adjust her mode of communication so that it is more inclusive of others and their beliefs and viewpoints.

The Geisha life and the Courier life both have the connecting theme of speaking out. Because the Gemini SN is in the first with Mars conjunct and the ruler is also in the first house, in these past lives she was immediate, brazen and forceful in her approach.

While all past life and subconscious content is a part of our personal shadow, some past lives are harder to look at than others. These lifetimes are often the ones where we did not handle ourselves well or where our actions harmed others. The qualities we displayed in those past lives are often the ones we project most strongly onto others in our current lives. We see others as intolerant, cruel, selfish, greedy or arrogant staying blissfully unaware that we often have those same qualities buried or suppressed within ourselves. This client's empowered qualities of Leo and Mars/first house courage combined with her natural Gemini curiosity gave her the impetus to also explore these darker corners of her psyche.

She was the son of a medieval baron landowner who was given a serfdom to take over and run. Since he was just a young man who had lived too comfortably under his father's care, he felt unprepared for this task. He was aware of his incompetence and felt highly unqualified (contrast to Gemini tendency to know it all). Pluto in Leo in the fourth relates to the Gemini SN – insecurity about power and knowledge). But it was his birthright (Leo ascension to the 'throne' in the fourth – ancestral inheritance). Also Saturn (father, responsibility, lineage) squares Pluto and opposes the ruler of Pluto's sign, the Sun). Further, the Mars/first house signatures relate to being thrust into something prematurely before one is fully prepared. Because of his insecurity he went overboard in taking charge, 'my way or the highway' became the rule (Leo and Mars/first house).

After he was in charge for a time, the crops started to fail, people were getting poorer and they meekly tried to advise him on changes he could make to improve the conditions for all. He totally shut out any input and became even more controlling (Pluto in the fourth – control because of insecurities along with Saturn and Taurus). He quickly became an autocratic tyrant – Leo, Saturn, Mars/first house. He oppressed all education and all forms of learning and eventually it got so bad he attempted to forbid communication as much as possible, (the ruler of the SN, Mercury, is also inconjunct the Moon in Capricorn and Saturn as the focus point of a yod). People were forced to stop speaking out; if they did they were killed, and his method of doing that was to have their heads chopped off (Mars/first house).

The people became immensely frustrated with him and his oppressive regime and started to ambush him whenever he was riding around his territory. Unbelievably they didn't kill him, they just beat him up and ran away. This happened many times and each time it did he would go into town with his army in a rage and rampage (Mars/first house) and attack people and kick some of them out of their homes. Some of them died because of this.

One day three men did ambush him and kill him. He died enraged and in the spirit world remained that way, quite nasty and still not wanting to hear anything anyone had to say. The spirits of those who killed him were asked to come forward. He saw them as deformed 'Quasimodo types', mocking them and calling them ugly and stupid. "You are idiots and have nothing to say that I want to hear". The spirit guides eventually got firm with him and said, "OK, if you want be so stubborn…" (Taurus Sun Square Pluto – also the ruler of Pluto's sign), "we can stay here for all eternity; they can keep beating you up until you start to listen". "This will be your eternal reality here in the spirit world".

He finally heard that and was directed to look in the eyes of the ones who killed him. They started to communicate to him what their lives were like before he came; they were prosperous and knew how to get the most out of their lands (empowered Taurus). They said, "We could have taught you but you wouldn't listen". He started to soften and felt ashamed. Interestingly, as he started to change his perception of them, they also started to change form and morphed from looking like 'Quasimodo' into healthy strong young men. Now he started to realize that how he saw the entire situation was wrong. He realized his whole view of reality was just in his mind (Gemini) and not the truth of the objective reality (Leo is subjective reality; polarity point Aquarius is about embracing the objective). His whole world view had been colored by his Leo/fourth house insecurities.

More villagers started to come forward and as one made himself known the client realized this one spirit was her present day son. She broke down crying, as she said in their present day life together he was always saying, "Mom you don't listen and you never let me speak". She was sobbing and apologizing for her ignorance to the villagers and her son. An interesting astrological correlation is that her son has a NN in Aquarius in the third/SN in Leo in the ninth. Part of his karmic issue is also about coming forward and finding new ways to communicate his truth and be heard.

Adding to the experience this soul has had with the themes of communication, she also had lifetimes where she was tortured for knowledge and in one life she died saying, "I don't know the answer, I don't know anything". In another life she was gagged while being tortured so was unable to speak at all. She also had two lifetimes where she was mute.

We can see from these past lives, that this soul, imbued with a healthy dose of the Gemini archetype, has experienced many sides of communication issues in an attempt to fuse all the various angles into wisdom (Sagittarius). Her soul has fluctuated as a way to learn all that is possible within this theme, which is not only a Gemini principle, but a common principle in souls' histories. In order to fully manifest and master the power of the polarity point, all the experiences of the archetypes representing the past must be in the soul's memory. In her current life she struggled with an intrinsic paradox that she felt unheard when she spoke out, yet others told her she was not listening to them. This caused her to fluctuate between extremes of being too shy or overly bold when communicating. We can see from her past lives how this complex was formed. As she worked through these layers in regression, her natural abilities as a teacher started to manifest. She found she was not only comfortable communicating what she knew but people wanted to hear it!

4

Cancer/The Moon and the Fourth House

"There was a child went forth every day;
And the first object he look'd upon, that object he became;
And that object became part of him for the day, or a certain part of the day, or for many years, or stretching cycles of years."

Walt Whitman – *Leaves of Grass*

Keywords

Cardinal/Yin/Water	Conditioning	Emotional Memory
Ego	Pregnancy	Imprints
Womb	Sensitive	Neglect
Childhood/Lunar Inner Child	Protection	Helpless
	Early Environment	Needs
Isolation	Mother	Emotions
Children	Family/Clan	Dependency
Home	Ancestors	Self Image
Roots	Inner space	Touchy
Formative	Nurturing	Subjective
Security	Protection	Gender Roles
Baby	Child-like	Housewife/Husband

The Natural Archetype

After the flurry of Gemini, energy returns again to the inner self in the yin sign of Cancer. The rationality of Gemini now meets the non-rational, with the ever changing tides of emotional reaction. In Gemini the ability to take in and react to stimuli mentally is highlighted, in Cancer the reactive and formative nature is purely emotional. The second of the yin signs, Cancer picks up where Taurus left off and complements the feeling nature with the ability to emote.

Within the archetype of Cancer the preceding signs coalesce and consolidate. Aries is the spark of the self, spontaneously arising out of the cosmic womb of Pisces. In Taurus the spark of self becomes a felt sense of being that is then grounded into feeling. Within Gemini, 'I think therefore I am' becomes the predominate theme. These first three signs are imbued with the energy of spring. There is newness; a promise of things to come; a nascent energy that seeds the following signs with potential that later ripens. Cancer is the second of the cardinal signs and begins the energy of summer. In gardens in the northern hemisphere, June and July herald the first pick of the growing season. Thus Cancer is simultaneously about birth and fruition.

One interpretation of the glyph, or symbol for the sign of Cancer, is that it represents the interconnection between male sperm and the female ova in the process of fertilization. The place where male and female seeds meet are in the womb, and from understanding the processes that happen at this stage of the very beginning of life, we delve deeply into the meaning of Cancer. Symbolically the potential of the previous archetypes consolidates in the womb and gives birth to the human child in Cancer.

In the archetype of Cancer/Moon and the fourth house our inner world is formed; our emotions and our self image (the foundations of ego). Since Cancer is at the IC of the chart in the natural zodiac, our roots also include not only that of the family we are drawn to be born into, but also our ancestral lineage and our own personal karmic history. These pre-existing conditions form the template for the hard outer shell that encases our sensitive inner self, just like the crab that symbolizes Cancer. The crab is not born with a shell but forms one in the early stages of its life from a soft template, and it is at this point that it is most vulnerable. The type of conditioning that is experienced in Cancer can be described as imprinting, which comes from the early environment. Beside the pre-existing conditions, the infant forms its first awareness of itself through the symbiotic relationship with its mother. At this stage it is theorized that the infant experiences the mother's reality as its own, and only progressively discovers itself and its own identity as it grows apart from her.

A similarity of the Cancer/Capricorn axis is that conditioning is a part of each of these archetypes. In Capricorn, Saturn gives form and structure and aside from making order, the quality of conformity is also a part of this archetype. The father is often associated with Saturn and it is the archetype of Father that models the way we are in the outer world (society at large). Ancestral and cultural traditions are also in the realm of Capricorn and in following them (consciously or unconsciously) we find we become shaped and molded and even confined by their conditions.

In his poem, *Leaves of Grass*, Walt Whitman writes, "And the first object he look'd upon, that object he became". The Moon-ruled element of water within us shapes itself by the surroundings. This follows the natural square from Aries, where identity is in a constant process of being formed, so that in Cancer that propensity gives us the openness to introject feelings and emotions that are not fully ours in an attempt to form who we are. The receptivity and changeability of the Moon makes us impressionable. Cancer is the Lunar Inner Child, who retains all the emotional imprints from childhood, starting with those that were formed in the womb. Researchers that work with non-ordinary states of consciousness therapeutically have consistently reported that the experience in the womb is as formative as our early childhood experiences.

One pioneer in this understanding is Dr. Stanislav Grof, who first through LSD research and then breath work with thousands of clients, mapped out various stages of the pre- and perinatal experience called *Basic Perinatal Matrices*. Grof's research revealed that individuals had similar archetypal experiences emerge from the unconscious while 'regressing' to various stages of pre-birth and birth. These ranged from feelings of oneness and unity with the cosmos, to titanic struggles of life and death. What his research showed is that consciousness in the process before birth is receiving imprints and impression from the collective root memory of all of humanity. In the womb, the consciousness is 'downloading' the previous experience of all humanity along with individual karmic conditions, and this forms a template of the shell that will grow and harden after birth and through early childhood. The water triad is connected through this theme of birth. Pisces is the cosmic womb, where consciousness is born out of the collective unconscious that contains all the archetypes possible for life on earth. Cancer is the physical womb, where the collective and individual consciousnesses merge to create a form that can be born into the world – this form is ego dominated. Scorpio is the place where we birth ourselves, purifying impressions, desires and intentions to birth a soul-dominated consciousness that is aligned with divine will and prepares us for the return to the cosmic womb.

Dr. Grof has Pluto, Jupiter, Sun and Mercury in Cancer opposed by Saturn, which is conjunct the Moon in Capricorn in his natal chart. It is not hard to see why the foundation of his life's work was the study of conditioning (Capricorn) that happens in the womb (Cancer). Dr. Grof's findings also showed that womb experiences quite easily flow into past life memories and that a part of our biological birth process includes being re-imprinted with our personal karmic history. Experiences that happen in the womb to us, to our parents and events in their environment, mirror our personal past life history. This is also the experience from those who work in regression therapy; myself included.

Cancer in Past Life Experiences

The Cancer archetype is a part of the karmic axis when:

Pluto is in Cancer or the fourth house or
The South Node is in Cancer or the fourth house or
The ruler of the South Node is in Cancer or the fourth house or
The Moon aspects Pluto, the nodal axis or rulers of the nodes.

Imprinting in the Womb

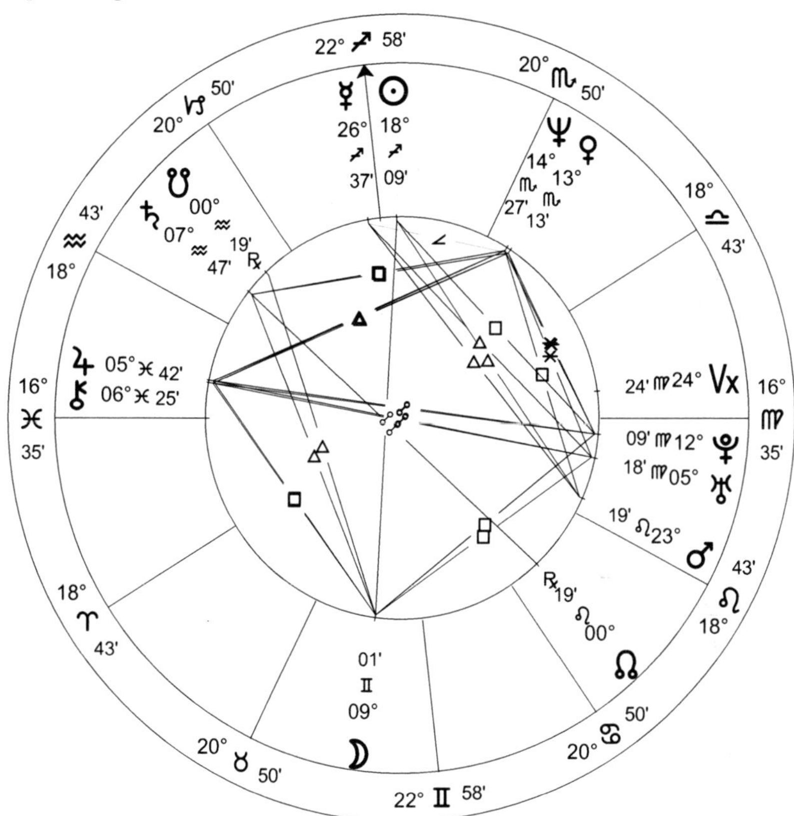

Chart A (Porphyry houses)

Chart A

This client regressed back to the womb spontaneously during a session. While focusing on a feeling of being constricted she curled up into a ball and began rocking back and forth saying, "I don't want to do this". With natal Pluto conjunct Uranus square the Moon, all the Cancer/Moon themes of mothering/childhood become a part of her karmic axis. In fact in her current life she was adopted and did not know anything about her birth mother. As her regression experience illustrates, the issue of abandonment (Pluto square Moon) was imprinted in her womb experience and was also a part of her karmic history.

As she repeated the phrase "I don't want to do this" her awareness suddenly jumped to the fact that these were her mother's thoughts when she was in the womb. Therapists who work with regression to the womb commonly report that the fetus is not only aware of the mother's psychological state and is affected by it but also by events that happened to and around the mother during her pregnancy. Many times clients recall during regression events and details that were intimate only to their mother or father, which they had no knowledge of but were later able to confirm.

It seemed that this client was recalling the later stages of pregnancy and the depression and desperation that her mother felt as the time of birth approached. The feelings she continued to recall from her mother were a confusing mix (Pisces planets also square the Moon from the twelfth house) of not wanting the baby yet feeling helpless to do anything about it as if it were forced upon her. As a result the mother also seemed to fluctuate in and out of states of dissociation (possible drunkenness) which the client as the fetus registered as further abandonment, (Pluto, Uranus and Chiron square Moon).

In the midst of this recall, spontaneously, she flipped back into a past life memory as a woman living in a remote region with her husband and two small children. She was standing in the doorway frozen in shock and overtaken with a sense of being overwhelmed as she was watching her husband leave in a wagon. He was leaving her for good, and she looked frantically back and forth from him to the two small children standing behind her in the house. She started to shake and sob saying, "I can't do this". The reality of her situation was that she was totally isolated (Uranus/Pluto and Aquarius SN) and was already living a hard life working from dawn to late in the night, just to get by (Saturn conjunct SN and Pluto in Virgo/sixth house). As the days went on, the sense of being overwhelmed went from frantic worry to a complete nervous breakdown resulting in a state of temporary insanity (Uranus conjunct Pluto in the sixth house – Gemini Moon/Aquarian SN). She locked the two children in a room and spread cooking grease around the house and set it ablaze. She did not attempt to escape but lay down on the floor in futility just wanting to die (Saturn conjunct SN – Chiron in Pisces opposite Pluto).

She died with a deep sense of guilt and shame for what she had done, and as a spirit did not want to move on, but instead remained hiding in the ashes of the burnt-down home. Eventually with further work she moved to higher planes and re-met the spirits of the children. Upon seeing them she realized that one of them was her current-life birth mother. The dominos started to fall in place as they dialogued and she realized that she needed to come into this life with the imprint of abandonment to balance out the karma between them. Interestingly the night before this client had this regression, she had a dream of a spiritual figure named Mother Mira, and did not know why this being had appeared to her. After this regression she realized the dream contained a humorous spiritual pun that Mother Mira's name sounded much like Mother Mirror, and that now she knew her mother's experience of her in the womb was a mirror of her own past life experience, with the roles reversed.

She did meet her mother a few years later and her mother confirmed that she was torn, as she did try to keep her as a baby yet felt overwhelmed with the thought of it. She had become pregnant through a one-night stand and the father of the child was not in her life. She did drink during the pregnancy and said she barely remembered anything about the birth (she was dissociated). She also admitted that after she gave birth she felt deep anger towards the client, which she could not explain and could not seem to bond with her. Her mother had feared that if she kept her, she might have harmed her, yet had no logical reason to explain this as she already had one other child and didn't have those same feelings towards him. As a result of this strong emotional reaction, her mother had taken her home from the hospital intending to keep her but gave her up for adoption less than a month later. After doing this she was so conflicted she went back to re-claim her, took her back, only to give her up finally for adoption eighteen months later.

Her mother was also born with asthma (her past life death by fire as a child). It was clear to my client that it was her mother's own past-life child self who reacted to seeing her again (this time the roles reversed), and was thankful to both her mother and the grace of the universe that spared them from completing their karma in a more destructive way. There were other lifetimes, not detailed here, that revealed a sacrificial theme between the two of them, and perhaps they were at the end of enacting this now. In this client's chart, Pluto squaring the Moon signifies the darker emotions her mother had about her and the fact that there was a karmic theme with her birth mother. Jupiter and Chiron in Pisces, in the twelfth house, squaring the Moon and opposing Pluto, alludes also to the sacrificial theme, but also adds the quality of grace and potential for healing. A few further aspects of the client's Moon in Gemini in the third house are not only the dual emotions her birth mother felt, but the fact that she does have two mothers in this life, as she was adopted into a family at the age of two.

Another client, whose case is also in the Pisces chapter, remembered struggling for her life in the womb during her birth process, as her mother was drugged and possibly even unconscious. This birth drama was a re-enactment of past lives where the client had given up in hopelessness, and also had felt guilty about not being able to 'be there' for her own children. Her mother, during the birth process, was enacting her unborn child's karma. When this client regressed back to this womb memory, she relived the panic and horror she felt when her mother's contractions stopped. She remembered feeling that she had to fight to get out of the womb in order to survive. These birth events seemed to be a divinely choreographed drama which forced the client to begin countering her own karmic patterns from past lives of hopelessness and 'giving up', even before she got out of the womb.

The image of mother as a mirror beautifully sums up the idea that the imprinting that happens in the womb is not the primary cause of issues, but the continuation of karmic themes. Psychoanalytic development theory states that the mother is the first mirror of the infant and the infant's image of itself is formed through interaction with her. But taking the reality of the soul's prior incarnations into account this is only a part of the dynamic. As our birth charts reflect we are all born already with karmic patterns in place, our womb experience as well as early childhood in part, re-imprint these previous conditions. This is the deeper meaning of emotional memory that is carried by the Moon, and subsequently by the Moon's nodes.

Since the lunar nodes are not planetary bodies, but rather are sensitive points on the ecliptic (the Sun's path as seen from the earth), where the pathway of the Moon crosses the course of the Sun, they metaphorically represent another dimension of her meaning; karmic memory. The Moon also as we know, is the only planetary body that exerts a measurable gravitational force on the earth. The Moon's force of gravity is greater than the Sun's, and it is interesting to note that the term 'karmic gravity' is often used to describe the spiritual force that pulls us repeatedly into incarnation. The Moon as a symbol for our current childhood conditioning has a gravity that can pull us back in time, and we find ourselves well into adulthood and often in dismay, repeating old unconscious patterns that were formed there. The lunar SN is the weight of unfinished business from past lives that we struggle to free ourselves from.

Sun sign Cancer is often described as approaching life and situations indirectly; this analogy is drawn from the crab's ability to move and run sideways. This indirect approach also points to the way that growth occurs for this cardinal sign. Like the actual crab during the molting process, when the new shell is ready to emerge, the old shell cracks and the crab progressively backs out of it. Going two steps back to make one step forward is the way that progress happens for Cancer. Specific to the Cancer/Capricorn axis this also points to the fact that for real growth to occur we must 'regress' and revisit our past (our childhood, family patterns and personal karma) with new awareness, otherwise we are doomed to repetition.

Birth and Conception

Cancerian past life imprints involving the womb extend also to how one gets pregnant or is conceived. This client (chart B) came to me because she had tried *in vitro* fertilization twice already, with no success. We can see that with her Pluto conjunct Uranus in the second house, fertility might be an issue. Combined with the Scorpio signatures in her fourth, making Pluto also the ruler of her SN, it was not surprising when she told me that she had had surgery (Scorpio) on her ovaries when she was younger which made her unable to conceive in the normal way. Medically she was cleared to be able to conceive through *in vitro* means, but since each attempt was very expensive and she had tried twice before with no success, she wanted to address any issues that may be blocking her before she tried again. Furthermore, Jupiter in Cancer in the twelfth house is loosely squared by

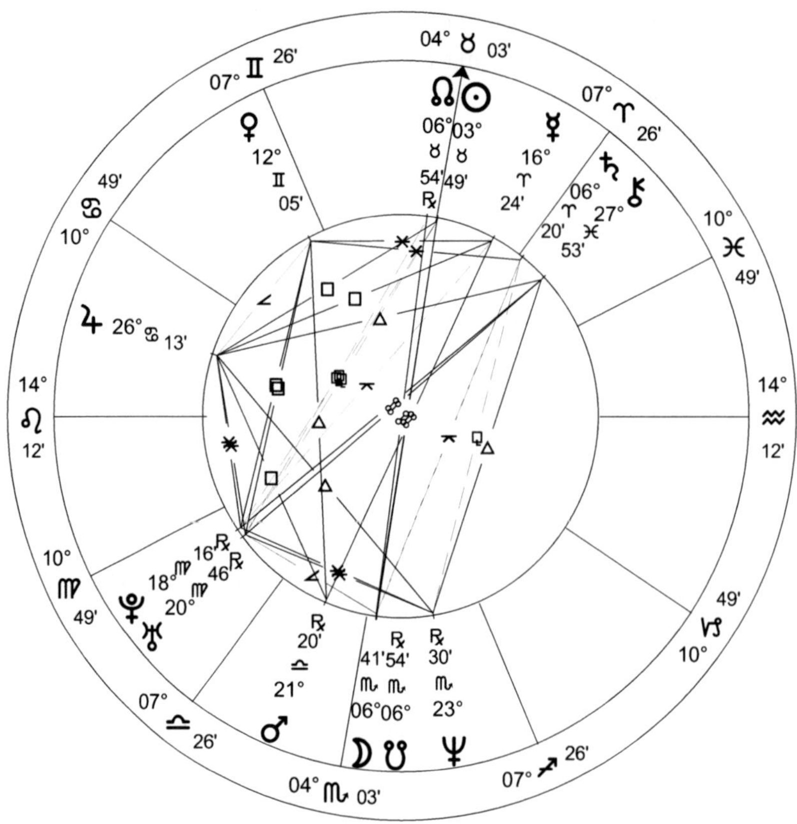

Chart B (Porphyry houses)

the nodes, and is in full orb of squaring the Sun, which conjuncts the NN and opposes the SN and Moon.

When we explored her past lives around childbirth she went into a past life experience as an African woman who was captured by a warring tribe. She was about four months pregnant at the time, and the tribe that captured her wanted to use the fetus for a magical practice (Scorpio/Taurus axis – ritual magic). It happened so quickly after her capture that she had no foreknowledge of what they wanted to do. They simply held her down while they cut the fetus from her and threw it onto a ritual fire during a ceremony. She died soon after in shock and horror. The suddenness of what occurred (Pluto/Uranus) did not allow this part of her soul to fully grasp what had happened and because of this a soul fragment was still frozen in horror beside the fire. We worked with this part of her soul, and after she was able to fully process what had happened, that part of her was ready to move on. In the spirit world some strong African grandmothers came to her holding the spirit of the unborn child, who was radiantly happy to see her again. The child assured her it was okay, and the grandmothers worked to heal the subtle body wounds that the client still carried from that life. They told her to reconnect with them in her present through drumming, and by that means they would work with her to get pregnant and help her through the pregnancy. This was a bit of a surprise to this client as she was an upper-class white woman who had never attended a drumming circle, but she was open to the idea and promised these past life 'ancestors' she would honor their wisdom and help in this way.

Quite frequently I find past life connections with Africa in the Cancer and Leo archetypes. The archetypal association with Cancer comes from Africa being referred to as the birthplace/motherland of all humanity (the womb). With Leo, the association comes from Africa as the homeland of the lion, and the inherent natural dignity and nobility of its people. This client did follow the advice she received in the spirit world, and several months later came back for a session while she was pregnant. She wanted to make sure all the residues were healed so that the baby would feel safe coming to term.

We worked with another past life where she and a child had died in childbirth (Scorpio SN in the fourth). She died in that past life with the imprint that giving birth is deadly (Scorpio SN in the fourth house). After healing her own past life character from these imprints, we worked with the spirit of the past life infant. It was indeed the spirit of the same child that was about to be born to her again in this life. This spirit assured her that it was strong and confident this time around and told her not to worry. My client was struck with the calm confidence, strength and radiance of this incoming soul, who showed herself as a little girl. She did give birth to this baby girl without complications.

In this client's chart we can see that the NN in Taurus in the tenth house required her to have persistence and determination to fulfill her desire to be a mother. In fact all those involved in her process, including her husband and the spirit of the child, echoed this determination by persisting with this intention even when she did not conceive after her initial attempt. With Jupiter in Cancer in the twelfth house in aspect to the NN and Sun conjunction, it is also not surprising that help from the spirit world was involved in her fertility and pregnancy, (Taurus/Cancer).

Death in childbirth, as either the mother or child, can carry into the current life as fear of birthing on all levels. As we can see in her chart, all the yin signs (Taurus, Cancer, Virgo) in the lower half of the natural zodiac were involved in her karmic axis. These signs share a common theme of a reluctance or fear of 'emergence'. Another client with the same archetypes had a Cancer SN in the second house and its ruler (the Moon) in Scorpio in the sixth. She went into a past life experience as a fetus in the womb. Unfortunately her mother died when she was about six months along in her pregnancy and this client, yet unborn in that life, went through a long painful death process along with her mother. The issues of survival (Taurus) combined with the incomplete birth process (Cancer/Scorpio/sixth house) stayed with this woman in her current life as a fear of 'coming out' in any way. Also because she experienced her death in that past life womb as the inability to get out, this contributed to current life claustrophobia. Her Pluto was also in Leo in the fourth house and in the next chapter about Leo, the ideas of coming into one's own powers are discussed; this was also part of her current life issues.

Childhood Wounds

Our lunar inner child stays with us our entire life and Cancer's polarity point of Capricorn is the energy that urges us to grow up ourselves and parent this inner child so this part of us can also mature. We can have many inner child selves that completely or partially 'split off' at different ages, each of them carrying an unfulfilled need which must be completed by our adult selves. This is the crux of the Cancer/Capricorn axis. Quite frequently when Cancer/the Moon/the fourth house are a part of the karmic axis, the need to actively work with the lunar inner child is highlighted. In our past lives, we were all children many times, but the main imprints that are carried into future lives are not always those that were formed in those childhoods. When the Cancer archetype is a part of the karmic axis, it appears that wounds sustained in past life childhoods have frequently imprinted the soul deeply, and are still in need of healing.

This following case shows the impact of a past life suppressed childhood trauma and how it affected the person in the past and present life.

Chart C

This client came into therapy discussing his awareness of how he does not make clear boundaries for himself (Neptune in Libra square the nodes and SN in the twelfth house). He said, "In order for me to claim my own space or point of view, or stand up for myself without feeling guilty about it, things have to build up, until I feel I'm going to explode".

We can see that his natal Moon is in Aries (anger/rage) but in the fixed house and sign of Scorpio. Pluto is also in the first house square Mars and his nodes are squared by Neptune in Libra, so the conflict of expression of anger and denial of it is also a karmic theme. We had already worked together on a different past life that represented another layer of the 'rage complex' he was now describing.

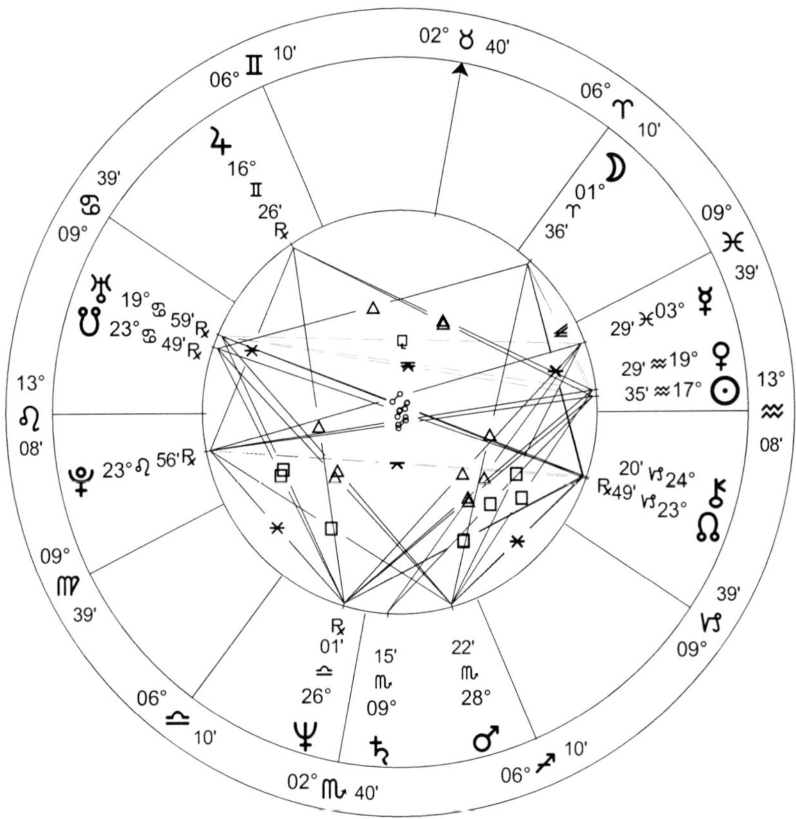

Chart C (Porphyry houses)

He said further that, "All day I have been having the most disturbing images pop into my head of blood, gore, bodies dismembered and I have had to keep pushing it out of my mind". It is not uncommon that when we go to healers or helpers with our issues, in the days or hours prior to the session subconscious material starts to bubble to the surface. As it turned out, this imagery was tied into his past life experience that began with the body sensations of a tight stomach and a crushing feeling on his hips and pelvis. He said, "It's as if my whole lower body is missing". He also felt paralyzed with fear. This led immediately into a past life scene where he was hearing the sounds of explosions around him and was dying with an immense pain in his lower body, but was also saying, "I don't feel anything", (Neptune and twelfth house – dissociation, also Aquarius planets opposing Pluto – shock and fragmentation).

We moved to an earlier time in that past life and he found himself as a young man who was a dock worker in a port city. He had been working there for a bit of time and had ambitious plans for his future. His plan was to join the Royal Navy and "shoot cannons". As the inner life of this past life self was revealed more, it became clear that he had an urge to kill, and joining the Navy was going to allow him to do so. (SN – double signature of water [navy]; Pluto in the first square Mars – violence/war; ruler of the SN, Moon in Aries in the eight house – murderous intent).

When I asked him about any family he left behind (nodes Cancer/Capricorn), as the past life character he curtly responded, "I don't want to remember that". Because of this resistance I guided him to do so. He went back to a memory of when he was fourteen. His father was yelling at him and he felt a rage inside himself, but also a simultaneous feeling of numbness. He said, "This is what it is like all the time, my father is a drunken slob", (another aspect of Neptune and twelfth house), and "I hate him, but I can't do anything about it" (powerlessness – Cancer, Neptune/twelfth house and Scorpio – power/powerlessness). "It's like I have this hatred but no power. I want to leave but I can't cause I'm afraid my father is going to kill my mother", (Cancer/Capricorn – SN ruler in Aries in the eighth – Pluto square Mars). He said, "I feel dead inside, as if a part of me is just not there", (dissociation – Neptune/twelfth house). I directed him to go back to when this dead feeling started.

He immediately went back to about four years of age. He was in his house with his mother and everything seemed fine. After a few moments his father burst through the door, pushed him out of the way and started beating his mother. As this young child he was horrified, frozen in shock, as it all happened so fast, (Uranus conjunct Cancer SN – child frozen in sudden shock).

His mother fell to the floor and despite his fear he rushed to her and found her face all bloody and some of her teeth on the floor. He was sobbing as he picked up her teeth, holding them and crying. (This is the moment of the deepest wound of this past life child – Cancer). His father had left and he was alone with his mother, who was unconscious. He was sobbing pitifully, "Mommy, I'm so sorry. I couldn't help you. I don't know what to do. Mommy please don't leave me. I'm so scared" (Cancer).

This was where his life force simply went away, leaving him with the lasting imprint for the rest of that life of feeling dead inside, yet still having the subconscious urge to defend his mother uncompleted. His anger at his own helplessness as a small child (Cancer SN in the twelfth) became the core of the complex, which was a blend of rage and powerlessness. Later in his life, this was the fuel for his obsessive urge to kill (Aries/Scorpio). He did eventually leave home at about age sixteen and after working at the docks joined the navy. Just before he did, he fantasized aloud about what it was going to be like and said, "I imagine myself being on that big boat, I like the ships, they move, I like the feeling of rocking", (Cancer/twelfth house, Neptune square the nodes and eighth house of water all emphasized, and again his own little wounded inner child still seeking comfort).

He did succeed in working his way up in the military saying, "I know I would never be able to be in charge, like one of the officers, but I can get to control one of those cannons", (Scorpio/Capricorn – ambition and control), and he became obsessed with this idea (weaponry – Pluto in the first, ruler of SN in Aries in the eighth – obsession).The cannon also had a phallic reference for him that became clearer at the end of his story.

After his training he did get to control one of the cannons, and because of his obsession, we learned a lot about daily care of them, how to load them, all the precautions you need to take when firing them etc. (We laughed about this later, as neither one of us had much of an interest in cannons and their care). Eventually his ship became engaged in battle, others were killed around him and in the midst of battle the hull of his ship was hit and a huge timber pinned him at the pelvis crushing him to death. This was the memory that first surfaced when we started in the story. He died next to his cannon, full of the rush of battle fresh in his consciousness (first house/Aries), and was angry that he died so young. He screamed in rage, "This isn't fair, I died too young!" Aries/Mars SN and Mars/Pluto aspects can indicate lives that end too soon, violent past life deaths, and certainly deaths in the midst of battle.

While working in the afterlife bardo with the many imprints from that life, at one point he became aware that he died a virgin before he ever got to have sex. That was also some of his Scorpio/Aries unspent youth/libido that never got expressed and was channeled into his obsession with 'firing his cannon'. The bloody imprints with which he started this story he associated less with the end of his life, but more from when he was a young boy holding his mother's teeth. How, at that moment, his absolute powerlessness was combined with defeat and rage, and the sight of his mother's blood, all simultaneously imprinted in a flash. Here we can see how the Cancer SN conjoined by Uranus could indicate mother experiencing a shock, as well as his own inner child past life character being shocked by what happened to his mother. The part of him that went away is also indicated by Uranus conjunct the SN (soul fragmentation caused by shock and trauma) and the Neptunian/twelfth house tendency to dissociate… go away. Further, it was the little boy part that dissociated (Cancer SN and Pluto in Leo). He was able to reunite with his mother, who helped him overcome his feeling of responsibility for her (Cancer/Capricorn nodes). She helped him to soften from that hardened life and embrace his own lost child self. With her help we did much work in reintegrating this lost inner child. (When he dialogued with this part it told him, "I am bringing back to you the ability to be open to love again").

After finishing that past life he said, "I immediately see that one of the main themes of my past lives has been about the wounds to my ability to love", (Pluto- Leo). "Because of this, I hide my sensitive side and avoid my emotions", (Cancer SN in the twelfth). "But now I see there is power in my emotions and I don't need to be afraid", (empowered Cancer and ruler of the SN – Moon in Aries in the eighth).

Emotions

As this case also points out, when the archetype of Cancer is a part of the karmic axis, the person can come into this life feeling that their emotional reality will not be accepted, and most likely, in various ways, 'reality' will bear this out. This points the way to a blending of the Cancer (emotions) and Capricorn (reality) archetypes, that individuals on this axis learn through the course of their lives – that it is safe to bring their inner world into the outer world. Commonly the larger arena of society doesn't allow for full emotional expression; women (Cancer) in the workplace (Capricorn) find this out all too often. And often with this axis the individual finds that their current life early childhood environment did not validate or allow them free emotional expression. The healing is in recovering and meeting the needs of the lunar Inner Child for oneself. This is the promise of the Capricorn polarity, the ability to re-parent the inner child from the inner adult self, with the conditions that it needs.

As in the previous case, commonly when one's emotional nature has been wounded the response is to deaden, harden, retreat or dissociate from the emotional pain. The reality is that, even though these defenses allow one to 'get on with life' (which is one way to incorporate the Capricorn polarity), they do not meet the needs of the inner child. Through the natural square to Libra often those needs can be projected onto 'the other' through relationships, and the person can become overly needy, unconsciously expecting others to fulfill the inner child's longings.

In fact this was also a dynamic in play with the client from the previous case, as he constantly was told by women that he was "too needy". We can see by his Neptune in Libra square to the nodes, how easy it is for him to project his unconscious, fantasy-like (Neptune), and child-like (Cancer), expectation onto others (Libra). In esoteric astrology, via Alice Bailey, Neptune is the esoteric ruler of Cancer. Esoteric rulers of signs are said to symbolize a dimension of the soul's reality and its interplay with the current life personality. This makes part of the lessons in the Cancer archetype similar to those of Libra (where Neptune is the higher octave of Venus). For Cancer, the ultimate Neptunian realization is that only the divine Mother/Father can truly fulfill their needs. Any parent or partner will fall short, just through the nature of their humanness. The integrated axis of Cancer/Capricorn can allow the lunar inner child to face the reality that no one person can meet its needs unconditionally. Ultimately, as the re-parenting of the inner child takes place, the archetype of the 'divine parents' can be tapped into, to sustain and nurture the lunar needs.

In his past life, his own sensitive inner child did meet with a cold hard reality (Capricorn); that of his father's brutality. Because none of the trauma was resolved in the past, as he grew up in that life he became more and more like his own father. As Carl Jung said, "You always become the thing you fight the most". This illustrates the power of how we become conditioned by our experiences and others who shape us, especially our parents. How often have children said, "I do NOT want to be like my mother/father", yet to their horror they find as they grow up, they are enacting all that they rejected in their parents. The Capricorn polarity offers the potential to give a boundary to all that Cancer has unquestioningly taken and the foundation to start to define one's own reality. A keyword for Capricorn is 'integrity', which one often thinks of in ethical or moral terms. But integrity, as Virgo, another earth sign reminds us, also is about wholeness within oneself. In Cancer, that sense of wholeness and self-security comes from the healing and integration of the emotional body.

Chart D

It is not uncommon for people with past lives that include the Cancer archetype to have had significant karmic experiences as both mother and child that affect them in their current lives. With a quick glance at the karmic axis of this chart, the archetype of Cancer is not so pronounced; but the fact that Pluto is in the fourth house and the Moon squares the Cancer ascendant, brings this archetype into her past life experiences quite strongly.

The first of this client's past life experiences arose spontaneously while I was doing energy work with her. There was no particular issue that we went into the session seeking so there was no formal induction into the past life memory. She was in a co-dependant relationship at the time with an alcoholic and drug abuser, (Pluto is in Libra and Neptune conjuncts her SN). In the first scene in her past life she was clutching a baby in her arms as men were wrapping chains around her and the child. This was the moment just before her death, as the men threw her and the baby into a body of water and the weight of the chains drew them down to the bottom, drowning them both. She died with a simultaneous imprint of wanting to hold onto the baby to protect him, but feeling guilty that she was unable to let him go to save his life.

As we went back earlier in the story we discovered that the baby was a product of an illicit love affair (Pluto in Libra square Venus in Leo) with a village priest (Sagittarius SN – sixth/twelfth house axis) and that she was

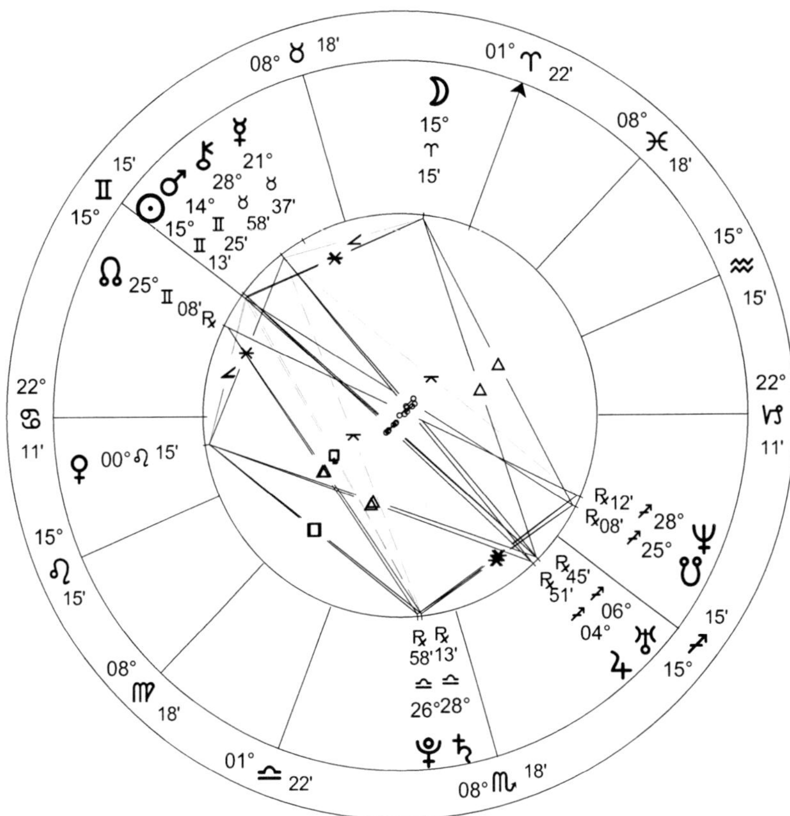

Chart D (Porphyry houses)

drawn into sleeping with him because of her naiveté (Neptune conjunct SN). As her pregnancy began to show, the priest feared being outed and accused her of having the Devil's child; stirred up the villagers and they quickly did away with her.

I find that the Scorpio archetype in past life experiences is prone to being accused of being evil, and in this chart we have Pluto in the fourth house so the child carried that projection (Libra) along with the mother. This child in the past life was her current life boyfriend, which was one reason why she was still caught in the dynamic of trying to save him (Sagittarius, Neptune and sixth house). One can see how issues of mothering or needing to be mothered could play out in the arena of relationships with Pluto in Libra in the fourth house. Despite the obvious betrayal that she died with, this was not her focus at all and in the spirit world she had no concern for the people who killed her, or the priest. She simply was sobbing with the grief of not being able to save the baby, and feeling guilty that she caused his death. Saturn is conjunct Pluto in the fourth house, so the issues of responsibility and protection combine with the sixth house signatures, causing further feelings of guilt and failure. Because she died with him in her arms, with the chains holding him in place, her spirit was frozen in that moment and it took significant healing and help in the spirit world for her to release the death grasp she had on the child. Once her spirit was able to realize that despite her torn intention (Libra) of holding him or letting him go, the chains would have prohibited her from doing anything to save his life, she was able to start to release some of her guilt.

Helpful mother and grandmother spirits came in the spirit world to take the baby out of her arms and it was at that moment she realized he was her current life boyfriend. After processing this, she was able to let him go and turn him over to the care of the spirit helpers. This also broke the spell of their co-dependency and shortly thereafter, with gentleness, she ended their relationship. In the couple's composite chart (not shown here) they have a Pisces Moon square the nodes!

In another past life experience other aspects of the Saturn conjunct Pluto in the fourth house continued. She was a pioneer woman (Venus in the first, square Pluto), who followed her husband out into the wilderness to stake a claim on land and start a family. They had a whirlwind romance prior to leaving that was full of hope and promise for the future (Pluto in Libra – Venus in Leo square, ruler of the SN, Jupiter in the fifth). After she had three small children her husband started drinking and gambling (Neptune conjunct SN and Venus in Leo) and she found herself sinking into despair as he broke one promise after another (Pluto in Libra). "This was not what I expected" (Pluto in Libra) she sobbed, as the reality (Saturn) of her situation became clearer to her.

As time went on, her life became more dreary. She was torn (Libra) between her maternal instincts to love and care for her children and the weight of the responsibility taking care of them entailed, which made her want to run away (Sagittarius SN). While her children were still small her husband failed to return from one of his drunken outings, as he was killed in an accident. Now that she was left to care for the three children alone, she cried, "I have to keep going on; I have to give up all hope of life as I wanted it to be and just work". Her shattered expectations and disillusionment at the loss of her dreams are represented by the Libra archetype and Neptune conjunct the SN. Unlike the first case presented in this chapter from another client in a similar situation, she did not have a complete nervous breakdown, but rather sunk more and more into depression, which progressively made her unfit for mothering.

As her eldest child grew up, this child stepped into the role of caring for the younger ones, and resented the mother because of it. The rest of the client's life went on fairly uneventfully and she died as an older woman, depressed and alone (Saturn). Underlying her depression she felt ashamed and guilty that she had not been there for her children, as she would have wanted to, and died with these imprints. This past life, combined with the previous one, seemed to have solidified in her soul the feeling of guilt around children and the need to atone for this, by trying to save them.

In the next past life we worked with, she came to me during an emotional crisis. She had already in her young life (she was only 24) volunteered one summer to go to Guatemala to work in a home for children who had Aids. She was currently working in a daycare program in the United States for children of Mexican illegal immigrants. Transiting Uranus was in orb of squaring her nodal axis and she felt she was in the process of some sort of mental/emotional breakdown and was having panic attacks. In many cases, when transiting planets aspect the karmic axis, karma is released quite dramatically into the current life. The nature of the transiting planet has a lot to do with the quality of what is being released. In her case, while the Uranus transit was causing upheavals in her life, ultimately as her next two stories will show, the higher intention of Uranus, namely liberation, was the result of this transit. Her current life situation was not horrible; she had a recent breakup with a boyfriend that obviously was triggering deeper material. She felt overwhelmed at work, but this was more from a sense of emotional overload than the actual responsibilities. She said simply, "I cannot seem to meet the demands of anything in my life right now".

In this memory she went back to a past life as an African woman in apartheid South Africa. As mentioned earlier, often African lives relate to both the Cancer and Leo archetypes, which are both present in her karmic axis. She was a teacher in a classroom (Sagittarius/Gemini nodes) in a poor shanty town. In her first past life scene she was in the middle of a lesson when uniformed men burst in, firing guns and killing a few of the students in front of her while the rest of them scattered. She was in horror, screaming, "They're killing all the babies". It seemed that it was during a time of uprising in the area and the uniformed men were looking for 'insurgents and protestors'.

Again she felt totally responsible that she was unable to save them. She was arrested on the spot but instead of taking her to prison or a jail they transported her to a distant township, and simply left her there. She had no means of support and was a total stranger in this desolate town, (Sagittarius SN – foreign trauma, also ruler of SN Jupiter conjunct Uranus). She was in total shock from the killing she had witnessed and wandered the streets of the unknown shanty town. Beside the grief she had about the children, as she wandered she cried also for her people and their loss of pride and dignity (Venus in Leo square Pluto). She didn't last long as sickness soon claimed her life, and she died alone in the streets. She had already given up by this point so she welcomed death as a relief from her immense suffering (Neptune conjunct SN). As we worked in the afterlife to help her heal, even after re-meeting the spirits of the children, she remained stuck on the last moment when she saw them being killed and kept repeating, "They're killing all the babies". It was apparent there was another past life memory that was equally important to explore that was connected to this phrase so I directed her to follow it.

She immediately went into the body of an infant past life self that was about to go under the knife as a sacrifice, (Venus and Leo are both associated with the heart in the first house; violence/knives – the square by Pluto from the fourth). Her theme of sacrifice and needing to 'save the children' was taking on another twist. Now it was her that desperately cried to be saved, and although the memory was from a time when she was pre-verbal, she screamed, "I want my mommy. Mommy where are you?" She died quickly as her heart was cut out, but was in absolute infantile panic and fear. The afterlife was not any better as she went into a 'hellish' state in the bardo, which was full of blood and screaming babies. This part of her soul was stuck with the other infants that had died as she did. I worked with her to release her and the others from this horrible state.

We were able to reunite her with the spirit of her mother from that life who expressed that she felt terribly guilty for having turned her over to the priests for sacrifice. As they worked together to heal this guilt and soothe the infant part of her that needed her mother's comfort, her mother told her how she felt she had not had any choice and that it was the social conditioning (Saturn conjunct Pluto in the fourth) and beliefs (Sagittarius) of their people at the time. During this healing process with her past life mother, she became aware that this was her current life mother and made connections about a mutual 'hero/savior complex' that they shared. In fact, because she was in a current life crisis, she had called her mother in panic before the session with me, and her mother was on the way from a few states away to come and stay with her that evening!

In the composite chart (not shown here) they also have a nodal axis of Sagittarius SN but in the fourth house and Gemini NN in the tenth, squared by four planets in Virgo in the first house. It is interesting to know that the transiting Uranus in her natal chart that was triggering liberation from her own hero/savior complex was also squaring the nodes in their composite chart. After working with this story, the feeling of panic subsided; it was clearly the infant past life of absolute helplessness and vulnerability that had been taking over her current life consciousness. Because she had remained in a state of panic, with other souls in the same situation in the afterlife, this had only magnified her emotional sense of being overwhelmed.

In the afterlife, light beings came to her to help further her healing. They told her that in this lifetime she can work with children, but that she did not need to sacrifice herself to do so. They pointed out to her that in this life she had only experienced working with wounded and displaced children and that she might also want to connect with children in another way to balance this out. She became aware of how much of the children's pain she carried psychically and emotionally and it became clear to her that she needed to have better boundaries (Neptune conjunct SN), and maybe she needed to mature more herself (tenth house polarity point to Pluto) before she could become immersed so much in others' problems.

The spirit helpers reminded her of her own creative inner child, and told her not to lose touch with that. In fact she is quite naturally talented in many different art forms including the performing arts (Venus in Leo in the first and her Libra Pluto in the fourth). She was starting to feel that working with children to help them bring out their talents and creativity would be a direction she would now want to explore, rather than solely being involved in the social services' side of working with them for the present moment. Because her Pluto is conjunct Saturn in Libra, certainly it is necessary for her to balance out these extremes. A timeline would indicate that her life as the

African woman was her last life before the present, and this would be one reason why her desire to work for social causes started early in her life. With her four planets in the eleventh house and her nodes on the sixth/twelfth house axis it seems that as she finds the balance of her own boundary she will still continue to contribute to social causes and the healing of others.

5

Leo/The Sun and the Fifth House

"Our deepest fear is not that we are inadequate. Our deepest fear is that we are powerful beyond measure".

Marianne Williamson A *Return to Love: Reflections on the Principles of* 'A *Course in Miracles*'.

Keywords

Fixed/Yang/Fire	Generous	Fame
Creative self – actualization	Subjective awareness	Romance
Solar Inner Child	Creativity	Child prodigy
Ruler King/Queen	Artist	Joy
Personal Power	Inflation – positive and negative	Magical
Arts	Involvement	Gambler
Drama	Approval	Actor/Actress
Integration	Exhibitionism	Risk taker
Purpose	Applause	Affairs – Adultery
Heart	Being noticed – special	Mistress
Full of self	Recognition	Children
Grandiose		

The Natural Archetype

Following Cancer and the understanding of the lunar inner child, Leo represents another aspect of this inner self – the Solar Inner Child. Having formed an emotional self and a self image, the ego now seeks acceptance of its being by others. The Sun principle within us is meant to shine. Many analogies exist about the Sun as a non-partial generous being, shining light upon all without prejudice. In their heart of hearts this is what Leos hope for – to receive appreciation and love and to give it freely. It was largely the Pluto in Leo generation's coming of age that created the 1960s' hippie counterculture of 'Free Love'. The dynamic of the 1960s shows a generational progression from Pluto in Cancer to Leo. Leaving behind the rigid roles of homemaker (Cancer-Mother) and breadwinner (Capricorn-Father), the youth of the 60s embodied the Leo/Aquarius axis by rebelling against the social norm and embracing a vision of life that was truly a revolution of self-expression.

Our solar inner child can be equated to about the age of three to five onwards. This is the age when we start to meet other children on equal terms in pre-school and kindergarten, we leave the exclusivity of the home environment and immediate family (Cancer), our inner world expands and others now become part of our formative years. The approval this solar child needs now extends beyond the home life. Teachers, other children and their parents, and other caretakers enter our orbit, and we need them and their love to grow into the fullness of ourselves. We are urged at this age to create, finger paint, sing songs, draw, play, and generally express ourselves, as we look to the adults around us for approval. We come home from school proudly with gold stars on our masterpieces that become enshrined on walls and refrigerators. Our little hearts are filled with joy, when we hear 'ooohs' and 'ahhhs' of appreciation for what WE have created, and this helps us form our sense of self-esteem, as our ego expands. We might even participate in our first school play around this time. What a joy to look out and see all those loved ones adoring us! We explore costumes and dressing-up, playing roles as we develop ideas about who we are and who we want to be. Through creativity we are expanding our world view and the messages we get during this time about how we are received by the world are crucial to our ongoing sense of self.

Appropriately named Leo Buscaglia, pop psychologist of the 1970s, writer and lecturer of many books about the creative loving child within and the power of living from the heart, tells a story in his book *Living, Loving and Learning* about what happens when a child receives her first lesson in conformity versus creative self expression. In his story, a little girl in grade school is terribly excited when the teacher announces they are going to draw a tree. The teacher draws an example of what a tree looks like on the blackboard and then passes out the crayons. This little girl draws the most outrageous tree, full of every color in the box. She used pinks, blues, purples and every shade that could capture her true feelings about trees. When the teacher saw her drawing she gasped in disapproval, "Oh My God!"

Leo Buscaglia goes on to ponder the dual message this teacher exemplified, 'be yourself – but only if it fits the system'. So life goes on for this little girl as she progresses from grade school to college, and each step of the way, in order to pass and fit in, she needs to bargain away her unique self.

Leo Buscaglia may not have known astrology, but his thinking clearly exemplifies the Leo/Aquarius axis. Our unique individuality (Aquarius) and creativity (Leo) feed each other, and when our individuality is not validated early in life, or sustains wounds from past lives, a part of our solar self retreats behind the clouds, and healing work is needed with this solar inner child before it can emerge again.

A core desire in the Leo archetype is for personal creative self-actualization. Realizing oneself and potentials through creative works (or offspring) is a direct expression of the deeper art of letting one's Sun shine. Living life creatively is not only about producing works of art, but can also be seen in the bravery it takes to summon from within new ways of self-expression. Leo is a fixed sign, in the previous fixed sign, Taurus, one was meant to discover inner value and worth. With this integrated within, one then has the foundation to share and reveal what makes one so worthy. The rootedness within oneself that was found in Taurus, breaks out of inner isolation and shoots up like a sturdy tree. Its many leaves can photosynthesize the power of the sun, harnessing the light energy of life and creating personal vitality. Creativity is the very light of life that keeps the Leo in all of us vital.

Marion Woodman, a world renowned Jungian analyst and teacher, reminds us that, "The creative process shrivels in the absence of continual dialogue with the soul. And creativity is what makes life worth living". If the process of creative self actualization is enacted only from the ego it will lose its natural 'life giving' capacity creating a vacuum of narcissistic self absorption. This can become problematic in the Leo archetype if one forgets that everyone has an inner Sun, and a right to vital self expression. This is where the Aquarius polarity, when integrated within Leo, allows for equitable sharing. When the Leo archetype is expressed in a healthy way, true nobility and generosity of character shines forth, which acts as an inspiration to others.

Leo in Past Life Experiences

The Leo archetype is a part of the karmic axis when:

Pluto is in Leo or the fifth house or
The South Node is in Leo or the fifth house or
The ruler of the South Node is in Leo or the fifth house or
The Sun aspects Pluto, the nodal axis or rulers of the nodes.

Creative Self-Expression

This following case contains the theme of the unique creative self that meets with disapproval and the consequences of such. This woman's chart has a Leo NN in the fourth house with Pluto in Leo conjunct to it. Because Pluto is conjunct, we know that the NN has already been worked on in past

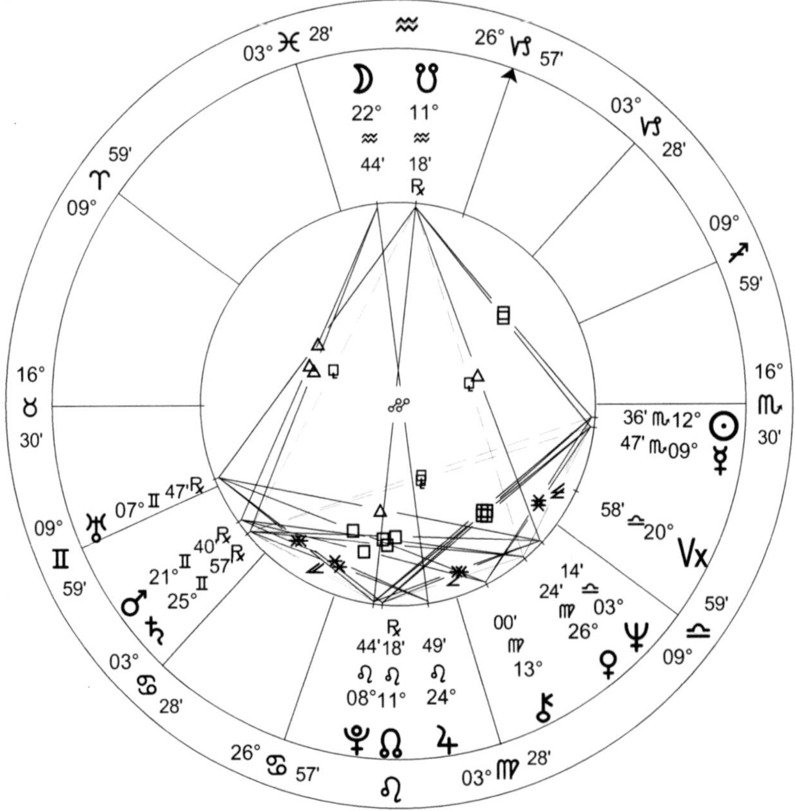

Chart A (Porphyry houses)

lives and that the polarity point to Pluto as a direction for evolution in this life does not apply. This does not mitigate the SN or its house and sign as an element of past life experiences, it only means that in this lifetime she is meant to continue to work on the Leo and Cancer archetypes. The nodes are also squared in this chart, so both nodes have also been active in the past. This case follows nicely from our understanding of Cancer to Leo, as the client has the combined signatures of Leo and Cancer via the fourth house placements. The healing of the solar and the lunar inner child are both emphasized.

Before going into her past lives, we did some current life inner child journey work. Although it wasn't planned this way, with the combined signatures of Cancer and Leo the need for such work was strongly indicated. During this process a seven year old inner child self came to the forefront to be worked with. This seven year old self was very sad. As we explored the causes, we found this child felt she was living in a 'cloud of nothingness'. By probing how this cloud formed, her mother's voice emerged saying, "You are nobody special".

My client remembered that when she was young, her mother used to say this to her whenever she tried to share her creative expressions. The client had internalized this message, which was at odds with her authentic self, causing her to feel as if she was "a nobody – a nothing". After working more with this child fragment, we recovered her essential self, which was quite mischievous and precocious. This was the essence that had been hiding behind the clouds, forgotten. During our work a spirit animal came in spontaneously to help. It was a peacock that communicated to her, "It's okay to be special; you are somebody". This guide was a wonderful symbol for the inherent potential this woman had to show her own true colors! Joy started to return to this child self and we were able to remove the cloud of 'nothingness'. Finally this child part was happy to rejoin with the adult self of my client, clutching her peacock feather with enthusiasm and excitement about being able to bring back joy, magic and specialness into her life now.

Discussing the themes of this journey together and the work that happened, she said that she was now more aware of how she grew up with a sense of guilt and shame about just being herself. She affirmed that she was mischievous when she was young and that this part of her had become lost (her Sun in Scorpio in the sixth house squared the nodes, along with Mercury conjunct the Sun). Her inner solar child has the natural qualities of deep perception and a quick mind, but also could internalize criticism easily. We ascertained that she was simply too intelligent for the adults in her life, so they were threatened by her, especially her mother. Subsequently she suppressed all these natural qualities to fit in and earn mother's love.

It was how she learned to receive love, which can be a karmic Leonine theme, Leo ruling the heart – wounds to the giving and receiving of love. The suppression of her uniqueness and innovative intelligence, as a karmic imprint, is evidenced by the SN in Aquarius in the tenth house. The Moon (mother) is also within orb of a wide conjunct.

When parents or caregivers are insecure themselves, even if they do not overtly suppress us, there is often an unspoken childhood 'contract' that we will not outshine them or achieve greater things than they did. In these instances, one can suppress natural childhood abilities, often throughout adulthood, because the child part has felt that to outdo the parents means to lose their love and care that are needed for survival. The lunar needs of nurturing and caring outweigh the solar needs of approval and self-expression.

In this client's case, her mother was the early oppressor, as she was frustrated with her own life. Despite this early conditioning my client had pursued her creativity as an artist, writer, and teacher, but also had many blocks. Several of her creative projects felt oppressively laborious. She said that each creative impulse was met with an equally resistant force, yet she knew in her bones she had to live a creative life, and through creativity she had achieved many things. It was a mix for her of creative success and feelings of massive difficulty and failure, which is not unusual in the artist's psyche or the creative process in general. The clash between bringing the creative self onto center stage with the presence of inner and outer blocks is often at the root of Leonine insecurity. Often this insecurity is over compensated by constantly seeking approval from others. Because the solar inner child's need for approval was not satiated enough to build authentic confidence, the need for others to approve can create a vacuum and a constant need to 'have the applause of an audience'.

With her Pluto conjunct her NN in Leo in the fourth house, the client knew deep in her soul that despite obstacles, she had to continue to work from an internal space of creative self actualization (Leo) and build her own foundation of emotional security (fourth house – Cancer) to support this ongoing process. Because Pluto conjuncts the NN, there is no Pluto polarity point activated for her evolutionary direction, and all of her current life focus is meant to evolve the Cancer/fourth house and Leo/fifth house archetypes. She demonstrated this clearly by the way she chose to live her life following her soul's urging to pursue her creativity. Each block she met and overcame was a part of her healing to facilitate this process and reintegrate the lost child self.

The client said during our review that she had felt poisoned as a child, that her early emotional environment felt toxic, (Pluto in the fourth squared by Scorpio planets from the sixth). We discussed the meaning of the peacock as a power animal and did some reading together about it and were both amazed to find out that there is a legend about the peacock which says it is able to eat poisonous snakes and be unaffected by their poison. What an appropriate spirit animal guide he was for this now restored child self! A wonderful affirmation from the universe occurred for her about a week after this session. She called me to say that a student of hers had just given her a peacock pin as a spontaneous gift of appreciation for her as a teacher, which she was now proudly wearing on her purse.

It is important to understand that the individual creative process also meets blocks of another kind. When people are too absorbed and personally inflated with the process of self as creator, the universe will remind them in various ways that ultimately power comes from another source. As this quote from William Blake says, "The pride of the peacock is the glory of God".

Integration of the polarity point in Aquarius also offers detachment from one's works offered as a gift to humanity, just as nature's beauty displays its magnificence for everyone's benefit, impartially and for a greater glory than itself. Leo works best when it is involved in creative pursuits simply for the joy of creating, without personal attachment. This is a difficult balance for the fullness of Leo, but a lesson that in some lifetime will be learned.

In the natural zodiac Leo is followed by Virgo, where humility is learned. In essence, Leo becomes deflated in Virgo, and in this last client's chart we see the combined signatures of Leo with planets squaring from the sixth house. Her fifth house cusp is ruled by Virgo, and Chiron and Venus are there in Virgo. Many of my clients with Pluto in Leo but in the sixth house, or Pluto in Virgo in the sixth house and other karmic combinations of Leo and Virgo, feel they tread a narrow path of self expression or its surrender through humility to a higher source, as if they need to meet both urges in their soul and develop both simultaneously.

Royalty

Since royal bearing and dignity are intrinsic to the Leo archetype, I have seen quite a range of different types of monarchs in Leonine past life experiences. A common image of royalty is a monarch in a red robe with a crown. This is a European image, but many cultures and civilizations had kings and queens, and tribal cultures have monarchs, otherwise called chiefs. The variety of ways clients have expressed this type of power in past lives varies from the benevolent ruler to the autocratic tyrant.

One such benevolent queen came from the past life of a client with a Leo SN in the eleventh house. The queen was a woman of Polynesian tribal royalty. She lived a life of service to her tribe with ample time to be worshipped and adored as a source of grandmotherly love for her community (Leo/Aquarius). This was an empowered past life that had no particular tragedy in it, except that internally this client felt uncomfortable with standing apart from the tribe. This is a reflection of a common denominator of the Leo/Aquarius axis. In Leo one can stand apart because of personal talents, gifts, 'specialness' or fame, and be either comfortable with it or struggle with self expression. While in Aquarius one can feel the pain of alienation of standing apart from others, or one can be comfortable as a rebel or even an aristocrat. In this client's case in relation to that single past life and with her NN in Aquarius in the fifth house, she can draw upon this past life as a resource to continue to blend the ability to share of her love yet still feel she belongs as an equal.

An example of a Leo type king or emperor who was full of the glory of himself was Napoleon Bonaparte. He had a Leo Sun with an MC also in Leo. He is quoted as saying, "If I had to choose a religion, the Sun as the universal giver of life would be my god". This statement shows how pervasive the Leo and Sun archetypes were in his consciousness.

The association of the Sun, as a supreme deity and ruler, pervades cultures all through the ages. Napoleon identified himself progressively with the archetype of the solar deity, culminating with his self coronation as Emperor. The two most widely used birth times for Napoleon (August 15, 1769, Ajaccio, France) are 11:00 am or 11:30 am. Using the 11:00 am chart, this self coronation occurred as transiting Pluto was three degrees into his fifth house! France is a country ruled by Leo, as is Italy, both of which Napoleon came to rule over. France also had another sun-king prior to Napoleon – Louis XIV, le Roi Soleil. Napoleon resurrected Louis' autocratic style of governing during his (Napoleon's) own reign. Louis, with Moon conjunct Venus in Leo, was born into royalty and reigned over a culturally rich era of France's history. Louis also archetypally embodied strong Leo characteristics as he was known for his extravagance, mistresses, patronage of the arts and his claiming of divine right to rule as an absolute monarch.

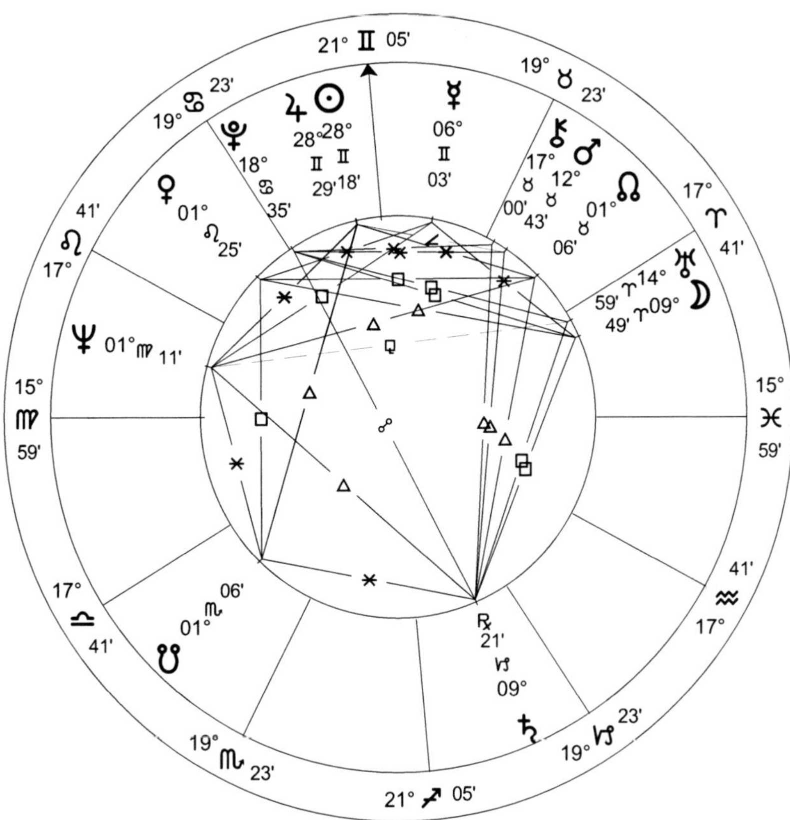

Chart B (Porphyry houses)

Chart B

This case is the story of a past life monarch who became consumed with the love of power to the detriment of his own life and humanity. The key astrological signatures of this story are Venus in Leo in the eleventh house square to the Scorpio/Taurus nodes. Both Venus and Leo have an association with the heart. This client came to me with a fear that his heart would stop beating. In fact this had happened to him in his current life twice, once as an infant and also in his fifties. As we explored this from the past life perspective, he went back to a time when he was born into royalty. His upbringing was devoid of love and nurturing (Pluto in Cancer in the tenth house) as he was being groomed solely to become a monarch who could wield power in a turbulent time.

This cold childhood brought out the worst Leo and Scorpio qualities in him, particularly a ruthless lust for power that drove him to murder his father so that he could take the throne himself when he was in his late teens. He became a tyrannical ruler (Pluto in the tenth and Leo) and died on the battlefield, not surprisingly by a spear through the heart. This fatal physical wound not only carried forward into his current life, but also mirrored the state of his psychological heart in that lifetime. The healing that needed to happen primarily involved the inner child (Cancer/Leo) of that past life self.

Working deeper with key moments of this child's experience revealed a craving for love that was never fulfilled in that lifetime. His mother and father were largely unavailable to him and he was given over to servants to be raised from infancy. Although he was royally pampered, most of them were indifferent to him, except one woman who he described as beautiful and caring. By the age of eight it became obvious that this servant had become the target for all his displaced emotions and needs (Pluto in Cancer and Venus in Leo in the eleventh house). His longing for love was projected onto her alone, and he obsessed about her daily (Scorpio). Frequently when she was unaware, he followed her, and one night spied her making love to a man.

He was consumed with jealous rage (Pluto squaring the Aries archetype) and having no other outlet for this emotion, he strangled a pet cat to death. This incident became the turning point in that lifetime because he was not able to deal with the vulnerability of his feeling and emotional nature. He became detached (eleventh house), repressed (tenth house) and shut down (second house).

In the afterlife, aside from healing the physical wound to his heart from that lifetime, it was essential that his 'lost heart' was returned to the young boy (Venus in Leo in the eleventh – soul fragmentation). Once this reintegration happened, he started to come to terms with his misuses of power and began to make reparations in the spirit world with those he had harmed. With his restored heart he also was able to grieve for this past life self and for his current life experiences where he felt 'heartless' and unable to participate in the flow of giving and receiving love.

Fame and Talent

In current times monarchy is not as prevalent, but shades of it exist in other areas of society, such as the Leo-ruled entertainment industry, where fame and talent allow an individual the personal power to rule kingdoms of fans and personal 'attendants'. Through entertainers' lives we also see the shadow sides of fame and fortune, from the drama-laden prima donna to the tortured, tragic fading star, (as Joan Crawford was portrayed in *Mommy Dearest*). Leo's association with applause, talent, and the solar inner child shows up sometimes in past lives as having been a child star or prodigy. But these sorts of past lives can be just as tragic as a current-life child star's can be.

Chart C

This client with a Pluto in Leo in the fifth house square the nodal axis, had a past life as a child star. She grew up as a peasant but was a child prodigy, gifted (Leo) beyond her age in music and verse. With the ruler of the SN in Aquarius in the eleventh, and additional planets in Aquarius squaring the nodes, she felt different and ahead of her time. Around the age of six she was sent into the streets to beg (Taurus SN – poverty) to help support the family. Singing to entertain herself, she quickly drew a crowd and soon became a local legend. Shortly thereafter she was 'discovered' by a gentleman who brought her to the royal courts of her time. Her parents were happy to let her go as they were paid a handsome sum and they now had one less mouth to feed.

At first she was stunned by all this. The combination of the Taurus and Leo archetypes made one part of her shy and isolated, while the other part was comfortable and longed for the spotlight. The adoration and attention lavished upon her soon outweighed any shyness she had about herself, as she completed one brilliant performance after another. Although she was surrounded by attention, she also was unable to form relationships with any other children because it seems they were jealous of her (Scorpio) and teased her, only adding to her inner feelings of alienation (Aquarius/eleventh house). As a compensation for this alienation, she became overly inflated with her 'specialness' (Mars/first house and Leo) and saw herself as far above others (also Aquarius). "Who needs them anyway?"

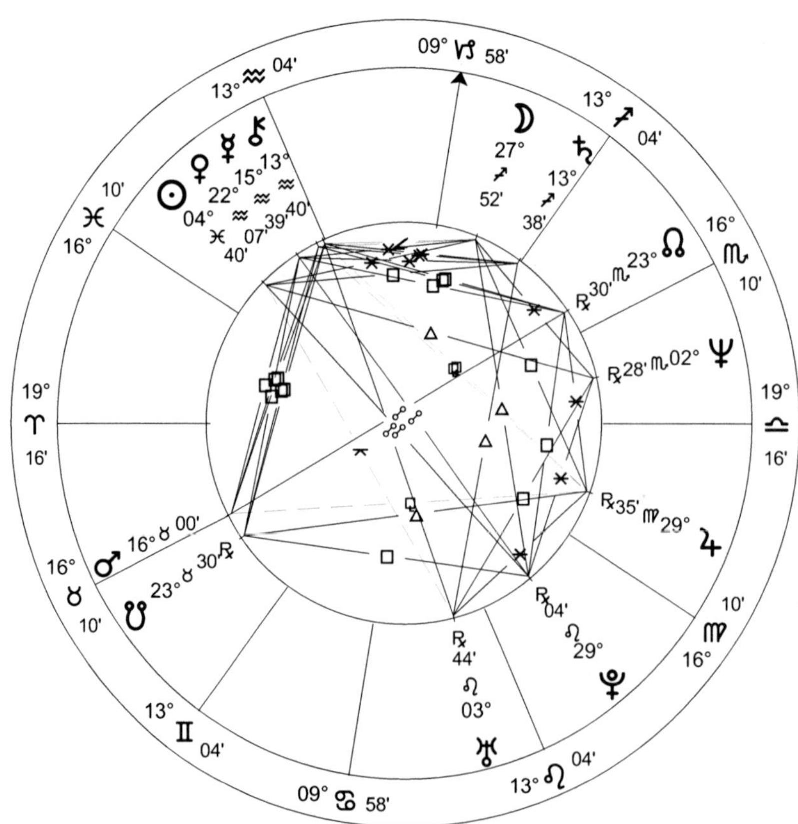

Chart C (Porphyry houses)

As she grew into her young teens, she became quite attractive but also vain (Venus square the nodes and Pluto in Leo). Unfortunately she drew the attention of an older man in the court who violently molested and raped her, (Taurus/Scorpio nodes, Pluto square Scorpio NN and Mars opposing Scorpio NN). The shock (Aquarius/eleventh house) of this was devastating to her and caused her to develop a phobia about performing, internally concluding that, "Drawing attention to myself is dangerous". Eventually her agent, caretakers, and the court abandoned her (Scorpio) because they had no more use for her (Taurus/Scorpio), and she was cast out into the streets. The mental shock (Mercury conjunct Chiron in Aquarius square the nodes) caused her to have a breakdown and she died in the streets, insane and destitute.

In her current life she was a professor of art history. She said she was always drawn to the arts of all kinds, yet had terrible fears of pursuing her own talents. This past life was certainly behind those fears and, as her chart pattern indicates, she also could have had other lives as a 'starving artist' type. This would cause her in her current life to further fear that talent cannot bring resources (Leo – Taurus/Scorpio).

As a professor she was able to be detached (Aquarius) yet involved in creative works and to support herself financially. The issue of involvement versus detachment is also a core theme of the Leo/Aquarius axis. Her current life as a professor allowed her soul also to detach from the drama of the arts so that it could objectify what the past life experiences had been.

Part of the intention of the Aquarius polarity point to Leo is about gaining the ability to objectify, as the Leo consciousness is highly subjective. The healing of the trauma of this past life character allowed her to put aside fears of 'not belonging' because of a talent, and to feel safe enough to explore her creativity more.

Pride and Dignity

The entire Pluto in Leo generation intrinsically has the combination of Leo and Scorpio as past life archetypes. Through that, one can pair any of the empowered Leo characteristics with the experience of loss (Pluto/Scorpio) to understand a range of possible past life experiences. The characteristics of dignity, nobility and pride are central to Leo the lion. The effects of the loss of dignity and natural pride can penetrate to the core of the individual and linger in Leo-type past lives. Many past life scenarios can be the cause of such wounds.

One archetypal situation that is an oft-repeated theme in human history and is still perpetuated today is enslavement. The combination of the Leo/Aquarius archetypes with Capricorn, Virgo or Scorpio can describe a life as a free and proud tribal person who is captured and forced into slavery. In the face of such trauma, dignity can be strongly held onto, slowly eroded or instantly crushed. Dignity is intertwined with the personal sense of self, purpose and meaning. When dignity has been lost or wounded in past lives, it may be hard to form a current life purpose. One may also be born with a pervasive aura of shame around the very sense of self, which makes it hard to live the present life fully and freely.

We can see this issue collectively in the history of many countries and peoples. In particular, the USA has an Aquarius SN with a Leo NN and struggles with the effects of the consequences of its history of slavery. A shadow side of the USA's Aquarius SN – freedom and liberty for all (but not blacks and women) – has been expressed in her history, with the Leo NN pointing the way to the healing necessary to reach an actual state of equality that will let all people have rights and dignity equally. When the US is able to make equality less of an ideal and more of a reality, then she will have succeeded in a healthy integrated expression of the Aquarius/Leo axis.

Until that happens the African American people are left to struggle with the collective ancestral wounds of slavery and being severed from their roots and culture. As Pluto was culminating its transit of Leo in the mid 1950s, Rosa Parks refused to go to the back of the bus and thus sparked the Montgomery bus boycott. As a result of her actions, not only Martin Luther King Jr but also the entire civil rights movement was catapulted into the national spotlight. Then again, as the Pluto in Leo generation started to come of age, 'Black Pride' was born in the midst of this movement. This was a step in the right direction because the only way to heal lost dignity is to reclaim it. At the time this book was written Barak Obama had not yet been inaugurated and time will tell how his presidency will affect these racial scars. He shares the same nodal axis as the United States (Aquarius SN, Leo NN). Beside all the hopes placed upon him, and how he may or may not be able to fulfill them, his election has already served to further the racial healing process, by restoring a sense of pride and dignity for African Americans.

Empowerment and Personal Power

The final case presented here is actually from two separate individuals. Born within two days of each other, these charts are very similar as were their past life stories, making this an interesting study. To make sure they maintain their sense of personal dignity (intrinsic to the Leo archetype), instead of naming them A and B, I have given them pseudonyms, Verna and Julie.

In both charts Pluto is in Leo in the fifth house. The SN is in Virgo in both but in different houses, and the ruler of the SN for both is in Aquarius but also in different houses. Both individuals came into therapy discussing a similar core issue: "How do I bring myself and my gifts out into the world?"

Here we see the dilemma of Leo combined with Virgo: the fullness of the self (Leo) and the deflation of that self in Virgo. Both these women suffered in past lives because of their gifts (what made them special), and this lingering issue is part of their current life journey to heal so that a secure, self actualized self can embrace the polarity point of Aquarius and pour those gifts out to others. With the SN in Virgo, both women's past life stories showed not only feelings of persecution because of their past life gifts, but also the desire to use those gifts in service to others in the past.

Both their north nodes are in Pisces, with the ruler Neptune sextile Pluto. This shows, as their past life stories illustrate, abilities in psychic realms and a continuation of this in the current life. This Pisces/Virgo nodal axis also indicates healing abilities.

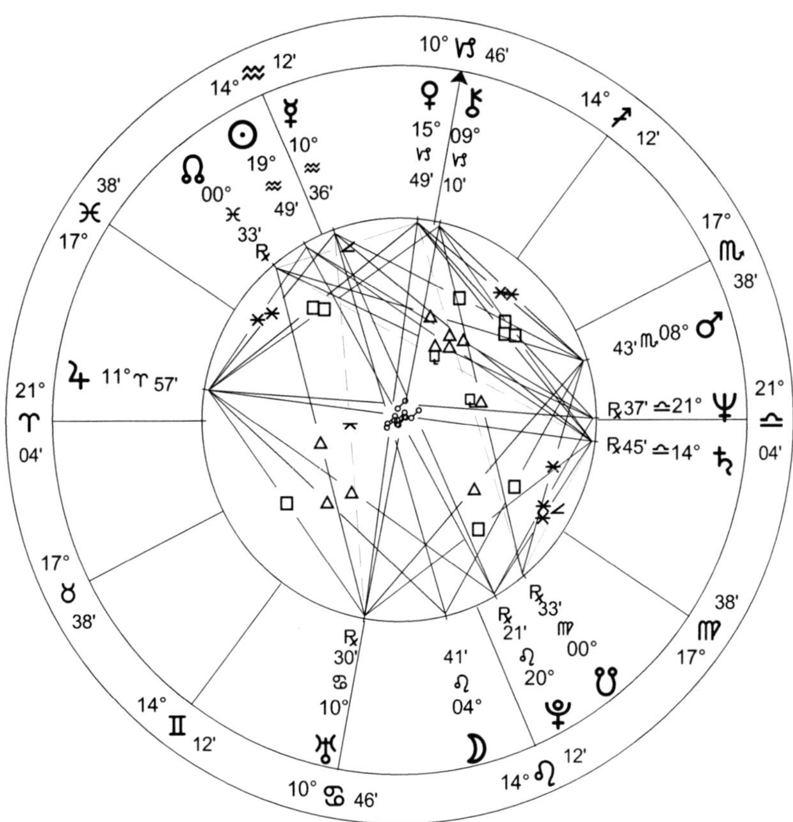

Chart D: Verna (Porphyry houses)

Verna

When Verna came into therapy, after some discussion about her life and what she wanted to work on, she concluded that because she was in transition in her life, just having recently divorced, her most pressing issue was, "I want to just be me". With her Pluto in Leo and SN in Virgo in the fifth house, it is not surprising that such a Leonine dilemma would be plaguing her. As an observer, I felt she was internally comfortable with herself and that her anxiety was about self-actualization. She simply had not brought out enough of her inborn abilities yet to test them in the external world.

She went back into a past life memory, as a young girl of about five years old in a South American tribe, (ruler of SN in Aquarius – tribal life), which seemed Mayan. Her father was the chief of this tribe (Leo) and she was quite happy. Her mother had died and her grandmother was raising her, and was very nurturing and supportive, (Moon in Leo and fourth house connected to the karmic axis by opposition to ruler of the SN). The loss of her mother could be indicated by the Moon squared by Mars in Scorpio.

As this young girl, she had the natural ability to talk to plant spirits and was recognized early in life for this gift (Leo). She also talked to the spirits of the dead (Pluto sextile Neptune) and had a personal relationship with a male tree spirit that acted as a guide and friend for her.

As she grew up, these gifts were carefully cultivated by her grandmother who was a healer. Within the cultural context of this past life, it was clear that while she had these gifts, and was cultivated because of them, her 'specialness' was not out of balance with other tribal members who had their own talents and were recognized for them, (empowered aspects of Virgo SN, Pluto in Leo and ruler of SN in Aquarius). In fact, the energy of her story thus far was that all this was quite natural, and there was no internal or external conflict.

She grew under the tutelage of her grandmother and support of the tribe until the time she was about seventeen years old and her grandmother died. While this was a sad occasion, again in the cultural context it was understood to be a natural rhythm of life, and she continued to have contact with her grandmother's spirit after her passing. She then stepped into the role (Leo) grandmother prepared her for as a healer (Virgo/Pisces). She traveled to other tribes to serve them (Virgo SN) with her gifts of healing and communication with the spirits, and she became fairly well known regionally (Leo – fame). Several years into this, her tree spirit gave her a vision of blackness in the form of images of foreign people coming as invaders (Mars in Scorpio square SN ruler). She also saw the spirits of people already killed, and these spirits seemed to be in shock and frozen in terror (Aquarius).

Eventually the invaders came and overran the village she was in. The conquistadors ended up keeping her alive, along with others they wished to keep for slavery, but killed all the rest. She and the surviving people were horrified – all of this was so alien to them (Aquarius). She was deeply grieved (ruler of SN in the tenth) but maintained a personal sense of power and dignity (Leo). It seemed the conquistadors had heard of the gifts of the indigenous healers. They recognized her as a healer and wished to use her abilities for their own ends, (singled out as special – Leo-Aquarius, and Mars square SN ruler).

After she was captured and traveled with them, it seemed they wished to test her skills; they gave her a young native boy who was on the edge of death because he was badly wounded, to see what she could do. She tended to his body and spirit and succeeded in bringing him back from the edge of death. After this, the conquistadors slit his throat in front of her, which caused her to fully feel the depth of their brutality (ruler of SN in the tenth squared by Mars in Scorpio). She concluded as a result of this, "These people are brutal and it's not safe to be who I am".

At the conquistadors' settlement, she was taken to the one in charge (again aligned with the ruler of a people – Leo and ruler of SN in the tenth) and was told to tend to a woman who was pregnant by him, but was struggling with her pregnancy. This became a huge source of conflict and tension for her. It was revealed that the pregnant woman had been brutalized, and had taken natural poisons to kill the fetus because she did not want to give birth to the leader's child. This is another layer of the opposition of the Moon to the ruler of the SN.

She tried to talk the woman into having the baby. It was important to her at this point in the past life to not let herself and others be overcome by the soullessness of the conquistadors. Yet in her exchanges with this woman, she subtly mirrored the brutality of the oppressors (ruler of SN in the tenth). Here her Leo and Mars square Mercury is very vocal. She said, "We must preserve our people's ways and not be overcome. Stop being so weak".

She urged this woman to get strong and fight back by regaining her dignity (Leo/Aries). She was feeling the strength of the tradition of her people (Mercury in the tenth) deep within her as a source of power, and she was exhibiting a warrior attitude (Mars square). The pregnant woman though had already given up and was determined not to bring this baby to term.

Also during this time, the healer was losing contact with her helpful spirits and began to feel very disempowered because she could not connect to the source of her power (Pluto in Leo – loss of power). It also became apparent that bringing this baby to birth was a personal matter of life and death, (Mars in Scorpio square ruler of SN). She knew that they would kill her if she didn't succeed. As it turned out, the baby was premature and stillborn, and the healer was quickly killed because of this.

Although violent (Mars in Scorpio square Mercury), the imprint carried in that death experience was not particularly traumatic. This is often the case in past lives lived in more natural ways because the fear of death was not as pervasive as it is in modern societies. She was immediately met on the other side by her grandmother, who helped the transition and brought her joy (Leo). The healing from this lifetime involved being able to reunite with her tribe and lost father, and the reconnection with her spirit helpers. In the spirit world she was still angry with the pregnant woman, who she declared, "was not strong enough". This woman mirrored her own deep unconscious fear – the loss of power (Pluto in Leo) that she fought not to feel in that lifetime. We worked with this further and also with her fear of showing personal power and what the consequences had been.

"Coming into one's own power" is a phrase that is used quite frequently in our times. Verna's past life story touches upon the choice we all have in expressing this power. Verna's story outlines the various levels of personal power as they are reflected in the Leo/Aquarius archetypes (Sun in Aquarius opposing Pluto in Leo), each of which she has the choice to enact in her current life. Can she come from the place of natural inborn talent that is inclusive of others (Aquarius) and is equally supportive of them, like her childhood in that past life? Or will she manifest her personal power from the place within her that fears losing it? Her power can manifest in a variety of ways, such as ruthlessness or with the unconscious attitude that is predominate in our modern society (as the conquistadors in her story represented) that there is a limited source of power, so people must grab what they can with no concern for others.

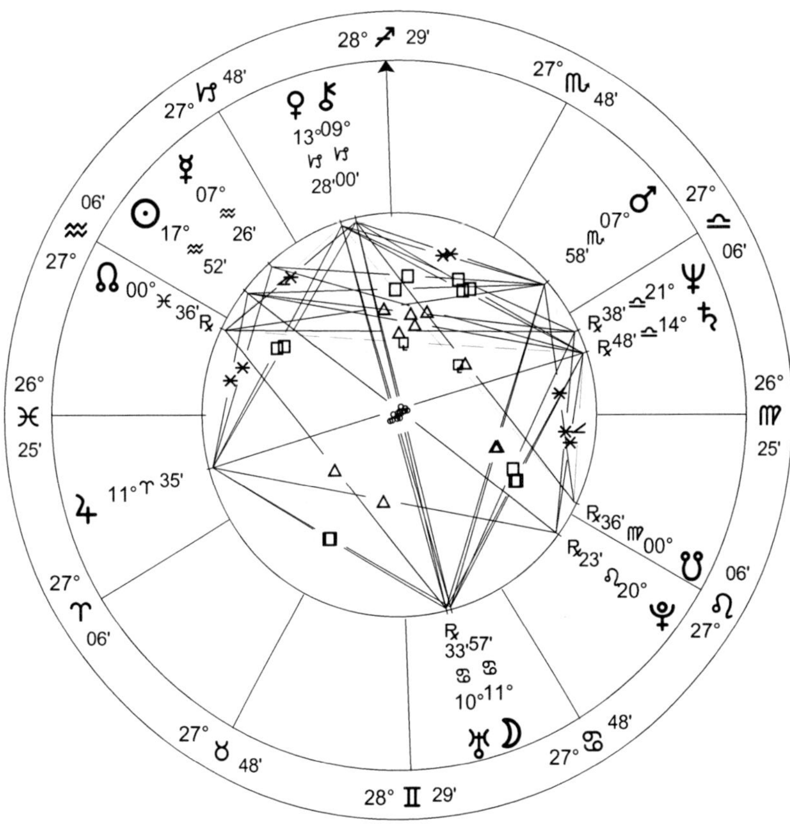

Chart E: Julie (Porphyry houses)

Julie

Julie came into therapy with the same issue as Verna, a desire to express who she truly is to the world. Her fears were more acute and focused on feelings of inferiority than Verna's. With her SN in Virgo in the sixth house instead of the fifth, her psychic structure was different. Julie had already been working in various forms of healing work, yet also held a job doing office work. Her urge to express herself creatively (Pluto Leo/fifth house) through spiritual work was at odds with the typical Virgo/Pisces anxieties of 'coming out', 'being seen', and not feeling good enough. As a present life signature, her Pisces ascendant with Virgo on the descendant brought these issues even more to the forefront of her consciousness. Further, Julie described a core feeling of aloneness that is at the heart of the Virgo consciousness.

Julie found herself in a past life in which she was chosen for a special school at a young age. The setting was in a Celtic culture during a time of circles of women's mysteries and priestesses. Her experience and imprint of this training was very Aquarian (the ruler of her SN in Aquarius and the eleventh house) as her consciousness was totally subsumed in the connection with her community of like-minded women. Her training also happened within a natural context involving healing, prophecy, worship and dedication to the Goddess. Aquarius archetypally is associated with matriarchal and matrilineal societies. The Moon is also in Cancer in the fourth house with Uranus inconjunct the SN ruler. Again, all went well until about the age of seventeen, when her community became aware that a shift was happening. They perceived a coming 'blackness' and were concerned with the preservation of the wisdom traditions they held. In their tradition the elders were the living vessels of this wisdom, but the younger women were also believed to be equally strong and capable.

Because of this, it was decided that the elders must depart and initiate the younger women into the deeper mysteries before they left. They believed that the coming invaders would see the younger women as more pliable, and thus spare their lives. The younger women would, however, remain dedicated to their ways. Internally this young priestess felt the weight of the coming task, but told herself, "I can hold this together, it is my service to do so", (Virgo SN in the sixth – Leo 'can do' attitude).

Mars in Scorpio in the eighth house and squaring the ruler of the SN adds to the gravity of this initiation, with the threat of life and death circumstances. Just as she was put into a position of power, the invaders came and slaughtered most of the remaining sisterhood. The invaders spared the lives of those who showed the most power, because they wanted to bend the women to their own needs. The invaders believed that by co-opting their spiritual power and authority, controlling the people would be easier. In contrast to the overt brutality of the conquistador invaders in Verna's story, once in control, these invaders were more manipulative (Mars in Scorpio in the eighth, square ruler of the SN).

During all of this, the young priestess maintained her sense of Leonine purpose ("I can do this"), combined with the energy of Virgo. She worked behind the scenes and internally without being noticed because her focus was on service. The invaders adapted the existing rituals of the sisterhood but imbued them with their own energy. She went along with this, but secretly and covertly (Scorpio and Virgo) tried to energetically infuse the rituals with the original love and intention of the Goddess. This became an immense psychic strain on her as she felt she had to draw the black intent of the invaders into herself to transform it (Scorpio and Virgo – purification and perfection of the negative). She lived for five years like this, slowly wearing down with the struggle. Her once strong sense of purpose faded and was replaced with guilt and shame (Virgo). She felt she had let her people down and failed her cause. When she became less useful, they killed her. By that time she was quite ready to go.

She was met in the afterlife by the sisterhood, and healing work helped her to release her personal and psychic trauma. She had carried so much of the collective (Aquarius/eleventh house) hopes of her sisterhood and her people, that her sense of personal purpose and power had become eclipsed. Instead of having been able to experience a fulfilling and lasting connection with the sisterhood and the people, she had sacrificed herself and carried their collective trauma. This was an unhealthy imprint she internalized about how to 'belong' with others, and it contributed to the core sense of aloneness she talked about before the session.

In the spirit world, very wise healing beings came to deliver a profound message for her Leo/Aquarius axis: "You must learn that you can still be an individual and remain connected". With this understanding, she was able to begin to reclaim herself. She then could recognize that she had used her power wisely in that past life, and her shame started to fade (healing of the Virgo archetype). Because she had been manipulated by the conquerors, she had to wear a false face to her people (duality of Mercury), and she also felt shame about that. She was able to re-meet them in the spirit world and show her true self to them, which was empowering for everyone.

Both these stories show us that personal power is not easily manifested. But it is necessary to embrace personal empowerment to be able to balance the Leo/Aquarius axis. The Aquarius polarity shares with Leo the desire for increasing individuation and revelation of self-potential. The Aquarius polarity urges Leo to break out of its own orbit and share its personal gifts and talents so all may benefit. In that light, the self-empowered individual, through their own creative self-actualization, can then turn to serve humanity; the act of self-actualization can be of itself an act of service.

6

Virgo/Mercury and the Sixth House

"We awaken in Christ's body
as Christ awakens our bodies,
and my poor hand is Christ, He enters
my foot, and is infinitely me...

...where all our body, all over,
every most hidden part of it,
is realized in joy as Him,
and He makes us, utterly, real,

and everything that is hurt, everything
that seemed to us dark, harsh, shameful,
maimed, ugly, irreparably
damaged, is in Him transformed

and recognized as whole, as lovely,
and radiant in His light
he awakens as the Beloved
in every last part of our body."

We Awaken in Christ's Body -
Saint Symeone (949 AD)

Keywords

Mutable/Yin/Earth	Victim	Self Improvement
Inferiority	Persecuted	Existential Void
Service	Self Sacrifice	Aloneness
Servant/Slave	Discipline	Inadequacy
Apprentice	Shame	Lack
Humility	Perfection	Self-improvement
Humiliation	Place in Society	Health

Critical	Holism	Discernment
Guilt	Nurse/Medicine	Nun
Masochism	Healing	Virgin
Crisis	Craftsman	Martyr
Gestation	Reality	

The Natural Archetype

Following upon radiant Leo, the humble Virgin is poised between the upper and lower spheres of the natural zodiac wheel. Virgo returns us to the idea of pregnancy but she represents a different kind of birth than Cancer. What grows in her womb is the potential of the birth of one's own 'Christed consciousness'. While the Pisces/Virgo axis is associated with Christianity the concept of Christ is not confined to this belief system. A fully realized and awakened spiritual being is a 'Christed' individual. The personal egoic self is born in Cancer, but it is the seed of the spiritual self that is gestating in Virgo. That is why symbolically, the fruit of her womb is not a product of human intercourse but of divine communion. Her virginity is not about being sexless but harkens back to the archaic meaning of 'being whole unto oneself'. Only the divine can create souls and spirit and only we can reveal that within ourselves through our spiritual evolution. Through the upper interpersonal and transpersonal half of the zodiac the spiritual self will be born, developed, tested and manifested. Because she is a transitional archetype she is still in gestation, it is the promise of what is to be born (the potential for greater consciousness). Alice Bailey comments in *Esoteric Astrology*, "The sign Virgo is one of the most significant signs in the zodiac for its symbology concerns the whole goal of the evolutionary process which is to shield, nurture and finally reveal the hidden spiritual reality".

The esoteric secret of Virgo is that for something to be revealed it must be hidden first. Virgo as an earth sign aligns it with the body and all of matter. Virgo demonstrates that the material world is not in opposition to the divine, but is an intricate part of its plan (Pisces/Virgo). Matter (especially that of the body) is not 'bad' and spirit 'good', it is the container that hides the inner light which is meant to be revealed through a progressive progress of the evolution of consciousness. The Virgo/Pisces axis is intimately tied into the union of 'mind/body/spirit'. As consciousness expands, we increasingly recognize the divine in everything (Pisces polarity), including ourselves. The world did not change, just the perception of it did. We awaken to the divine, as it awakens within us. Virgo contains the germinating seed of this expanded consciousness but just like the Virgin Mary pregnant with child, Virgo is not quite sure what is going to be born or if she's really ready. Therefore she focuses on preparing the 'vessel' of her body, purifying, refining and improving upon herself.

Virgo sits midpoint (naturally sextile) inbetween Cancer and Scorpio. Virgo as a Mercury-ruled sign makes her an ideal mediator between these two water signs. Cancer represents the birth of the human and the personality self, while Scorpio is where the personal will meets the higher will and through trials soul consciousness is finally birthed into awareness. Virgo culminates the developed personality and through her humility prepares the egoic consciousness to recede into the background, making way for the revelation or birth of the soul. She also makes a fine mediator for the emotional/psychic processes that happen in Cancer and Scorpio (and Pisces by opposition) as she is meant to shine a light of intellectual clarity.

As was discussed in Gemini, Mercury's rulership of these two signs gives it an archetypal association with Alchemy. Turning lead into gold is a metaphor for a psycho/spiritual process of the revelation of spirit (gold) within form; the process of en-light-enment. Alchemy involves various stages in this process. The stage commonly associated with Virgo is Distillation, where the fermented solution is agitated and boiled to bring out impurities and prepare it for the next step. Psychologically this has to do with sublimation of the ego and its purification and also correlates to digestion and discernment. Virgo governs the intestines and digestive system. Because it is an earth sign it also aligns with matter and the body, and is actively involved with the sanctification of matter (Pisces/Virgo) through what is taken in (diet) and the purifying processes, as well as the revelation of spirit in matter.

Mercury as ruler of Gemini was busy gathering massive amounts of information, facts and various points of view. This is the outer form of Mercury. In Virgo, the inner form of Mercury develops the capacity to assimilate or digest what has been taken in. Through testing information by critical analysis, experimentation and practical application, the higher function of discernment arises. Virgo separates the wheat from the chaff and refines what is retained by putting it into practice and practical use.

These natural processes associated with Virgo also earn it the reputation for being critical and overly discerning. Every quality has its shadow manifestation. Criticism of self and others is a manifestation of Virgo's desire for perfection and arises from Mercury's analytical ability. In order to perfect something one must be aware of the flaws. This can lead to a propensity to focus on what is wrong or missing, exclusive of what is present in totality (Pisces). This 'lack consciousness' is endemic in Virgo and can lead to an underlying complex of never feeling good enough or that nothing is fulfilling. This is also part of the idea of gestation where one is in a process of becoming but is not yet 'perfected' enough to give birth.

Virgo in Past Life Experiences

The Virgo archetype is a part of the karmic axis when:

Pluto is in Virgo or the sixth house or
The South Node is in Virgo or the sixth house or
The ruler of the South Node is in Virgo or the sixth house or
Mercury aspects Pluto, the nodal axis or rulers of the nodes.

Inadequacy and Guilt

When Virgo/Mercury or the sixth house are a part of the karmic axis the feeling of being 'imperfect' or that every situation is 'lacking' in some way is deeply imprinted in the consciousness. This next story shows how such a complex can be formed.

This chart (Chart A) has a Virgo SN in the fourth house with Pluto (not conjunct). The nodes are squared by the Moon and the combination of the Moon and fourth house with the Virgo archetype contributed to a "feeling of being inadequate as a mother".

In this short past life story this client went back as a woman to a time in northern Europe where she and her husband had to escape by boat with their infant child to get to safety. Before they were able to make it back to land this small boat was pulled out to sea (Pisces/Cancer) by strong currents. She was terrified but focused her fear on caring for her infant (Virgo/fourth house). After a few days their supplies ran out and the combination of her fear, anxiety and stress of the situation caused her breast milk to dry up. Her husband also became ill but still continued to struggle to get them back to shore.

Several more days went by and unable to feed the baby it died from starvation/dehydration and exposure (Pluto fourth house/Virgo). She was deeply traumatized by this and went into dissociative shock (Pisces NN)

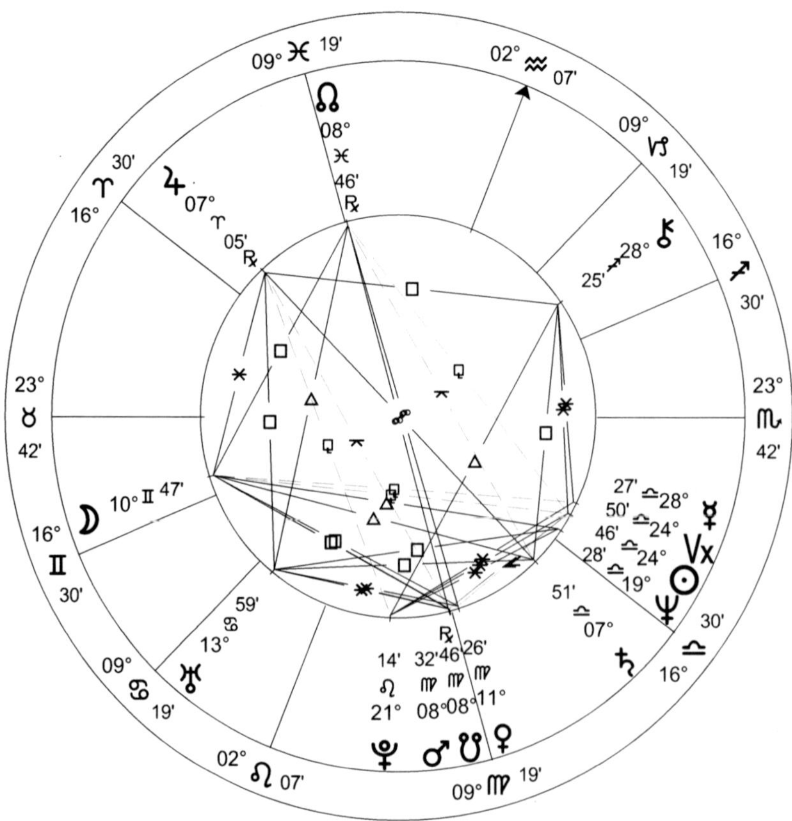

Chart A (Porphyry houses)

when she had to release the baby's body into the ocean. She and her husband did make it to shore several days later but she never recovered from this loss. She never had any other children in that life and died feeling completely guilty and inadequate (Virgo).

Her healing came when she learned from the higher guides in the afterlife that this baby had its own lessons to learn and dying that way was a part of its evolution. In essence she needed to 'surrender' her guilt complex by embracing the truth within the Pisces NN, that there is a larger divine orchestration that is often beyond our limited understanding. Walt Whitman captured this, saying "What is good is perfect, and what is called bad is just as perfect". In her current life the client had a pattern of forming relationships with critical men unsuitable for partnership, who only mirrored her complex back to her (Libra planets in the sixth house). This created a vicious cycle of feeling intrinsically inferior and constantly being told that she was.

My Virgo cases are full of clients who can easily identify a pattern of thinking, "I'm not good enough". They are often born into this life with this inferiority complex already developed from past lives. Deep feelings of unresolved guilt within the psyche cause one to feel they need to atone for some past misdeed. Quite often, like the mother in the boat, this guilt is unwarranted and arose from situations beyond one's control, yet remains deeply embedded in the consciousness. We often judge ourselves quite harshly, and can carry this self-criticism, mistaking it for fact, through many lifetimes.

Virgo SN can find some karmic relief in embracing the Pisces polarity point, by tapping into the infinite grace and forgiveness of the divine and applying it to oneself – if only she could feel worthy enough to do so! What needs to be remembered is that natural humility is not the same as atonement. In fact, a guilt complex that is overblown is just as much an inflation of the ego as Leo's magnanimous sense of self can be. Psychology recognizes these states as 'positive and negative inflation'. Since Virgo is meant to trim down the positive inflation of the ego self which was developed in Leo, inflation can also carry forward into this archetype. Being too full of oneself is simply the flipside of feeling totally inferior; in either case the focus is still excessively upon oneself. Both positive and negative inflation are recognized as 'self delusional' ego states that attempt to maintain control of the psyche instead of allowing spiritual growth to occur.

The 'martyr complex' and more generalized 'victim complex' finds a home in the Pisces/Virgo axis. But we need to look at ourselves and others compassionately and with understanding when assessing how we might be held in the sway of such complexes.

Christianity and Guilt

Outside of personal karma formed from past and present lives we also participate in collective patterns. For the last 2,000 years with the influence of Christian dogmas (coinciding with the current Age of Pisces), collectively the victim/martyr and savior archetypes have been activated in our consciousness. Furthermore, with the uniquely Christian doctrine of Original Sin, we are born already guilty and flawed. These archetypes have empowered and wounded aspects within them. The martyr for example can be an exemplary archetype as to how to commit oneself to a just cause or principle enough that one would die for it. On the other hand when guilt seeps in, the martyr not only stumbles through life with the weight of the world on its shoulders, but makes sure everyone else shares in the suffering. Even if one has not been raised in this belief system, it is as close to us as the air we breathe when you live in Western societies. To recognize the difference, one would have to spend time in cultures that are not defined by Original Sin such as in the East.

Central to Eastern religions like Buddhism or Hinduism, is the belief that one is born intrinsically good. We may be ignorant of this fact, but the true essence of each being is purity. Contrast this to the idea of being born intrinsically bad, and it is easy to see how deep the wound of guilt goes. The underlying neurosis that arises by the belief that at one's core we are flawed, guilty and imperfect, is rife in Christianized societies. The Dalia Lama was once asked a question about self-loathing by an American seeker and he had to ask the translator and questioner to clarify what that meant. Until he had been further exposed to Western societies this concept was foreign to him! His view on self-loathing contains the roadmap for Virgo's healing: "The antidote to self-hatred would be to reflect upon the fact that all beings, including oneself, have Buddha Nature." In other words, focus on the positive, the potential, not what is lacking. [1]

Because astrologically we are currently near the end of the Virgo sub-age of Pisces (980-2060 AD), it is hopeful to see an increasing number of books authored in the last few decades dedicated to exploring 'authentic' or 'esoteric/mystic' Christianity as opposed to the altered forms that have dominated since the Council of Nicaea (325 AD) or when Saint Augustine (354-430) introduced the doctrine of Original Sin.

Archetypally, the institution of the Church can be looked at as the 'ego' form of Christianity that hides the spirit within, just as our personal egos do not always reflect the reality of our soul/spirit. In essence the outer church hides the light of Christ as it also serves its Virgonian purpose. To get to the hidden Christ (Pisces) one must grow beyond the outer form (Virgo). In all spiritual traditions there is an exoteric (outer) and esoteric (inner) teaching. The outer teaching contains the dogmatic approach and is meant

---

1. *The Art of Happiness: A Handbook for Living* by His Holiness the Dalai Lama and Howard C. Cutler, M.D. Riverhead, Hardcover, 1998.

for the masses; the inner teaching, in esoteric initiatory practices, is often called the 'inner temple' or the 'holy of holies' that only initiates can enter. This is true also in Christianity as those who evolve to a mystic union with the divine often fall away from the established church as it serves no purpose anymore; they have entered the inner temple. The personality or ego form of the church no longer holds power when one has entered the heart of the mystery. Mysticism (which is Pisces ruled) is an individual calling, which one must pursue despite the Church (Virgo – the form). Looking at the historical actions of the church, like the Crusades and the Inquisition it is easy to see how far it has fallen from the simple message of love. The healing for this belief system, as well as for anyone resonant with the Virgo/Pisces axis, is to return to the essence of love which the life of Jesus exemplified...

"I understand your wounds that have not healed.
They exist because God and love
Have yet to become real enough
To allow you to forgive the dream"

Hafiz... Sufi Mystic

Persecution

Karmically those with this axis, if they have had past lives within the last 2000 years, have most likely crossed paths with Christianity and have some level of this conditioning in their soul. My Virgo cases are full of past life nuns, monks, Christian martyrs and those persecuted by Christianity (Inquisition, witch burnings etc.) This is also true for the Pisces SN/Neptune/twelfth house cases (see the Pisces chapter).

Chart B

This client came into therapy discussing a "nagging negativity" which she said caused her to feel, "I'm never good enough". She also said she had a lifelong compulsion to "make things right" but "no matter what I do, it always feels not good enough". Her SN in Virgo in the ninth house squared by the Sagittarian Sun points to not only (Pluto in the eighth) compulsive caretaking, but the type of hero/savior complex discussed in the Sagittarius chapter. The square to the nodes also brings in Pisces as a part of the past life experience. All of her themes coalesce within the Virgo complex of inferiority and inadequacy and this story also shows the damage to the soul that happens through persecution.

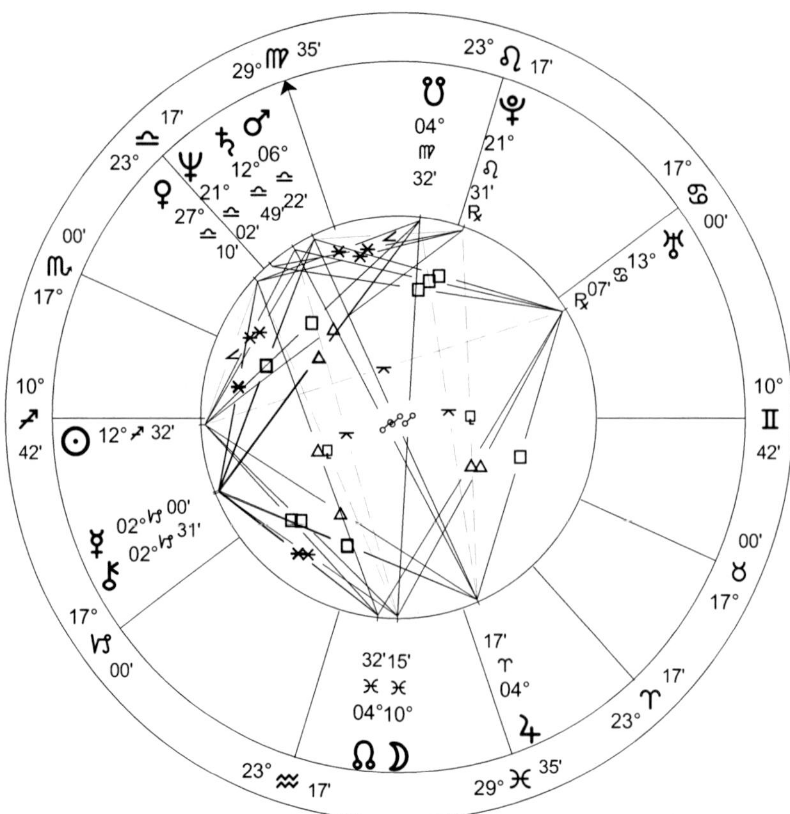

Chart B (Porphyry houses)

In this past life she was a young man in the Cathar sect. Historically the Cathars were a medieval Gnostic (mystic Christian) sect living in the Languedoc region of France. In 1208 they were deemed heretics by Pope Innocent III, and in 1209 a papal army of tens of thousands descended upon the region in the Albigensian Crusade, slaughtering the Cathars en masse. The killing and persecution continued for a further 35 years, in a combination of outright slaughter and inquisition. It is estimated that over one million died.

This young Cathar man was in a cart racing to get to his sister and her children (third house siblings and Moon in third – children). It was during a mass slaughter and he was frantic saying, "There's not enough time, I've got to get there before they are killed". (Sagittarius Sun square from the first house – hero racing against time).

When he got there his sister was dallying getting the children and things together and his anxiety, fear and impatience (Virgo and first house) almost caused him to lose consciousness (Pisces). Dizzy with fear, he finally got all of them into the cart and took off through the forest. His sister started to get the idea of how dire and urgent their circumstances were as men on horses started to pursue them. He assured her, "I'll take care of you" and as the men got closer, he decided to throw himself from the cart to act as a diversion, so his sister and the children could get away (self-sacrifice – Pisces/Virgo).

He was captured and brought to the inquisitors. He knew no matter what he said he was doomed (Pluto, eighth house) so he decided to be strong and stand by his beliefs (Sagittarius/ninth house). Being persecuted for one's beliefs is also the combination of Sagittarius and Virgo.

Under torture he faded in and out of consciousness and dissociated (Pisces) to the degree that he was unclear of what was real or unreal. The monk inquisitors eventually took him to a public square and burned him at the stake with several others. Half-conscious, he still had the conviction of his beliefs enough as he called out, "Queen of Heaven be with me and give me strength". He died as the monks taunted him repeating his 'heresy' and telling him he was evil and would go directly to hell. In the trauma of his death, one part of him felt at peace but another was tormented because he had introjected the inquisitor's beliefs that he was evil.

This is a common effect of dissociation that happens under torture and abuse, and is also intrinsic to the Virgo/Pisces axis. Further, it is also a tendency to the Scorpio archetype to believe that some part of oneself is evil. Dying with such an imprint often leaves a part of the consciousness trapped in the horror of the torture, and in his case, a part of his soul stayed in the flames, believing he deserved to 'burn in hell forever'. We can see the distortion of his belief system (Sagittarius) that happened through the ruler of the SN, Mercury, with Chiron conjunct in Capricorn, combined with Virgo/Pisces.

The part of his soul that had stayed trapped was worked with in the afterlife and eventually found solace in the presence of the Divine Feminine. This presence told him, "You are free in this life to have your beliefs". The client said that hearing this felt like a huge piece of "something that had been missing for a long time, came back into my heart". What was being returned to the client, was her own truth that had been tortured out of her in that lifetime (Virgo SN in the ninth). The spirit of an older wise healing woman also came to her in the spirit world. She took oils and anointed her heart and forehead, which initiated a rush of energy that the client said, "Instantly purified me, I was returned to a state of knowing how wondrous and beautiful the divine and my own soul is."

This is an empowered Pisces NN and it is also interesting that Cathar in Greek means purity. I have to mention that the main inquisition of the Cathars happened by the Dominican order and this woman today was teaching in a Dominican school! This is discussed later in more depth but working with this past life helped this woman to clarify her own beliefs which she had been too afraid to 'come out' with, in her current life (Virgo SN/ninth house).

Assimilation and Introjection

Virgo and Pisces share an openness to others' attitudes that is easy to see in Pisces, but not so obvious in Virgo. Outside of its resonance with criticism, being a yin inner-focused sign, Virgo also internalizes much of the surrounding psychic environment in an attempt to purify it as well. In this way she shares in Pisces' lack of boundaries, although is often unaware that much of what occupies her interior space may not actually belong to her. This is where a refined and subtle sense of discernment is needed, which is an empowered aspect of Virgo but also often needs to be developed. Separating what belongs to one and what doesn't, becomes difficult when that ability has been clouded in past lives, like what happened to the Cathar. The natural sense of discernment is often wounded in some way when Virgo is a part of the karmic axis. Since Virgo is a transitional archetype that precedes the Libran lessons of inter-relatedness it has shades of the co-dependent nature, which is in full flower in Libra.

The Pluto Virgo generation for example has a double signature of digestion and assimilation as Scorpio (Pluto's sign) is also associated with the excretory system. This lends a natural tendency to subconsciously internalize toxic psychological processes, to digest them as if they belong to oneself, in an attempt to bring them to resolution. Doing this consciously is a developed skill, but for most people this happens unconsciously which leads to a negative aspect of the Pisces polarity – self-undoing. Wikipedia describes this aspect of introjection as "a defense mechanism which handles threats from the outside that can potentially cause anxiety by infolding them into the internal world of the subject, where they can be neutralized or alleviated".

The Cathar's story was an example of this in an extreme form, which carried over into her current life as an 'identification with her persecutors' which is a form of Stockholm Syndrome. Her soul was still trying to discern the truth of her own beliefs, and she found herself in her current life right in the midst of those who caused the confusion. In day to day life this happens by internalizing critical attitudes and negative beliefs that someone else may have about you, as if they were your own. For example a child who wants to go out and play, but is scolded by her mother to stay in and clean up her room, experiences a level of anxiety about this conflict. She does not want to anger mother so she may tell herself she was 'wrong' or was a 'bad girl' for wanting to go out anyway. For Virgo this manifests often as an ever present sense of self-doubt, because what has been internalized overrides one's own inner alignment. Self-cancellation is another form of self-sacrifice. Many of my Pluto Virgo clients have done this chronically in their past lives through various means; they are meant, in their current life, to come back to the wholeness of self that both Virgo and Pisces represent.

Self-Doubt

Returning to the idea of gestation, Virgo often feels that if only she can learn one more thing, or improve upon one other aspect of herself she will be ready to act. This leads to a fear of action that both Pisces and Virgo share. Pisces can give up in face of adversity easily, while Virgo can create adversity making mountains out of molehills. Both archetypes can overcome this by utilizing the higher octaves of themselves, Pisces can tap into the flow, like Tao, and swim around what seems like an obstacle, or relinquish that which it has no control over anyway, because it can surrender. Virgo can identify what is wrong and move through it, because it can analyze how to do so. When Virgo is able to surrender self-doubt and throw aside the 'paralysis of analysis' her practical 'can do' nature shines. The balance of both these higher octaves working in unison is perfectly reflected in the Serenity Prayer – 'God, grant me the serenity to accept the things I cannot change; the courage to change the things I can; and the wisdom to know the difference'.

A fear of 'coming out' also stems from the idea of gestation. Virgo is associated with apprenticeship and developing oneself to perform skilled labor. Past lives often reflect this theme as one may have been an apprentice and thus has great skills to bring forward into the current life.

One client with a Virgo SN apprenticed in an ancient Greek school of architecture. After many years of study he was ready to oversee his first project and with his teacher's approval he sailed off with plans in hand. On the ship he was anally raped by some 'barbarians' and all his hopes for the future evaporated as he was never the same again. When he arrived at his work site he was unable to measure up to the task. He was deeply shamed by not only the rape but his inability to actually do what he had trained so long for. He ended up drinking himself to death and died in a state of hopelessness. In his current life he was terrified of 'being seen' for his skills, thus he had created all sorts of distractions to keep himself away from what his real life work was. When it comes to manifesting one's purpose, busyness is not the same as getting down to business. With Virgo's emphasis on work and service, past lives such as this last one are common.

A past life inability to complete what one felt their purpose was can linger as a subconscious fear that paralyzes the ability to act in the present. When several lives repeat this pattern, an added layer of feeling that one has never lived up to the task they were born for can leave one thinking they copped out on themselves in the past or are fundamentally inadequate. Similar to the imprints left by being persecuted for one's beliefs or skills, a cloud of guilt and shame can eclipse the natural joy of performing right work or service that springs from one's soul.

In truth, we are often wounded the deepest in the place of our greatest gift. This is a principle of healing that Homeopathy is founded upon and is a way that the soul stimulates growth and healing. For example, one persecuted for 'speaking out' in the past is most likely meant to manifest that gift of communication in some way in the current life. In trying this, what is often first felt is the wall of fear, shame or guilt that has been built up around the gift. Many pause and retreat at this phase and fall into 'victim mode' letting the fear run the show.

One way to dismantle fears is to allow them to have a voice. Going into the fear rather than avoiding it will allow one to speed its resolution. In past life work a first stage of identifying what the fear is really saying, is to ask, "what is the worst thing that would happen if you…" A person who is terrified of public speaking may not be aware of why they are afraid but if they allow the irrational fear to have a voice it might say, "If I am in front of a crowd speaking out, they'll kill me". Now the fear is clearly identified as a voice from the past. If one chooses to explore that past life or not, this stage of identifying the fear also allows one to know it is not a present day truth. Most likely if they give a lecture at their local Rotary Club they are not going to be killed. This is also a natural ability of Virgo, to use one's own mind to analyze such things and put them in perspective. The fear will make it feel like a mountain, the right perspective will let one see it is only a molehill. From this view they then can 'feel the fear but do it anyway'. A further prescription for healing the paralysis of fear of action that happens in Virgo is given by Jeff Wolf Green…

> "The antidote is to just keep putting one leg in front of the other…Even though the sixth house and Virgo are intrinsically feminine or yin in nature, they are also mutable. Movement or action promote clarity and understanding…The intrinsic motion of an action allows for a processing with respect to that which is being analyzed".[2]

Finding the center within movement is a natural strength of the mutable signs. In other words "Just *do* it!"

Service and Subservience

Past lives of subservience, servitude, slavery and being at the bottom of the heap are common in this archetype as it is naturally aligned with humility and service to others. Mother Teresa with her Sun, Mercury and Mars in Virgo exemplified an elevated form of humble service. The inferiority of Virgo is meant to evolve to a state of natural humility. Humbleness in service to others does not lay claim to the outcome, but works from a detached attitude that surrenders results (Pisces polarity). Virgo past lives often involve being in the midst of chaos or overwhelming circumstances while trying to help others. These lives often result in either burnout or an inability to actually help, which can leave a person frantically still trying to complete that in their current life. One Pluto in Virgo client was a physician in the American Civil War who just couldn't keep up with all the dead and dying amidst horrific conditions. He worked himself into a nervous breakdown (Virgo rules the nervous system), which caused him to not be able to help anyone. In her current life the client was not only a healer but a compulsive helper. She would go to the far ends of the earth for her clients or anyone she felt she could help. But the universe had devised another plan for her and little by little nothing she was doing seemed to

---

2. Green, Jeff Wolf, *Pluto, the Evolutionary Journey of the Soul*, Llewellyn, MN, 1998, p.120.

work, which was what brought her, immensely distressed, to therapy. Her learning from this past life came in the afterlife, when the higher guides told her, "Sometimes a little is enough; you did your part". She realized she was learning limits of her own abilities (Pluto) in that past life, and surrender to what was beyond her control. The ability to bring order out of chaos is a Virgo gift but can only be enacted effectively within limits or else more crisis and chaos ensues.

Another client with Pluto in Virgo in the sixth house square a Taurus SN/Scorpio NN had a past life in a holocaust work camp. He took it upon himself to become responsible for seeing that what limited food and medicine was available was distributed equally (Scorpio/Taurus/Virgo – efficiently managing resources). This was a hopeless and daunting task as there was never enough to go around (Virgo/Taurus) and people were starving and dying daily. This nearly drove him insane as he tried to devise one system after another to try to help everyone. In the afterlife he was able to laugh at himself because he realized, "It was my arrogance to think that I could figure this out and make sense of it, or even feel it was all my responsibility". Of course in the face of such an overwhelming atrocity, it was his attempt to gain some sense of control. But he recognized this as a current life pattern that might have been appropriate then, but not now.

Healing and Holism

Virgo is aligned with holistic and natural healing also and many gifted healers are to be found on the Virgo/Pisces axis. In fact the Pluto-in-Virgo generation has brought forth many healers and many who struggle to bring their abilities into the world. The archetype of the wounded healer, associated with the centaur Chiron, is also significant for Virgo/Pisces. Homeopathic medicine, which works with the subtle energy bodies to bring about healing, is based on the principle that healing is found within the wound itself. Since the discovery of Chiron in 1977, healers, helpers and counselors who have all been wounded themselves and through their own healing process turn to serve others, have emerged in society in great numbers. Several years earlier, Carl Jung described the wounded healer archetype and his understanding became the basis of illuminating the dynamics of counter transference.

Counter transference happens when the counselor's own wounds are activated by their client's process and potential problems, but also the potential for healing occurs because of this when it is used with conscious awareness. Jung also observed that, "Only the wounded physician heals. But when the doctor wears his personality like a coat of armor, he has no effect". In other words one who has done their work and is actively engaged in their own ongoing healing process from a soul level can then serve as a fitting guide to others. But the wounded healer archetype can also describe a process, when one tries to heal their own unconscious wounds by 'fixing' others. The difference is the degree to which one is conscious and working on their own woundedness. When past life wounds exist in the areas of service and healing, and remain in the subconscious unresolved, one can either find themselves in overdrive about helping others (savior/fixer), or absolutely fearful of doing so (the reluctant healer).

Chart C

The Virgo/Pisces pattern in this chart is obvious by the Pluto/Chiron-Saturn-Mercury opposition as well as the nodal axis being placed in the sixth/twelfth houses. This client described some of her current life patterns as "feeling it's all my responsibility" (Saturn in Pisces in the tenth, opposite Pluto in Virgo), and "people always want to tell me their problems, I can't get away from it".

Her pattern is one of the 'reluctant healer' and the more she tried to avoid being in the position of being sought out for help, the more it showed up in her life. She had gotten to a point of conflict about this, as her back very painfully started to give out (fear of responsibility – Saturn, and feeling overwhelmed – Virgo/Pisces). As we explored the past life roots she went back to a time when she was a young girl within a gypsy-like culture and was apprenticing with an elder healer (Virgo). She had a natural psychic ability (Pisces/Scorpio) to 'see into' illness and disease and know what remedy to give by this energetic information. She was able to communicate with helping spirits and plant spirits.

Her mentor needed to travel for a time and left her in charge feeling she was sufficiently prepared. This young woman did not believe that herself (Virgo – self doubt) and felt her teacher's confidence in her was misplaced. She begged her to not leave or to let her go with her, but neither happened. "Don't worry, you have spiritual guidance", her teacher assured her. Within a short amount of time this young woman started to feel overwhelmed with the responsibility (Saturn/Pisces/tenth house).

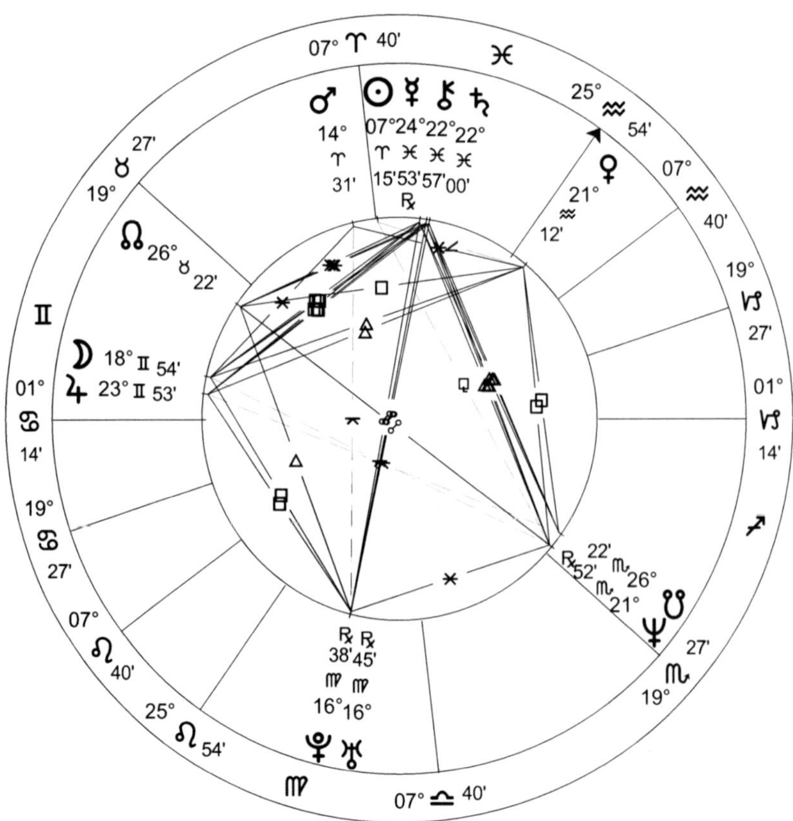

Chart C (Porphyry houses)

This theme is very archetypal for Virgo and I have seen many such stories, but what was slightly different about this one was that it was purely her own inner state of anxiety (Virgo) that was disabling her, as no mass disease or trauma descended on her tribe which is often what happens in such scenarios. She started breaking out in hives and picking at her skin reflecting her nervous state (Virgo). "I can't deal with this, I can't do it". She decided that her current spiritual guides were not helping her and did a ritual (Scorpio/Taurus) to invoke a 'powerful guide' that would help her (Scorpio). Unfortunately, she did not do this with proper discernment (Virgo/Pisces) and drew a powerful yet malevolent entity who ended up partially possessing her (Scorpio). This caused a near nervous breakdown, but fortunately her teacher returned with a cousin who was also a healer and they were able to release her from this entity's grasp (a little Jupiterian luck). After this ordeal she empathically stated, "I will never do that again". She renounced being a healer and decided to take up weaving and raising children.

She never changed her mind in that lifetime and it seemed the universe was still 'pushing the envelope' on her past life adamant refusal. As was mentioned in Gemini, past life vows or statements made definitively may have seemed appropriate in the moment but they linger and often need to be reworked in other lives. With Jupiter in Gemini at the focus of a T-square to the Virgo/Pisces opposition it was obviously up for review in her current life.

She admitted rather reluctantly, that in her current life she was very psychic but did her best to keep it at bay as it scared her. It was clear that this was an ability she could use in her current life, minus the past life mistake of feeling that the more subtle and humble forms of guidance are "not powerful enough". The self-doubt and anxiety of the past life woman was alleviated when she met her true spiritual guides in the afterlife. She cried when she saw them in their purity and felt the unconditional love they had for her. This returned her to an earlier state of innocence that she had in that lifetime, experiencing the simplicity of her connection with the nature spirits and spiritual guides. The polarity point to her Scorpio SN is Taurus in the twelfth house which is a double signature of simplifying and trusting. The Pluto polarity is also Pisces but in the tenth house which in relation to this past life, was about her taking responsibility for past mistakes (Gemini) with her psychism (Pisces). This allowed forgiveness to happen and through that learning; allowing a more mature expression of her 'right work' (empowered Virgo and tenth house) to manifest.

In this next and last case we see other aspects of imprints left by healer and helper past lives.

Chart D

In this chart Pluto is in Virgo in the eleventh house and the SN is in Aries with Mercury and Venus conjunct in the sixth house. The nodes are squared by Saturn in Capricorn, which like the previous case leaves a strong imprint around a sense of responsibility. This client described a pervasive sense of "I'm not good enough; I'm going to screw up".

In this first past life she was a nineteen-year-old southern woman who came from the upper class (Libra). She grew up on a plantation and her

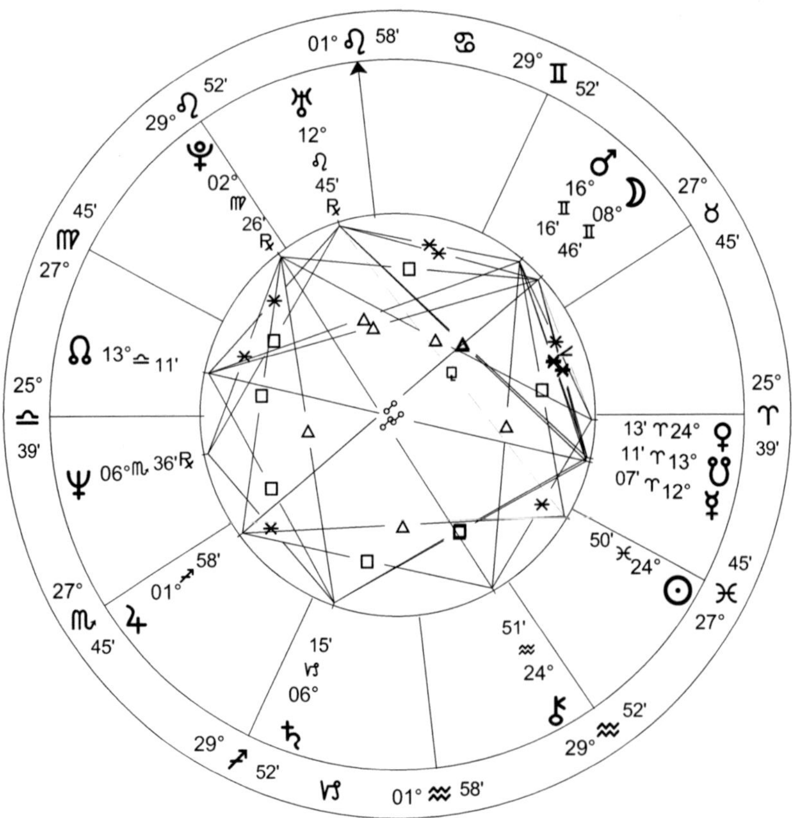

Chart D (Porphyry houses)

family were slave owners (Virgo/Capricorn). From the time she was young she preferred to be with the slaves. She said, "They embraced life in a way we didn't". Although slave ownership was the cultural norm (Capricorn) she always felt it was wrong. She was promised in marriage by her family to a man to a man who lived in the north many miles away, and she married him out of duty and familial obligation (Capricorn/Libra NN). Her husband was also a slave owner.

After she was married and moved away with her husband, she met some people who were involved in the Underground Railroad, liberating slaves (Pluto in Virgo/eleventh house) and joined them secretly in their efforts. She kept this from her husband, but one day when she was going down to the river to bring some slaves food, her husband followed her. He beat the slaves, and in the fray shot and killed them. While she witnessed this, she collapsed into guilt. "If only I hadn't done this, they would be alive". She also felt that she had let her husband down and that she had betrayed him (Virgo – introjection).

He then took her to a council of men in the church so her punishment could be decided (Capricorn/Virgo). She felt deeply shamed and humiliated (Virgo) as she stood before them while they decided her fate. They said they had to make an example of her as this was going on too much and they needed to stop it. They threw her in a root cellar and locked her in. In her imprisonment (Capricorn/Virgo) she berated herself, "If only I hadn't done that; Who was I to think I should make a change in the system" (Virgo/eleventh house/Capricorn). After some time she started to suffer from dehydration and eventually died.

It took a long time in the afterlife for her to unravel her self-doubt and self-punishing attitudes (Capricorn/Virgo). With help she came to her first major realization, "I need to let this go" (Pisces/twelfth house surrender – NN). She learned in the afterlife that, "Nothing is a mistake; it's all a learning process" (third house Saturn square nodes). Through this she was able to start forgiving herself and releasing her guilt.

She said that this woman's wounds had carried into her current life as a fear of action. "I felt I had no right to effect change in anyone's life". This relates also to the Aries SN which in its empowered form is the ability to act, but its wounded aspects can cause a fear of initiating action. Her feelings of having done something wrong in that past life stayed with her as an abject fear of action (Aries/Virgo).

In another past life she was a Native American man who was trained as a medicine man. Native American lives are most common in the mutable signs, also Pluto in the eleventh relates to tribal lives. He had received a vision of his life's work on a vision quest early in his life, and grew quite naturally into his role. His tribe had already had contact with white people, but his trouble started when he had a vision of future problems that the white people would bring to his people. He saw his people become ill but he doubted this vision and kept it to himself. He felt inside the white men should not be allowed around the tribe, but also told himself, "but they are bringing us things the people like and need". He also desired peace, so his instinct (Aries) was at odds with his humanity (Libra and eleventh house). The tribal leaders were not conflicted about their contact with the white man, and this also contributed to a fear of causing a conflict (Libra).

Because he felt torn (Libra and Saturn in third house) he never shared his vision and soon his people started to fall ill from smallpox.

His guilt was amplified because he was also a medicine person dedicated to his people's health. He berated himself, "I knew what I should have done, but I didn't follow through; I had the vision (Pluto in eleventh square Jupiter), I let spirit down because I doubted it (Virgo)".

He did what he could as a medicine person and tended to the ill, but had to watch his own family die. He eventually also contracted the disease, at which point he could not help anymore, which only made him feel guiltier. He died with all these imprints and was adamant as a spirit that he would not leave his tribe. He stayed earthbound, feeling "I have to do what I couldn't do before, I have to protect them". He was angry with the white men but was angrier at himself (Aries/sixth house). This earthbound fragment was worked with and eventually the tribe and the elders came to him in the spirit world. With quiet dignity and grace they simply passed him a peace pipe. They said, "We accept this as it was" and urged him to "let it go". Feeling embraced by their forgiveness and compassion he was able to progressively work through his guilt and anger. He finally surrendered to peace (Libra NN in the twelfth) and came to the realization, "Things happen and have a purpose in the spirit; we don't always know the whole picture". He was relieved to let go of his need to know (third house/Virgo/Mercury) and took comfort in the peace of his tribe.

Reflecting on these past lives the client said, "One had to do with the fear of action and the other was the absence of action". Both were active in her current life, as she said she felt she "lacked the courage to follow her own heart, because of the fear that someone would get hurt or that something was going to go wrong". The polarity house to her Pluto is the fifth, which along with an empowered Aries SN, is the ability to act with courage and heart. She said working through these wounds enabled her to "reignite my passion and drive" (Aries) and her fears around 'doing' were gone. She said she also learned that "we do the best with the gift we have, we just need to do what we can, and keep moving on". This is an empowered Virgo/Pisces attitude.

7

Libra/Venus and the Seventh House

"The best relationship is the one in which your love for each other exceeds your need for each other." Unknown

"The entire population of the Universe, with one trifling exception, is made up of other people." John Andrew Holmes

Keywords

Cardinal/Yang/Air	Denial	Boundary-less
The 'other'	Mask/Persona	Social Grace
Social	Relativity	Partner
Objective awareness	Relatedness	Fantasy
Relationship	Mistress/Lover	Damaged trust
Inclusiveness	Peace/Harmony	Intimacy
Comparison	Diplomacy	Allure
Others needs	Co-dependency	Casanova/Flirtation
Projection	Choices	Philanderer
Pleasing/Nice	Flirt	Idealism
Listening	Beauty	Greece (Ancient)
Extremes	Surface	Appearance
Polarity/Split	Promises	

The Natural Archetype

In Taurus we looked at the inner, yin side of Venus. Venus as the ruler of Taurus represents what we find within ourselves such as what we value, what internal resources we have to survive, and how we meet our own needs. In Libra the energy of Venus is yang and turns outward, so we seek more than just what we can provide for ourselves – we look to 'the other' also for fulfillment. When Libra is the active archetype from the past life perspective (SN in Libra or the seventh house/Pluto in Libra or the seventh house/Venus involved in the karmic axis), complications can arise from having been too open to others in all sorts of relationships.

The natural impulse of Libra is toward inclusiveness and socialization – the intention is to open beyond the boundary of oneself to others (opposition to Aries). As natural ruler of the seventh house, Libra is the sign that is just above the horizon, the first sign where we emerge from the lower half of the chart (our inner world or private self) to the world at large. Frequently Libra is associated with partnerships and marriage. While this is true, Libra is the precursor to the deep committed, intimate bonding that happens in Scorpio. The urge to merge is seeded in Libra and reaches its apex in Scorpio. The allure of Venus/Libra is the promise of the delight of a relationship, the flirtation that draws us with attraction to another, like the worm on the hook. In Libra one might nibble a little here a little there; in Scorpio, shortly after you bite, you can find yourself in a life or death struggle.

Needs are deeply tied into our sense of security and survival (as we saw in Taurus and Cancer). When the fulfillment of needs is taken out of the realm of the 'known' (ourselves) and projected into the realm of the 'unknown' (others), it can open Pandora's Box. Hence our relationships are complex but are also such fertile grounds for deep personal growth and awareness. Most of the time, the needs we project are subconscious. Therefore digging deeper into the dynamics of how we relate to others can be a great source of self-discovery, bringing what we are unaware of into the light of consciousness. With a self-aware and self-reflective consciousness, relationship provides a possibility of deeper self-discovery: seeing oneself through the mirroring of another. But because we are looking at a reflection, the potential for distortion exists. Separating out what belongs to oneself or to the other person in relationship can be a Herculean task.

Ideally, when self-worth and self-reliance are intact (the inner side of Venus in Taurus), they complement the outer side of Venus (Libra) and we can relate to others from a place of strength within ourselves. The more the felt sense of self is established and functioning (Taurus), the less of our interior world is then projected onto 'the other' (Libra). But relatedness is a learned thing.

Imagine just in your current life, how all your past relationships with others have altered you, and how your reactions and behaviors are a result of those relational experiences. Even if you narrowed down this focus to just romantic relationships, imagine how your ability to relate to others would be different… If only your past partner hadn't been abusive, or an alcoholic, or cheated on you, or broken your heart etc. How might you be different as a person in this moment? How might you be different in relationship?

Ultimately, as we remember and heal past relational wounds, the journey back to the self (Aries) happens. As we further integrate the Aries/Libra axis, self love becomes the foundation of our ability to have healthy relations. A natural quandary of the Aries/Libra polarity, that beckons us to further integration, is how to have the freedom to be ourselves and still be in relationship. It takes a lifetime, even many lifetimes, to learn how to be fully yourself with another person, to be able to be open and not lose your center but also simultaneously not to be too self-focused so that others can't get in. To accomplish this is a balancing and synthesis of the Aries polarity of (self-identity/independence), the inner side of Venus/Taurus (self-reliance), and Venus/Libra (reaching beyond the boundary of the self). A further intention of Venus/Libra is to form relationships of equals, being neither greater/lesser, dominant/submissive, dependent/independent, or various other roles and polarities we can get involved in.

> "Not every relationship between two persons is an 'I-Thou', nor is every relationship with an animal or thing 'I-It'. The difference, rather, is in the relationship itself. I-Thou is a relationship of openness, directness, mutuality, and presence, [i.e. a relationship of equals]. I-It, in contrast, is the typical subject-object relationship in which one knows and uses other people and things without allowing them to exist for oneself in their uniqueness…"
>
> Martin Buber – Philosopher. 1947

We can start to imagine now all the ways relationships that are 'I-it' based can go wrong. Two people coming together with 'I-it' scripts will never see each other outside of the mental construct they believe, think or want the other to be. We have to consider that, Eros aside, Venus/Libra, is an air sign, and falling in love or lust with what one thinks the other is and not a whole person, is a self-deceptive way to avoid growing beyond oneself and entering into real relationships!

The 'I-it' relationship is in fact a relationship with oneself; it is not a dialogue, but a monologue. In this kind of relationship, one person is more a satellite to the other than an equal partner. But it can also be subtler than that. Even the person who appears to be the caring, supportive one can have an 'I-it' script going on. The other is an 'it' to be fixed… to fulfill an unconscious need to be needed, or further, to use the other and fixing his or her problems as a way to avoid one's own problems. This is a learned pattern of relating commonly called co-dependency. In modern psychology it is theorized that co-dependency springs from the conditions and roles one played in one's family. It is often our childhood (Libra natural square to Cancer) and then social conditioning (Libra natural square to Capricorn) that we are not to be accepted as we are, but need to change or conform to some other standard, or another's needs, to gain acceptance or love. When we are raised this way ourselves, the model is then in place in our subconscious that this is the only way to have a relationship.

Venus as ruler of Libra has Neptune as the higher octave – conditional love that has the potential to evolve to unconditional love. Further, Neptune's relationship to Venus would ultimately lead one to the awareness that the primary relationship is that with the Divine, which is the true source of unconditional love. Without this connection we find ourselves 'looking for love in all the wrong places'. Our experiences with our first care-givers (parents/family) form the blueprint about love that colors our mode of relating; think of the natural square to Cancer (mother) and Capricorn (father). Below is a list of unspoken family rules that shape the way that relationships are expected to happen within the family, which have been identified as childhood causes of adult co-dependent behavior. In parenthesis I have added some Venus/Libra correlations.

- It's not okay to talk about problems. (Pleasing aspect of Venus)
- Feelings should not be expressed openly; keep feelings to yourself. (Socially adaptive mask/denial)
- Communication is best if indirect; one person acts as messenger between two others; known in therapy as triangulation. (Non-direct, distorted form of being heard or hearing)
- Make us proud beyond realistic expectations. (Conforming to expectations)
- Don't be selfish. (Denial of Aries polarity)
- Don't rock the boat. (Further denial of Aries polarity)

✦ Above all be NICE! (Libra desire for peace and harmony)

(http://www.allaboutcounseling.com/codependency.htm)

It can take a lifetime of serious inner work to heal destructive childhood conditioning. To further complicate this, we have learned these ways of relating from past lives also. Our current life circumstances only reinforce past life conditions.

Libra in Past Life Experiences

The Libra archetype is a part of the karmic axis when:

Pluto is in Libra or the seventh house or
The South Node is in Libra or the seventh house or
The ruler of the South Node is in Libra or the seventh house or
Venus aspects Pluto, the nodal axis or rulers of the nodes.

Being Nice

The adopting of a mask to be fully accepted is often what we have learned to be socialized means. We experience many messages of this type daily: one must look a certain way to be lovable or one must act a certain way to fit in. In past lives, some literal versions of this type of conditioning show up in Libra as lives spent as a Southern Belle or Gentleman, a Geisha/Concubine, or a Victorian societal lady or gentleman. In these lives, appearance (part of Venus) was more important than the full range of humanness. This leads to an adaptive form of being; pleasing others, conforming to expectations, and suppressing or distorting one's own needs to maintain a relationship (Libra). The 'need to please' also can lead to an inner state of inertia, as one may get trapped in constantly comparing themselves to others in order to try to live up to unspoken expectations.

One woman with the SN in Capricorn, with Venus conjunct in the seventh house, had a past life as the wife of a southern gentleman. It was an arranged marriage based on their societal positions (arranged marriages are common in both the Libra and Scorpio archetypes). It was a 'proper' marriage with little love, in which she felt bound by duty (Capricorn). Her entire life was lived being nice and proper, she was unable to say no to anyone including her children. Her husband had affairs, but they were never mentioned, as it wasn't proper to do so. She felt pity and empathy for the slaves they owned and for their captivity (certainly a reflection of her own state of being), but was unable to help herself much less them. Ownership of slaves was the societal norm (Capricorn in the seventh). Commenting on her past life self after her regression, she said, "I was so nice, I just wanted to slap myself!"

The complex of 'nice-ness' goes beyond just pleasing others. At its core it is a true loss of the self. Think of Venus as the lower octave of Neptune – keeping an appearance (Venus) can dissolve (Neptune) one's own boundaries of self. Trying to fulfill other's expectations, when distanced from personal needs, reinforces the creation of a false identity. Because we are all in a process of becoming, we wear different masks to present ourselves in different social ways, and we need a persona to allow us to interact with others. This is not pathological. Ideally the persona is the vehicle through which we carry the self into the world, as much as the other signs on the cardinal cross represent the formation of an ego (Cancer – the inner self) that allows one to meet the conditions of society at large (Capricorn – the outer self). To varying degrees, our masks and personas hinder the expression of the instinctual self (Aries), but in a healthy psyche the masks are adaptable, used only when needed, and the authentic self is also expressed through and despite them. By evolving deeper into the integrated Aries/Libra axis, one discovers that the authentic self can emerge onto the social scene and find its ability to love and be loved equally.

In Taurus we explored the imprint of shutting down the feeling nature to survive; Venus as ruler of Libra can manifest as a denial of feelings. When we meet a friend who asks us, "How are you?", and despite what we are really feeling we parrot our social conditioning, "Just fine, and you?" – we are wearing a Libran mask. From the pathological to the mundane, and all the shades inbetween, these are the ways we deny our true selves.

Bonding and Relating

Often when Libra is part of the karmic pattern one can find themselves born into a family with a narcissistic streak, or may (subconsciously) choose an intimate relationship with a very self-absorbed person as a way of re-imprinting the personal karma of adaptability to other's needs in order to feel accepted and loved. The evolutionary intention is to cause the Aries polarity to come forth in the Libra-type's consciousness, and to establish the boundary of one's own self and needs and to make appeasement secondary. Because of such present and past life conditioning, the Libra SN will often feel that asking for anything for the self is downright selfish! They learn, through the course of their lives, to first identify what they need and then ask for it, without a sense of shame or feeling they are 'breaking the rules'.

Neptune's relationship to Venus as the higher octave brings the Pisces archetype into the mix, as potential confusion about where self ends and other begins, and the illusion of idealization.

Neptune's influence in relationship also causes what John Bradshaw (popular writer on the dysfunctional family unit and the creation of co-dependency through shame bonds) and psychiatrist R.D Laing refer to as "Mystification and the formation of Mystified bonds". I also noticed these kinds of relationships formed from Libra and Scorpio past lives, and named them 'fantasy bonds' and 'fixated bonds.' Most people who re-meet the people they formed these sorts of relations with in past lives, are shocked because they almost immediately slip into a karmic fog again in relation to that person, and replay dynamics from the past either metaphorically or sometimes very literally, regardless of how much they may try not to.

The Venusian and Neptunian idealization of the desired soul mate in our current culture leaves one longing for the familiarity that comes with past life experiences with another. The reality is that many times there is serious karma to be worked through, and the initial feeling of familiarity morphs into the replaying of old karmic patterns, just as modern psychology would explain that after the idealized image starts to fade in a relationship, the old childhood patterns arise and control the relationship. The following cases clearly illustrate the past life dynamics of the types of bonds that carry from life to life.

Chart A

This is a story of a 'possessive' relationship that illustrates the combination of Libra and Scorpio causing a fixated bond. It started as my client regressed to being a young woman in a tribal society (SN and its ruler are both in the eleventh house). Her mother had died (Pluto in Cancer in the eighth) and her father arranged a marriage for her at around age 11, and she was literally given away to a Mongul warrior (Libra SN/Pluto in the eighth – arranged marriages and marriages of convenience).

In this loveless and abusive relationship, he often beat her into submission and let her know that she was nothing more than his possession (Pluto in eighth/Saturn opposition from the second house). Despite this

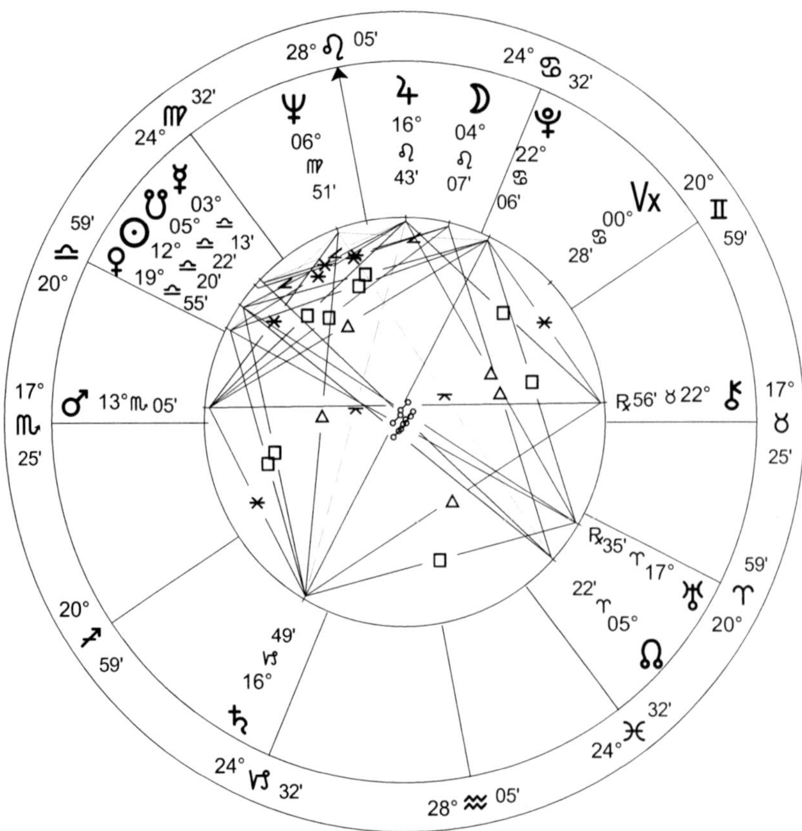

Chart A (Porphyry houses)

treatment, she still maintained a state of inner rebellion (eleventh house), even though he terrified her. When she had time to herself in that lifetime, she dreamed up alternative fantasy lives (Libra SN and Neptune semisquare to Venus). She hoped for a more ideal life (Uranus opposite SN and ruler of SN – Venus – in Libra in the eleventh house and Neptune aspects). He went to battle at one point, leaving her in the care of a trusted house servant. A relationship between the two of them developed (another form of the Saturn and Pluto square Venus – relationship in captivity). It was a sweet relationship, and it was amazing that she still had the heart and trust to be open to anyone at all (Libra). They sneaked time together when her husband was away and avoided each other when he was around.

Eventually the husband found out, killed her lover in front of her, and then beat her to death (Pluto/Saturn). During this time he was enraged and screamed at her, "I trusted you!" (when in actuality he most likely did not). She took this in as though she had betrayed him rather than the other way around. Here we can see the receptivity of Venus/Libra squared by Pluto in Cancer in the eighth as a signature of a past life Stockholm syndrome (a psychological response of hostages, captives and other victims of abuse or torture to form a bond with the abuser). This type of complex arises as the psyche's way to make sense of, or have a semblance of control in overwhelming circumstances. She took all the blame, recriminating herself, saying she was wrong to have broken his trust. Self blame and recrimination is also common in the Capricorn archetype, Saturn in Capricorn opposes Pluto.

Trust and wounds to trust, are another expression of the Venus/Libra archetype and in this story it became distorted, as she took responsibility (Saturn) for his projections onto her (Libra and Uranus and the eleventh house – projections). Because she witnessed the death of her lover, she also died with an imprint of deep guilt (Saturn – "It's all my fault"). As a result, a part of her spirit stayed captive with the Mongul (soul fragmentation – eleventh house) and a part of his spirit continued to possess her (Pluto in the eighth). It became apparent in the session that his angry voice had been in her head for most of her current life, causing suicidal thoughts, taunting her to kill herself (presumably so that he could have her in the spirit world again fully). He was still full of rage and was still trying to punish her, (he fit perfectly into the role of her Uranus in Aries opposite Venus and the Pluto opposition to Saturn). After some therapy with the Mongul, and additional help from the presence of his parents in the spirit world, he found resolution for his own pain allowing him to let go of his rage, along with his need to possess her. His healing allowed him to move on in the spirit world and he left her.

Working with the client on her side of this attachment revealed further layers of her dependence on him (Pluto in Cancer in the eighth and Libra). It was revealed that he had been acting through many lifetimes as a 'pseudo protector spirit' that had kept her from forming relationships with men in her current life. In a co-dependent way she had subconsciously wanted him to stay with her, even though it was tortuous, to keep herself away from the pain and vulnerability that she would experience if she opened to another relationship. She confided in me that she had felt his presence with her most of her life, although she didn't know who this spirit was as she had not been conscious of the past life story previously. Symbolically, he also represented the energy of her Aries NN and Uranus in Aries that she had been unable to express fully in her current life and had disowned in that past life (her own anger/rage, ability to fight back/warrior spirit). In subsequent sessions we worked together to find and express her own anger, and through this process she also connected to her own inner warrior, which helped her further to access the sense of self indicated by the Aries NN in the fifth house.

In the client's current life, her mother was not the reincarnated spirit of the Mongol, but she served to re-imprint the karma of this past life with stunning similarity. Her mother was an abusive narcissist and this client had a co-dependent, co-narcissistic relationship with her. At one stage the client believed that she had re-met the spirit of the man who was her secret lover in the 'Mongul' past life. He was a school counselor and helper for her in her college years, who guided her into starting to come to terms with the wounds from the abusive relationship with her mother. It would seem their bond of caring for each other, yet not having a relationship, served them both to heal from that past life. He was able to complete the past life scenario of not being able to protect her, and she was able to receive his caring and direction in relation to healing the shame from her relationship with her mother, which was a reflection of the unconscious shame she carried from dying in the past life with the feeling that it was all her fault.

Another example of a fixated bond mixed with the imprint of fantasy bonding, this time non-abusive, comes from a woman with Saturn conjunct the SN squared by Venus and Neptune in Scorpio in the eighth. Because the issue of relatedness is so prominent in the Libra archetype, I have added a look at the composite chart of the couple.

This woman (Chart B) met her husband-to-be in a foreign country shortly after moving there for business. It was love at first sight. She was ill at the time and psychologically vulnerable because she was trying to adjust to life in a new country. They quickly fell into a mutual self-sacrificial dynamic. In the composite chart (Chart C) Pluto is in Virgo, opposing Chiron in Pisces, with composite Venus also in the twelfth. As she tried to adjust to life in his country without success, they moved and he tried her country, but also

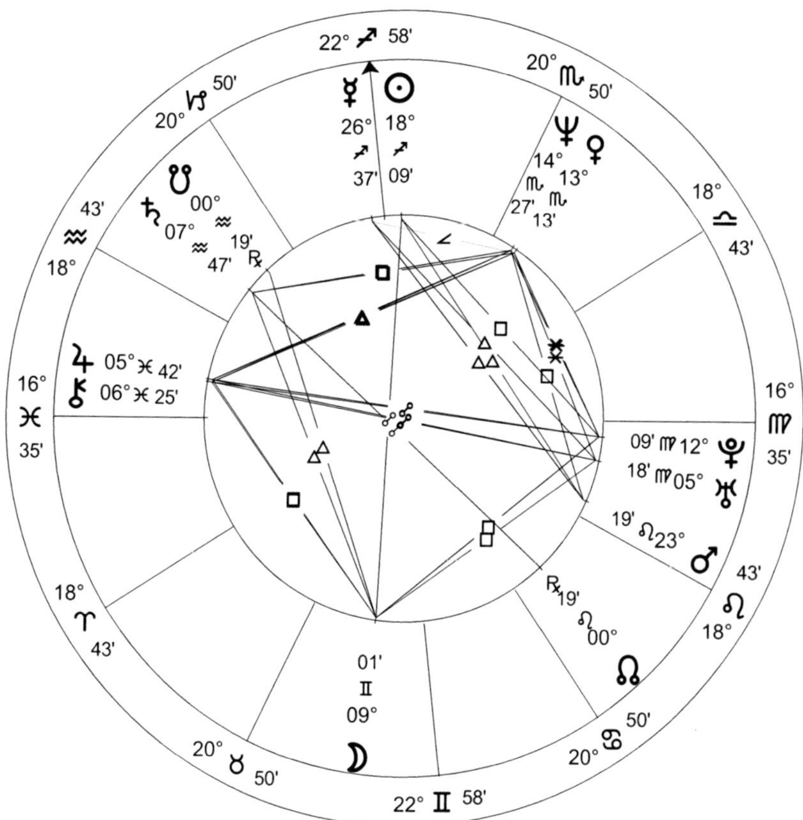

Chart B (Porphyry houses)

found it too difficult. With her mutable cross being tied into the karmic axis via Pluto, the attempt to find orientation by moving was triggering her subconscious past life trauma of alienation (SN in Aquarius in the eleventh and Pluto square Sun in Sagittarius in the ninth – foreign trauma). Each time they tried to move to find a happy medium for both, one of them would feel as if their life was stalled and that they had to sacrifice who they were to try to stay. In the couple's composite chart the mutable axis is tenanted by Chiron in Pisces and Pluto in Virgo in the third/ninth houses. Venus in Sagittarius in the twelfth house is also square Pluto and Chiron.

The regressions with her happened a few years after the couple decided mutually and amiably to split, and served her to complete the grieving that she had over the loss of the relationship (Saturn square Venus in her chart).

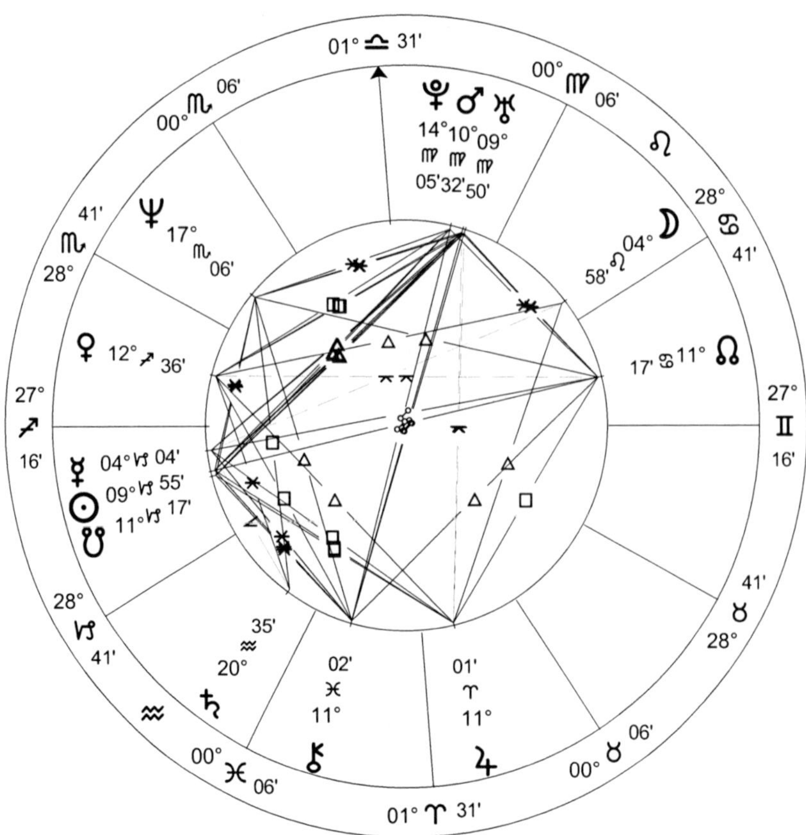

Chart C. Composite chart. (Porphyry houses)

The work served both in their growth, as they remained in touch as friends. Her work on their past lives together, helped to clear the energetic bonds of the sacrificial karma they were enacting and the idealization of the fantasy bond that was formed from the past. One source of these dynamics became clear in a regression where this woman went back to a life as a male slave in an Egyptian quarry; slavery in past lives is associated with the Scorpio, Virgo and Capricorn archetypes. Because Saturn is conjunct the SN in her chart, it is a part of the karmic axis. Saturn squares Venus in Scorpio and Pluto is in Virgo in the sixth. Many different sorts of slaves from all cultures (Gemini-Sagittarius) were kept in this quarry, and only one from this man's own tribe was present (Aquarius). This was a woman who he saw daily (her present-life husband), but as the slaves were forbidden to speak with each other, he never got to have real contact with her. Saturn here is the external limitation of the ability to bond with another like one's self (tribe), being in Aquarius and square Venus and Neptune in Scorpio.

She became a sort of compulsion for him, as all his fantasies were projected onto her (Venus/Neptune – Scorpio). At night when he lay on his mat alone, he would think obsessively about her. This was a way for him not to feel the pain and grief of his own captivity, and she became a symbol of his only reason to live day to day. He did not allow himself to think of what his life was like before, because the pain of the loss of freedom was too great (Pluto square the Sagittarius Sun), he would only think of the precious moments he could have each day when he might just glimpse her, or maybe brush against her if he got close enough. Life went on this way, but as time progressed, the Egyptians came to take the woman away to be a house servant. He saw this happening and was almost in rapture with happiness for her, that she was going to have a better life (Neptune conjunct Venus – selfless love). But all too soon as she disappeared out of sight, it suddenly hit him, "How will I live without her? What about me?" In shock (Aquarius) he collapsed and gave up (Neptune/Pisces). The slave drivers beat him to make him get up and continue working (Saturn), but his shock and collapse into the reality of his own grief was too great (also Saturn). Unable to get him to move, they ended up rolling a large boulder over him, crushing him to death (Saturn).

Having died with these imprints unresolved (especially the unrequited love – Venus), when the client met him again in the current life, it was all too easy for her to let him be the center of her life and vice versa. Their moving from country to country, was a replay of the trauma of being taken from one's culture that both experienced in that past life (composite Pluto in the ninth – Sagittarius foreign trauma, as well as Venus in Sagittarius in the twelfth). The fixation of the bond between them equated in her subjective experience to each holding the potential of life or death for each other (her Venus in Scorpio in the eighth). This was active in the current relationship as each was holding the potential for who the other was, yet neither was able to fulfill the potential while they were together (in the couple's composite chart their Pluto is in Virgo in the ninth house – potential, and SN is in Capricorn – limitations, grief, duty to each other).

The couple's SN in Capricorn is in the first house with the Sun conjunct, which equates to a mutual karma of suppression of who they each truly were because of a sense of responsibility to each other. Venus in the twelfth (self sacrifice) squares the planets in Virgo, including Pluto. The Pluto square also shows that in many lives they were unable to complete the relationship and suffered separation and loss of each other.

In another lifetime they were brother knights who spoke a vow to each other, "I will die for you" (a spoken vow of sacrifice, Chiron in the third in Pisces opposite Pluto!) They both went off in different directions on a crusade, never seeing each other again, and each feeling the loss as if losing a part of themselves (emotional enmeshment). The composite NN is in Cancer in the seventh, and because it is squared, it is also part of the past life experience. These self-sacrificial imprints were replayed psychologically in the current life as both being unable to fully have a life of their own, when they were together. The crusader vow played out in their current lives as each 'dying' for the other every time they moved trying to find a place where both could be happy. The formation of a mystified fantasy bond is clear from the slave past life. Since the slave could not have her, he fantasized about her (composite Venus in the twelfth and her natal Venus conjunct Neptune). The fixed bond was formed by the conditions of mutual slavery (composite SN in Capricorn in the first – limitation of freedom).

In another past life together, during a time of war, she was his mother (the composite nodes are on the Cancer/Capricorn axis and Jupiter squares from the fourth house, which implies they were together in a family in more than one past life). While he was just a small infant she gave him over to others to care for so he could escape to safety. She knew in doing this she would certainly be killed (more self-sacrifice), and shortly after she was indeed captured and shot. In their current lives she was a model of his mother and he was a model of her father. While not uncommon (it is often said we marry our parent of the opposite sex), the Cancer/Capricorn nodal axis, and the square to the nodes from the fourth house, shows that unresolved emotional dynamics from their current life childhood(s) were also very operative in this relationship.

It would seem for this couple, although bittersweet (Venus square Saturn in her chart), that letting each other go in the current life was a way to enact true unconditional love, (Venus/Neptune in her chart and the composite Venus in the twelfth). Loosing each other from the limiting bonds from the past allowed both to be free to become themselves (Jupiter in Aries). The issues of individual freedom and personal identity and moving beyond the past and present life conditioning, are emphasized in the composite chart by the Aries/first house signatures and Sagittarius/Jupiter/ninth house. The composite nodal axis is in angular houses, as is the square to the nodes by sign and house, indicating that this life was the beginning of a new cycle for them and an ending of old patterns.

Fixated bonds can form when people are together in extraordinary, stressful or life threatening situations. The bond that is formed has a trance-like, compulsive quality, equating it to Scorpio and Pluto quite easily. In the case of the Mongol, as the perpetrator he also had a fixated bond to the client, formed out of his displaced and suppressed rage. Relationships that occur in past lives in extreme repressive or dangerous situations such as captivity, concentration camps, refugee situations, battle fields, or even growing up together in an abusive family can form these sorts of attachments with others. The victim and perpetrator can also form a very fixated bond that lasts through lifetimes.

The fantasy bond has more of a Venusian/Neptunian quality – an idealization of what the other is dreamed and hoped to be. Projected needs are prominent here and the 'other' is strongly felt to be needed as a completion of oneself. Past life scenarios can include the relationship of the artist and muse, unrequited love, or a little girl's longing love for an absent daddy. When someone is longed for so profoundly, we are often not really seeing the person, but shadow boxing with our own unconscious needs, hopes, potentials and expectations. The term 'outer dependence', along with co-dependence, seems to most accurately describe this aspect of Libran Venus.

Following One's Heart

Conversely, one cannot deny the truth of heart bonds that are formed and last through lifetimes. In Taurus, the aspect of the etheric body that attaches to a person or object, and feels it as oneself, was discussed. This is the same Venus energy that forms a real energetic cord, heart to heart, with another (Venus rules the heart chakra). It is also this kind of relationship that the Venus in all of us thrives on. Venus wants nothing more than to embrace the world with heart wide open, and hopes that the world will respond in kind. If somewhere, in the reservoir of our soul's memory, we had never tasted this sweetness, why would we follow our hearts anywhere? The following story unfolded for my client very much like a Harlequin romance, but ended with a strong spiritual message for her, about the sanctity of honoring the power of love.

When this client (Chart D) came for a session she had two clear and specific questions: "What is my mission?" (Aries NN) and "Why do I feel so alone in life?" (Libra SN – seeking the other, Pluto/Virgo – aloneness, also SN in the eleventh with Uranus conjunct – feelings of alienation). With these concerns in mind we began the regression.

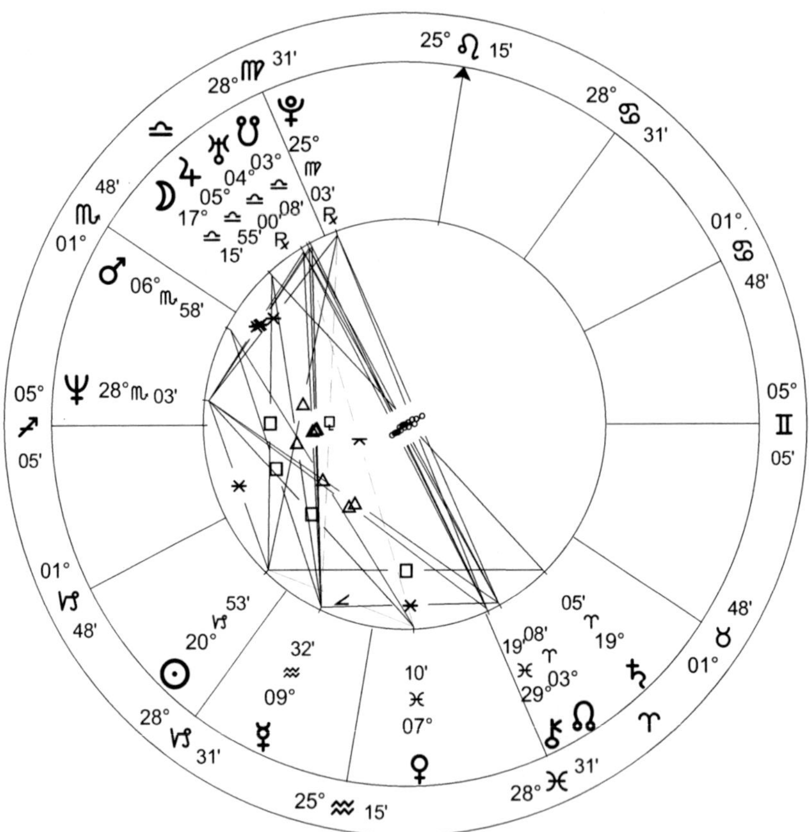

Chart D (Porphyry houses)

In the first memory of the past life she came upon a burned-out, war-torn village. She was filled with deep grief (tenth house Pluto). She wanted to help the people, so she started burying the dead and saying prayers (her Virgo desire to serve, plus soft-hearted Libra with ruler in compassionate

Pisces in the fourth). She was not thinking of her own safety. A soldier came upon her – it was love at first sight. He beckoned to her that he would take her to safety, but she feared that if he took her back to her village, the people there would kill him, because he had helped to destroy neighboring villages. Her heart was torn. She was attracted to him, but he was a part of the enemy army that did this (Libra – decisions). In Libra-type past lives, the difficulty of making a decision or feeling spilt or torn internally about a situation is typical. He did take her back to her village where she found that her mother was accepting of him, but it was dangerous for the soldier. Again she was torn because he had offered to take her away to his town, a bigger city with a better life, yet she didn't want to leave her mother (ruler of the SN in the fourth).

So she tortured herself a while with this process (Pluto/Virgo) and finally decided to go with him. Of course her fellow villagers cursed her, bidding her never to return (alienation of the eleventh). However, her mother blessed her on her way because she wanted her daughter to have a better life (Venus, ruler of SN is in Pisces in the fourth). We see a Piscean overlay of mother sacrificing her relationship with her daughter for her daughter's sake.

The daughter arrived in his town and found he was a man of means, fairly wealthy (certainly by her past standards) but also found her future mother-in-law didn't like her much because she was from a different/lower social group (Virgo – not good enough, Libra and tenth house – social standing and more alienation). Regardless, he wanted to marry her and she stuck in there and had several heated exchanges with the future mother-in-law. A poignant phrase that came up during one of these arguments was when she exclaimed to the mother-in-law, "I'm not here for the money, I'm here for the love!" (Libra/Venus – following her heart).

Eventually they married, had children and she became a sort of social worker, and advocate for the poor (Libra and ruler in Pisces in the fourth). Her husband supported her but continued his military career, even though she implored him to stop fighting and being a part of war (Libra – peacemaker and Aries/Libra polarity – love or war). At some point he went on a military campaign and never came back. She grieved a long time. As life went on she eventually met someone else, but not like her first love. They married and she died a peaceful death of old age (no one likes a happy ending more than Libra, or maybe Pisces). In the afterlife, she found that her lesson in that life was to follow her heart no matter what, and that she had been able to keep her heart open despite alienation and judgment (eleventh and tenth houses).

In the spirit world an image of Jesus appeared to her and she had quite a profound experience, as he blessed her for the work she did in the past life and told her she was to continue healing work; that her mission in this life is healing with His love. Interestingly, her urge in the current life had been to get a degree in psychology so she could help people, but up until that point she doubted herself (Pluto in Virgo in the tenth). Her NN in Aries has Chiron conjunct in Pisces, and Chiron's ruler is in Scorpio (psychology) in the twelfth. This chart also reflects Neptune as the higher octave of Venus (ruler of her SN is Venus in Pisces). Her feelings of aloneness faded with her encounter with higher love, and her own capacity to be a channel for love increased.

War and Peace

"Make Love Not War" was a popular slogan in the 1960s' Vietnam protests, that if not invented by a Libran was widely popularized by one; John Lennon who has Sun conjunct NN in Libra. But even before John Lennon coined his own similar iconic phrase, "Give Peace a Chance", those with Libra south nodes and Libran signatures in the karmic axis lived lives dedicated to these very principles. Luminaries such as: Pluto in the seventh house – Mahatma Gandhi; Mars in Libra – Nelson Mandela; seventh house SN – Martin Luther King Jr., and several of my clients, have felt the consequences that the world sometimes offers those who choose the path of peace and reconciliation over war and strife.

One woman epitomized the conflict between peace and war as an internal and external struggle in one of her past lives. Her chart (not shown) reflects this paradox with her SN in Libra in the first house, which combines the Aries and Libra archetypes. In one of her past lives she was a young man in a Greek society who was part of a very peaceful and harmonious school of higher learning (all of this is very Libran). At one point a war broke out on the edges of their territory and the choice (Libra) came down to war (Aries) or diplomacy (Libra). He advocated very strongly for diplomacy (Libra) amongst his peers as a way to solve this potential danger. Eventually he convinced them, and became involved in active negotiations (Libra) with the potential invader (Aries). Thinking he had found a solution, all went well for a short time, but as it turned out, the enemy invaded anyway. The young man's people were unprepared for this and were overrun. He was left with a crushing feeling of having made the wrong choice (Libra), thus leading to a wound in the client's current life around trusting her own decisions. In her afterlife review, her spirit guides delivered a succinct message that summed up her way to integrate this Aries/Libra paradox in this life. They said, "You need to trust your instincts and not compromise them away. But you also need to listen to others so that you don't shut them out".

Another client with Neptune, Jupiter and Chiron in Libra square his nodes and Mars was also caught between war and peace, and found himself in a past life as a white man during the times that the Native Americans were being overrun. He became dedicated to finding a fair solution, as he didn't agree with the atrocities he witnessed. He became a self-styled diplomat saying, "I want justice for them" (Jupiter in Libra). It was a short-lived mission. He entered a native camp with a proposal for peace that he wished to sell to both sides. Due to his naiveté (Neptune) he walked into a hornet's nest (Mars square). Unbeknownst to him, this group of Native Americans had suffered a recent incursion by the whites. He became the target for their anger and they killed him. His dying thought was, "It isn't fair; I was just trying to make peace". It was necessary for him to help this inner character resolve the unfinished urge to see peace prevail, as this deep uncompleted desire was ruining his life. After this work he said he could now see that his desire for equanimity and peace in all situations and relationships had been causing him to be a doormat. He could now walk away from situations that he felt were unfair without sacrificing himself and feeling he had to fix them. Ultimately his lesson was about having balance while seeking balance!

This story underscores another quandary of the Libra archetype that is often associated with inherent balance – hence the symbol of the scales. But the reality of actual scales is that the point of balance is tenuous and temporary. The slightest shift of weight on either side causes it to be lost. A more accurate image for Libra would be a pendulum, swinging to extremes and eventually settling in the center. More often than not, my Libra SN clients describe themselves as having lived lives of extremes.

One client of the Pluto in Libra generation described her life experience as one of extremity. She said, "I am aware of my insane part and rational part, aware of the extremes of light and dark in myself and my murderer part and victim part". It is a good thing she had this awareness. When one is not aware of such traits and denies such internal tension, the personality splits.

It is notable that as a constellation, Libra did not always have a distinct identity and in ancient times was a part of the constellations of Scorpio and Virgo. It was once known as the claws of Scorpio and later became the scales held up by Astraea (who is now Virgo), showing that not only can Libra create an identity from those around it, but a split nature can also be a part of this sign.

Chart E

Earlier in this chapter I discussed the dynamics of the natural squares of Cancer and Capricorn to Libra, as well as the ongoing look at Aries as the polarity. In this chart we will see how these archetypes worked together, and were at odds with each other in one client's past life story. It is not always the case that one single past life story demonstrates most of the symbols that are a part of the karmic signature, but this one does so quite clearly. In this chart Pluto is in Libra in the fourth house. The opposition from Mars/Sun/Venus creates a tension between the fourth/tenth and Aries/Libra, bringing into focus the quandary of war/violence and peace. The nodes are squared by Chiron in Taurus in the eleventh, bringing in issues of survival, isolation, individuation and alienation, which relates also back to the SN in Aquarius (placed in the seventh house adding to the overall signature of Libra in this chart).

Our session started with the client talking about a pervasive fear of imminent violence that he had been aware of for most of his life. "I feared that I would find myself, or be forced into a situation, where I would have to defend myself to survive, that I would have to die or be killed" (Pluto/Mars opposition, Chiron in Taurus square the nodes, also ruler of the SN in Scorpio). He went on further saying, "It feels as if 24 hours a day my body and some level of my consciousness is in fight or flight mode" (past life PTSD). It is clear from his chart that warrior karma (discussed in depth in the Aries chapter) is part of his history (Pluto opposite Mars in Aries, and the NN in the first house; Chiron square to nodes makes NN part of past life experience also).

In the first scene of his story, the client found himself as a teenage boy lying on the ground, bloody and with his clothes torn. He was sobbing and shaking with a mix of anxiety, confusion, shock and grief. He was thinking,

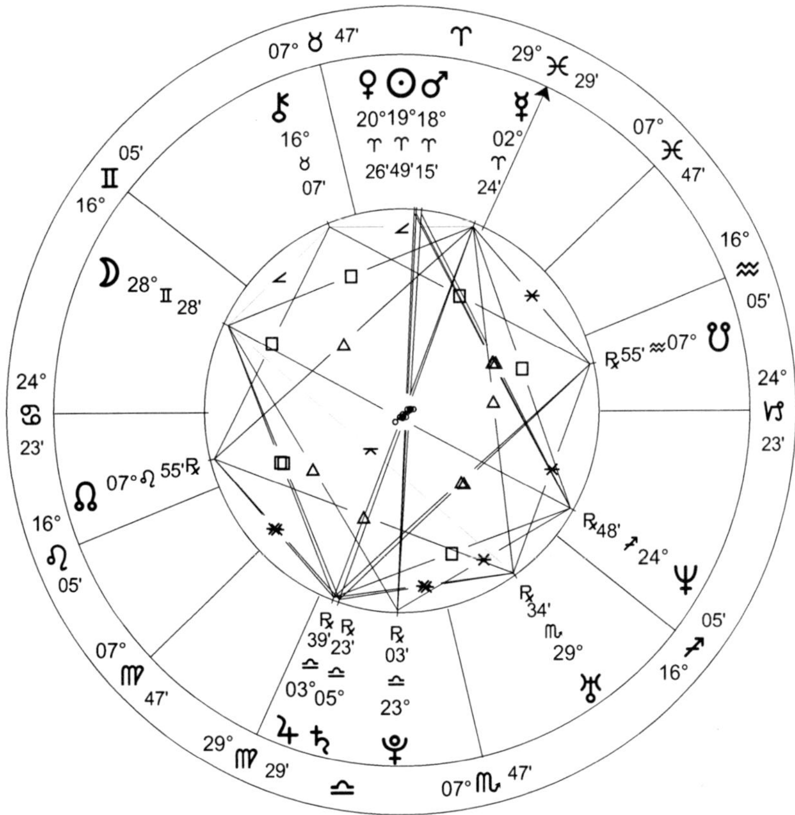

Chart E (Porphyry houses)

"Why did this have to happen? They're all dead, they made me kill them". The client said, "I feel emotionally devastated" (Pluto in the fourth). To start to learn more of what brought him to this point, we went back earlier in the past life.

The client went to a time when he was about six years old and was in a courtyard of a large house compound, in an Asian culture. He was there with his father and was being instructed by him in a form of martial arts (Pluto/Mars opposition – father, tenth house). His father was hitting him with a rod while telling him to control his emotions and anger (Mars in Aries in the tenth). This young boy felt anger arise in him, but his desire to please his father (Libra) was so strong that he quickly became torn (Pluto opposing Venus – split in feeling nature). He was also aware of the fact that he was only a small boy, and helpless to really do anything about it (fourth house), and he just wished that this would stop. This was nearly a daily ritual that this young boy grew up with, and since they seemed to be of some sort of ruling class (Leo NN and ruler of SN in fifth house/ Libra and tenth house – social standing/status), he lived a very isolated life with little or no contact with peers (Chiron in Taurus in the eleventh square the nodes, also SN in Aquarius). His mother was a solace to him as she was caring and affectionate (Libra/fourth house) but she was only a woman in a strict patriarchal system and had no ability to change the situation for him (Libra – societal/cultural conditions and gender roles/familial conditioning of the fourth/tenth house axis).

As he grew into his early teens, he was very aware of real feelings of hatred for his father despite the warrior honor code (Aries and the tenth house) he had been subjected to. He began to tell himself he wanted nothing to do with it (rebellion and individuation of the Aquarius SN and square to the nodes from the eleventh). When he was around 14 he ran away from home. At this point in his life he was subjectively aware that he felt emotionally numb and that this was a defense against the rage that was seething below the surface (suppression and repression of the tenth house).

In the next significant moment in the story, he had arrived in a village that was out of his home district but in the same culture. Because he came from a different class, he was dressed differently than others, and drew unwanted attention to himself, as he clearly didn't fit in (alienation/social standing – Aquarius/Libra/tenth house). One day while he was in the village, some boys around his age started to tease him. He tried to ignore this (Libra – denial), but it escalated to the point where they surrounded him and started to physically provoke him.

It is important to note how projection in the Libra archetype is functioning in this situation, as his own denied anger was now being mirrored by others in his environment. When we efficiently deny and repress something, not only do we project qualities onto others and see them as the one with the problem, but the environment will also respond by sending more people into our sphere with the exact quality that we avoid in ourselves. In the case of the Libra/Aries polarity, it is often provocative anger and selfishness that the Libran meets in the Aries type.

While the boys were pushing him, he was trying as hard as he could to not react (this was a replay of his childhood conditioning from that lifetime

– fourth/tenth house). He was trembling with the conflict of feeling he would need to fight for his survival (Aries/Taurus) yet wanted to maintain peace (Libra). He knew he was skilled in fighting arts, and feared what would happen if he let loose. He said through clenched teeth, over and over, "Don't make me do this".

The boys pushed him to the ground and started kicking him. At one point, he was hit sharply in the head and started to bleed (Aries) and it was as if a switch was thrown. Later he described this like "being possessed by the rage", which can happen when repressed energy is loosed (Mars/Aries tenth). Now all of his warrior training kicked in and he tactically (tenth house) singled out the boy who was leading the others, hoping that if he took him down he would be able to end it quickly and escape. The fight only escalated further as weapons were produced (Aries) and he stabbed the boy, feeling instantly shocked and devastated. Slaying the leader did not have the effect he desired, and the other boys continued to come at him. He started to lose his grip on reality, as he killed several more. Local people ran to the scene and he knew he would shortly be totally surrounded. When he saw his chance, in the ensuing confusion, he ran.

This is now the point where we started the story as he made his way out of town, found a place to hide and collapsed in grief, devastation and confusion. As the rest of his life went on, we find out that he lived most of it with the fear of feeling pursued and found out to be a murderer. He wandered from town to town, staying on the fringe as much as possible (Aquarius). Going back home was never an option as he felt a deep sense of shame, not only about having killed, but because he violated the honor code his father beat into him. He felt he had failed to live up to what was expected of him (Libra – expectations, and tenth house – failure), despite his attempt to rebel against it (Aquarius/Chiron in eleventh house). He lived to be an older man but died destitute from an illness. By that point in his life he didn't want to live anymore anyway (Chiron in Taurus – shut down/tenth house repression). As he left his body in death, his spirit felt despair and anger. He was angry with God, and felt betrayed by having had such a life (ruler of SN in Scorpio). His Libran consciousness felt that none of this was fair.

We now started to work in the afterlife, because part of his soul from that past life was stuck in a bardo of anger and despair. He re-met the spirit of his father and he was able to rage at him (releasing and restoring the suppressed instinctual nature – Aries). Once the rage was released he and his father had a conversation, and his father was understanding yet stated he did this with his son's best interests in mind. This was the tradition the father was raised in and it was his duty to pass it on to his son (tenth house). He and his father were at an impasse in the spirit world as the son did not agree with him. Because this conditioning was a matter of a larger cultural order and obvious lineage (tenth house), I asked for the spirit of his father's teacher to be with the two of them.

As it turned out, his father's teacher let them both know that the father's methods were a distortion of the true teaching. Repression and denial of emotion were not the true aim, and that his father had misunderstood these methods. The teacher assured the client that having emotions is okay (empowerment of the wounds of the fourth house and Venus feeling nature). Further, the client worked with the spirits of the boys and was surprised that the boy who was the leader was quite repentant for what happened. They all came to reconciliation (empowered Libra).

Further, spirits of many different warriors joined the client in the bardo. Some of these were parts of his own past life selves, and others were models of true and empowered warriorship. They worked with him further on his healing and spoke with him about what it means to fight and be noble (Leo NN in the first). They honored the fact that he had the instinct to be noble, despite the conditions of the lifetime. They told him that he had learned the lessons of violence, and that this life brought an ending of a karmic cycle (Pluto is angular by sign and house, nodes are angular by house – new evolutionary cycle).

One spirit warrior stepped forward, telling him that he will be with the client in this new cycle as a teacher. Oddly, my client described him as not looking like a warrior at all. He was short with balding hair, but he described his eyes as emanating deep strength, love and compassion. This new guide told him that the lessons from that lifetime didn't have anything to do with the courage to fight, but it was about him finding the courage to love (Leo NN in the first, Pluto in Libra) and that in this lifetime his work was to learn the ways of the spiritual warrior. Also, as a reflection of the polarity point to Pluto in the fourth, this teacher told him that there remains some reality (tenth house) about his karmas that he needs to deal with from other past lives, but not in this session.

Several months after the session this client told me that the fears of impending violence had lessened greatly, but what he found to be more profound for him was, in his own words, "I now have the courage to be open, to be noticed, and to embrace life in a way that was not possible for me before" (Leo NN in the first house). We can see that healing this past life was part of his process of de-conditioning (tenth house) from familial and societal expectations (fourth/tenth and first/seventh houses), to individuate (Aquarius SN, Chiron square from the eleventh) and embrace the potentials of his NN.

8

Scorpio/Pluto and the Eighth House

"Out of the night that covers me,
Black as the Pit from pole to pole,
I thank whatever gods may be
For my unconquerable soul.

In the fell clutch of circumstance
I have not winced nor cried aloud.
Under the bludgeonings of chance
My head is bloody, but unbowed.

Beyond this place of wrath and tears
Looms but the horror of the shade,
And yet the menace of the years
Finds, and shall find me, unafraid.

It matters not how strait the gate,
How charged with punishments the scroll,
I am the master of my fate;
I am the captain of my soul."

Invictus, William Ernest Henley, 1849-1903

Keywords

Fixed/Yin/Water	Shadow	Magic/Curses
Commitment	Intimacy	Corrupt power
Fear of entrapment	Fear of Intimacy	Manipulation
Spy	Sex	Alchemy
Betrayal	Shared resources	Loss
Compulsions	Resourcefulness	Abandonment
Obsessions	Psychology	Merging
Fear of Vulnerability	Power/Powerlessness	Metamorphosis

Taboo	Sexual violence	Fascination
Penetration	Phobia	Macabre
Covert	Paranoia	Violence
Secret	Priest/Priestess	Evil
Transformation	Egypt	Destruction
Darkness	Intensity	

The Natural Archetype

Up until the 1930s, when Pluto was discovered, Scorpio was ruled by Mars. The poem *Invictus* conjures an image of Mars as ruler of Scorpio. Mars is always up for a battle, but unlike in Aries, which is yang and the battle happens 'out there', the battlefield in Scorpio, a yin sign, is ultimately within oneself. The poet himself wrote *Invictus* from a hospital bed during a recurrence of childhood tuberculosis, which caused one of his feet to be amputated. His life long struggle with his illness and handicap imbued him with Scorpio qualities of true personal power that arises out of powerlessness. The *Invictus* warrior uses adversity and confrontation to forge the realization that it is oneself that must be mastered, to become the captain of one's soul. Echoing the polarity point of Taurus, Scorpio moves beyond just survival to the transformation of limitations. This mirrors the natural order, as within the Taurus archetype the strategy is preservation of the species through procreation and in Scorpio it is evolution that ensures survival.

Mars, representing our personal will, meets the force of evolution of the soul (Pluto) in Scorpio, and often the result is a life and death struggle as to which will reign. Pluto, as the higher octave of Mars, leads beyond the sphere of ego desires to transform the personal will and align it with Divine will. The inevitability of evolution is that, no matter how many lifetimes it takes, the soul will emerge the victor, as the soul is the only part of us that is invincible and unconquerable (Invictus). Pluto's mode for accomplishing the revelation of a greater reality than just the egoic, is often experienced as ruthless.

A natural tendency of Scorpio is to penetrate the surface to get to 'the bottom line'. This energy can be used in any direction that Scorpio turns its attention. This is why depth psychology, investigation, and all things mysterious and esoteric, are associated with this archetype. As a yin sign, Scorpio seeks not only to reveal the depth of what is outside of itself, but also the personal hidden realms of the psyche. When Pluto's power is consciously focused inward, the ultimate bottom line that is reached is nothing less than the soul. But in order to find the gold in the mine, one has to descend into the underworld.

If we look at the glyph of Scorpio (♏) we see an M with an upward pointing tail. Symbolically this shows the passage of consciousness from the heights and the depths to a final resurrection. This ultimate resurrection culminates at the end of the zodiac wheel in Pisces, which is the final water sign. It is only through this sort of journey that the soul is made free to permanently reunite with its source, the Divine. This also mirrors the soul as the intermediary energy, which travels from the spirit world to the material and back again as it moves through the cycles of reincarnation. Scorpio is said to have three aspects – the scorpion, the eagle and the phoenix. These three symbols of the decanates can also be looked at as phases of this journey.

In the scorpion phase we are focused deep within, examining motives, confronting our own dark places in the psyche and recognizing the limiting nature of past wounds and separating desires. Held in the scorpion's claws we feel the repeated sting of all the aspects within ourselves that are dysfunctional. Hopefully, this births the desire to transform what has been keeping us enslaved. If this introspective process results in disentanglements from desires and fixations which no longer serve us, we become the eagle where we taste the heights of our potential to truly become the transcendent self. The eagle allows the vision of the higher reality that inspires us to want to soar above the limitations of the small self. The eagle's eye allows it to take in a panoramic view without losing detailed focus. This symbolizes Scorpio's ability to evaluate both the inner world and external simultaneously, which results in keen perceptions. The scorpion to the eagle represents a leap in consciousness that arrives at the conclusion, 'There is something more than this'. This leads again to descent, to the energy of transmutation and transformation – the phoenix. Now that we know there is something more we must make the conscious choice, with the higher view now in mind, to throw the dross of our lower nature into the fire; to willingly go into destruction to arise in permanent resurrection.

> "Only if we venture repeatedly through zones of annihilation can our contact with Divine Being, which is beyond annihilation, become firm and stable."
>
> *The Way of Transformation*, Karlfried Graf von Durckheim

This is the esoteric meaning of the death and rebirth that happens in Scorpio. The small self (the ego) will continually meet with its own death as a part of the evolution to soul consciousness. In *Esoteric Astrology*, Alice Bailey writes that it is in the archetype of Scorpio where the 'crisis of soul' ensues, as the battle between personality (ego) and soul begins. The soul, as energy, cannot be destroyed, only transformed. From the soul's perspective, destruction is impossible, but to the personality or ego level of consciousness, which is impermanent, even the smallest threats of change can be felt as annihilation. The fixed nature of Scorpio often plays out this conflict by obsessively holding onto anything that it feels would ensure its security.

Scorpio is similar to Cancer in this regard, which is the first sign of the water trine. They both will grasp and tenaciously hold in their claws whatever represents security from the past. Both Cancer and Scorpio, like the Moon (and its nodes) and Pluto, represent retention of emotional memory from the past. Even when it doesn't serve us, the past is what is familiar, and our rate of evolution beyond it is directly proportionate to how firmly we hold onto it. While we can understand metaphorically that parts of us must die for a greater reality to emerge, we often don't go through those deaths and losses gracefully. In our process of evolution, when we are mainly identified with our ego selves, the movements of the soul are perceived and often experienced as forceful. Until we willingly cooperate, Pluto can be felt as the 'tough love' of the divine. Having our growth in mind, when even we don't, it will sweep away, often dramatically, the people and things we hold most precious to us, which is how the experience of loss becomes a part of this archetype.

The development of the ego self is represented by the archetypes of the lower half of the chart. All the conditions for the birth of the ego self coalesce in Cancer. In the next sign, Leo (another fixed sign, that is naturally square Scorpio), the ego self is 'pumped up' so that the essence of the self can shine forth. In the transitional archetype of Virgo the preparation begins for the gravity of the consciousness to move from the lower half of the chart to the upper transcendent, transpersonal sphere. Libra initiates that experience with the awareness of the duality of self and others, and proposes challenges of how to balance the two, which are played out in the dynamics of relationship. The balancing of opposites that Libra represents continues and deepens in Scorpio, to become deep intimate bonding in personal relationships, but ultimately the real duality experienced in Scorpio is that of the ego and the soul. In alchemy (also associated with Scorpio) the 'great work' of merging these two has often been referred to as the sacred or inner marriage.

Scorpio has Taurus, which is Venus ruled, as its polarity point. It is an interesting dynamic that Scorpio, being co-ruled by Mars, associates it with the archetype of Aries. Aries also has Libra, the other Venus-ruled sign as its polarity point. As Aries integrates this polarity, it gains from Venus the ability to step out of the sphere of 'only the self' to embrace 'others'. Scorpio, following Libra in the natural zodiac, has intrinsic within it already the inclusiveness of others, but needs to learn the lessons of the 'inner marriage' – self reliance that is based on an internal relationship with one's own soul and divine will. This inner side of Venus – the relationship to oneself, is a part of the Taurus archetype. This is a difficult task for Scorpio energy that is associated with shared resources. Merging with another through the basic resources needed for survival (Taurus) implies a deep level of committed involvement and also opens up a can of worms. We can see in couples that when joint accounts are opened, or real estate is purchased together, the emotional investment in each other intensifies, as do the fears. In divorces or even in inheritance, dividing the resources is often when the stingers come out. All levels of power games, manipulations, betrayals and deceits can emerge from the darkest corners of the psyche.

Scorpio in Past Life Experiences

The Scorpio archetype is a part of the karmic axis when:

Pluto is in Scorpio or the eighth house or
The South Node is in Scorpio or the eighth house or
The ruler of the South Node is in Scorpio or the eighth house or
Pluto aspects the nodal axis, or rulers of the nodes.

Power and Powerlessness

In past lives, when Scorpio/Pluto or the eighth house is involved in the karmic axis, one has often met power shadow qualities in interpersonal relationships, either as the victim or perpetrator, and most likely in the total soul's history, one has been both. Frequently issues of power struggles from both sides of the spectrum are a repeated theme in past lives. The courage to face one's own shadow is an admirable quality of Scorpio that feeds the ability to uncover and understand underlying motives. Examination of motives leads one to realizations of what desires lie behind one's actions. But when one is unaware, or in denial that they also have shadow characteristics within themselves, they project them onto others and often meet these qualities externally, in full force. As Pluto acts to make the hidden apparent, rooting out the personal shadow is a critical part of real soul work. Carl Jung summed up the intention of this saying, "One does not become enlightened by imagining beings of light, but by making the darkness conscious". Pluto is the great equalizer, and the need for balance that started in Libra reaches its crescendo in Scorpio. The common understanding of karma as an equalizing law is part of Pluto's domain. As mentioned in other chapters, karma is not solely about an 'eye for an eye', it is also about the repetition of wounds so that healing and resolution can occur; this is also an expression of an equalizing force and is an intrinsic part of evolution.

It is necessary then to understand the wounds that are carried into the current life from both sides of power struggles. These two charts reflect the intrinsic Scorpionic issues of power and powerlessness.

Chart A

This chart has a Scorpio SN with Mars conjunct in the sixth house. The ruler of the SN is Pluto, which is in Virgo in the fifth house with Uranus conjunct. Along with the Scorpio themes that are illustrated through her past lives, the Virgo/Pisces issues of lessons of discernment, victimization, sacrifice and service have also been a part of her past life experience. This is illustrated by the nodes being on the sixth/twelfth house axis and Pluto/Uranus in Virgo in opposition to the Pisces planets. The residues carried from past lives when one has been a victim of power games can lead to present day mistrust of others' motives, secrecy and even paranoia.

This past life along with several others of hers has to do with wounds associated with entanglements with black magic. Involvement in ritual magic or with magicians is not an unusual theme in the Scorpio/Taurus axis. This is easy to understand in light of the fact that the Scorpio archetype is where the personal will and divine will intersect. In a simplified sense, the practice of magic has two expressions, white and black. The dividing point has to do with whose will is in control – the divine or the personal. This is represented symbolically by the pentagram used in both white and black magic. When the single point of the pentagram is pointed upwards, symbolically it forms a triangle showing that the point of power is in the

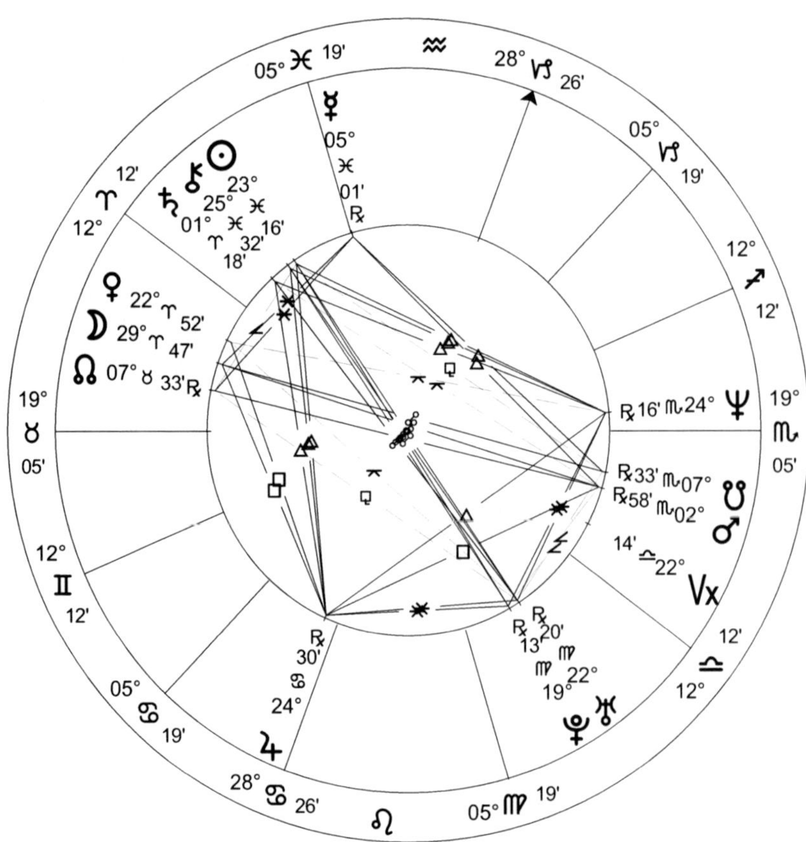

Chart A (Porphyry houses)

'heavens' and it is divine will and its expression through the individual that is being sought. When the single point is facing downwards, it forms a funnel, which symbolizes the intention of gathering divine power unto oneself and bending it to personal will. The classic clash of light and dark, good and evil is also strongly represented in the Scorpio archetype and has to do with the energy of ascent and descent, as well as separation from the divine and returning. Like the Devil card in the tarot deck, Scorpio represents the fact that we have freewill as we move through a world defined by duality, and we are always presented with choice.

In this past life she was a young girl living in Egypt (also associated with the Scorpio/Taurus axis). She was in her late teens and was a very attractive young woman. One day while she was in the market with her father she caught the gaze of a man and was instantly transfixed. She described this as an "instant seduction", like a "hypnotic trance" (all very Scorpionic). Her father disliked this man, but as she had already fallen under his sway, a relationship was inevitable. She left her home to live with him.

This man was a magician who already had a 'harem' of women and she was at the center of this group. He made her feel special (Mars) and protected and it was her desire for this, coupled with her Piscean naiveté (Pluto opposing Sun/Chiron in Pisces), that formed the hook in her psyche that allowed him to progressively possess her. Before she was aware of what was happening she was involved in group ritual and because of her entranced state she blindly went along with this, even though her own instinct felt there was something wrong (Mars – instinct, in sixth house conjunct SN). She described that during the ritual they would enter an even deeper group trance and a "dark force" would take over (Scorpio – possession and entrapment). The intention of their ritual was to capture and use raw life force. Sex and young children were involved in the rituals. Youthful life force, sex and its power is contained in the symbol of Mars in Scorpio; the Moon is also in Aries opposing this Mars.

At one point during a ritual she said, "My heart started to wake me up, I suddenly knew what we were doing was wrong". The power of this heart-centered knowing is represented by Pluto in the fifth house. Once this inner knowing started to awaken in her, the conflict between the 'dark and light' forces caused an all-out inner war (Scorpio SN in the sixth with Mars conjunct). Sudden realizations (Uranus and eleventh house) struck her about what they were doing, the nature of what this man was really about and what she had become involved in. It caused a shock of disillusionment (Pisces planets in the eleventh opposed by Pluto/Uranus). She did not survive the strain of this conflict and went insane. This signature is represented by the same factors – Uranus conjunct Pluto/the Sun conjunct Chiron in Pisces in the eleventh house (dissociation and fragmentation, and madness/ insanity). She said, "It felt as if I blew up internally and shattered into little bits" (Mars/Scorpio/Uranus/eleventh house).

She ended up on the ritual altar herself and was stabbed to death while being raped (Mars/Scorpio). The work in the afterlife had to do with disengaging her from all the forces that had possessed her, including the man, and bringing back and reintegrating the fragmented parts of her psyche. This is the empowered aspect of Virgo/sixth house, the ability to reassemble that which has been dissociated (Pisces).

If we put this past life into a linear time in her soul's history it was an ancient life. Subsequent lives have borne out the themes of victimization and absolute powerlessness and were frequently repeated (Scorpio/sixth house – Pluto in Virgo). The trance-like quality that she described falling into, was extended through many lives, and shows the fixed nature of a Scorpio SN and the tendency to form fixated bonds with others. The abusive man in this past life represented on a symbolic level the power her soul desired to regain for itself. Not that she would need to become an abusive magician to regain power, but that she had swung so far to the other side of the spectrum, all her sense of power was projected onto others. The natural tendency in the Scorpio archetype is to become magnetically attracted to something in another that we are unconscious about in ourselves and form a relationship with that quality through them (osmosis). It would seem her soul also became fixated on being a victim (Virgo/sixth house), possibly as a form of atonement (Virgo) for her own past misuses of power. With her Taurus NN in the twelfth house, it also shows that the blueprint for her to do this is to realign with the gentleness of the divine and to regain trust.

Another past life that she re-experienced illustrates this clearly. She was raised in a Goddess-oriented culture and was a young woman preparing for a sexual initiation rite (Mars/Scorpio SN) that was intended to unite God and Goddess within (inner sacred marriage). It was a period of history where patriarchal ways were gaining power over the more earth-centered cultures, which often manifested, as it does in our current times, as an overpowering of the feminine principle by force.

As she ascended the steps to meet the priest who was enacting the ritual, she sensed that something was wrong. She doubted her own instinct (Mars in the sixth house) and told herself, "But I am going to experience the Goddess, this can't be wrong". She was given a ritual drug (Pisces) and just as in her other life, she became a ritual sacrifice. This time though she was internally enraged as it happened (Mars/sixth house) but because of the drug she was powerless to fight. She died fighting internally though, screaming, "You will not take my soul". She was also overcome with the realization that this was an often repeated pattern: "Not this again; How could I let this happen?" Dying in this state of rage actually showed growth from the previous life, as her personal will was more active and engaged. Anger creates a boundary which isn't there when we have felt invaded.

She died also with the belief that the Goddess had failed her, that she wasn't strong enough, and this needed to be healed in the afterlife. Her soul, weary from the battle (Mars) not just from this life but many lives, needed to find a place of peace in the spirit world. A female spirit helper came to bring her to a place of lush green nature (Taurus NN) in the spirit world. She lay on the welcoming grass soaking in this support, while receiving healing. Through this, she was able to experience pure energetic sensuality (Taurus). She reconnected with the energy of the divine feminine in the spirit world, and received further healing. She realized that in that life, although she had been raised to honor the Goddess, because of the times it was more conceptual than an actual experience. In the spirit world, when she was able to connect through direct experience (Scorpio) she said it became a "visceral knowing" (Taurus) that was beyond anything she had experienced before. She said, "My sensual nature had become numb and it needed to be revived" (Taurus). Through this she came to realize how deeply her trust in the divine had been wounded (Scorpio) and that she could now begin to heal that. Because she is actively on a spiritual path in her current life, her nodal pattern shows that regaining trust and having faith (twelfth house) in the power and abundance of the great Mother Goddess (Taurus) is exactly the intent of her NN in the twelfth house. Her ability to find self-reliance (Taurus) is directly connected to this inner relationship with the divine.

The intensity that Scorpio consciousness contains from lives of living on the edge meets a challenge when integrating the Taurus polarity, whose message is, 'Let it be gentle'. Essentially the Scorpio consciousness needs to learn from Taurus, to slow down and find the gentle rhythm of the sensual earth within itself. In both these lives recounted here the safe home of her body was invaded (Mars/Scorpio). This leaves a karmic wound of feeling that nowhere is safe and can leave one in a state of paranoia. Scorpio shares this tendency with Aries when it's a part of the karmic signature, and the individual can come into life with the 'volume turned up to one hundred'. One can see how Taurus is the antidote for that, urging one to slow down. The healing she found through the support of the sweet green Goddess also represents a reunification of soul with body, which is a part of the Scorpio/Taurus axis as well as Virgo/Pisces.

Because her Pluto is in the fifth house and her SN is in Scorpio, lessons about the nature of power and self-empowerment have been a part of her karmic history. Power and powerlessness are both a part of Scorpio as it evaluates what it means to have true power. Another lesson that these last two past life stories show about the Scorpio archetype is the necessity of learning the difference between power and force. All levels of power and force are explored by the soul on this path to hopefully come to the truth that the power of love trumps the love of power.

This next chart also illustrates the lessons of power, and one of this client's very early past lives echo the experience of the previous chart. In this chart Pluto and the SN are in Leo in the eighth house but not conjunct. The nodes are squared by Venus in Taurus in the fourth house.

Chart B

In this past life, set in an early civilization, the woman was a sorceress of sorts. She was betrothed to a man who was her partner in magical practices. There was no love in this relationship as it was solely power based and she described it also as sadistic (Leo/Scorpio). This is an extreme form of mutual misuse akin to Scorpio. Like the first story of the previous chart their magical practice involved taking life force from children. She said, "Through sex (Scorpio) we would create life (children – Leo and fourth house) only for the purpose of cannibalizing them for their essence". This very dark practice ate at her mind and soul, and drove her to eventually murder her mate, as she reached a point of insanity (Aquarius NN). She did not survive her attempt to kill him, as they engaged in a life and death struggle with each other, which resulted in a mutual murder. This part of her soul stayed in a dark place for a very long time, until it was worked with in the afterlife.

The theme of seeking power through killing continued in another lifetime, when she was a male Native American who took part in many war parties and scalping raids. He particularly focused on scalping women. She said, "I felt victorious and proud" (Leo/Scorpio). Hair is archetypally associated with one's power, like Leo's mane, and scalping is another form of taking the power of one's enemies. She said, "The more scalps I had the more powerful I felt".

In one raid this warrior came upon a woman with small children; she was kneeling begging for mercy and something about her broke through to his heart (Pluto Leo/Venus). What he was suppressing (Chiron in Capricorn is inconjunct both Pluto and the ruler of the SN as the tip of a yod) was the pain and anguish of the loss of his own family, when they had been raided

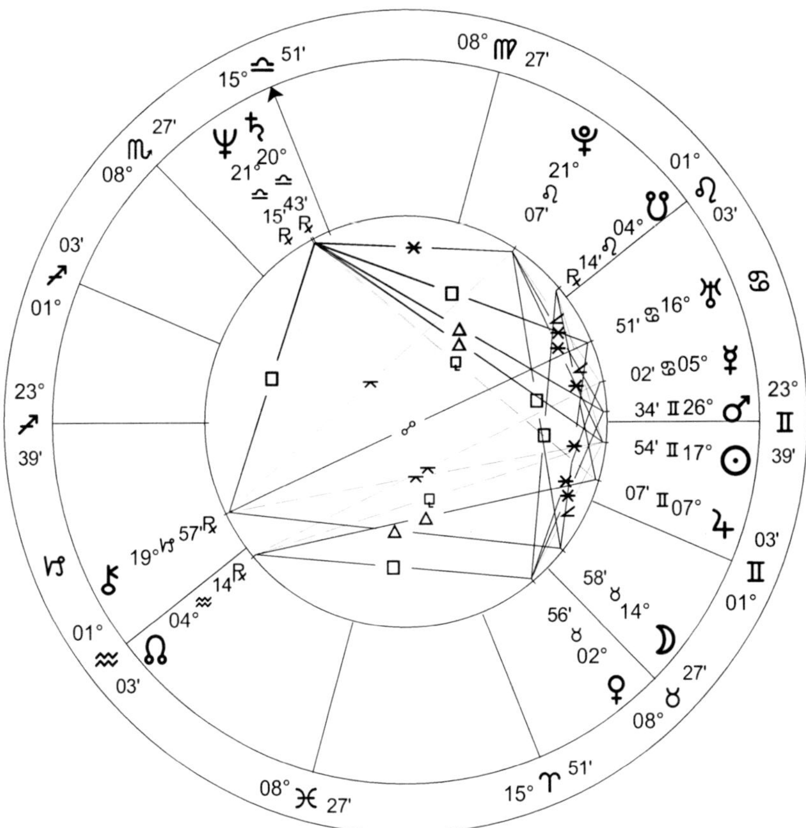

Chart B (Porphyry houses)

years earlier. He had sworn vengeance (common in Scorpio – especially when Mars/Aries/first house is involved) and had channeled this rage into his warring (first house). As he broke through to his pain, he grieved for his misdirected rage (Capricorn/first house), and for the anguish he had caused others, especially the previous women he had scalped and killed. In the spirit world after his death he begged to reconcile with the spirits of those he had wronged. He was able to do this, and was also able to see that as a soul he could kill no more. It was this lifetime that was a turning point and where he laid aside vengeance to become a peaceful warrior. The displacement of emotion is also indicated in this chart by the Venus in the fourth house. This man had been unable to deal with his loss (eighth house) so he projected it (Venus) onto women (Venus/fourth house) and in killing them he was actually trying to kill his own pain.

As a continued experiment with the limits of power, this soul also had lifetimes of absolute powerlessness, where she was the victim of manipulation, sexual abuse, betrayals and murder. As a result, in her current life she has had a deep fear of 'owning her power' (Leo/Scorpio). Her soul nonetheless has laid out a plan for her with the NN in Aquarius in the second house which is also the polarity point to Pluto, by giving her the opportunity to manifest visions of change. She is a healer and teacher in this lifetime, whose main focus is teaching an alchemical process of transformation. A deep part of her healing in this life has been to regain trust in herself; that she has learned to manage power and that her motives are aligned with higher will. She said, "I had to redeem myself".

Further to that, with the Venus in Taurus square the nodes, her feeling of deserving love was deeply wounded and some of her power-seeking lives may be looked at like the rebellion (Aquarius) of a lonely child who constantly tests the love of the parents by acting up. Because she has felt so undeserving (Taurus) it has been a part of her path to realign herself with the steadiness of divine love (Pluto and SN Leo/ Venus in Taurus in fourth house) both in receiving and giving. There were several lifetimes where she had mental breakdowns (Aquarius and ruler of SN in Gemini/sixth). She said the effect from those lives was that her link with the higher community (spiritual connection) was broken. She said, "I had to re-stabilize myself (Taurus) in this life and repair that connection (Aquarius)". By doing this, teachings have flowed through her that she is now in the process of preparing to write about. This is reflected not only by her Gemini planets but that through her own alchemical transformation (Scorpio) she can create from a place of joy and communion (Leo/Aquarius) to create a durable/tangible work (Taurus) that serves others (Aquarius/sixth house).

These stories and the previous case also illustrate the principle of 'soul theft' that shamans have described. Black magic practices, since they are not aligned with true power, are informed by a fear based on a belief that power is limited, so they resort to the theft of power. While one may not in their current life actively engage in black magic practices, there are many ways we enact stealing power from each other. Back-stabbing, violations of trust (betrayal), deceit and manipulation are some of the strategies we use to pry power away from others for ourselves. The power games that we play stem from a basic fear of loss and can be seen in the way we view and garner resources. This is seen collectively in the massive misuse of natural resources.

The integrated Scorpio/Taurus axis represents a trust in abundance, and an economizing of the earth's wealth (shared wealth). On a personal level one can evaluate their own wise use of power by looking at how many 'win-win' situations they seek to create as opposed to 'win-lose'.

Exposure

'Intense' is a word that most people use to describe Scorpio. This description works also for Scorpio past life signatures. One can imagine what some of those lives must have been like when Scorpio is part of the past life signature. People with Scorpio in the natal charts often have an 'all or nothing' attitude. The concentrated intensity gives them focus, but also can mean that in past lives they have met the darkest corners of human nature head-on. This extremity of experience follows on from Libra's swings between extremes to find balance.

Scorpio's intent to penetrate to the bottom line echoes Taurus' ability to simplify. When one has been in extreme situations that strip one to the core of existence, the myriad distractions of life are instantly removed and a basic reality is revealed. This opens the possibility to 'be real' with oneself and others, which allows for deep bonding to happen. In Scorpionic past lives, destructive and annihilative forces have often been met literally. When one has experienced total destruction and devastation, such as plagues the effects of war or monumental personal losses, an 'Armageddon consciousness' can be formed and carried into future lives. This can cause an acute fear of death or a perpetual feeling that one's demise is imminent. It also can contribute to a 'screw it all' attitude that pushes the limits and provokes disaster to happen (a death wish). As one client with three planets in Scorpio square his nodal axis said, "All my life I've been itching to stare down evil", which reflects a confrontational energy found in Aries that is also a part of Scorpio.

This confrontational nature also happens through Scorpio's propensity to expose others while keeping itself hidden. Past lives as inquisitors or spies sometimes display this literally. Past life deaths by exposure from either the elements, being 'outed', tortured for information, or even literal disembowelments, leave a deep seated fear of exposure of any sort. This adds to the need for secrecy, as a means of protection, and a compulsive drive to get others to face what one fears within themselves.

One client with a Scorpio SN in the tenth house was a gay man during the Nazi regime. He tried to blend in, but as many minority groups were actively pursued, he was outed and killed. This translated into an absolute fear of being 'seen' or noticed in this life, and a shame around sexuality (Scorpio/Capricorn). In his current life he was a psychologist (also ruled by Scorpio) who delighted in his own ability to tear down others' defenses with his penetrating insights. This was a misinformed use of his natural skill, simply because his own fears of exposure had not yet been dealt with. When these fears of exposure are healed, Scorpio can enact a higher octave by turning that penetrating gaze inwards to identify what needs to be personally purified. When one has truly walked through one's own fires, it then flows easily and naturally to help others navigate the same terrain with gentleness (Taurus) and compassion. Further, when one has been exposed in many past lives to the darker aspects of oneself and others through the Scorpio archetype, Taurus also acts as an antidote that shows in this lifetime that it may be time for one to start looking for the beauty in all.

Abandonment and Loss

Many of my clients with Scorpio in their karmic axis have abandonment complexes that were rooted in past lives. One client with a Taurus SN/ Scorpio NN squared by Saturn had enacted a pattern of sabotaging (Saturn) every relationship that threatened to get too intimate. When we explored the fears behind her fear of being left she said, "If he leaves me, I'll die".

The past life that contributed to this fear was one of a young woman who had been abandoned as a child. She was left on the steps of an orphanage when she was a baby. Fortunately she was adopted and brought up reasonably well. She loved her father very much (Saturn) and he was in the military. When she was about six years old, she was out on a horse with her father having a wonderful time. Suddenly her father was killed by a gunshot and she fell to the ground stunned but unharmed. She felt it was "all my fault" (Saturn) because she begged her father to take her riding that day. Her mother did not cope with the loss very well and silently blamed the little girl. This, coupled with the pain of the loss, resulted in her shutting down (Taurus) and repressing the memory of what happened (Saturn). Because of this she was doubly abandoned. Later in her life she met the love of her life. This was pre-WWI and he was also a military man. Shortly into their young marriage he was called into duty. She had become pregnant and was loath to let him go, but had no choice. Inevitably he never returned, and when the soldiers came to the door to deliver the news the wound of loss and abandonment was re-opened. She was overcome with grief (Saturn) and re-enacted her own early life abandonment by killing herself, thus abandoning her infant daughter.

This had stayed in her present day consciousness as, "If I am left I will die". As well as, "I cannot be trusted with myself or with love" (Scorpio mistrust). After she had worked through many of these wounds in the afterlife, wise guides came to advise her about the meaning of that past life. They told her, "You have to go back and face reality (Saturn)". Which is what she did as she was alive now. They also told her, "You are learning the lesson that love does not come and go even though people do". They were pointing out the durability (Taurus) of bonds (Scorpio), that when they are formed in love, are eternal and can be trusted.

Loss in general is a common theme in the Scorpio archetype from the past life perspective. The intrinsic lesson of rebirth from the ashes of destruction is learned through loss, although the path to healing after loss is often a long one. This past life story shows that through the pain of loss, growth is stimulated, which illustrates this basic Scorpio theme.

Chart C

In this chart Pluto is in Leo in the eighth house along with Mercury, which is the ruler of the SN. This client went back to a past life as a young woman living a normal medieval peasant life. She lived in a countryside town with her parents and a younger sister. Everything was fine until a plague (Scorpio) broke out and people started dying rapidly. She, along with those that were still healthy, were left to care for the dead and dying.

She became quite involved in being as helpful as she could (Virgo SN/ Moon in Pisces opposing), gathering herbs, baking foods and tending to the sick. The fact that she was in a role of service to others in a life and death situation is also reflected by her Virgo SN and its ruler in the eighth house. It was only a matter of time before the sickness affected her family. Her father succumbed first and simultaneously her mother and sister became ill. She had no time to grieve the loss of her father, as she became even more consumed with trying to save the rest of her family. "I've got to save them" (Virgo/Pisces – helper/savior, and ninth house – hero. The ruler of the SN is also opposed, out of sign, by Jupiter in Pisces in the second – survival). The situation in the rest of her village became even more dismal, as piles of bodies were burning everywhere and there was no escaping the stench of

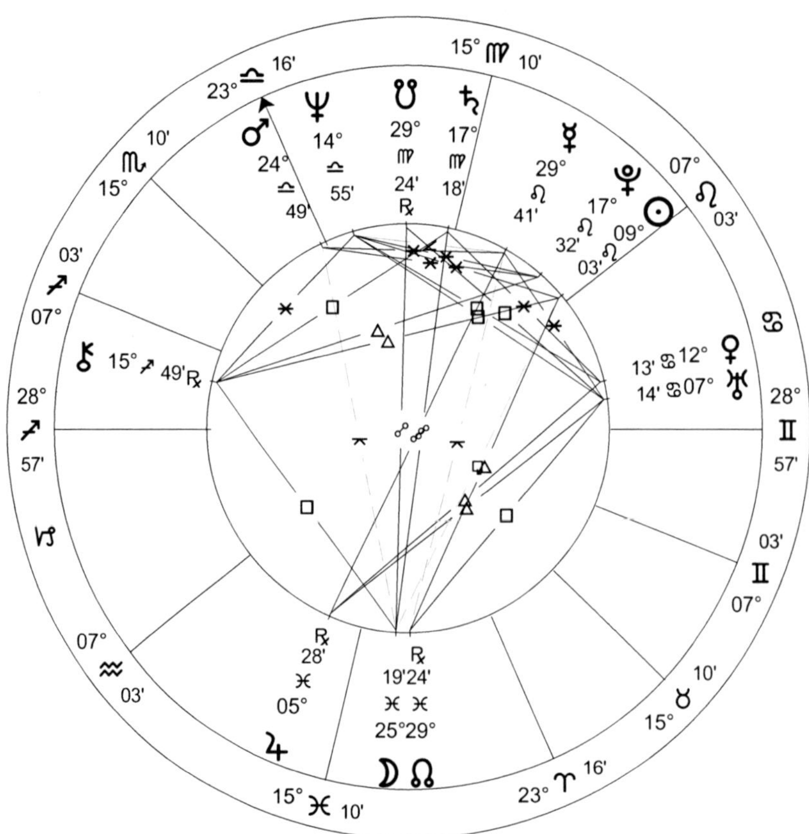

Chart C (Porphyry houses)

disease and death. As her mother neared death, the pain of the inevitable loss combined with exhaustion took over and she collapsed into grieving, "Don't leave me; I won't let you go". The loss of her mother was heart-wrenching, in fact this regression took place in a workshop with the group observing, and nearly everyone was weeping along with her. Despite her personal pain, she renewed her fervor and stepped up her effort to keep her sister from death. She desperately tried everything she knew, yet was powerless to keep death at bay (eighth house). She clutched her sister as she died in her arms, again wailing, "Don't leave me". She was overwhelmed (Pisces Moon) with the pain of the loss, "I'm all alone", and wished that she was dead instead of them (Scorpio – death wish).

This is a common effect that the loss of loved ones can have on the living. In shamanic cultures it is understood that an actual piece of the soul can split-off and follow the departed into the afterlife. This is part of the intention of the elaborate death and grieving rituals that these tribal societies perform; to protect the living from trying to follow the dead, and to keep the dead from trying to take the living ones with them, thus maintaining the balance between the two worlds. While this young girl sobbed for days she was utterly alone in her grief, and had no support from the community that was now in chaos (Virgo/Pisces). It wasn't long before the plague consumed her also and she died feeling devastated and completely alone (Scorpio/Virgo).

The gravity of the life and death situation caused her natural desire to serve (Virgo) to become stuck on overdrive and was carried into her current life as a savior complex, (Virgo SN in the ninth/Pisces Moon opposing SN). With her Virgo/Pisces axis she naturally gravitated towards healing work in this lifetime, but because this complex was unresolved she was still trying to 'save her family' through her clients. She repeatedly gave more of herself to others than she could afford and it had affected her health. In the past year a friend of hers had died from an illness and she had invested herself deeply (eighth house) in trying to save her. It was not planned this way, but as a part of divine synchronicity she did this regression the exact day of the one year anniversary of her friend's death. It was apparent to her that her friend had been her sister in that past life, and as she worked in the afterlife she saw her savior pattern in a way she had not been able to before. In a deeply touching moment her friend's spirit came to her during the work and told her that yes, they went through the loss again, but this time the one who was being saved was her. Her friend told her it was time for her to start caring for herself (polarity point of the eighth is second house – self reliance) and that she needed to let go of being the 'savior'.

What an interesting view of her Pisces NN with Moon conjunct; she needed to surrender being the savior (Pisces) and turn her compassion, into her own nurturing (Moon conjunct). After this work the client said that she now planned to make more time for herself and her own healing, and as a part of this process she was considering taking up writing (Pisces NN in the third, also an empowered Pluto and Mercury in Leo – creative self actualization).

Fixated Bonds

Entrapment is also a part of this archetype which manifests in past lives as literal lives of slavery or being someone's possession, as well as having been held in the clutch of psychological manipulations. One client with a Leo SN in the eighth house with Moon conjunct, went back to a life as a middle-aged man who had been psychologically and sexually abused by his mother (Moon). Since he was a young boy he was seduced by his mother as she fed him a steady diet of, "I'm the only one who truly loves you; Be Mommy's good boy and never leave me; You're mine". The possessiveness and dark entanglement of this relationship trapped this young boy between the almost irreconcilable polarities of simultaneously loving and hating her.

Being in double bind situations is most common in the Scorpio and Capricorn archetypes. Because of this he grew up unable to form any relationships, but the natural 'urge to merge' came out in compulsive and obsessive ways. He found himself fixated on little girls, like a pedophile. While he was not predatory (which would be a possible manifestation of this), he often just watched them from afar. Because of the abuse he had suffered since he was young, he was psychologically stunted and although he was a grown man in his thirties his emotional state was that of an eight year old. Eventually he made friends with one young girl and did end up fondling her. He instantly felt nauseous and sick by this, but was also unable to control himself. By this point in his life a psychological double bind had been formed in his consciousness that said, "In order to get love, I must do something evil or bad" (Leo/Scorpio). His own feeling of being evil (common in the Scorpio archetype), obviously caused other adults his age to be repulsed by him. One day when he was out in the village some men who had just left a tavern, cornered him and beat him to death.

His healing in the afterlife involved disengaging and unraveling all the entanglements formed with his mother. His own inner child (Leo and Moon) was worked with, and the little girl that he had fondled even came to him in the spirit world to forgive him. She and other children came to also help him feel joy (Leo) and the freedom of childhood that he had never had. It was the light of their unconditional love that released him from the twisted conditional love (Scorpio/Leo) that he had been trapped in all his life.

As discussed in Libra, the two types of karmic bonds commonly formed with others are fantasy and fixated bonds. As a cardinal sign Libra initiates the exploration of one's self through relationship. Scorpio as a fixed sign deepens the experience that happens in relationship. When Scorpio/Pluto or the eighth house are involved in the karmic axis, fixated bonds with others can be a part of the karmic theme.

Excerpt from the Libra chapter...

> "Fixated bonds can form when people are together in extraordinary, stressful or life threatening situations. The bond that is formed has a trance-like, compulsive quality, equating it to Scorpio and Pluto quite easily. Relationships that occur in past lives in extreme repressive or dangerous situations such as captivity, concentration camps, refugee situations, battle fields, or even growing up together in an abusive family can form these sorts of attachments with others. The victim and perpetrator can also form a very fixated bond that lasts through lifetimes either repeating the same relationship or even switching roles".

Several of the cases already shared showed different types of fixated bonds. When one meets a person in their current life with whom this sort of bond has been formed in the past, circumstances that reflect the past karmas will play out again.

Chart D

This woman met her husband-to-be and within a year they were married. Shortly after their marriage, both their finances started to crumble. She was in real estate which was experiencing a downturn at the time, and her husband had lost his job and was looking for employment. Her income was sustaining them, but their shared anxiety was affecting the relationship. She said, "I feel as if we are on a downward spiral that there is no escape from". She was considering leaving him so that she could regain the sense of financial security she had before she married. This caused deep conflict in her, as she loved him, but the fears of 'losing it all' were also great; she felt trapped.

This chart has a double Scorpio signature as Pluto is in the eighth house and the SN is in Scorpio. In this past life they were husband and wife, although their roles were reversed and she was the husband. They were living during a time when the economic situation was declining. Fortunately for him, he had come into a small inheritance (Scorpio) so was able to provide for his

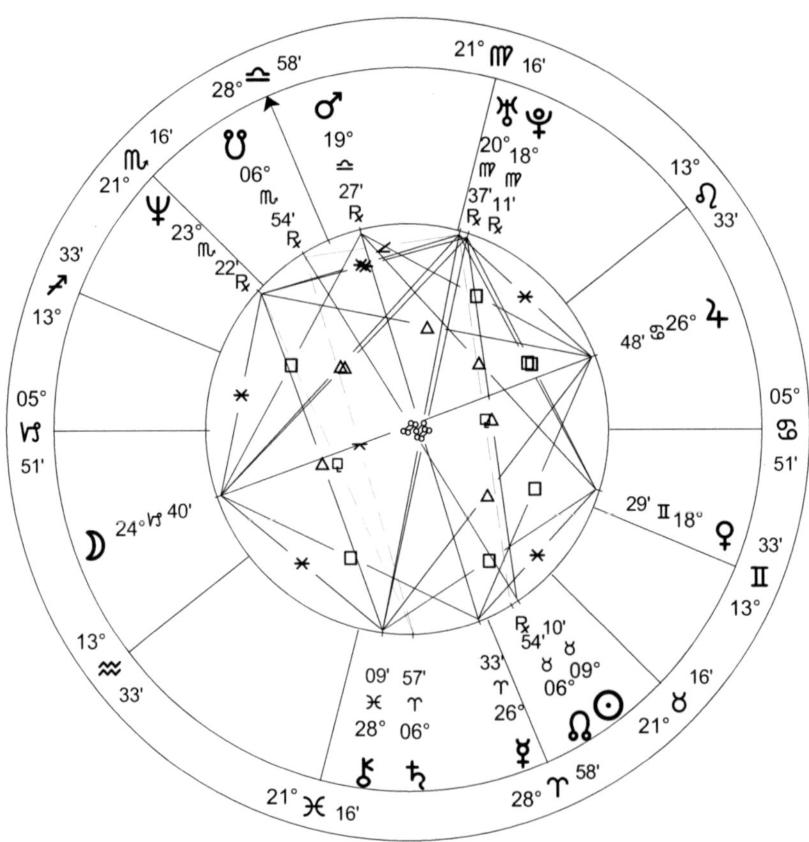

Chart D (Porphyry houses)

wife. Unfortunately, it was a dangerous time to have a better-than-peasant-class income. Political powers were changing (Scorpio SN in the tenth) in the time frame of the early 1900s in Russia. Soldiers stormed their house in the middle of the night, seized their property and possessions, declared them to be 'enemies of the state' and took them away to a work camp.

Overnight their world went from relative comfort to absolute destitution (Scorpio loss). They were separated into men's and women's camps never to see each other again. He was devastated, as not only had he lost everything, but he was unable to protect his wife (tenth house). Life was horrible at the camp and his grief put him into a state of numbness and shock. The only way to survive was to repress (tenth house) the memory of what had happened and concentrate on his own survival (Taurus Sun opposing SN).

He also felt guilty about his past inheritance (Pluto Virgo/eighth house) as it was part of the indoctrination at the camps that to hold wealth was against the state (Scorpio SN in the tenth). At one point he became responsible for dishing out food to the other prisoners (Scorpio – shared resources). It was a task he hated and it amounted to intense psychological torture for him, as he was acutely aware that there was never enough (Virgo in the eighth) to go around. Every ladle of food he spooned out felt to him as if he was making life and death decisions for others (Pluto/Virgo/eighth house). He tortured himself with the feeling that if he scooped out more for one person than another he would be responsible for their death. The pressure became too much and he started to have a mental/nervous breakdown (Venus in Gemini in the sixth square Pluto and Pluto conjunct Uranus). He pushed over a pot of food in a small act of rebellion (Uranus) and was taken outside and shot.

As he was being dragged out he felt simultaneously filled with grief, but relieved that it would soon be over. His immediate thoughts at death were, "I made them kill me", and "There was no choice". Because of the hopelessness of his situation he had enacted a subconscious death wish, effectively forcing his captors to kill him instead of him committing suicide. This reflects the combined signature of Scorpio and the tenth house. This lifetime represented for this client being pushed to extremes on many levels; and meeting her present day partner, who was the wife in that past life, re-triggered many of these dynamics for both of them. As we worked through the different imprints carried from that life, including the guilt, the conditioned negative messages of 'wealth is evil' and the effects of the massive losses, she was finally able to feel a sense of relief in the spirit world.

Guides came forward to assist with her healing and assured her that the fear of losing everything belonged to that life and not this one. She came to a realization that she and her husband were being challenged to economize and simplify their lives (Taurus NN) but that it did not mean they would not survive (Taurus NN). Utilizing her empowered Scorpio resourcefulness, combined with the tenth house and Virgo ability to plan and strategize, she immediately started to imagine ways in which cutting back could actually make her feel more secure (Taurus NN in the fourth). In the spirit world she was also able to see that the fact of her income supporting them at the moment was a way for that past life character to complete his feelings of guilt at not being able to protect and provide for his wife. This also helped her to feel the mutual nurturing (NN in the fourth) that the relationship did have instead of only seeing what was missing (Virgo).

Another Taurus lesson for Scorpio is to learn the ability to simplify. Many of my clients on this nodal axis often come to a point in their lives where paring down their existence to focus only on their basic needs is felt as a relief. Taurus in this way represents the energy of non-attachment, which may seem paradoxical for a sign associated with possessions. The Buddha, whose birth, death and enlightenment is celebrated on the May full moon when the Sun is in Taurus and Moon in Scorpio, demonstrated through his life and teachings this essence of non-attachment.

9

Sagittarius/Jupiter and the Ninth House

"This above all: to thine own self be true,
And it must follow, as the night the day,
Thou canst not then be false to any man."
William Shakespeare

Keywords

Mutable/Yang/Fire
Adaptability
Beliefs
Dogmatic
Philosophy
Optimism
Wisdom
Meaning
Goals
Expansion
Exaggeration
Trust
Faith
Religion
Truth
Intuition

Possibility
Honesty/dishonesty
Long Journeys
Pilgrimage
Multicultural
Foreigners
Immigrants
Ideals/Ideas
Nomad
Homeless
Explorer
Inspiration
Honor codes
The Hero
Restless

Wanderlust
Hope
Zealous faith
Missionary
Priest
Convert
Sales
Freedom
Half Truth
Silver-tongued devil
Charmer
Guru
Teacher
Natural Law
Shaman

The Natural Archetype

The intensity of Scorpio takes a much needed vacation and lightens up in Sagittarius. Echoing Scorpio's eagle aspect, consciousness in Sagittarius is uplifted to embrace possibility, hope and an optimistic bigger picture. The arrow of the archer in the actual constellation is pointing to the heart of the Scorpion, alluding to the fact that once one's own demons are confronted and slain, the path becomes even clearer. Sagittarius is not predominantly concerned with the present but more the distant potential that the future holds. The much sought-after future is often somewhere 'over there' and in pursuit of that Sagittarius gallops off on one journey after another. Both Gemini and Sagittarius share this restless seeking nature. While Gemini is more akin to The Fool who sets off on a journey simply for the sake of the adventure, Sagittarius often has a purpose in mind. The search for meaning is the ultimate quest of Sagittarius and through that philosophies and over-arching world views are formed. Through the history of humanity we can see that the search for meaning has birthed many different religions. As humanity has sought its place in the cosmological order it has created systems of religious belief whose limitations seem to be paradoxical to Jupiter's expansiveness, but both the energy of seeking greater truth and limitation by dogma belong to this archetype. The esoteric ruler of Sagittarius is the Earth, which gives us a clue to this paradox.

The centaur is often said to represent animal earthly nature at odds with spiritual attainment. Another way to look at this is that the spiritual instinct of human nature can either align with natural law or attempt to control it. In the next sign, Capricorn, man-made systems and structures arise to create social order. Earth, as the esoteric ruler of Sagittarius, aligns it with natural law. We can see how this has manifested by looking at earth-based religions.

Our ancient ancestors' systems of belief were aligned with natural law much more than our modern society's. Through their animal nature they were able to find a place in the cosmos, and it was their reverence for the spirit in all things that kept the societal order. Spiritual discovery meant the revelation of how spirit manifests in the physical. This is the integrated centaur not at odds with itself, but manifesting the higher Sagittarian aspects of synthesis. The human animal nature that gets out of control may not be the so-called 'base desires' of the flesh, but the need to wrestle away power from nature and the divine, rather than align with it. In Sagittarius the seed of the desire to control is present in the mental nature as the man-made systems of belief effectively create God in man's image; after all, Jupiter's tendency is towards inflation.

When one supplants the divine, someone has to stand in its place, which is how priests and preachers came into being as a part of this archetype. This sets the stage for other phenomena such as dogma and fanaticism to arise.

We only have to look at Pluto's transit through Sagittarius from 1995-2008 to see this in action. On a global scale two of the world's major religions, Christianity and Islam, engaged in a new crusade. The result was an increase in fanaticism on both sides. Mega-churches sprang up all over the United States and radical Islamic groups were at an all-time high of new recruits. Conversely, during this transit, many fell away from organized religion, to begin a quest for personal contact with the divine. There was a resurgence in the interest and teachings of Shamanism (Natural law), Wicca and Earth based religions. The wisdom of the indigenous people's elders was also prized by spiritual seekers of all kinds. Pluto's transit through Sagittarius energized humanity's relationship to its spiritual beliefs, bringing out the best and the worst equally.

The 'me-ness' of the other fire signs Aries and Leo continues into Sagittarius when it comes to beliefs. Since Sagittarius is the final fire sign, it culminates and refines the lessons of the previous two. To sit with the question, "Do I belong to the cosmos? Or does the cosmos belong to me?" is an appropriate contemplative meditation for Sagittarius. Whatever the orientation, beliefs display the same characteristics. They can be a guide to establish one's own moral compass or a platform to preach from, to convert others to one's own idea of morality.

Generalizations are akin to Sagittarius, and in general the archer is only aiming to indicate there is a path. In his purest form he is the refined energy of aspiration itself. Truth is in the eye (or heart) of the beholder. This is an insecure position for many who hold spiritual beliefs dear, and the lesson of the relativity of truth needs to be integrated from the Gemini polarity. There are many paths to the same goal. Gemini's ability to see many view points, when integrated in Sagittarius, gives it broad tolerance instead of narrow adherence to doctrine and the belief that, 'My way is the only way'. The single-pointedness of Sagittarius can either be the energy that carries one along any given path with focus, or it can make one a fanatic.

The student and teacher are other archetypes that belong to both Sagittarius and Gemini, which represent the natural impulses of the acquisition of knowledge and the desire to share what one knows. The integrated axis realizes that the student/teacher relationship is a circle; being a teacher means that one is also perpetually a student. In India, the planet Jupiter is called 'Guru' and carries all the attributes of an ideal spiritual teacher as a source of divine knowledge and guide to awaken spiritual insight.

When this archetype is part of the karmic axis, complications of student/teacher relationships can be a part of the past life experience. Sometimes there is karmic propensity to give oneself away to teachers and when this is the case, the lesson that needs to be learned is a positive reclaiming of one's own truth. In other cases one may be full of their own truths from past lives as a teacher, and may need to learn to be more inclusive of others' knowledge and points of view.

In contrast to Gemini's left brain orientation Sagittarius is associated with the right brain. Thought that is holistic, conceptual and intuitive is characteristic of the right brain. Gemini's rationality and classification of knowledge lays the foundation for the Sagittarian ability to synthesize and 'connect the dots'. Sagittarius focuses the gathering of information to synthesize it into a meaningful construct. The conflict of bridging concrete and intuitive thought is highlighted on the Gemini/Sagittarius axis and is often manifested as a difficulty in communicating one's inner intuitive knowledge.

Sagittarius in Past Life Experiences

The Sagittarius archetype is a part of the karmic axis when:

Pluto is in Sagittarius or the ninth house or
The South Node is in Sagittarius or the ninth house or
The ruler of the South Node is in Sagittarius or the ninth house or
Jupiter aspects Pluto, the nodal axis or rulers of the nodes.

Learning and Beliefs

Higher learning is a part of this archetype and in past lives there may have been difficulties in acquiring knowledge, or difficulties because of such knowledge. One client with a Sagittarius SN with Mars and Venus conjunct in the fifth house and Pluto in Virgo in the second house had a past life as a woman in Asia who was sold to an older man at a very young age as a sort of concubine. She was brought up in a decent household and was educated, but was trapped (limitations of both Virgo and the second house). She was fiery as a young girl (Sagittarius/fifth house/Mars) but had to confine that part of her nature as she grew older so as not to upset the order of the household and threaten her own survival. It became sublimated into her learning and education, which pleased her 'lord'. This was the only place she felt she had some freedom to soar (in her mind) but she was not free to explore subjects or interests that were not appropriate for women in that society. As she grew she also learned to shut down her own desire for knowledge, tragically giving up the only thing that had a semblance of freedom. As a result of that past life, in her current life she had a fear of both freedom and learning, as in her subconscious it was associated with being trapped.

Chart A

This case makes for an interesting study to understand the dynamics of the Gemini/Sagittarius axis as in this chart the nodal axis is squared, which brings both archetypes into the past life experience.

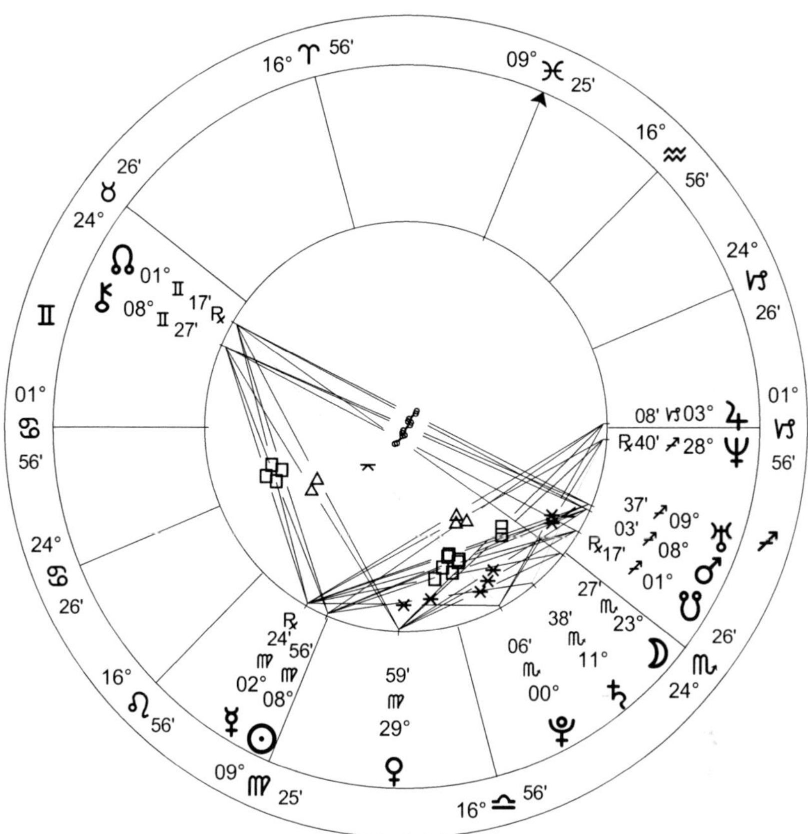

Chart A (Porphyry houses)

This client had a past life as a Native American youth who was in training and apprenticeship to become the next shaman (Sagittarius SN in the sixth). One day while he was in the mountains he was attacked by a bear, which resulted in permanent damage to his ability to speak (Gemini/Mercury square the nodes). After the attack he was in and out of consciousness and was tended to by the shaman, who was his mentor. In essence, the attack was a shamanic initiation (Mars conjunct Sagittarius SN). In this chart the archetypes of the mutable axis are all emphasized, their combination here underscores the traditional 'making of a shaman' as there is often a life-threatening illness or crisis (Virgo/sixth house) that brings one into the other worlds (Pisces/twelfth house). After such a process, both worlds are synthesized (Sagittarius) as the shaman stands as a symbol of the wisdom of the natural and spiritual worlds. He acts also as a mediator (Gemini/Virgo) and as a channel for the knowledge and application of natural law.

Eventually he healed from this attack but was unable to speak. Shortly after he recovered, he was with a friend and they saw strange ships in the water in a bay near their village. These were the ships of settlers (another aspect of Mars conjunct the Sagittarius SN – foreigners coming as invaders), and as was discussed in Gemini, these invaders caused a clash of two divergent worlds or cultures. As the client and his friend were watching from a hill, some of the men from the ships sneaked up behind them and attacked them. They were unarmed and caught off guard and were quickly overcome. His friend was slain in front of him. He was enraged (Mars) and also frenzied as he was trying to scream but was only able to produce grunting sounds. The settlers killed him by spearing him through the diaphragm up into his heart. He died not only enraged about his life being cut short (Mars) and his friend's death, but incomplete in his initiation (Mars in the sixth house) into becoming a full-fledged shaman, thus he felt thwarted in his ability to 'be in his power' (Pluto in Scorpio in the fifth house and the SN in the sixth house). The Scorpio and Leo themes of personal power and powerlessness were prevalent in many of his other past lives but are not outlined here.

In his current life he said he finds it hard to give words to what he knows, yet he has a wisdom that goes far beyond his years. Since Sagittarius is about intuitive non-linear ways of knowing, the Gemini polarity and its ability as a master of words has to be worked on to bring the Sagittarius wisdom into a form that can be communicated and shared with others. He also said in his current life he has difficulty expressing his thoughts and opinions. He has

Chiron conjunct his NN thus in opposition to the SN and Mercury and the Sun in Virgo in the third house squaring the nodes. This represents the past life wounds to his actual ability to speak. The loss of his voice and finding his voice are all represented by the Gemini NN and the square to the nodes, both literally and metaphorically. In his healing work in the spirit world, it was important to him to be able to say the things he had been unable to say in that lifetime to his friend, his mentor the shaman, and the settlers. After doing this he had a spontaneous realization that he does have the opportunity in this life to express himself even if he has to work at it. This is part of his evolution in this lifetime.

In that past life he had looked forward to being initiated fully into the ancient natural wisdom so it was imperative for him to complete his initiation in the spirit world. This unfinished initiation was also part of the reason why he has difficulty expressing his 'inner knowing'. He said that working with this past life allowed him to validate an internal knowledge of "something more natural, a connection with nature and a deeper spirituality" in his current life. He felt he was able to recapture the enthusiasm he had in that past life without a feeling of trepidation, and embraced the deep wisdom that was in him already in a new and more profound way. Another past life also showed that his tolerant belief system as the Native American and who he is today was something that he evolved towards. In an earlier life he was a priest (Sagittarius) in Egypt (Pluto/Scorpio) who was completely dogmatic in his service to his deity. In fact he was quite power hungry (Pluto in Scorpio in the fifth house) and was aligned with the darker aspects of the god Set. There was a power struggle during his life between temples, and he was slain.

Because he died as a result of his beliefs (common in the Sagittarius archetype) and his need to cling to power, in death he was quite fixated (Pluto Scorpio) on his own truth (Sagittarius). He also felt his god was invincible and would protect him, but despite that belief, he was killed, so he also died feeling betrayed (Pluto/Scorpio). His healing in the afterlife resulted in him coming to the realization that all the gods are just a reflection of a greater truth. None of them contain the whole truth or complete power. He was able to transcend his narrow views and expand them (Sagittarius), to start to perceive the divine behind the idols (Gemini NN in the twelfth). His distrust in his own vision of the divine melted away, as he started to understand the personal limitations of power (Pluto/Scorpio/fifth house) and realized that this was a main purpose of that lifetime.

Sagittarius is the truth seeker, and often souls with this archetype as a past life signature have explored many diverse belief systems. Because of this they often have in their karmic history past lives like the Egyptian priest. My cases have many Sagittarian preachers, missionaries and even Puritans (especially when combined with Virgo or Capricorn). One client with a Pluto in Virgo in the sixth house and the ruler, Mercury in Sagittarius in the tenth, had two past lives as a puritanical judge and as a revivalist style preacher. Both were steadfast in their beliefs and absolutely intolerant of others to the point of persecuting them (Capricorn/Sagittarius and Virgo).

As any soul can experience polarities in its many lives on earth to come to a complete balance of any archetype, she also was persecuted in several lives for her beliefs. Like the previous case and many others, in her current life she had a tolerant belief system aligned with the oneness of truth in all beliefs. This type of reversal and result of having experienced both sides is often the hallmark of a more mature soul, but not everyone alive today has had this experience in their soul's history. This is why we see religious wars and persecutions still very active at the present time. As the mutable cross culminates in Pisces, this shows that all belief systems eventually will need to be transcended to come to the realization of true oneness.

Intuition

When Sagittarius is a part of the karmic axis one may have spent many lifetimes in cultures or communities that were oriented more towards the intuitive and the non-linear. The intuitive function, although natural to Sagittarius, is often wounded in some way from past life experiences. Past lives, such as one in which a person had a vision or inner knowledge that they tried to share but met with persecution, ridicule or alienation, can be such a scenario. Because of this, healing and trusting one's own inner direction and voice, is often a lesson for the Sagittarius SN.

Chart B

This following story illustrates the nature of intuitive beliefs versus dogmatic thinking. The SN is in Sagittarius in the seventh house, which also brings the Libra archetype into the karmic axis. The nodes are squared by the Moon in Virgo in the fourth house and by wide orb, Mercury, which makes the archetypes of the NN and SN part of the past life experience. Pluto is in the third house opposing the Sun and Mars in the ninth, further emphasizing the Gemini/Sagittarius polarity.

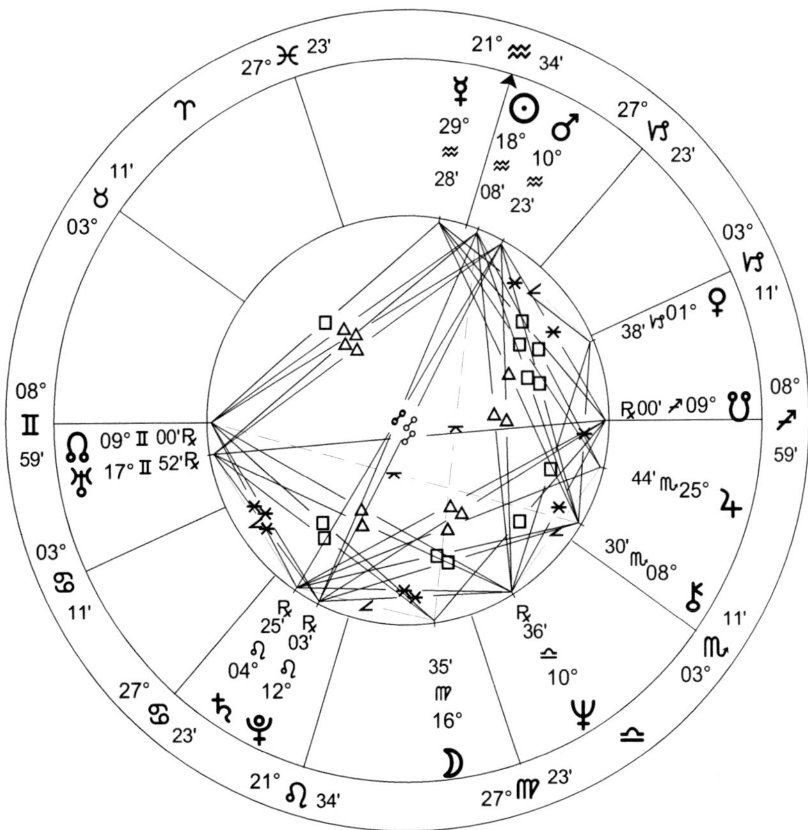

Chart B (Porphyry houses)

As a young man in the past life, he entered the monastery seeking to serve God (ruler of the SN is in the sixth and the Moon in Virgo squares the nodes). The Virgo/Pisces, sixth/twelfth house axis is also associated with Christianity. His life was spent in prayer, study, meditation and chores; he described his daily existence as communal and harmonious. He also worked as a scribe (Gemini) copying spiritual texts that were brought to the monastery. His life was deeply contemplative and he enjoyed studying and learning (Gemini/Sagittarius). His belief system was Christian, but since he had exposure to different spiritual sources, his thinking was eclectic (Uranus conjunct NN) and unconventional. Occasionally he shared his thoughts with his brother monks, but mostly he lived in silence. The abbot who ran the monastery died and was replaced by another who came from outside the order. Under this new abbot's influence, things changed in the monastery and became very dogmatic. It seemed this new abbot was less mystical than the monks; he was all about rules, order and dogma. He imposed new rules and seemed to be hunting for heresy within the order. As time went on, the previous idyllic life they lived was eclipsed by a shadow of fear and growing suspicion of each other that turned brother against brother (ruler of the SN – Jupiter in Scorpio). Any unity that existed before quickly disappeared. All of this was totally at odds with this monk's personal spiritual life and he was greatly pained and increasingly disillusioned as time went on. He felt split between fulfilling his vows of service and obedience (Gemini/Virgo) and honoring his own belief system (Sagittarius). As was mentioned in the Libra chapter, feeling split and conflicted because of trying to conform to what is expected of one is a part of the Libra/seventh house archetype. Duality is also a part of both the Gemini/Sagittarius archetypes.

As they mostly lived in silence, he was unable to share this with his brothers, but found a few occasions to speak to others about it. He was reported to the abbot because he did so, and was called in and questioned by those in power. The new abbot was already aware that forbidden knowledge had been a part of normal life here before, and told the monk he must renounce all his past knowledge. He was given time to make up his mind and was torn (Libra) with the weight of the decision. He was wracked with self doubt and questioning (Virgo) but when the time came to deliver his answer, he said he could not refute what he had come to believe (his own truth – Sagittarius) for what was now described to be the truth. Although he was not unshaken in his conviction, he stated to the abbot, "The God I know is not here anymore". The courage to speak out despite his growing self doubt and fear is an empowered aspect of the Pluto in Leo in the third house.

He was deemed a heretic and cast out of the monastery (sixth house/ Virgo – persecution). He felt totally lost outside the monastery walls, but was fortunate that a local family took him in for a time. The family was Jewish and to his surprise he learned that even his own belief system was limited and that God is larger than just the Christian God (ever expanding beliefs – Sagittarius). He was humbled by this awareness (Virgo) but also it revived his love of learning (Gemini/Sagittarius). He started to preach locally, but it seemed these were dark times of persecution. He was captured and taken into custody and again accused of heresy, tortured and died on the rack. He died confused and angry, but with work and help in the spirit world, the monk was able to reconnect with his own 'direct knowing' of the divine. This is the empowered Sagittarius that is able to transcend mental limitations through direct experience.

The client said that in her current life she always had a strange mix of attraction and repulsion to the church. While she considered herself to be deeply spiritual, and had wanted to express this through Catholic faith, she found she could not even go into a church without strong negative emotional reactions. It became clear these were a carryover from the life as a monk. She also said that she gravitated towards more non-conventional churches. However, before she knew what she was doing, she would always find herself in the position of challenging the priests on rules and doctrine. This was certainly her Gemini NN in the first house acting out from the wounded monk's perspective. It would seem this past life monk living inside her was still trying to find healing. After working with the monk she found that the need to confront religious authorities to 'prove' her point lessened, as this part of her was now healed and at ease with its own truth.

Truth

'To thine own self be true' is an appropriate dictum for Sagittarius. This truth-seeking aspect of Sagittarius also relates to one's own internal beliefs about oneself that may not be aligned with 'truth'. Both Sagittarius and Capricorn are associated with integrity, honor codes and an essential form of truth or honesty that needs to be realized and actualized in the consciousness. While the polarity point Gemini is associated with outright lies because of its duality and trickster nature, Sagittarius also can bend truth by exaggeration, compensation and self-righteous justifications. Believing in an inflated ideal more than what actually is, can cause the truth itself to become misshapen. Essential honesty about oneself and others is necessary for Sagittarius' psychological health. When Gemini/Sagittarius are a part of the karmic axis, issues of truth versus mistruths come to the forefront.

The Hero

> "There is another way if you have courage...
> [The way] is unknown and so requires faith
> The kind of faith that issues from despair
> The destination cannot be described;

You will know very little until you get there
You will journey blind
But the way leads towards possession
Of what you have sought for in the wrong place"

T.S. Eliot *The Cocktail Party* (1949)

In contrast to the immediacy of its opposite – Gemini, long range vision and distant goals are the fuel for Sagittarius' fire. Gemini often cannot see the forest through the trees, but Sagittarius does the opposite, and needs to learn to see the trees in the forest. This is often expressed in past lives as not having been able to see what was right in front of one. Like Dorothy and her journey through Oz, or knights off on long quests, one often comes to the conclusion that what they were looking for 'out there' was always within their grasp if only they had looked in the right place. Often the journey ends up pointing one back to oneself, to the power within. This relates to the search for the authentic self which is a hallmark of Sagittarius and is reflected in the archetypal Hero's Journey.

Sagittarius concludes the interpersonal segment of the zodiac wheel and as a transitional, mutable archetype, opens the way to the transpersonal development that happens in the final three signs. Sagittarius has elements of the hero's journey in it, and in past lives either literally or symbolically, it was necessary to set off on a journey to meet with challenges and find the ability to overcome them to discover a truth or power about oneself (the authentic self). The Hero's Journey was a favorite topic of Joseph Campbell, whose book *The Hero with a Thousand Faces* popularized the term and has now become a classic. Joseph Campbell outlines that many myths have a universal theme that could be boiled down to what he described as the stages of the hero's journey.

A few modern myths such as the *Star Wars* and *The Lord of the Rings* trilogies reflect an archetypal rehashing of more ancient stories. George Lucas in fact credits Campbell at length for influencing and informing his creation of *Star Wars* and J.R.R. Tolkien was well versed in ancient Norse and other mythologies. I have noticed in my ninth house and Sagittarian Sun sign clients, that many of them have missing or distant fathers which causes them to either seek the archetype of father internally or externally. But this is much like the classic hero who is often fatherless, like Frodo and Luke Skywalker. Often in myth the budding hero is mentored or protected by a wise male elder such as Gandalf or Yoda. These mentors represent the father that the hero must learn from, but whose qualities he eventually must find within himself. In Sagittarius the quest begins, and continues into Capricorn where one eventually becomes the wizened authority themselves. The Sagittarian stage of the hero's journey is what Campbell names 'The Call to Adventure'. The budding hero receives his calling and either reluctantly or enthusiastically sets off on the journey. The entire journey will ultimately bring the hero back to himself, in a new and more authentic way.

The Capricorn leg of the journey calls forth not only self-determination and strength forged by tests, but the integrative stage that Campbell calls 'Atonement with the Father' or at-one-ment. The hero must reconcile not only the positive, but also negative aspects of the father within himself. This is the de-conditioning that happens in Capricorn, where confining external structures are internalized and eventually cast off. Having internalized the father archetype and matured because of the trials of the journey, the hero can begin to embody what was sought after, in his own way. Further individuation takes place in Aquarius. The hero's journey also often requires that he return home with his new powers or gifts and in doing so must face how to integrate these two worlds. This phase leads to the final two stages where after integrating this acquired power and growth he is able to pass between the realms and becomes the 'Master of the Two Worlds'. He is like the fish of Pisces here, able to swim in both directions, and also like the integrated centaur, able to bridge heaven and earth.

The ultimate goal of the hero's journey is to accomplish 'The Freedom to Live'. In this stage the hero is now transfigured and is beyond death himself (immortal), he has transcended his limitations and is even beyond the struggle of duality (again the duality and potential integration of the centaur, and Pisces). The hero is also required to share with others what has been learned for the benefit of all; this alludes to not only the natural teacher of Sagittarius, but Aquarius who through his own individuation is able to share his gifts with all humanity.

The final stages of the journey are represented clearly in *The Lord of the Rings* by Frodo's conflict when he returned to Bag End. Frodo returned home, yet was still weary with his journey and as part of his process he wrote about his travels. This stage is Gemini/Sagittarian as it represents his process of learning to integrate the two worlds by putting it into a tangible form of communication. After completing his writing Frodo was eventually granted the boon of leaving Middle Earth with both his 'earthy father

(Uncle Bilbo)' and 'other-worldly father (Gandalf)' to the eternal realm of the elves. Leaving behind his knowledge, in the form of a book to be continued by Sam, he passed on his wisdom. Frodo's leaving on the ship represents the hero's final transfiguration where he and the journey are no longer separate; he has gained mastery of the two worlds and is now released from his strife with the 'Freedom to Live'. His very essence radiates the wisdom gained as there is no more conquest, he has relinquished 'doing' and is now pure 'being' (Sagittarius culminating in Pisces).

While heroism in epic myths underscores a symbolic journey we all might take, we can also get stuck in an unhealthy hero role. Like its cousins, the Helper (Virgo) and the Savior (Pisces), one can express heroism to the detriment of oneself. It's not unusual that people in the helping and healing professions struggle with different degrees of savior or heroic complexes. This next case shows a version of 'atonement' with a missing father, and how the eternal bonds of love between a father and son resulted in both of them being saved by a mutual hero/savior complex.

Chart C

This chart shows the main imprints of Savior and Hero coming from the Pisces and Sagittarius archetypes. The nodal axis is squared by both Venus and Jupiter in Pisces in the seventh house, bringing all these archetypes into the karmic history. The ruler of the SN is Mercury in Aries in the ninth house. Transiting Pluto was activating his nodal axis and Venus square at the time of these sessions as it was 17 degrees Sagittarius, also culminating its fourth house transit. It was certainly an opportune time for this man to heal familial karmas. A little current life background is needed to understand the past life scenarios. This client had always had a desire to help others in crisis situations. He had been a lifeguard and emergency ambulance worker (EMT). But since his father died three years earlier he had become very depressed and seemed to have lost his direction in life. Before his father's death, they had an argument on the phone and instead of visiting him later that day, as he had planned, he didn't because he was angry. That day his father died suddenly of a heart attack. The client had immense buried guilt that he was in denial of, and unconscious about (Pisces planets in the seventh house). He also mentioned that since his father's death he had often felt the father's spirit around him, and a few times his radio had turned on by itself, playing a song that was significant to both of them. This was comforting to him, and I confirmed that when spirits have the ability to cross between the worlds in a positive way, they are showing that they are okay on the other side.

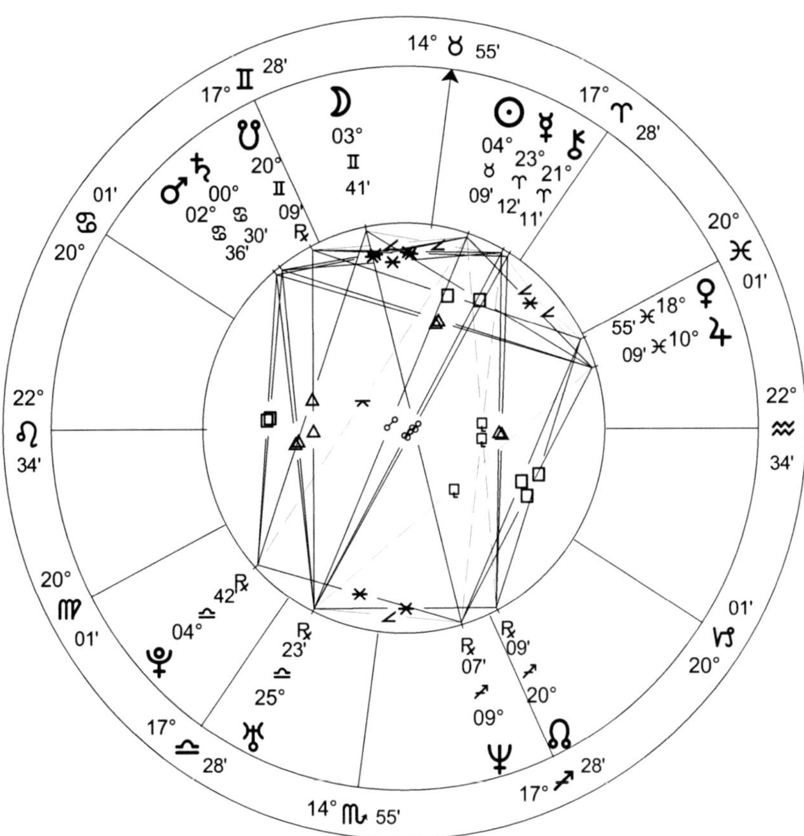

Chart C (Porphyry houses)

This first scene of this past life started in the after-death state as a young woman sitting in a rocking chair, seeming to be in a state of shock, rocking back and forth muttering, "Why, why, why?" It became obvious she was already dead, out of her body but still earthbound in shock. Going back to what had happened, she had hidden under a table and witnessed her son and husband murdered by an attacker with an axe and then was murdered herself. Immediately the client said, "My husband in that life, was my father in this life". As the woman in that life, she had died with the thoughts, "Why me? I could have saved them. Why didn't I do anything?" She had judged herself as being a coward (fifth house/Sagittarius), and was angry at herself that she hid.

In reality, as we went back through this past life, it was plain that the woman had been in no position to have done anything. She had lived with her husband and son in a cabin as a happy young family. A man from a neighbouring town that they had some business with, became infatuated with her (Venus in Pisces in the seventh). This man had come to the cabin a few times, and on the third visit her husband made the boundary clear and threatened to hurt him if he came back again. It was this man who brought her family to a sudden, violent end (Pluto square Mars in Cancer in the eleventh). After working in the afterlife with this woman, my client still was unable to let go of the guilt, despite the spirits of her husband and child affirming that it was not her fault. In therapy, this is often an indicator that more than one past lifetime is involved in this imprint.

In another past life he found himself as a young man with his father in a car that had just been in a serious accident in the 1930s. He lay there nearly dead waiting for help. Again he was in shock (SN in the eleventh), knowing that his father had died but not wanting to accept it (denial of Pisces and seventh house). Eventually he died just as people came to help.

As a spirit, he stayed around the accident scene after his death, confused and in a daze (Pisces). In working with him, I reminded him that he had died, and that his father had died also. He was guided to join the spirit of his father and after their reunion he and his father's spirit went into the light. This was the same father from his current life and he started to see him as he knew him before. On seeing his father, he started to deeply sob and poured out his heart to him. It brought up the repressed guilt and he told his father how guilty he felt, that he hadn't been there to save him in that lifetime. His father told him that it had been his time to die and that he could have saved him this time (his EMT training) but it had been arranged on other levels for him not to be there when he died.

His father told him there were other lives, beyond the ones he had just re-experienced, where he had seen him die many times before, that he wanted to end that pattern for both of them. His father further revealed that in another lifetime he and his son were soldiers together but not related. In that life his father was in a position to call for a retreat during an ambush in which his present life son was a part of the platoon. As he directed his men to make a desperate retreat, they were overcome and slaughtered. He watched the whole platoon be destroyed and was wracked with guilt before he was killed. This had also contributed to the pattern of his father feeling he needed to 'die in front of his son' to atone for his guilt. So this current life action was freeing for him also, and he said the next time they met they would not have the complexities of this issue between them (completion of a co-dependent sacrificial pattern – Pisces/seventh house). This pattern of a soldier being slaughtered on the battlefield is present within the son's chart (SN in the eleventh – mass trauma; the ruler in Aries – the warrior and life cut short; killed during a retreat – ninth house).

The unconditional love between them was palpable and so was the grace and compassion that filled the room during this session (Venus conjunct Jupiter in Pisces in the seventh). This exchange allowed him to finally forgive himself and find peace with his father's death. Further, the part of him that was stuck in overdrive as a hero and savior could now ease, as he and his father were both free. This had been the evolutionary intention already indicated by Pluto's transit to the Sagittarius NN and karmic axis, which is why he had lost all his zeal for his previous heroic roles, although until these imprints were resolved he had been depressed by this. Now it was clearer to him that he had to find new ways to express himself without these roles (fifth house). He is also a ninth house Sun which follows what was written on the fatherless hero's journey, although his once earthly father was now a spirit guide for him. The past life scenarios with his father are also indicated by the Pluto/Saturn square, but additionally Saturn in his chart may be looked at as a symbol for his current life father. It has not only the nurturing and caring of Cancer but is also a force of liberation that the eleventh house represents. Saturn is also at 0 degrees which is a culminating signature.

Freedom and Travel

Literal past life journeys are a part of this archetype, as is the search and need for freedom. The Sagittarian soul has explored not only diverse belief systems but also many different cultures. In past lives, issues of immigration and nomadic lifestyles come into focus. Often the desire for freedom is what drives such a journey. The wide open plains of the Wild West in the USA, conjures such images and by astrological geodetic equivalents, that area is ruled by Sagittarius. Pioneers are most common in the Aries archetype but also show up in Sagittarius, especially when the past life was in the United States. Just as Native American lives show up frequently in Sagittarius so do cowboys, mountain men, outlaws and other mid-western lives.

Immigration involves a long journey to a foreign land and often immigrants are filled with optimism and hope. But difficulty or deaths during journeys in a past life can squash such hopes and leave one with a present life dread of travel.

Forced immigration is another issue that often involves combinations of Sagittarius/Capricorn/Scorpio and Taurus and can include lives as a refugee. One client with a Sagittarius SN and Saturn conjunct in the eleventh house was a small child on the run (Sagittarius) with family and a group of Jews during the Holocaust. Their short-lived attempt to flee to freedom (Saturn/Sagittarius) was thwarted when they were captured. Prior to the capture this young boy had become ill and was already struggling to stay alive and keep up with them (Saturnian burden). As the group was being prepared to be transported to a camp, he died. His own trauma (eleventh house) of flight and then capture was further complicated by the group's trauma (eleventh house) as he died in a cloud of their collective thought, "Were doomed, there is no tomorrow". Carrying this into the current life he had not only an underlying anxiety about any travel but also a pervasive fear of the future.

Another client with a Pluto in Virgo in the ninth house, had a past life as a man assisting slaves to freedom in the Underground Railroad. This particular past life was not traumatic but working with it rekindled a floundering passion for his current life work as a social worker assisting homeless African Americans.

Another version of travel and journeys is reflected also in the action of running away. This echoes not only Gemini but the escapism of Pisces. The issue of self-judgment is often operative as the person may consider themselves to be a coward, because they ran away. Several of my Sagittarius SN clients have had lifetimes where freedom was more important to them than what was immediate (Gemini polarity) and they simply ran away from the challenges presented. One such story is recounted at the end of the Aquarius chapter (Sagittarius SN in the eleventh house). The lessons of the Gemini polarity in these instances is about learning to face what is happening in the now.

Chart D

This chart has a Sagittarius SN in the twelfth house with its ruler Jupiter in Libra in the tenth. Jupiter is squared by Saturn which is conjunct Mars. Many of this client's past life stories take place as either a soldier/warrior or a monk/priest. Since Pluto is in the seventh house and Jupiter is in Libra the issue of swinging to extremes to find balance is a large part of his karmic history. Involvement in Christianity and the church comes from his nodes being on the twelfth/sixth house axis as well as the Sagittarius archetype. One of his past life monk stories is shared in the Pisces chapter along with his chart, shown also below.

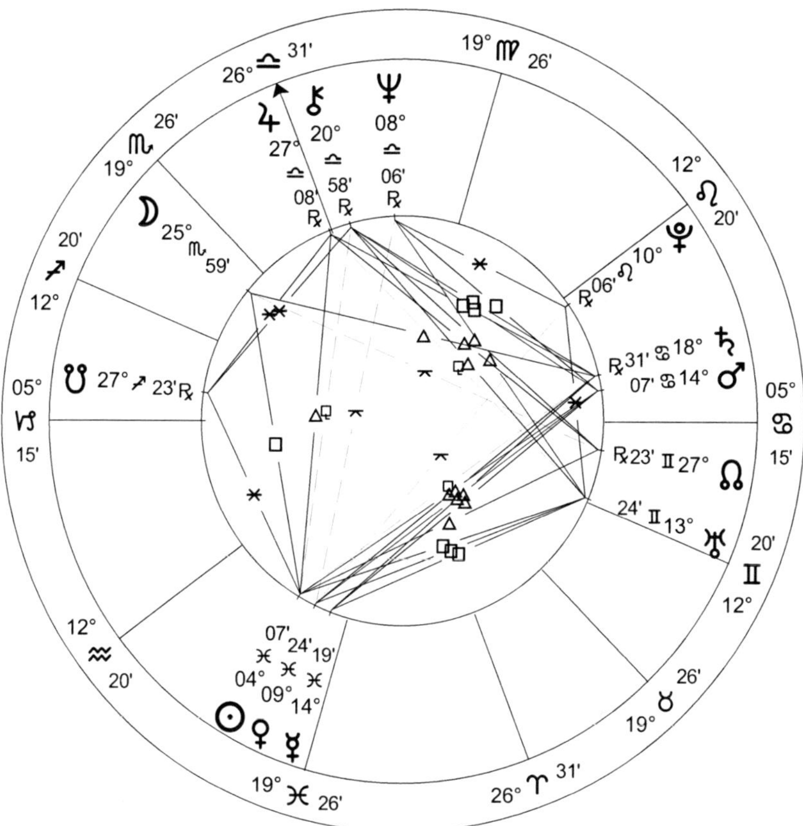

Chart D (Porphyry houses)

In one past life, in the midst of the battlefield, he had an epiphany about the nature of beliefs (Sagittarius). He was a young religious man in the Middle Ages, who was invited to a special meeting at the church one day. At the meeting he was asked if he wanted to become a soldier for Christ (ruler of SN in the tenth). He commented that, "I loved the church, but I also was young and wanted something more adventurous" (Sagittarius/twelfth house). Feeling completely inspired he signed up to become a future crusader. After several years of training he was knighted and set off with fervor (Sagittarius) to take back the Holy Land. He proved to be a heroic skilled fighter and also self-righteous in his beliefs. He said, "I live and die by the honor code. I lived for inspiration; it was like food to me", (both Sagittarius and tenth house).

Several years and battles later, his epiphany came in the midst of raising his sword to slay an enemy. In one instant he said, "I looked in his eyes and saw he had intense light. He was just as inspired as I was. I realized we were fighting for the same reason, but we called God different names. We both were aiming for the same goal". (Sagittarius SN in twelfth). This realization of oneness devastated him, as the insanity of it all exploded into his awareness (Sagittarius/twelfth house – revelation of truth). The 'enemies' spared each other's lives and he collapsed on the battlefield.

After the battle a captain came to him to see what was going on and the crusader poured his heart out to him, with tears in his eyes (Pluto Leo in the seventh, also Jupiter in Libra – heart and feeling). "We all come from the same God; we all belong to the same light". This outpouring was met with tenth house disdain and the captain screamed at him, "How dare you spare an infidel", and whacked him in the knees with his broadsword (also Saturn/tenth house ruled), as if trying to knock sense into him; spat on him and abandoned him there. Left on the battlefield, the crusader was crippled (Chiron conjunct Jupiter) and alone.

He eventually was able to make his way into town, but feeling dishonored he never rejoined his order. He lived the rest of his days as a beggar filled with remorse and shame (Saturn/tenth house). The disillusionment (twelfth house) followed him into the afterlife and his healing there consisted of having a direct contact with the light again. His shame was lifted and he was assured by his beloved Christ that his realization was true and that his intention was honorable (Sagittarius/tenth house and Pisces). He re-met with his former enemies and they clasped arms spontaneously in an act of spiritual brotherhood (Sagittarius – the brotherhood of humanity). This lifetime, like the next one recounted here, was about his 'unlearning' of the man-made systems of belief. He had to come to the truth of the relativity of beliefs (Gemini). Capricorn/Saturn and the tenth house are archetypes of 'de-conditioning' from such artificial structures. The operative mode was through disillusionment (twelfth house) which brought him to the clear-eyed reality of the sixth house.

In another lifetime he was a young man in Italy in the early church who joined the priesthood full of devotion (Sagittarius/twelfth house). Unfortunately through the politics of the church (Jupiter in the tenth) he became corrupted, and his spiritual devotion turned into a love of power. As he moved up the ladder of success (Saturn/tenth house) he became unrecognizable even to himself (loss of authentic self – Sagittarius in the twelfth). He commented that, "In the act of forgiving people you could control them. You could sell them indulgences, like candy to children". The control issues of Saturn and the tenth house are inflated by Jupiter's presence. He was also very charismatic and used this to his advantage frequently (Libra and Sagittarius). He died in old age as a high ranking church official, but was only a shell of a person. In the afterlife he was filled with remorse as he reviewed his life from the spirit world. He said, "We created an entire structure – the church, and it was all a lie. It's only use was to control people and make money. I believed this lie, I lost my true meaning, I knew the truth and I gave it up for the form". He said his learning was about not being deluded by appearance (Libra/seventh house, and form – tenth/Saturn).

Like the crusader a large part of his healing was his ability to regain his original pure motive and intent (Sagittarius/twelfth house) and to be aligned with expansive universal truths. He sought for forgiveness in the spirit world from Christ also, and it was freely given to him. He learned that he had to reach the pinnacle of power so that he would learn how limited it is without real love. His Pluto is also conjunct the eight house cusp; both Leo and Scorpio's lessons of power are a part of his learning. His NN in Gemini in the sixth combined with its ruler and the other Pisces planets in the second house, implies a practical path of service, which happens in the here and now. It also has to do with his ability to embody his natural spirituality. His story in the Pisces chapter clearly illustrates this. Because Pluto is in Leo and the seventh house, several of his other past life stories have had to do with the lessons of giving and receiving love and also following his heart. In reviewing some of his karmic lessons he said, "I feel I've been trying to come to a balance between will and heart (Pluto on the seventh/first house axis). I've been learning to come from a place of authenticity and clarity. I've also been learning a lot about 'idiot compassion' as opposed to real service".

This last thought is a main lesson of the Pisces/Virgo axis – discernment. In his current life he was involved for many years in Theosophical study and was a minister of a Unitarian church. He also founded his own business to provide home-schooling materials for children, based on the Waldorf principles of education. His involvement with progressive and holistic early education is a beautiful expression of his manifestation of the Sagittarius/Gemini axis. Interestingly Rudolph Steiner (esotericist and philosopher who was the originator of the Waldorf schools and founder of his own form of Christ-centered theosophical thought – Anthroposophy) had his own SN in the ninth house with the NN in the third.

10

Capricorn/Saturn and the Tenth House

"Sometimes a man stands up during supper
and walks outdoors, and keeps on walking,
because of a church that stands somewhere in the East.
And his children say blessings on him as if he were dead.

And another man, who remains inside his own house,
dies there, inside the dishes and in the glasses,
so that his children have to go far out into the world
toward that same church, which he forgot."

Rainer Maria Rilke

Keywords

Cardinal/Earth/Yin
Honor
Social position
Authority
Judgment
Judge
Maturity
Old age
Structure
Reality
Repression
Responsibility
Oppression
Grief
Punishment
Discipline

Sobriety
Totalitarian
Fear
Authority
Rigid
Paralysis
Conformity
Isolation
Conditioning by
(family/society)
Man-made law
Ancestral
Tradition
Guilt
Self defeat/saboteur

Futility
History
Patriarchy
Experience
Suicide
Boundaries
Structure/form
Nationalism
Patriotism
Politics
Responsibility
Depression
Burden
'Fall from grace'
Accomplishment

The Natural Archetype

The expansiveness of Jupiter-ruled Sagittarius meets Saturn's boundary in Capricorn. Expansion and contraction are natural cycles in the material world. The atom which is the building block for all matter demonstrates this by expanding with heat (fire) and contracting with cold (earth). Capricorn/ Saturn and the tenth house represent the underlying structures existent in everything from matter to societal systems.

The mountain goat and the sea goat symbols for Capricorn both represent the process of ascent. The mountain goat which climbs the earthly mountain stands as a symbol for attainment of either material or spiritual wealth. The sea goat emerges from the watery depths onto dry land, showing not only the maturing process that the ego (the Cancer polarity point) undergoes through worldly experience, but also that one is equipped for the climb up the spiritual mountain to grow beyond egoic limitations. Sagittarius provided the vision of the mountaintop and the forward momentum; movement into Capricorn plunks one down at the base, to now apply all that has been learned and reach the top with permanence.

Capricorn awakens us to the higher frequency of spirit and the non-form. "In Capricorn we have the triumph of matter; it reaches its densest and most concrete expression; but this triumph is followed by that of spirit. There is full expression of the earthly nature in Capricorn, but also immense spiritual possibilities." (Alice Bailey, *Esoteric Astrology*)[1].

One either reaches the height of personal ambition, or relinquishes that to climb the mountain even higher, to become a spiritual initiate in Capricorn. It is simply a matter of what one desires and where one is in their evolutionary process. From the esoteric perspective, Capricorn is where the material world reaches its pinnacle of expression and butts against its inherent limitations. After surmounting all that the world has to offer one can go even higher.

Capricorn is also associated with old age, maturity and the end of life process. Archetypically, the end of life is when we prepare for the next stage of the journey into the afterlife. Our 'golden years', like the Golden Age that Saturn presided over, represents another type of enjoying the fruit of one's labors; the gains of earthly life morph into the wealth of spirit. Leaving behind our body in death is symbolic also for the many things we outgrow

1. Bailey, Alice A, Esoteric Astrology, Lucis Trust, NY, NY. (p.171)

during our lifetime. The physical rings of the planet Saturn are often said to represent the boundaries of ego consciousness (the limit of how much we can grow in our personality selves) and so is looked at simultaneously as the limitations and the mastery of the ego self.

The polarity point of Cancer is where the ego and self-image was formed. Mother is the dominate archetype there, as she models the inner world, and through her womb and our early childhood experiences, we develop the container (ego self) and emotional security to emerge into the world. In Capricorn it is the archetype of Father which is predominant. We learn from father how things work in the outer world. Our ego-self is tested and hardened through earthly experience and by meeting the conditions of larger society. Archetypically, it is the father that encourages and teaches the skills of adult adaptation, so that one can rise to a position of usefulness in the world. Through this he models and represents career, achievement, healthy competition and the voice of the laws, traditions and social norms that must be internalized to be accepted in one's culture. Cancer learns from Capricorn to reach maturity; to grow up. This means taking full responsibility for own lives, not only in the way we make it in the world but for the content of our character and the manifestation of our souls.

In Sagittarius the Hero's journey was discussed and this hero lives on through Capricorn. Sagittarius represented the beginning of the quest for the authentic self; the gaining of allies and also the integration of the journey after the return home. Capricorn represents the developed abilities that come from overcoming trial and challenges on the journey. Personal responsibility, discipline and mastery are forged by struggle. An important component of the hero's journey is the influence of the father or the mentor. Joseph Campbell named one of the many stages of the journey "Atonement with the Father". Often the hero is fatherless, which still shapes his psychology as it causes him to seek him in the external world. He often is mentored by a wise worldly or other-worldly substitute. This 'earthly' or 'magical/heavenly' father stands as a mirror, to reflect back to the hero what is already within him, but yet unrealized. The hero must overcome his own limitations to find the father's qualities within himself, by forging self-determination and stamina on 'The Road of Trials'. In myth the father can be either a helpful guide or a fearsome enemy. Either way, reconciliation allows the hero to become 'at one' with the father, which represents his initiation into maturity and results in him becoming his own authority.

The Cancer and Capricorn archetypes both are associated with conditioning received from family and society. Traditions and the way things 'should be' can be carried within, well into our adulthood before we start to question their validity for our lives. In Cancer the sensitivity of the psyche to imprinting is highlighted, while in Capricorn the ability to outgrow it is the desired aim. This is not to say that all tradition is limiting and must be cast off; there can be value to some of the psychic inheritance that is passed down by ancestry or lineages. But it is only when we consciously sift through these inheritances, rather than just unconsciously enact them, that we discover whose life we are really living. The maturing influence of Capricorn urges us to overcome the idealized image of our parents, to integrate the reality of their influence on us and to change what doesn't work for us anymore. When we outgrow these aspects of our child selves we discover it is possible to create our own reality.

Capricorn in Past Life Experiences

The Capricorn archetype is a part of the karmic axis when:

Pluto is in Capricorn or the tenth house or
The South Node is in Capricorn or the tenth house or
The ruler of the South Node is in Capricorn or the tenth house or
Saturn aspects Pluto, the nodal axis or rulers of the nodes.

Conditioning and Responsibility

An empowered aspect of Capricorn is the ability to take charge and responsibility. But it isn't hard to see how that can also become burdensome. In past life scenarios one may have been born into a role of responsibility without ever having the chance to question it. Just as Libra (another cardinal sign naturally square to Capricorn) has the propensity to conform to expectations from others, Capricorn will shoulder the responsibility of those expectations often without question, but not without cost to oneself. Evolutionary growth for this archetype involves a process of de-conditioning from previous roles. The Cancer polarity point can be looked at as the potential to birth oneself anew, just as the crab periodically sheds its shell to grow a new one.

Chart A

This following story illustrates the extremes of societal and familial pressures as a karmic pattern, as this chart has not only a Libra SN but also Pluto in the tenth house with Venus, which is the ruler of the SN in opposition, and Jupiter in Capricorn squaring the nodes. Thus he has a strong signature of Capricorn as it relates to his past lives. The wounded Capricorn themes of oppressive authority, repressed frozen emotions and fear are also very predominant. In this past life he was born into royalty (Pluto in Leo). Being born into positions of societal privilege such as a ruling or military class are also common in the Capricorn archetype, as it relates to political structures and ancestry. He had experienced his father as cold and authoritative since he was young and said he "rules by fear" (Leo/Capricorn). He described

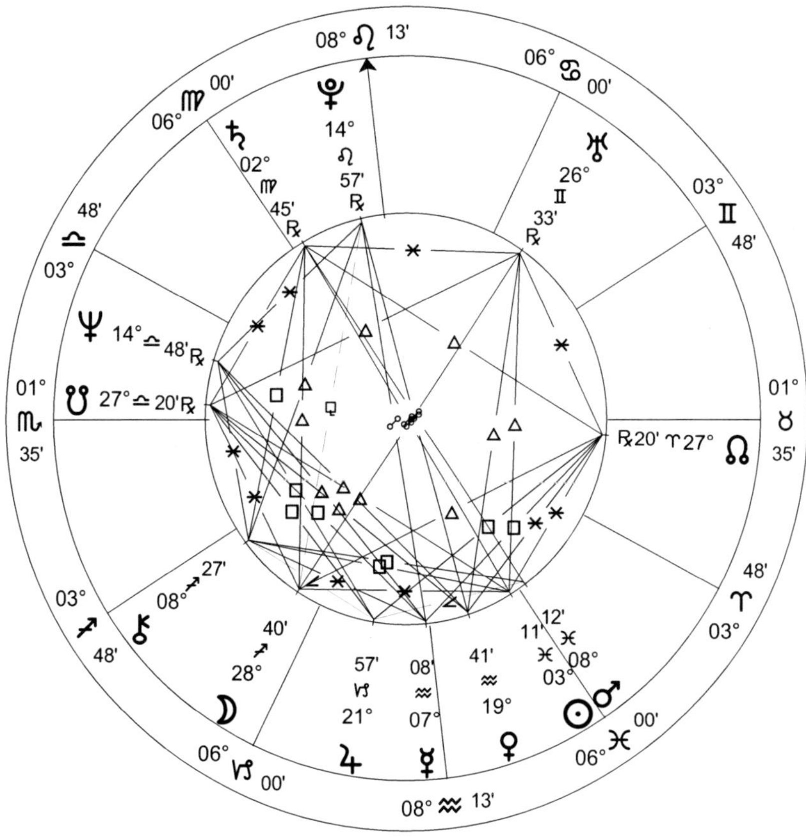

Chart A (Porphyry houses)

himself at the age of seven as already having no feelings. He said it feels as if "I am stone cold", there is "no love, no joy". This is the combination of the Leo and Capricorn archetype, the heart and joy of Leo in this early childhood was simply squashed, or in Capricorn terms oppressed. Venus (ruler of the SN) is also in the fourth in Aquarius – detachment. As he grew older it was ingrained within him without question that he had to keep with the family tradition and follow in his father's footsteps and he became a cold authoritarian type leader himself (Capricorn). The aspect of Capricorn conditioning was very strong in this lifetime, and the young man grew up feeling "there's no way out", which caused his sense of futility to be stronger than the ability to perceive other options (Jupiter in Capricorn in the third house).

As he grew into his position of leadership, he indeed did end up ruling mainly through the same control and fear he was raised with. He said at this point, "It's all about fear". He knew also that the people did not truly respect him; in fact he felt that they actually despised him (Capricorn wound to one's ability to have healthy authority). As his life progressed he fell into deep depression and self-recrimination, he actually despised who he had become, but felt powerless to change it (Pluto in the tenth and Capricorn limited options of the third house). Feeling completely hopeless, he decided he could not go on and committed suicide by stabbing himself.

One view of depression is that it is anger turned inwards; stabbing oneself to death is quite a literal expression of that. Past life suicide in the Capricorn archetype is often enacted from a place of futility, hopelessness and deep grief. For this single past life, the necessity for him to de-condition from unquestioned past life expectations from others (Libra) and from familial/societal roles (tenth/fourth house) is obvious. The 'hardening' of his emotions and feeling nature is also represented by the Venus in Aquarius in the fourth house opposed by Pluto. Rescuing his own past life inner child from oppression was a part of his healing from this lifetime, and represented Pluto's polarity point of the fourth house.

This story also points out the personal price that is paid when one's emotions are repressed. When Capricorn is a part of the karmic axis there is always some reclaiming of the emotional nature that needs to happen for healing and evolution to occur. Capricorn needs to realign itself with the emotional body, and through that, find an internal sense of security. One of the biggest fears in the Capricorn archetype is the loss of control, which is also a part of its healing. The Cancer polarity point beckons one to re-immerse themselves in the waters of emotion. The ebb and flow of its tides can erode and soften the hardened edges formed from lifetimes of emotional repression. This is hardly the solid rocky ground that Capricorn is used to, which is why it feels so scary, simply because emotions are unpredictable. The sea goat as a symbol for Capricorn has the potential to be both a land and sea creature, as does its polarity point, the crab. The image of the sea goat is showing that true mastery of emotions is not accomplished through control or repression but by becoming fused with them. It also is an appropriate symbol to show that no matter where you go, your emotions are right behind you, as are your early life (or prior life) experiences. As William Faulkner once wrote, "The past isn't dead and buried. In fact, it isn't even past". The exoskeleton of the Cancerian crab becomes the internal bone structure in Capricorn (which rules the skeletal structure) showing how our lives are built upon the foundations of the past and how deeply they are internalized.

The Holocaust

Past lives of hardship and over-responsibility can become so ingrained in the consciousness that one forgets over the course of lifetimes that there is comfort to be found through connecting with others and in the inner self. The self-care and nurturing that Cancer represents often needs to be rediscovered. Past life scenarios, such as responsibility thrust onto one as a child, can leave the eternal inner child within feeling quite undernourished and downtrodden. Impoverishment and deprivation of various forms comes under this archetype in past lives. Depression formed in a past life that is unresolved carries forward into the present, and one can feel they are born under a cloud of hopelessness, pessimism and grief. Since this archetype has durability, time and crystallization are a part of its associations. The imprints formed from past lives are not always from acute events but represent cumulative, long standing patterns that may have taken a lifetime or several to form. The effects of long standing depressive imprints are often felt as a lingering and pervasive grief. Oppression, depression, repression and suppression are the four apocalyptic horsemen in this archetype that lie behind such doom and gloom. In Capricorn there are some common past life scenarios that often carry all four of these imprints; slavery, imprisonment/captivity and lives in the Holocaust (or similar situations).

The most commonly used natal chart for old Germany is January 1, 1871, 1pm, Versailles, France. Alternately another popular one is January 18, 1871 at 12 midnight in Berlin. Either way, the SN for this country is in Capricorn with Saturn conjunct. The Sun and Mercury are also in Capricorn. The January 1st chart has the SN in the eighth house, combining the archetypes of Scorpio and Capricorn of which the darkest shadow of both were expressed through the Holocaust. Hitler also had a Capricorn SN along with Jupiter and the Moon conjunct. His natal Pluto was in the eighth house combining the same karmic archetypes as Germany's chart.

The Holocaust is not exclusive to the Capricorn archetype but does show up most frequently in clients' past lives with Capricorn, Scorpio (extremes of life and death), Taurus (survival) and Virgo/Pisces (victim). The Capricorn archetype as it relates to the Holocaust represents: repressive political regimes (dictatorship); oppression; tyranny; fanatical adherence to 'the law' and the normalization of such inhumanity (the ends justify the means). Germany as a society during that time, demonstrated the harshest aspects of a culture that prized conformity more than humanity. Capricorn Sun, Martin Luther King Jr, observed how easy it is to normalize atrocity by reminding us to "Never forget that everything Hitler did in Germany was legal". He also noted that, "The means we use must be as pure as the ends we seek". Capricorn can get into dangerous territory when its desire for accomplishment is not aligned with true honor and integrity.

Many of my clients with Capricornian holocaust experiences carried imprints into their current lives of a permeating sense of futility (depression), grief (frozen sadness) and a deprivation consciousness (impoverishment), showing that a current life pervasive feeling of "What's the use?" can have a much darker past life root. The polarity point of Cancer is present as a beacon for healing from such past life horrors. One who is born feeling "Why even care?" can find in the Cancer polarity point the essence of compassionate caring and ability to nourish one's past unmet emotional needs.

Imprisonment and Slavery

Past life death in captivity, slavery, imprisonment or even physically dying trapped, can leave a part of the soul still stuck there. This is another common root of current life depression and a feeling of general 'stuck-ness' I have seen in past life work and often Capricorn/Saturn plays its part.

One client with Saturn conjunct an Aquarius SN in the eleventh house had several lives of imprisonment and slavery. At the time of this regression she was at a stage in her life of expressing a greater sense of her individuality (Aquarius/eleventh house and a reaching towards the Leo NN) yet simultaneously felt fear and an unexplained guilt about it (Saturn). This underlies the fact that the archetypes of liberation (Aquarius) and limitation (Saturn) don't work that smoothly together, despite the fact that Saturn does co-rule Aquarius (this is discussed further in Aquarius). Prior to this regression, she described herself as feeling "deep sadness, as if I am looking up at a window filled with light that I cannot get to".

As it turned out in this past life, that image had not only a symbolic meaning but was also literal. She went back to the past as a young man in colonial America who was part of a Quaker group. Although this group was not completely outcast they didn't fully fit in (Aquarius), preferring to meet discreetly and keeping what happened behind closed doors to themselves. It seemed that the cultural environment was one of "don't ask, don't tell", which was not really tolerance but kept things running smoothly (Saturn). This young man also had quite a good career, as he was an accountant for his grandfather's shipping company (Saturn). He had lost his own father when he was young and went to stay with his grandfather (Saturn/Aquarius). His relationship with his grandfather was not strained but was mostly cordial and businesslike (Saturn – ancestral inheritance/elders). He often went to the docks to tally inventories of freshly arrived shipments for taxes.

He was rather shy and bookish and was easily intimidated by the ship's crew, and although they were not overt in harassing him, he felt their silent hostility (Saturn) towards him. They also were decidedly much more macho than he was. The crew started to smuggle goods in along with regular shipments. He noticed this during his inventories but feeling silently threatened by them, out of fear (Saturn) he overlooked it. This of course was what the crew wanted, so they kept smuggling and he kept silent. Eventually the authorities found out and arrested the young man as he was the one responsible for reporting all imported goods for taxation. He was quickly tried and imprisoned. During the trial he felt so shamed that he could not raise his eyes to the judge, or his grandfather. He refused to speak in his own defense, feeling that he fully deserved this punishment (Saturn – self sabotage/punishment/shame). There was also an element of being shamed as a man, as he felt internally that he had not been 'man enough' to stand up to the ship's crew, although he would never have broken the law himself. This represents another aspect of the Cancer/Capricorn axis; the balance of anima/animus. Thus he judged himself harshly (judgments, external and internal are also Saturn) feeling he had dishonored himself and his family.

He grieved intensely when he was locked up and simply wished he was dead. His cell had very high walls and a small window opened to the outside world letting in light about twenty feet up. This was the beginning image that the client used to symbolically describe her feelings, which in actuality was a past life memory. As it turned out, within several months this young man caught a severe respiratory illness and died in the cell gazing up towards that window. Feeling so weighed down by shame and grief, this part of his consciousness simply stayed frozen there looking up at the window (Saturn/Aquarius).

The healing for this young man's spirit consisted of getting him out of the cell and into the higher planes, which took some work, as he was full of self-recrimination (Saturn). His grandfather and father's spirit came to help. They informed him that the crew had framed him, with complicity from the broader authorities in an attempt to bring the whole family down (Saturn – politics and family honor). Part of their motivation was their own rebellion against the upper class (another aspect of Saturn/Aquarius), but another motive was born of religious intolerance. They assured him he was not to blame as he was "brought up proper" and that he did not dishonor the family, (honor codes also belonging to Saturn/Capricorn). In this case, this client simply needed to resolve old Saturnian guilt and shame and the imprints of imprisonment so that she could feel freer in her present self expression.

Another client with a Capricorn SN in the eleventh house went back to a past life as a teenage male slave in America. Being born into slavery caused this past life character to already be resigned to his life of drudgery at a young age. There were instances during the Revolutionary War when slaves were sent into military service in place of their masters (conscription/draft). This was what happened to this young man. Capricorn is often known for its wry and ironic humor, and the obvious hypocrisy and irony of a country fighting for freedom and liberty while keeping slaves and even sending them to the front lines for the cause, points to America's own natal Pluto in Capricorn. He was given the glimmer of hope that after a few years of service he would gain his freedom (eleventh house – promise of liberation).

Unfortunately, he never made it beyond a few months, as he was killed suddenly in an ambush. He died feeling that not only was his life cut short, but there was no dream he would ever accomplish (Capricorn/Aquarius). Working with this slave in the afterlife, we discovered he had an intrinsic gentle nature that he never had the opportunity to express in that life (unrealized potential of the Cancer NN). In the spirit world he was encouraged to go back in his racial lineage to the tribal roots that he had never known. African spirits came forward to help him rediscover not only the support of a tribe (Aquarius), but to break the chains that bound him in that life (Aquarius – liberation). He grieved for what he had lost, but through this process was able to reclaim his dignity (NN in the fifth house). In her current life the client was born into a tobacco-farming family and as a child was made to feel that her only purpose in life was to work in the fields, much like a slave. She had known and lived this past life slave's resignation all her life. Working with this past life dissolved the cloud of resignation and gave her a new sense of her unique and creative (Aquarius/Leo/Cancer) purpose in this life.

Slavery is not exclusive to this archetype, but the layer of resignation or hopelessness that settles into one's very soul from such lives is very Capricorn. Healing such resignation is difficult because it can hide underneath the cloak of duty and responsibility which are highly prized by Capricorn. A healing meditation for anyone with Capricorn emphasized in their chart is to change every 'should' to a 'could'. This is one way to start to separate out what responsibilities can be met with creative action (Cancer) as opposed to the ones that have been mindlessly internalized.

Work and Productivity

The essence of slavery is that one is valued only for work and productivity and not as a whole person. This can also carry over into the current life, making one a workaholic or a 'slave driver' boss. In patriarchal industrialized societies (Capricorn), many of them built upon the backs of slaves, it is easy to see how this principle has become a cultural norm. This norm of 'It's not personal, it's just business' is actually looked at as a valid reason to not only dehumanize others, but to achieve gains through any means possible. Corporations and industry, both Capricorn ruled, achieve their success through workers' productivity, who in turn are given pay to spend on products that are built by other workers' productivity, while the majority of the profit of this labor is held by the corporation. In fact capitalism and industrialism were born out of feudalism in Britain, during Pluto's last transit through Capricorn (1762-1778). This essentially transformed (Pluto) the way that work (Capricorn) was done. The United Kingdom is regarded as a country with Sun, Mercury and Venus in Capricorn and interestingly it was the Scotsman James Watt (also a Capricorn Sun with Mercury and Jupiter), who improved upon the steam engine during this time, giving it industrial applications, sparking the industrial revolution. Other inventions also spurred on industry, leading to global exponential growth. Uranus (invention/revolution) was also in aspect to Pluto during its transit through Capricorn several times by square and then trine. The Industrial Revolution led to an exponential increase of the rate and scale of manufacture, and the basic labor needed to work in factories. It also changed the underlying form of society, spurring on urbanization, changing the structure of the family, and making the acquisition of wealth and its subsequent prestige the new dominant goal.

We can see the earth trine here as a model of how work is manifested moving from Taurus – basic survival, to Virgo – skilled labor, to Capricorn – action = profit/reward. Further, within these archetypes are the ideas of job, career and dharma. Capricorn as the pinnacle of the earth trine contains the total spectrum of different forms of work, from slave labor to soul purpose. At the lower end of this spectrum duty is burdensome, at the higher end duty becomes, in the words of George Bernard Shaw, "true joy in life; this being used for a purpose recognized by yourself as a mighty one".

When one's vision and integrity is aligned with service to divine will, dharma is the natural result. Again, this is the theme of earthly power versus heavenly power. The work that one does, in whatever form it takes, becomes a joyful expression. One 'cares' (Cancer) about what one does and that caring feeds the soul; this reflects the integrated Cancer/Capricorn axis. This caring is naturally reflected in the outcome of one's labor, which in turn nourishes and provides for either one's biological family or the 'family of man'. The dharmic path also entails the surrender of outcome to the divine; this is also a lesson of the Virgo/Pisces axis.

Fall from Grace

Within Capricorn, work as a 'way to God' also can be enacted by the removal of one's work if it is not aligned with dharma or at the very least done with personal integrity. This can happen progressively over many lifetimes, or dramatically, as we often see in the lives of public figures that experience a fall from grace such as politicians, religious leaders and corporate heads. A recent example of this (2008) is New York's Governor Eliot Spitzer who during Pluto's transit to his natal Saturn in Capricorn was brought down in a prostitution sting. His own moral compass had clearly gone south, as he not only campaigned on ethics reform, but built his career and persona on enforcing the law – combating white-collar crime and securities fraud as a state attorney general, and organized crime as a prosecutor in New York City.

The Rosicrucians relate the tarot card of the Wheel of Fortune to Capricorn, reminding us that fortunes rise and fall as does our destiny. The only control we have in this process is to make sure that our conscience guides our actions. This natural expansion and contraction is reflected in one's personal progress as 'one step forward, two steps back'. This is an idiom that Capricorn or anyone with Saturn transits is intimately familiar with. Classically the sure and steady climb of the mountain goat does not include missteps, only because the goat will not only calculate each step but will backtrack to find sure footing. Anyone who was tuned into the financial markets when Pluto entered Capricorn (December 2007 with the intention to stay there at least until June 2008), saw the markets reflect a daily occurrence of one step forward two steps back. Pluto's ingress also happened shortly before the Capricorn new moon. The overly optimistic bubbles created during Pluto's transit of Sagittarius met the reality of recession/depression, regression and limitations. Sub-prime mortgages were the stated cause (Cancer polarity point – housing) and brought the world markets down with it. The talk of a global recession began early in 2008. The pessimistic (Capricorn) cloud that hung over Wall Street was reflected in some statements at this time…

> "The level of pessimism, the calls I'm getting, are it's like the end of the Western world".
>
> Alfred E. Goldman, Chief Market Strategist at A.G. Edwards & Sons Inc., March 15, 2008.

> [Today's economic condition is] "the most wrenching since the end of the Second World War".
>
> Former Federal Reserve Chairman Alan Greenspan in *The Financial Times*, March 17, 2008.

Pluto's initial visit into Capricorn brought a new reality in the financial world, reminding us not only of natural cycles of rise and fall, but the limitations of the material world and man-made systems. Just as Pluto exposed the dark underbelly of religion and fanatical beliefs during its transit in Sagittarius, through Capricorn it is exposing the underlying corruption of the global economy and the 'fathers' of industry – corporations.

Brutality

Returning to the theme of personal work and slavery, it is clear that labor that is brought forth by brutality and oppressive means is a barren breeding ground for soul purpose to be birthed. Lifetimes spent under such conditions can leave a cloud of resignation but also can make one ruthless in their worldly pursuits. As we can see in current life examples of those who have experienced brutality, they can also become the brutalizer. The sad fact is that much of human history includes slavery, servitude and the use of oppressive means to gain power. These elements are all part of a collective power shadow that the Saturn/Capricorn within us all either perpetuates or transforms.

Chart B

In this chart the Moon is in Cancer in the tenth house square the nodes, making the archetypes of Cancer/Capricorn prominent in the karmic signature. Further, this regression took place when transiting Saturn and Mars were conjunct the natal Moon, and square their own natal position. Transiting planets to the karmic signatures in the chart often indicate a release of karma into the present life. Natal Saturn and Mars are also a part of the karmic axis as they conjunct the NN and thus oppose the SN. With these transits it was an opportune time for this past life to be worked with.

In her current life she had cyclical patterns of being emotionally depressive and "dead and uncaring" (Moon/Capricorn). She said, "I feel as if there is a barrier around me, keeping me from enjoying anything meaningful in my life". When she went back to a past life she was a young man sitting on a horse surveying workers in a field. This young man was feeling very self important, arrogant (Mars and Saturn in Aries), and viewed these workers as far below him. As we explored his earlier life, we found that he had come to work on this estate with his mother, when he was young. His mother was a house servant, but also made money on the side as a prostitute. This made the young boy angry, but he quickly covered that up by saying, "That's okay, I don't care for her anyway. She doesn't mean that much to me". His emotional state at this point in the past life was already

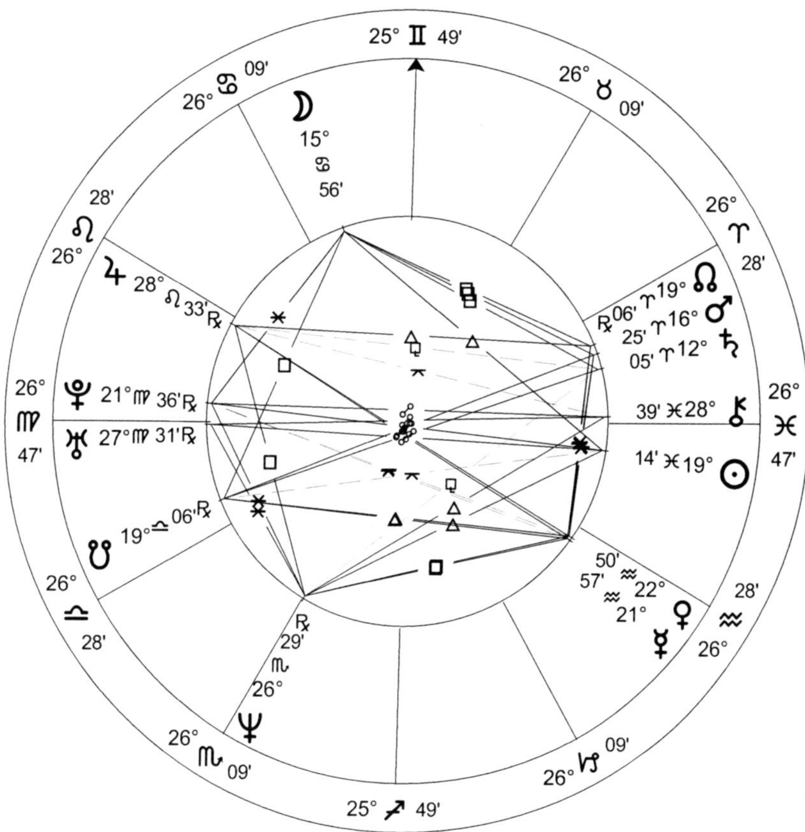

Chart B (Porphyry houses)

very hardened, so we went back earlier to see how this happened. It seemed that this imprint started in the womb (Moon/Cancer) as he was aware that his father was beating his mother, and that it was her pregnancy that was evoking his father's rage. This caused him great distress and as an unborn fetus he was desperate to help his mother. "I'm sorry Mommy; It's all my fault, I'll be good when I come out, I'll protect you". It is important to note that Capricorn/Saturn is also an archetype of protection in contrast to the deep vulnerability of Cancer.

The beating (Capricorn/brutality/Mars square) happened during his entire gestation period, so that by the time he was born he had already decided that he needed to be tough and could only rely on himself (tenth house, SN in first house). As an infant, he lay rigid in his mother's arms thinking, "I don't need you; I'll take care of myself". Libra and Cancer both relate to one's needs and his were clearly already suppressed (tenth house and Saturn) at birth. When he moved with his mother to the estate, all he focused on was working hard and finding a way to get ahead (Capricorn). At first he did menial chores but got a promotion to work in the stables. He did experience brutality from his overseers as they taunted him, and on several occasions beat him. This only made him more withdrawn and he focused all of his energy into working. Eventually he impressed the estate owner enough to work his way into becoming an overseer himself (Capricorn – climbing the ladder of success).

The other men of rank told him he had to be hard on the workers; "They are just animals". He didn't like that at first, as he was quite reclusive and not very expressive at all. But as he came into his position of power, his years of pent up rage (SN first house/Aries Mars conjunct Saturn and square Moon) started to come out and he enjoyed beating them with his whip. Years went by, and he progressively became more hardened, yet a small soft core within that he had tried to kill simply would not die, and this gnawed at him. In his thirties he had a breakdown, "My life means nothing, it's so hard to keep going. What's the point, it's all useless". Eventually he gave into this futility and shot himself.

In the afterlife this young man's consciousness was very resistant to accept any help, as he died truly believing that no one cared for him. Working through all the layers of rigidity slowly returned to him the ability to care and at this point the spirit of his mother from that past life came forward. It was revealed that this was the client's mother in the current life and that both of them were working on lessons of caring (Moon/Capricorn). It was important also to work with this past life character's own inner child to help restore the feeling nature that he had become so estranged from. The combination of the Cancer/Capricorn archetype in this past life represented a long karmic history of emotional repression and the effect of brutality on the client's emotional sensitivity. This relates also to the Libra SN and its ruler Venus in Aquarius in the fifth house, showing how detached the heart and feeling nature had become. This past-life young man surprised even himself in the afterlife, as he was able to not only grieve, but to reconcile with his mother and admit that he did truly care. Since Cancer/Mother/Moon is about the essence of caring, it was a breakthrough for him to realize this and express it openly. The pent up rage from that past life was also worked with, which further allowed the emotional body to soften to a state of receptivity (empowered Libra/Cancer).

Bitterness is a consequence of the loss of caring; someone who dies 'old and bitter' is also common in the Capricorn archetype as both are associated with it. But as this previous case shows, bitterness can set in at any age when the emotional body is in a state of rigor mortis. Active grieving is a way to start the waters of emotion flowing again, as is any form of emoting. Repression and suppression are secondary reactions to trauma and arise as a way for one to distance themselves from painful emotions or memories. As this past case shows, the effects of these reactions when formed in past lives, color one's present life as much as if they were happening now. Cancer represents the soft underbelly of such hardened imprints and its vulnerability needs to be felt, to restore stasis to the whole psyche. Just as food fuels the body, freely flowing emotions nourish the vitality of the soul.

Guilt and Failure

Because Saturn/Capricorn has responsibility at its core one can come into life feeling they owe a debt to someone or others in general. While this may be true, more often than not that feeling simply represents past lives where one was unable to complete something they felt responsible for. Failed attempts at trying to save others, or protect them (especially one's own children or family), can leave deep imprints of guilt that one may still subconsciously be trying to atone for. When Virgo is also involved in the karmic axis this dynamic is heightened. Past lives of failure can either have one in overdrive about accomplishing, constantly driven by the fear of failure, or can have the silent saboteur working in the recesses of the consciousness to ensure continual failure, or frequently a combination of both.

Chart C

This chart has a Capricorn SN in the second house and Pluto in Virgo is in the tenth, so there is a double signature of Capricorn. The nodes are squared by Jupiter in Aries in the fifth house, so the NN is also a part of the past life experiences. This is another chart that shows how transits and current events can act to release karma, as it was the events of September 11, 2001, that brought this woman into a state of a 'healing crisis' (Pluto in Virgo).

This woman worked directly across from the World Trade Center in New York City during the time of September 11th, in international finances. She

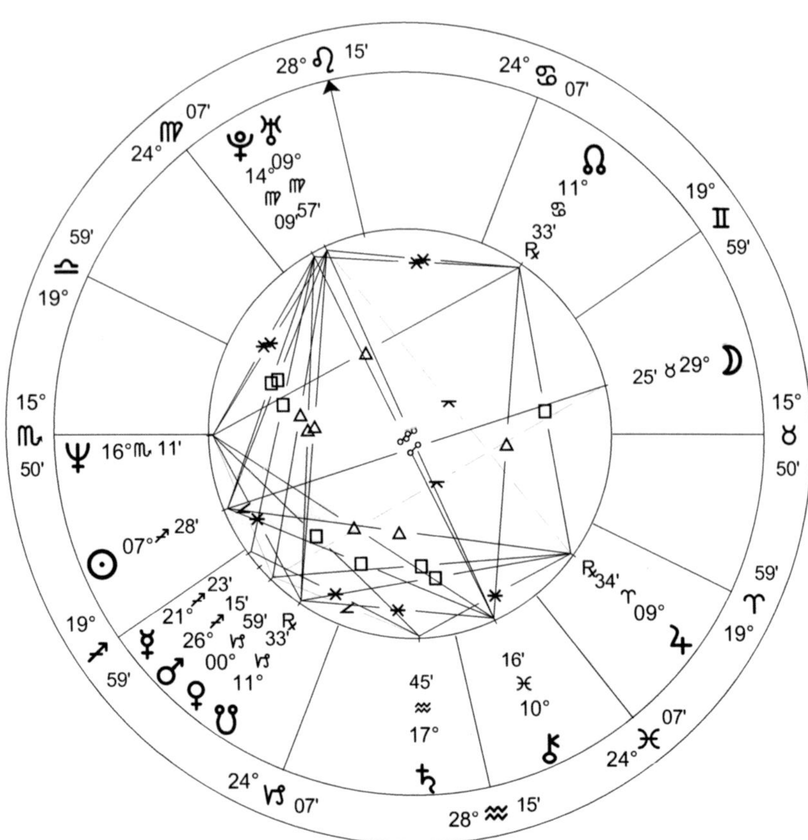

Chart C (Porphyry houses)

was traveling for business that day so was not in her office but her company's building was destroyed from the collapse and several co-workers died. Upon learning of what happened she went into shock. This is termed 'vicarious trauma', when one is a witness to another's trauma either as a bystander or as a caregiver, but nonetheless is impacted psychologically, sometimes as severely as if the trauma was one's own. In current life psychology it is said that this stems from an empathetic reaction. From the past life perspective, what is understood is that the traumatic events that one witnesses, even in a movie theatre or on the news, can trigger deeply personal buried past life traumas. In her case she went into 'soldier mode' for several years and then had a near complete breakdown. The combined signature of Capricorn and Aries is discussed in the Aries chapter as a primary indicator for warrior/

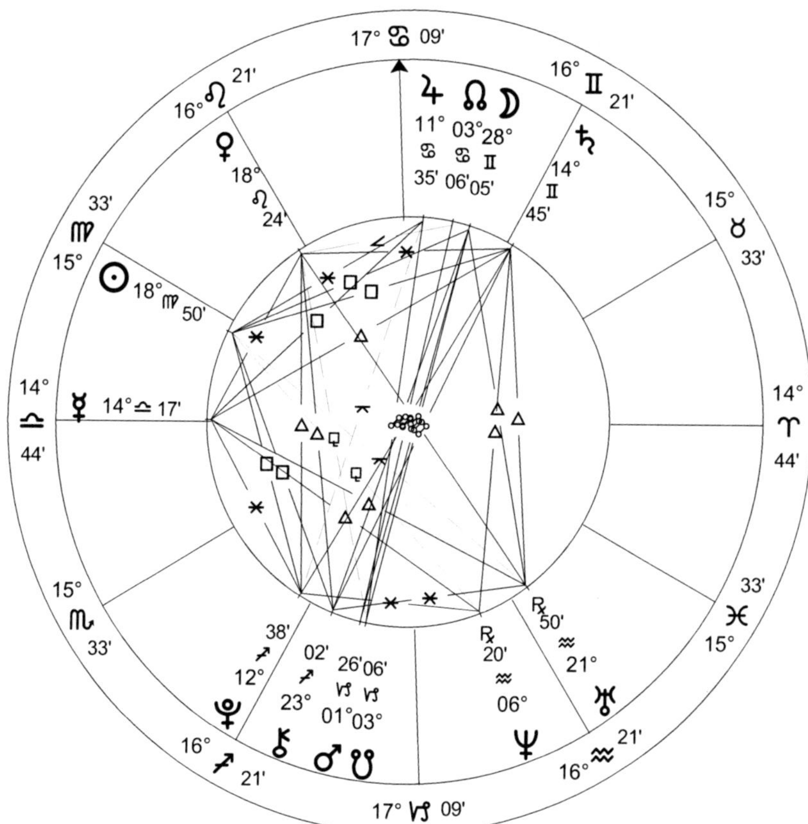

September 11, 2001. 8:48am. New York City, NY.

soldier karma as her stories will further illustrate. The case study at the end of the Aries chapter also has a combined signature of Capricorn and Aries and can be read to further understand these imprints. Excerpt from the Aries chapter…

> Capricorn/Saturn signatures are more often 'career soldiers'; those who are climbing the military ladder of promotion; patriots; and who have followed in the father's or ancestor's footsteps. The sense of duty/responsibility and honor plays a major role for this type of soldier. Equally, this signature reflects the repressive nature of Saturn and can be found in the past lives of those who were brutalized themselves or were conscripted/drafted into service. The Aries/Mars signature carries with it more the wound of the sheer violence of war… and the madness of killing.

The transits for September 11th show that she had already had her nodal return and Jupiter was exactly conjunct her NN. Jupiter's importance comes from the fact it is the squaring planet to her natal nodal axis. Mars was also just coming into orb of conjuncting the SN. It took her several years of standard therapy before she was able to even approach the depths of past life therapy, but when she did start it was in early 2008 when Jupiter had traveled half way across her natal chart and was exactly conjunct her SN! As these stories will also show, the traumas that were awakened within her and their subsequent resolution changed the course of her life and initiated her into the possibility of manifesting her NN.

After September 11th her company was nearly destroyed and the remaining staff rallied together to 'save the company'. She took much more responsibility (Capricorn) than her role dictated, but this was driven by her subconscious need to 'save' them. Note that Jupiter square the nodes, combined with the Capricorn signatures, indicates that the hero and savior are deeply active in her consciousness. She worked day and night under tremendous pressure and also with a nagging guilt that no matter what she did it wasn't enough (also Pluto in Virgo). Further, she was exhibiting classic signs of PTSD but she was attempting to override these through sheer will, emotional shut down and hyper focus on her duty (Aries, second house SN and other planets there and Capricorn). After about four years of this she neared break down and left the company for a hiatus. A few years later, when Jupiter was conjunct her SN, she started to work with her past lives.

The first past life she explored found her in charge (Aries/Capricorn) of a unit of about 300 soldiers in World War II. They had landed on a beach in the early morning (presumably D-day) and the mission was to cut a safe swathe through to a fence line to allow them, and others depending on them, safe passage during intense bombardment. She reported, "I was stunned by the noise and the carnage, but I had a mission and I just focused on the goal" (Aries/Jupiter). As is often reported by soldiers, there is no training that can prepare them for the reality of war (Capricorn). Accomplishing this mission was not easy, as there was chaos on the beach, and this commander was immediately presented with the reality that the majority of his men, and others relying on them to make the way safe, would not make the passage if he made the approach as was originally planned. The only way to accomplish the mission was to split them into two units sending one out as a decoy. He struggled with this decision but battlefields are not places for long pensive thought and "in a moment that felt like a lifetime, I ordered the second in command to lead a portion of the troops to the left. I was desperate to find another way; we both knew what was happening, but we also knew what needed to be done" (duty, honor – Capricorn).

That group of men was quickly slaughtered and unfortunately it did not stem the tide as he had calculated, as his group came under direct fire. He not only had to watch those men die, but now his remaining men were in danger of failing the mission, and losing their lives. In the midst of this he was shot and became paralyzed. In many charts Saturn/Uranus/eleventh house contacts often indicate past life paralysis. The client has this karmic signature as Saturn is ruler of the SN and is in Aquarius, and Pluto is conjunct Uranus in the tenth house. Despite his injury, his men tried to carry him, and their courage and devotion in doing this made him feel even more the failure (Capricorn). He died, as they tried to save him, feeling "They trusted me and I let them down; I got them all killed for nothing; It's all my fault; What a waste". All of these are Capricorn futility, guilt and failure imprints. Because he died in this state, this commander never left that beach and all this was activated in the client today when her commercial company was nearly destroyed. She made the current life connections quite easily, "I felt the whole company was my responsibility. I felt those who died were my responsibility and no matter what I did it would never be enough".

The soul fragment that remained in that state was worked with in the afterlife and a pivotal moment happened for the client when as the commander he met the spirit of a soldier who also remained on that beach but for different reasons. This soldier had a message for him saying, "I am standing sentinel here today, to guard the freedom you bought with your blood". This brought waves of tears of both grief and relief to the commander. Some of his own soldiers came to him in spirit form to let him know they won; it was not in vain. Now that he was feeling lighter, he was also able to help other sprits of soldiers that were still stuck on the beach in shock. After 'dismissing the troops' they were all happy to ascend to higher planes into the light. A further request came from this commander as he asked healing spirits to wash all the blood and horror away from his spirit body. This is an interesting spontaneous gesture, as in itself it has archetypal roots.

Many tribal societies recognized that the passage into warriorship must also have a return ritual after the battle, so that the warrior can again become a citizen. Symbolic cleansing and purification rituals that allow the warrior to leave the horrors of the battlefield behind are missing in modern warfare which also contributes to a psychic layer of PTSD and soul loss. The dehumanization of war needs to be reconciled in the soldier's own soul so he can claim his place in society again. As this story shows, even soldiers that have fought an 'honorable' war can die feeling dishonorable. As it related to this woman, resolving this past life commander opened the door to her own emotions again and helped her evolutionary process of movement to her Cancer NN.

During the time of her hiatus and therapy, she changed life direction to work in professional coaching. She said that because this past life commander was unresolved in her she had been "unable to let people in" as she felt "I can't be trusted" (NN in the eighth). His guilt had kept a protective barrier around her because subconsciously she feared she would only get people killed. Other connections she felt related to this particular past life were "an inability to really feel" (SN in Capricorn in the second) and "feeling everything is my fault", as well as an inability to be around loud explosive noises. "It's all my fault", is one of the most classic Capricorn karmic scripts. She found that her "limits of responsibility became clearer" and that it was a liberating feeling for her to realize how "out of control" the events of September 11th were for her personally, but that she had internalized so much of the responsibility (Pluto in Virgo in the tenth). The vicarious traumatic reaction from September 11th also eased for her as this commander was laid to rest. She had been unable to watch any news footage from that day and although it is still disturbing, as it is for anyone with compassion, it does not have the charge it did for her before.

The fact that the Cancer NN is also a part of her past life consciousness is clear when she describes herself as afraid to care or get close to others, but her actions do not reflect that. This past life commander clearly did care, but with the squared NN in the eight house, caring, which is the essence of Cancer, in the past had been a larger than life issue. For her, letting someone be close in her current life carried the gravity of personal responsibility (Capricorn) over life and death (Cancer NN in the eighth – caring equals death). When she felt the pain of the loss of her co-workers on September 11th, and how that affected her commercial company, she was deeply moved because her soul had already experienced the caring of the Cancer archetype. Transforming the way she cares is one potential of the Cancer NN in the eighth. The healing of her emotional body and its transformation is represented by not only the NN, but the polarity point of Pluto's house and sign, the fourth house and Pisces (with Chiron there).

In another lifetime the soldier/warrior theme continued but with a different twist. This was an earlier lifetime that took place in ancient Rome (also associated with Aries). She was a young man who was a scout party leader for a general. As it turned out the general was this young man's father (Capricorn) and his main goal at that time was to prove himself to him (Aries/Jupiter). "I want to carry my weight and make him proud of me". He set out with a small party of men and directed them to stay in the valley while he went up to a ridge to look around. While he was on the ridge, the men below were attacked and again as in the first story, he watched them get killed. There is an element of survivor guilt here (Capricorn SN in the second) but that didn't last long as he was soon ambushed and killed also. This did not happen before he had time to recriminate himself and feel, "What will I tell my father?" In this instance he died more with shame and an inability to complete his mission, which symbolically was his passage into manhood (being accepted by the father). "I failed my mission and my father". The incomplete initiation comes from Aries and the approval of the father is both Capricorn and the fifth house. He also died feeling that "I made a mistake" (ruler of SN in the third), and that "it was my need to show off that got us all killed" (Aries in the fifth house). This story led immediately into another past life of a young boy hiding in an alcove in a house, which also brings in elements of the NN archetypes Cancer and Scorpio.

This 'hiding' story took place also in Italy where the client was a young boy, about nine year's old, living in a simple home with his parents and two sisters. Roman soldiers came and obliterated the family, but he ran and hid. He heard the slaughter and he wanted to run out and save them (Jupiter/Aries) but he was frozen in fear (Capricorn/Saturn in Aquarius). After some time he came out and found them all dead. He felt not only that he should have tried to save them, but that his whole world was destroyed (eighth house). He also berated himself as a coward for running and hiding (Jupiter), when in reality he was only a small boy. Eventually a local priest came and took him to a dwelling with other priests. He missed his family terribly and although the priests took care of his basic needs (second house) he was never able to express or process the grief of his loss (Capricorn and eighth house). The only comfort the priests offered was, "They've gone to a better place".

This young boy so desperately missed them that all he wanted to do was die so he could be with his family again (Cancer/eighth house). He grew up feeling, "If I wash the floors well and say my prayers I'll get there too". Over time his earlier guilt about his family was replaced with a feeling of abandonment, "I must not deserve them; they left me" (second/eighth house axis). He made his way by doing menial work for the priests and was terribly lonely, numb and sad. He lived completely isolated (second house) except for the priests, and his life was uneventful. He died in his thirties from an illness. In the afterlife he did re-meet his family, and wonderfully the joy of this outweighed the misery he had felt during his earth life. The client said, "I was so happy to be loved again it was all I wanted. One of the things I had missed terribly was my mother's loving touch" (Cancer and tactile second house). She said that in her current life she had felt estranged from her family and unable to connect with them in a loving meaningful way. This currently was in the process of being healed in her life and working with this young boy also helped her to be open to their love more deeply (Cancer and healing of the fifth house – wounds to the giving and receiving of love).

It is doubtful that anyone has had no family contacts if they have had several past lives. But with Capricorn in the karmic signature, often issues of connectedness with family comes from past lives of failure with family; estrangement; loneliness even within the family; burdensome responsibility for family; orphaned or loss of family. All these scenarios can result in one coming into this life feeling that they don't know how to be a part of a family or to not even try to. The Cancer polarity point attempts to bring one into a familial circle of love, even if it is not with the biological family, but offers the promise that one can find that or create it themselves.

This next past life shows another imprint that is familiar to Capricorn; the feeling of being a fraud. Because the ruler of the SN is in the third house this brings the Gemini archetype into focus as well. Both these archetypes as well as the client's Jupiter contain various facets of truth and truth telling. In this very recent past life she was again a young boy. It is important to point out that the Cancer/Capricorn axis is also about gender roles, as is the entire Cardinal cross. We see the polarities of the very masculine Mars opposite Venus on the Aries/Libra axis and the Moon (mother) and Saturn (father) on the Cancer/Capricorn axis. Individuals with Cancer/Capricorn often have gender issues and they may feel they have newly arrived in their present gender. I have also had clients comment that they feel they are preparing in the current life to switch to another gender in the next life. One man who had a series of male-only past lives was raised by his mother and grandmother and six sisters in this lifetime. He felt that this was a way for him to learn about being female as he hadn't done it in a while, and felt his next life he would be as a woman. Many on the Capricorn/Cancer axis are in various stages of learning to balance the anima/animus within.

In the first memory of this young boy's past life, he was on a stage about to receive an award. He felt sick to his stomach as inside he felt "it was all a lie" (third house and Jupiter). How he got on the stage came from a previous incident where he and another young boy were running after a puppy in the street. He pushed the boy out of the way of an oncoming truck and ended up saving his life. Several adults saw this and hailed him as a hero (Capricorn and Jupiter). But how he described it was very different. "I pushed him 'cause I wanted the puppy, I didn't even see the truck". (Wound of impulsive selfishness – Aries). His dad was so proud of him and because of this he was unable to tell anyone what really happened. We can already see a replay from some of the earlier lives, but with a slight variation in this life. He kept the truth to himself and went on stage to receive the award in front of his whole school. What he didn't know was that the other boy had already told a band of his friends what happened and they blurted this out while he was on stage (public humiliation/ Pluto in Virgo and tenth house). His father took him home and beat him.

This young man never recovered from this and grew up feeling so shamed that he became a "loser and alcoholic", eventually drinking himself to death. The imprint again of dishonor is present but also this sort of event points out that when we don't live up to our own ideals, have unresolved guilt, or feel we have 'copped out' on ourselves in past lives it can leave a subtle imprint of fraudulence. Past lives of feeling one has failed is also an obvious culprit. This makes all forms of accomplishment tainted, and sets the stage for the Capricornian saboteur to dismantle achievements, sometimes before they even manifest. The saboteur is not exclusive to Capricorn, because ultimately the saboteur lies behind a broader fear of owning one's power, which relates to other archetypes as well. But in this archetype, the work in healing this saboteur is to align oneself with intrinsic integrity, which is a higher octave of Capricorn (and Sagittarius). The Jupiter in Aries is also about the ability to accomplish goals. The client was able to do so in her current life (her Sun is in Sagittarius in the first house) but she also had the unresolved feelings of fraudulence and shame tainting everything she achieved. She felt she constantly needed to prove herself (Jupiter in Aries), as a way to avoid the discomfort of feeling internally fraudulent and undeserving (Capricorn/second house). Clearing the shame that tainted her self worth (second house), allowed her to feel a deeper sense of authenticity (Jupiter/Sagittarius) that opened the way for her to truly accept others' applause and appreciation (fifth house Leo).

Interestingly, in the afterlife work the past life self was asked to let a spiritual guide come to him that would represent true accomplishment. Martin Luther King showed up. This client had no idea that Martin Luther King was bringing to her by his image the essence of empowered Capricorn Sun energy; but there he was!

11

Aquarius/Uranus and the Eleventh House

Keywords

Fixed/Yang/Air	Alienation	Fragmentation
Liberation from conditioning	Hopes	Trauma
Individuality	Ideals	Mass trauma
Individuation	Long-term memory	Splitting
Rebellion	Anarchist	Unique
Differentiation	Humanitarian	Shocking
Like-minded groups	Ostracized	Projection
Group hysteria	Cast out	Atlantis
Innovation	Group of One	Hyper activity
Secret Societies	Tribe	Prometheus
Reform	Community	Revolutionary

The Natural Archetype

In their hit song *Aquarius*, The Fifth Dimension certainly captured the essence of this sign with the thoughts "No more falsehoods or derisions… and the mind's true liberation" (from the musical *Hair*, 1969). Aquarius is about the free sharing of pure elevated thought, ideas and ideals; the Water Bearer pours out its gifts to all of humanity which is what also aligns this sign with the myth of Prometheus.

Prometheus was given the task of re-creating mankind out of clay by Zeus. After their creation Zeus was satisfied with leaving humanity to stay a primitive race, and had no concern for their evolution. Prometheus on the other hand was more attached to his creation (Leo polarity) and desired for humans to do better. After Prometheus angered Zeus by playing several tricks on him, Zeus responded by taking fire away from humanity. Mythically and literally for humanity, fire was critical to survival and civilization. Prometheus stole the fire from Zeus, bringing it back to humanity, and in various versions of the myth he also brought them gifts of the mind by teaching them the use of fire, the sciences and arts. This earned Prometheus the title of 'rebel god' and his punishment of being chained to the mountain.

This short recap tells us several things about Aquarius. Creating something out of nothing is a gift of the Leo/Aquarius axis. Aquarius lends the ability to not only innovate but to invent. While the creative arts, which are Leo ruled, are about personal expression, inventing something usually means it has a purpose and is useful for others. Leo wants its creations to be appreciated just because he made them, but Aquarian inventors and scientific innovators want their creations to add to the progress of humanity, or at least make life easier in some way. This hints at Aquarius' dual rulership of Saturn and Uranus.

Prometheus' action uplifted humanity and liberated them from primitive conditions. Bringing fire to humanity, because he had compassion for them, shows an integrated Leo (heart)/Aquarius axis more commonly embodied as a humanitarian. Liberation and limitation exist simultaneously in Aquarius. The sheer solidity of Saturn is matched by the Uranian urge to break free. Rather than the progressive de-conditioning process that happens in Capricorn, outright revolt is what is required in Aquarius. Historically, revolution or the urge to be liberated is born out of repressive (Saturnian) situations. Collective events (Aquarius), like the French Revolution bore the stamp of Aquarius/Uranus as the liberator. The Storming of the Bastille (July 14, 1789) happened while Pluto was in Aquarius, squaring the Scorpio/Taurus nodal axis. Widespread poverty (Taurus) and disease (Scorpio) and the inequity of wealth (resources – Scorpio) were the prevailing conditions that Uranus rebelled against. This revolution culminated in the eventual over throwing of the monarchy (Leo) and the establishment of a republic in September 1792, when Pluto in Aquarius was directly opposed to Uranus in Leo. The motto 'Liberty, Equality, Fraternity' first appeared during the revolution and represented the essence of Uranus/Aquarius to the tee.

On a personal level, the urge for liberation, when acted upon, results in the process of Individuation. Rebellion against the status quo that one has internalized through many lifetimes is what needs to be accomplished. Naturally, since Aquarius is a Yang outward moving sign, it often finds an outlet for rebellion in the outer world. In certain stages of individuation this is appropriate. Like a teenager who is testing the limits of their own freedom, for one to discover what they truly are beneath all the layers of conformity and conditioning, anything that restricts the discovery of individuality needs to be rebelled against. This stage though is decidedly still very egocentric. In the latter stages of individuation, one has not only developed and integrated their own individuality, but has also celebrated the uniqueness of others, finding a greater self in communion with the 'fraternity of humanity'. This reaches its culmination in Pisces, where the oneness of all is realized through the transcendent realization of the divine in all. Individuality and collective consciousness might seem to be at odds with each other, but as this archetype shows, they are intricately intertwined. Jung summed this up by saying:

> "Since the individual is not only a single, separate being, but by his very existence, also presupposes a collective relationship, the process of individuation must clearly lead to a more intensive and universal collective solidarity, and not to mere isolation".
>
> Carl Jung – *Psychological Types: The Psychology of Individuation* [1]

Saturn and Uranus thus describe this process eloquently, as one must develop along the prescribed lines of the cultural norm, which reaches its apex in Capricorn. Saturn brings this reality forth into Aquarius. The process of differentiation (what makes one unique) is the result of Saturn meeting Uranus in Aquarius, which often manifests initially as rebellion. The antagonistic stance of 'me versus the world' eventually must give way to further growth which becomes increasingly transpersonal and less self-oriented. This returns the individual back to the collective as a productive member who then is able to contribute to everyone's progress: this is the expression of Saturn and Uranus working in concert. As Prometheus showed us, one enlightened act can uplift humanity out of darkness.

These stages of personal growth are also reflected in our soul's total history as Uranus/Aquarius is associated with long term memory, which includes our individuated unconscious (the memory of our past lives). In our soul's total history we have undergone various stages of conformity and differentiation from it. Depending upon one's personal evolutionary state, one may still be in the stages of conformity which is aligned with Saturn; differentiation to collective consciousness (Uranus) or spiritual realization (Neptune).

---

1. C.G. Jung, *Psychological Types*, Harcourt Brace, New York, 1944.

Aquarius in Past Life Experiences

The Aquarius archetype is a part of the karmic axis when:

Pluto is in Aquarius or the eleventh house or
The South Node is in Aquarius or the eleventh house or
The ruler of the South Node is in Aquarius or the eleventh house or
Uranus aspects Pluto, the nodal axis or rulers of the nodes.

Alienation and Individuation

Past lives that describe the stages of conformity and its results were discussed in the Capricorn chapter. When Aquarius/Uranus and the eleventh house are a part of the karmic axis, lives that involve the development of personal unique qualities, separation and reunion with the collective come to the forefront. Separation of the individual from the collective in past lives is often represented by lives lived as an outcast where one suffers the wounds of alienation. Sometimes this sort of life is chosen, but more often than not it happens in traumatic ways. Uranus as a servant to the processes of individuation will also force one to navigate totally new terrain by severing all ties with the past to bring about its goal. When these lives have been a part of one's karmic history, the Leo polarity is pointing the way to healing these wounds to be able to reintegrate a sense of belonging again.

Chart A

This client with an Aquarius SN with Saturn conjunct in the eleventh house went back to a tribal lifetime as a Native American. Tribal lives of all sorts are typical in Aquarius. This young Indian had always felt different, as it seemed he also had a problem with clearly expressing himself (Pluto square to Gemini Moon and Sagittarius Sun). As he started to come of age within his tribe, he was unable to identify with any particular role or personal talent (Saturn/Aquarius – limitations of individuality, opposing Leo NN – self actualization). While his peers were clearly able to identify their paths as either budding warriors, canoe makers or other professions, he was stymied and felt massively inferior (Pluto/Uranus in Virgo in the sixth house).

The tension built day by day and was also intimately annoying as his brother (Gemini – siblings) was quite accomplished in his abilities as a young hunter. The young man became fixated on the symbols of power (Scorpio/Pluto) his brother possessed, such as his hunting knife and arrows.

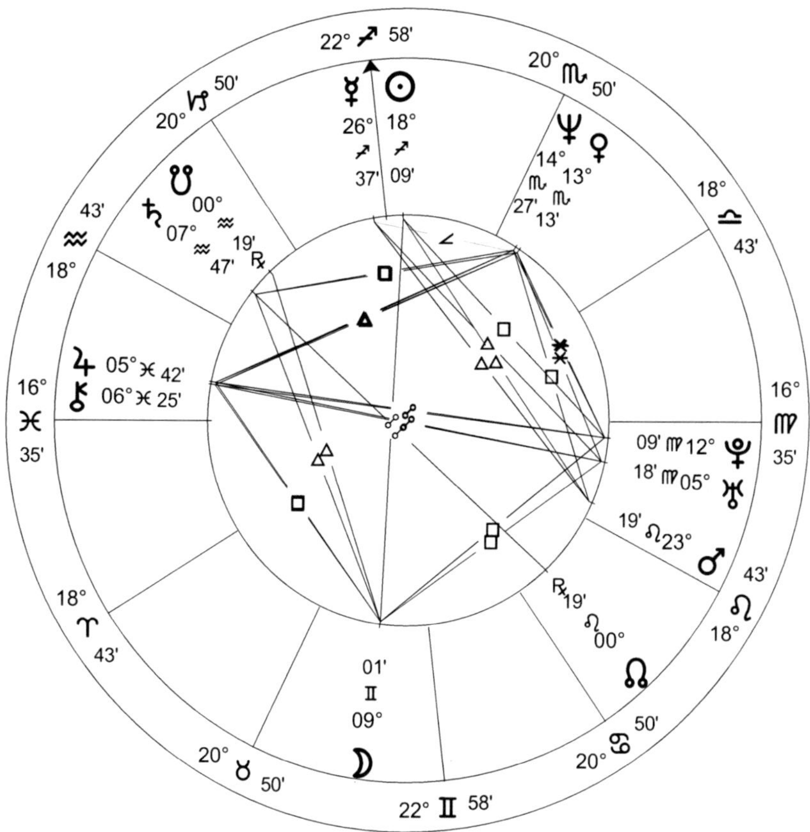

Chart A (Porphyry houses)

One day he stole his brother's knife (Gemini – thievery) and took it out into the woods to a secret place where he could hold it, hoping to absorb some of what it stood for. It seemed this was not so much a malicious act as one in which he desired deeply to have something concrete (Saturn) that would help him define himself (Aquarius) and gain acceptance (Leo NN) from the tribe. The tribe learned of this theft and quickly banished him by silently turning their backs on him. He immediately went into shock (Aquarius/Uranus) and with no other option (Saturn), he left in the canoe that they had packed for him with supplies. The trauma of grief (Saturn/Aquarius) was so great, that once he was off in the swamps alone he grieved for weeks. It was unclear if this banishment was meant to be permanent or just a temporary punishment but this young man believed he was never able to go back again. The loneliness (Saturn/Aquarius) of his existence plunged him into depression (Saturn) and also desperation. He had many ideas (Aquarius) of things he would accomplish (Saturn) to be able to return to the tribe. He imagined himself killing crocodiles or panthers and marching victoriously back to the tribe with carcasses slung over his shoulders, gaining their instant appreciation (Leo NN). Unfortunately he only ever dreamed of doing such things and never brought them into being (Aquarius). He was essentially crippled by his depression and grief. This underscores the challenge of this Saturn in Aquarius that ideas are meant to be manifested through a process of effort.

There were colonial settlements in the region and occasionally he would hang out on the edges and watch them, but never made any attempt to make contact. Since he wasn't a skilled hunter he sustained himself meagerly and this, combined with his depression, eventually killed him as he slowly starved to death. He died in a cloud of depression, distrust of others and loneliness and wanted to only be left alone in the spirit world. It took much to overcome this imprint, but eventually he was able to reunite with the tribe.

His parents from that lifetime came forward to apologize to him and the client had a stunning realization at this point. She was adopted in this life and the parents from that early life morphed into her adoptive parents in this lifetime. They told her, "We promised we would never outcast you again". She revealed that it was clear they had fulfilled their vow, as she had tested the limits of their love through much of her teenage years, and they were unwavering in their care for her. She sobbed as her heart was filled with the truth of the love that had been offered to her in this lifetime, to heal these past life wounds (Leo NN). The guides also offered her a further experience of belonging, as a pod of dolphins spontaneously appeared in the spirit world and invited her to join them. As she became one of them all the trauma of separation dissipated almost instantly. The dolphins were a fitting symbol of Piscean oneness which is the polarity point of Pluto. During this time in her life she formed a relationship with community of like-minded healers, which after clearing the wounds of separation from this past life, allowed her to draw deep sustenance from that support so she could bring her personal gifts into the world more fully; an empowered (Aquarius/Leo) axis.

This next story is an interesting contrast to the first as it shows a voluntary dropping out of society and the effects of such.

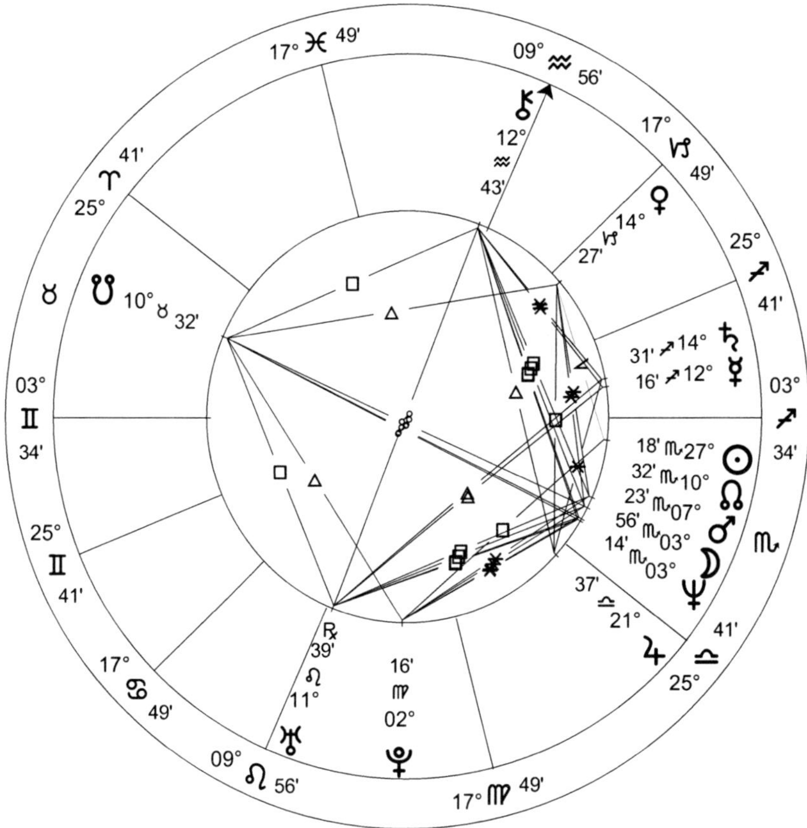

Chart B (Porphyry houses)

Chart B

This chart has Uranus in Leo and Chiron in Aquarius square the nodes. At the time this regression was done transiting Saturn was exactly conjunct the natal Uranus, so it's not surprising that the issues of conformity versus individuality were the theme of this past life. He was a young man born into Spanish nobility (Leo also Chiron in the tenth). He had many friends, who as sons of the privileged enjoyed intellectual pursuits, the arts and games. They frequently trained in swordsmanship, and had some military training although it was a peaceful time. His life was quite fine and he enjoyed most the camaraderie and 'brotherhood' with his friends (Uranus/Aquarius). This changed quickly when the country went to war and he and his friends were called into service. In the middle of the night he sneaked off and left behind his life as he knew it because he said, "I don't believe in killing", effectively becoming a deserter and walking away from his inheritance (Scorpio). He stayed to himself and lived in the woods or abandoned buildings, coming into villages only as he needed supplies, which he would barter for (Taurus/Scorpio). He was not deeply depressed but was lonely, missing his friends, and felt that "There is nowhere that I fit in".

It seemed that, unbeknownst to him, he was also a wanted man and soldiers came upon him one day and killed him. When he saw them approach in familiar uniforms he eagerly sought out his friends' faces amongst them but didn't recognize any of them. Nonetheless he felt a sense of kinship as they were fellow countrymen (SN in the twelfth – naiveté). He extended his hand to greet them and was instantly killed. He died absolutely stunned with the words on his lips, "But I'm one of you".

With his Taurus SN in the twelfth he was fairly naïve about the extent that people would go to defend their nation's dictates, as he simply had walked away without much regret. Even though he had many friends he had lived an isolated life (Taurus/twelfth house and Chiron in the tenth). The imprint that remained with him was a simultaneous double bind of "I want to belong, but my choices set me apart". The nature of choice and freewill is very Scorpio. This story helped him to reconcile that individuality has a cost, but it isn't life or death (Scorpio) in this lifetime. In his current life he was rigidly defensive about his individuality and was relatively anti-social as he subconsciously feared losing his individuality. He was living as a rebellious drop-out from society, and while this afforded him freedom, it was difficult to get by and he was often a victim of his circumstances (Pluto Virgo and sixth/twelfth house axis).

Both of these stories show that operating outside of the 'rules of the society' has a cost. In the first case the woman was at a stage in her current life that is typical of the Aquarius SN moving towards a Leo NN; needing to identify what gifts she had to pour out to humanity and finding the courage to do so. In the second story, also typically Aquarian, the man was at a stage of his life where he was trying to find a way to bring his individuality into a useful form within society. The Saturn/Uranus rulership shows that developing one's individuality brings up one set of fears and another set when expressing it in society. But the ultimate reality is reflected in the integrated Leo/Aquarius axis; that there is unity in diversity and by becoming fully individual all of society can be served. We only need to look at the diversity that is present in all of nature to appreciate the fact that, if a flower was not fully itself, unique from say a blade of grass, we would not even be able to enjoy the contrasts in a garden. The fact that each species is uniquely itself, while also a part of the larger landscape of creation, is what contributes to the magnificence of its totality.

As a whole, humanity hasn't fully gotten this truth yet, because in reality all of humanity has not yet arrived at the point of individuation. The majority are still in conforming states of evolution which causes a quandary for those who are not. Those who are different and unique and stand outside the status quo are often not looked upon kindly by past societies (or the present one). The one who sticks his head up above the crowd the highest is often the first to have it chopped off. Whenever one is a rule-breaker or rebel, it is often them and not the system that feels the pain. There can also be a past life cost of individuality that one can carry into the current life, which causes an underlying fear of 'being different'. My clients with strong Aquarian signatures in their charts often say within the first few minutes of a session, "I feel like I don't belong". While this is painful, it also is a necessary step of differentiation. There is a big difference between conformity and belonging. To get to the point of true belonging one has to break away from conformity.

Rebellion

My Aquarian cases are full of those who were slightly different in some way and were tortured, killed or completely outcast because of that. The mass hysteria of witch burning which also had misogynist roots was a clear example of this. History is full of such examples of either individuals or groups being singled out and persecuted for no other reason than that they frightened the consensus, because they were different. Anyone who has undergone such past life traumas will come into the current life with a fear of standing out, as well as a fear of groups or crowds because such past life deaths were often carried out publicly in front of a jeering crowd. This can leave one in a complete state of alienation even among like-minded others, as the fear of a crowd gone mad is present subconsciously.

Chart C

It must be shared that this client's real name, given to her at birth (and used here with permission) is Cassandra. Cassandra is a Greek mythic character who was known as the 'cursed prophetess' as she was granted the gift of prophecy by Apollo but when she refused him as a lover he took away her powers of persuasion. Thus no matter how accurate her prophecies no one would believe her. In her current life she was born into a family where denial was the norm. She said, "I'm the only one who will ever talk about the elephant standing in the living room and everyone ignores me". So it's clear to see she has lived up to her name. In her chart her SN is in the eleventh house and the nodes are squared by Chiron in Aquarius and Pluto in Leo.

In one past life she went back to a time when she was living in a simple farming community (Taurus). She was the wife of an abusive man who would often beat her and attempt to beat the children (violence by beating – ruler of the SN in Aries in the tenth). It was a close-lipped community where no one confided in each other on a personal level (Taurus/Scorpio and eleventh house). She was isolated within the community (Taurus/eleventh house) even though they knew what was going on. She lived in fear of her husband but also would stand between him and the children when he went after them. Her Aquarian rebellious nature simply would not allow her to be completely overcome.

There was another man in the community who was kind to her and over time they fell in love (Pluto Leo). They had to keep it very secret (Scorpio) which was hard in such a small community. Another woman who she had considered a friend but was secretly jealous of her (Scorpio) betrayed and 'outed' her (Scorpio – exposure). She was dragged out in front of the village, beaten and stoned to death, (stonings are also common in Capricorn/tenth house). She did not go down without a fight, and screamed at them for their cowardice and complicity and how they were hypocrites. "All of you knew I was being mistreated and did nothing to help me".

This past life character in the client represented a facet of her nature that actually is an empowered aspect. She said about her current life, "I have always rallied against patriarchal bullshit and won't stand to see women put down". But the fear of crowds and being persecuted by them was also very present for that past life woman and in her current life. She practices alternative forms of therapy in a bible belt area and while she has done very well and has not been persecuted, she lives in constant fear that she will be found out or "reported to the authorities".

It is clear in her chart that standing up for her own rights would also expand to the rights of others with her Taurus SN in the eleventh house. And

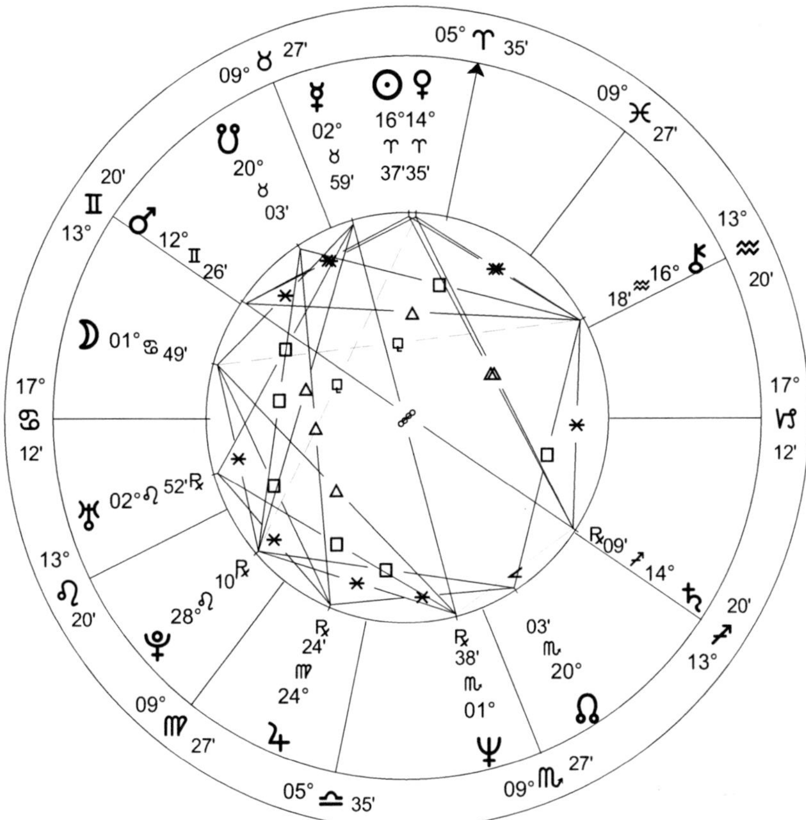

Chart C (Porphyry houses)

essentially this is an empowered aspect of Aquarius. Like Libra, the previous air sign, Aquarius also has the propensity to project and be projected onto. The various roles that belong to Aquarius, from the Revolutionary to the Visionary, can put it into the position of being a scapegoat for society's fear of change. It takes tremendous courage (Leo polarity) to stand up against a group for what one believes in. Many of my Aquarian cases were past life revolutionaries, social reformers, suffragettes and even those who helped in the Underground Railroad. Fighting for human rights and/or personal liberation is a common theme. As Aquarius shows us though, through Saturn, the road to liberation is often a hard one.

Liberation

Another client with Uranus and Saturn in Gemini square a Pisces SN/Virgo NN, had a past life as a young girl working for Boer plantation owners in South Africa. She was expected to work from the age of three which she did, but also she dreamed of better things. As she grew older she desperately wanted to learn, and also wanted to be free. Her grandmother secretly started to teach her to read when she was seven and this completely thrilled her. Unfortunately her mother was very downtrodden, sour and bitter, and when she found out what was happening she forbade it. This confused the young girl as she wanted to be a good child, but was also angry that her mother allowed such menial work to be more important than her learning and the freedom it implied (Uranus/Saturn). By the time she got to her teens, she had not lost her desire to have a life besides drudgery and met a young man. She said, "it was the first time I tasted sweetness". Again her mother found out and forbade her to see him. This infuriated her and she funneled that energy into inspiring a rebellion. It took some years and the work started to wear on her health but eventually there was an uprising and the slaves and servants took to the plains. It was a long walk in devastating dry heat. Sadly during the journey to liberation she collapsed with illness and exhaustion (Pisces/Saturn/Uranus) and the group was forced to leave her behind to die alone. She wanted them to go on to freedom, and watched them until all that was left were swirling dust clouds. She died, and in the spirit world, aside from her own healing, she worked with her lineage of female ancestors and mother from that lifetime, who were so beaten down they had no fight left. Liberating them was also liberating to her.

Just as this client helped her ancestors in order to further her own healing, it is often necessary to work with the soul fragments of others that may be attached to us, or stuck in a place where a trauma happened. In Aquarius, deaths that occur in mass traumas are common, such as natural disasters or human mass atrocities such as battlefields, invasions or genocide. When people die in groups, often the mass fear can trap parts of their souls in a cloud of confusion, as the energy of the collective trauma binds them together. When one has died in such situations in the past and these lives are worked with, one is able to liberate their own soul fragments and also others that are trapped along with them. In our current lives, one only needs to visit a site where such traumas happened in order to feel the clouds of soul bits that are still trapped and linger there in the trauma of the past.

Shock, Trauma and Soul Fragmentation

The Tower card of the tarot deck shows a volatile aspect of the enlightenment process. Lightning (Uranus) strikes the solid structure of reality (Saturn), which results in a fall from the tower, through which a sudden flash of realization is gained. Aquarius is associated with sudden flashes of insight, where divine inspiration is felt as lightning breaking through condensed solidified mental patterns. The shattering of reality to allow a new one to emerge is unsettling, as well as ultimately liberating. The interplay of Saturn and Uranus as co-rulers of Aquarius also show how sudden events that rupture our sense of solid reality can be traumatic. This is how trauma enters this archetype. Saturn as the ruler of structure and form also represents the structure of our psyche. When the integrity of our psychic structure (Saturn) is shattered by traumatic events, often the result is fragmentation (Uranus). The primary split that happens is between the mind and the body. The effect of fragmentation is called dissociation, which is also related to the Pisces archetype and is discussed in the next chapter.

> "A traumatic event is any overwhelming experience (physical, emotional, mental or spiritual) that has caused an inability in the psyche to integrate that experience fully and continue in the same manner as before the traumatic event was experienced. Thus trauma leaves a lasting and damaging impression that manifests as a combination of symptoms, including but not limited to chronic dissociation, anxiety, phobias, fears, hyper vigilance, inhibitions, paranoia, neurosis, avoidance, armoring or rigidity, suppression of emotions, emotional or physical numbness, mental confusion, compulsions etc. In psychological language combinations of these symptoms are classified as post traumatic stress disorder/syndrome (PTSD or PTSS)".
>
> See 'Past Life Wounds – Present Life Problems' in the Introduction.

Saturn also rules time and the chronological order of events which give us a sense of continuity and groundedness in space/time. The air signs are associated with mind; Uranus/Aquarius in particular relates to the 'observing mind/detached observer'; the natural witness aspect of our consciousness. While one may not be aware of this aspect of higher mind day to day, it exists, and because of that, when a situation is overwhelming a part of us can retreat to this distant state of mind, while the rest of us (mainly the physical body) is left to endure the event. This is reported in almost every account of trauma where the victim describes watching or observing the event from outside of the body, or going elsewhere with no emotional or sensate connection to what is happening (Aquarians in general are often described as emotionally detached). We all experience mild states of dissociation, when our body is doing one thing and our minds are elsewhere, and then we forget how we got to where we are. In traumatic situations, when the mind dissociates from an event while the body is left to experience it, what results is a personal fracturing or rupturing of the continuity of time, and subsequent memory. Often the part that dissociates does not stay around to observe what is going on, but goes into an alternate or fantasy reality.

Since Saturn also can be correlated to chronological memory or history, when the mind doesn't record events that happened by being fully present one's perceived reality is altered (Uranus). The part that 'went away' often has a different perception of the traumatic event and is not able to reintegrate into the body after the trauma, simply because its experience is incongruent with what actually happened. It remains frozen in time in shock (Uranus/Saturn). Traumatic memory is classically described as different than normal memory as it presents itself as fragmentary, isolated, incoherent and even amnesiac. Furthermore, when working with healing trauma what is clear is that the body and emotions can remember things that the mind does not.

This is the fragmentation (Uranus) that often results in a chronic state of dissociation (Neptune/Pisces). Severe forms of mental fragmentation result in psychological illness such as schizophrenia and multiple personality disorder. Abnormal mental states and insanity also belong to this archetype. Modern psychology has many descriptions for the mechanism and various phenomenological effects of trauma and dissociation, but it is in shamanism that the wounding to the psyche and soul is fully understood. The fact that there are other dimensions of reality is also the domain of Aquarius and Pisces. Because one may only describe or experience reality within Saturnian limitations, it does not discount the existence of other planes; it only means that a person has not experienced them. We are multi-dimensional beings existing in many planes simultaneously, whether we are aware of it or not. Shamans in particular are traditional masters of traveling in these 'other worlds'. Their conscious passage through these planes is often taken on behalf of an ill or disturbed person, to retrieve the fragmented parts of them that may have been lost in other dimensions.

> "Through his own initiatory experiences, [the shaman] knows the drama of the soul, its instability, it precariousness; in addition, he knows the forces that threaten it and the regions to which it may be carried away".
>
> Mircea Eliade, *Shamanism.* [2]

The shaman either invokes the lost part of the soul to return, or goes to retrieve it in a process called 'soul retrieval'. The lost parts are summoned or brought back to the present day consciousness and reintegrated. The person who has experienced trauma shares a symbolic resonance with the shaman. Typically, the shaman's initiation happens because of a life threatening illness, or as a result of a traumatic event that thrusts them into the other worlds. A stage of the shaman's initiation is known as dismemberment (fragmentation) where the individual is 'taken apart' and often devoured by the evil spirits. This also involves a descent into the lower worlds. Through the process of gaining spiritual allies, support of the community, being reassembled and mentorship, the shaman learns to 're-member' his self and master the other worlds, becoming a bridge between them. Through this process he undergoes a death and resurrection.

Those who experience fragmentation after trauma often describe that it felt like "a part of me died". The difference between the shaman and the trauma victim is that the former happens within a sacred context. The trauma victim is often left to suffer alone, and many times the only healing offered is medication or clinical help that does not address the essential soul loss. Only soulful means can enact soul healing. The trauma victim, like the shaman, knows through experience the precariousness of the soul and its fragility. In this next case we can see the shamanic parallel through the pathology of trauma, from fragmentation to the 'calling back' and reintegration of the lost soul parts.

Soul Retrieval and the Multi-Dimensional Psyche

Chart D

This chart has an Aries SN with its ruler, Mars in Cancer in the eleventh house, which squares the nodes. Mars is also opposed by Saturn in Capricorn and here is where we see the interplay of traumatic events affecting reality, causing fragmentation (eleventh house) and dissociation (Pluto/Moon

---

2. Mircea, Elidae, *Shamanism; Archaic Techniques of Ecstasy*, NJ Princeton University Press, 1972, (p.216).

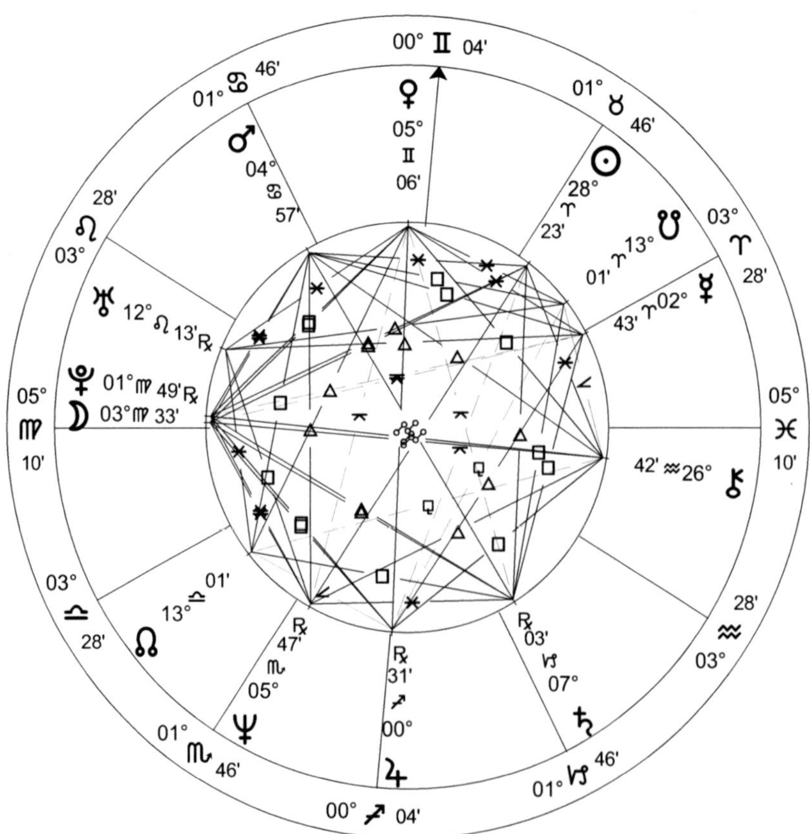

Chart D (Porphyry houses)

twelfth house). Also Pluto is opposed by Chiron in Aquarius. This case also moves through many different space/time realities (Aquarius/Pisces) as we worked in the client's own past lives, with attached spirits that were in her energy field and in her current life childhood.

This client started her session by reporting on her present state of being as "I feel like I am in the wrong story; My ground is gone; I feel like a starfish that has had all its arms cut off; I'm simply not all here… and I've felt this way for most of my life". Her chart also has a basic splay pattern of planets, which are literally 'all over the place'. This adds to the tension in her psyche of feeling scattered and pulled apart.

The first dimension of her issue that surfaced was the spirit of a farmer who was attached to her by a principle known as symbolic resonance. In the astral planes or spirit worlds 'like attracts like' (Uranus/Aquarius rules this principle), thus as will become clearer, her own states of shock and similar past life story resonated with this farmer's experience and subsequently he was drawn into her energy field, and was attached to her. The phenomena of spirits attaching to one's own energy field (also known as possession) in my many cases of working with them correlates most frequently to the Scorpio/Aquarius/Pisces and Libra archetypes.

The farmer had been out fixing his fence in the field and a truck carrying logs swung around the corner too quickly, dislodging the logs and instantly killing the farmer. He was in a state of shock, he didn't know he was dead and had no idea how he got attached to my client. As we worked with him regressing him back through his death several times, he was able to recover his own lost memory, realize he was dead, and was happy to move on. He was a very simple earthbound spirit to work with, as the main thing keeping him stuck was his amnesia and shock, which was fairly easy to remedy. We also worked with several other spirits attached to the client who were in various stages of confusion (she worked in a nursing home, where the elderly often die in amnesiac states) and in shock. With her personal twelfth house emphasis, Chiron in Aquarius and the Uranus/Neptune square, it's easy to see how such spirits would find her energy inviting.

The personal past life that came up was similar to the farmer's story. She was a young man, also a farmer, out riding his horse when he fell off and shattered his back (Mars eleventh house opposing Saturn/Capricorn) resulting in instant paralysis. It took him a long time to die as he cried, "I'm too young" (Aries SN – eighth house, life cut short). It resulted in his staying earthbound, as he never realized that he did finally die. He only remembered lying in the field in the process of dying. This was a fragmented part of the client's soul, from a past life that remained earthbound. Working with him to recover his memory also alleviated him from his earthbound condition, and he was progressively able to ascend to higher planes as we worked on various aspects of his healing.

After he was resolved, the client's back started to twitch in the same place as her past life character had been fatally wounded. Exploring this brought up a non-human entity (demon like – Aries/eighth house). The 'demonic' being was angry and said it was there to block her and was trying to kill her. Since these types of spirits also connect by a principle of resonance, I directed her to explore the angry feelings and go to a place when she felt like that. Instantly she was back in her current childhood when she was four years old. Her father was beating her (Mars/Saturn) while she was stamping her feet in rage. "How dare you be angry", he screamed at her. This was the point of fragmentation of this child self (Mars in Cancer in the eleventh house with Saturn opposing). Because she was expressing her rage she was fully present in her body and not dissociated, but unfortunately she was only four, and her father's rage and abuse hit her like a freight train causing her to fragment. When two solid objects collide with force, the weaker of the two will crack or shatter.

We can see how this was symbolically similar to the farmer who was hit by the logs and her own past life self who fell off the horse; as well as her current life little girl. This four year old self went to pieces and we had to work to collect all the fragments. The main part of her that fragmented went into a very dark place in terror, which was where the 'demonic' being got a hold within her psyche. It is interesting to note here that Leo, as the opposition to Aquarius, represents by its ruler the Sun an integrating force in our psyche. It is the center of our personal solar system. Aquarius' fragmentation is brought together through the solar nature. The same is true for the Pisces/Virgo opposition where the dissociated pieces find an integrating force in Virgo, who is associated with Isis who re-members the scattered pieces of Osiris.

For her own survival, that young girl had to cut herself off from her own anger (Mars in eleventh house) and repress it (Saturn) in the face of her father's unbeatable force. Part of the healing of this fragmented self was the reclaiming of her rage and anger (Mars). This 'woke up' the terrified little girl in the dark and brought her back into the client's body. It also released her from the clutches of the dark being who was a concretized thought form (Saturn and Aquarius) of her father's malicious intent, which had become embedded in her back when that part of her own energy vacated.

Transforming the dark being and releasing it also to a place of restoration and healing was possible at this point, and ensured that it would not trouble her again. Further work with the now returned inner child (Cancer and fifth house) helped her to integrate. It was also interesting that the little girl was pointing to her knees when she returned to the client. This inner child self was bringing back the energy of the right to stand up for oneself, which she had lost when that part went away. Capricorn/Saturn rules the knees. This little girl had been rebellious (eleventh house) and rightfully so, and now was bringing back to the client the ability to make a clear boundary (which had been damaged as her twelfth house planets show with Chiron opposition) and fight for her rights (Mars in the eleventh house). Spontaneously, in the bardo work, a panther and a mountain goat came. The panther was an ally to stay with her and protect boundaries and the mountain goat is clearly an empowered Saturn in Capricorn!

She said that since that event when she was four, she had never been able to express anger. With Mars in the eleventh house, squaring the nodes, her will had been traumatized and fragmented. With her Pluto conjunct the Moon in Virgo in the twelfth house, her tendency to internalize her psychic environment without any boundaries needed to be worked with, and clearing the attached entities was part of this process of restoring empowered Virgonian wholeness. The thought form that had stayed with her she said "was like a constant voice in my head saying you have no right to your feelings". That dark being had kept her estranged from herself and her own natural power. The fragmented inner child would never be able to return without removing this thought form, as she contained the very essence of the truth of her own emotions (Jupiter in Sagittarius fourth house).

Thoughts and Reality

The metaphysical idiom that 'energy follows thought and thought creates form' is also a part of the Aquarius archetype. This is commonly talked about in New Age circles as 'thought creates reality'. The creation of the dark being from the father in the last case, shows that strongly held thought, injected with powerful emotion and driven by intent, will create a living thought form with its own reality.

This means that anything humans are capable of thinking and feeling is projected with energy from their subtle body. These thought forms (Uranus) can be created intentionally, with the concentrated use of mental focus for higher or healing purposes, or with malicious intent and black magical practice they can become potent negative thought forms that once created continue to exist. The latter are often referred to as a class of dark non-human entities. Collectively, they can come from a variety of sources including wars, torture, mutilation and the horrors of suffering humans have caused each other over the ages. To a lesser degree, everyday, every thought and feeling we have can take form (Uranus/Saturn) in the mental and astral planes.

That thought creates form is a truism, but as Saturn/Uranus imply, this also happens within limitations. On the purely mental planes that belong to Uranus, thought creates form instantly (which is what happens in the afterlife when the spirit is no longer in the body), but once you add the dense vibration of matter (Saturn) this retards the process and for other limiting reasons, also hinders it. Thus the New Age idea that one only needs to think of something to bring about changes needs to be tempered with some realism, and sometimes some real work (Saturn). On the other hand, the principle of synchronicity seems to also fall into Aquarius' domain where the material world reflects back to us our interconnectedness with it through 'meaningful coincidence'.

Uranian alternate realities and power of mind show up in interesting ways in clients' past lives. One client with an Aquarius SN in the third house (a double signature of mind) went back to a past life where she was a part of a community (Aquarius) of builders who lifted massive stones only with sound and thought. It has been theorized that this was the way certain past civilizations built their temples and monuments. It has also been documented in the present, as Tibetan monks have displayed this ability to scientists.

Other Aquarian past lives frequently show a connection to alternate history (Uranus/Saturn) and take place in civilizations such as Atlantis, or even on other planets. Aliens belong to this archetype just as the feeling of alienation does. If one does not believe that Atlantis was real, it does not supersede the symbolic meaning that is so appropriate for us to revisit at this time of the 'dawning of the Age of Aquarius'. Misuse of technology, genetic manipulation and the arrogance of human intellect sometimes found in the sciences, when cut off from heart (Leo), can leave us also on the verge of destruction. Along with past scientific innovators in this archetype, I have also seen those who were deranged in their pursuit of scientific knowledge, such as Nazi experimenters. The detachment of Aquarius can go in very dark directions.

The Saturn part of Aquarius is a structuring/organizing principle that causes groups of people to come together because they share similar ideas or ideals. Any group of people that form a club, community, church or any other means of meeting are drawn together because they share similar likes, ideas or ideologies. This is true in all areas of society and is also true for sub-cultures or splinter groups. Standing apart from society with your own crowd is not only a way to differentiate from the whole, but it is also a form of rebellion. It also allows one to feel the comfort of belonging and to see one's self reflected through like-minded others (Leo/Aquarius). In past lives, belonging to secret groups, societies or communities that set themselves apart from the mainstream is common. Another form of this shows up frequently as aristocracy (as distinct from Leo royalty). This final case shows several of these Aquarian themes as this client's karmic history contains a long struggle between individuality and belonging.

Chart E

This chart has a Sagittarius SN in the eleventh house with its ruler Jupiter in Taurus in the fourth. Further Aquarius/Uranus karmic signatures include Pluto conjunct Uranus, and the ruler of the SN, Jupiter, squared by Saturn in Aquarius. Her first story shows the Sagittarian themes of the search for the authentic self; running away; combined with Aquarian alienation.

In one past life the client was a male Russian aristocrat. He grew up under the care of servants but even at a young age he appeared to be completely distanced from everyone (eleventh house also SN ruler in Taurus/fourth house – emotional 'poverty' squared by Saturn/Aquarius – deprivation). As a young boy he really wanted to learn (Sagittarius SN) but was mistreated in school by the teachers as he "couldn't sit still or do what I was told". (Aquarius hyperactivity related to repressed trauma/rebellion). His inner attitude was, "You're not going to get to me" (Taurus and Aquarius combined) which was a combination of emotional shut down (Taurus) and rebellion as self protection (Aquarius/Saturn).

As he grew older, he never recovered his emotions. He was married but it was an arranged marriage (eighth house) and he ignored his wife, choosing to have affairs (Sagittarius non-committal – playing the field). There was a revolution in the country against the bourgeoisie and aristocracy and a part of him sided with the revolutionaries although he was of the upper class. They reflected his own state of rebellion, but he was trapped in the middle and actually felt quite powerless (eighth house). By this point in his life he felt he didn't fit in anywhere; he didn't belong to his family, class, the revolutionaries or even himself. His love affairs were not pursued with passion as he was quite unable to feel (Aquarius – detached, Taurus – shut down, Saturn – repression). The uprising intensified and his home was attacked, he left his wife and children and ran away (Sagittarius). He did

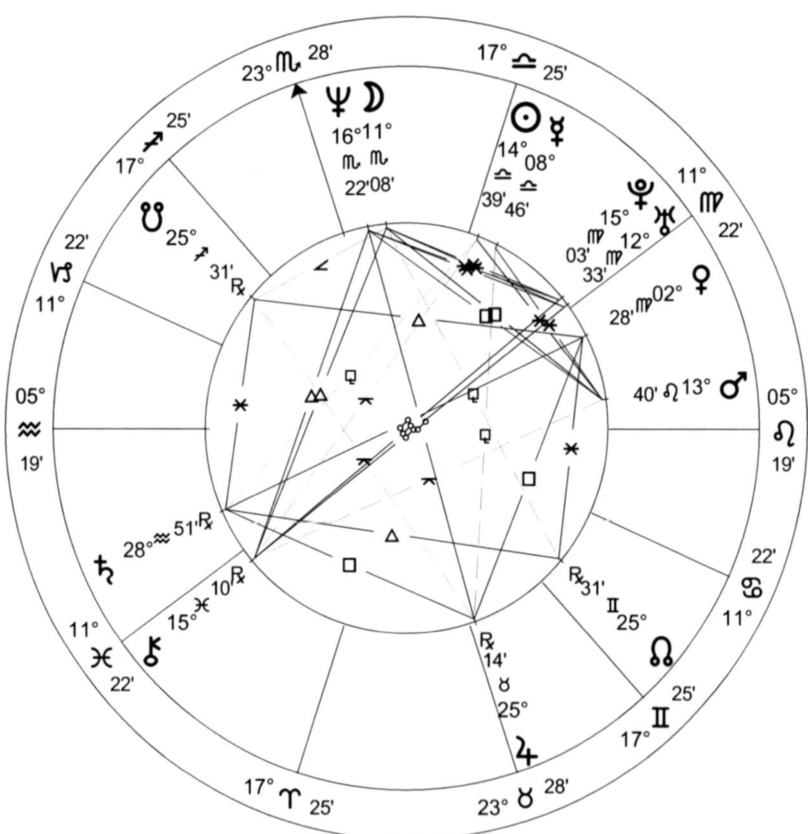

Chart E (Porphyry houses)

not escape as he was overrun and captured by the revolutionaries, who shot him and threw him in a pit with other bodies.

In the afterlife he remained stony and uncaring and was still in shock. After working with his shut down, a turning point came when he went back in his memory to when he was six. He sobbed for himself because he started to remember that he had been a very sweet and sensitive child (Pluto opposite Chiron in Pisces). He had lost this part of himself with his cold and detached upbringing and subsequently he became just like his guardians. This return to his 'authentic self' (Sagittarius) brought that lost boy back into his heart, restoring what had been lost (NN in the fifth). He then was able to feel and face the remorse he still had about his marriage, and his abandonment of his wife and children (eighth house and Sagittarius). He told his wife, "I did love you; I just didn't know how to feel it". He saw that she was a good wife, and let her know that he now appreciated her. He also apologized for being a coward and running away (Sagittarius). After they reconciled, he was able to reflect on the meaning of this life and said, "No one ever really cared for me, so I decided to hide and never show my real self. It was painful as I really did have a good heart but I was divided from myself". The aspect of hiding oneself relates not only to the emotional shut down and loss of the authentic self but also to Virgo in the eighth (hiding) and the potential of the NN in the fifth house.

As the client reflected on that life she realized that the aristocrat "just wanted to be who he was but his school years also forced him to rebel against feeling he was being forced to perform". This is an expression of the eleventh/fifth house axis and interesting that in this life she is a performance artist who employs 'shock value' in her performance to "get people to think outside the box". (Gemini NN in the fifth house). She has struggled with many layers of fears as an artist about being seen, being rejected and performing, but her eighth house emphasis, and Scorpio planets, give her the current life capacity to confront the fears and dark places within herself. Both her polarity points (fifth and second house) relate to a healing of her heart and feeling nature. She said, "I feel in this life I have been learning about my emotional nature" and also "the equalizing of power".

This last statement leads to another life where she was a servant (Virgo) in a castle, who joined a rebellious uprising that killed their employers. As a group they ran off and lived like gypsies (Sagittarius). The reverse themes of this lifetime compared to the aristocrat are interesting. She said in her current life, "I was never even aware of how much class systems and the inequity of wealth and subsequent power was in my consciousness, but I lived it daily". She came from a working-class family, but her father did quite well and she said, "I always felt guilty about having" (Taurus and Scorpio).

In other past lives she experienced severe mental trauma (eleventh house/Aquarius/Uranus) which resulted in insanity. She said that in many lives she either went into "frantic insanity" or "complete shut down and dissociation". One of these was a slave lifetime. She was a member of an African tribe (Aquarius – tribal), and was taken by her own people (Scorpio betrayal) and put on a boat. She was sold to a man who had a large farm and became trusted as a servant, which gained her some liberty and freedom

(Sagittarius/eleventh house). She was allowed to go to town and run errands and one day tried to escape. She was captured and was put into a cage, constantly being taunted to the point of insanity. Her memory of going crazy was like "something in me splintered and I just went frantically insane (Uranus)". She said that this played out in her current life during her higher education years (Sagittarius/Gemini) as she said, "I constantly felt like I was being poked at, no matter what I did it wasn't good enough and my work was constantly torn down".

In another life she was a tribal (Aquarius) medicine woman whose people were struck with a plague of smallpox (eighth house). There was more going on behind the scenes, as another tribe was also cursing them through magical means, and they believed that the plague was a result of this power struggle (eighth house). She was absolutely overwhelmed (Virgo/Pisces) with trying to save her people (Virgo/Sagittarius) and stave off the power attacks. She felt alienated yet immensely responsible for the tribe (Aquarius – Saturn in Aquarius). She said that her learning from that lifetime was about knowing the limits of her own capabilities and power (Scorpio). And that there really was nothing she could do, which is also a lesson of Piscean surrender.

The astrological themes are easy to see in her own summation of her karmic history. "I've been learning that it's okay to be seen and to have personal power (fifth house). I now understand the nature of being empowered instead of having power over others (fifth house and Scorpio)".

The wounds of alienation and the ability to come forward as an individual to be seen for her gifts are also an empowered expression of her eleventh/fifth house axis.

12

Pisces/Neptune and the Twelfth House

"Having removed any view
in terms of self,
always mindful, Mogharaja,
view the world as void.
This way one is above & beyond death.
This is the way one views the world
so that the King of Death does not see one."
The Buddha

Keywords

Mutable/Yin/Water
Disillusionment
Victim
Persecuted
Martyr
Savior
Illusions
Monk/Priest
Alcoholism
Mystic
Medium
Psychic
Astral glamour
Addiction
Drugs
Escape

Hopeless
Helpless
Weak boundaries
Surrender
Subconscious
Transcendence
Wounded
Madman
Lost Identity
Guilt (individual/collective)
Masochist
Fantasy
Naïve
Poet
Musician

Loss/erosion
Isolation
Confusion
Dreamer
Dissociation
Disbelief
Visionary
Melancholy
Otherworldly
Imagination
Compassion
Sensitive
Suffering
Innocence
The Fool
Suicide

The Natural Archetype

Pisces and the twelfth house, as the last of the zodiac wheel, culminates all the previous signs. Pisces is like the color white, which is a combination of all the colors of the visible light spectrum, yet technically is not even a color itself. Because of this composite nature, Pisces is a little bit of all that comes before it and also not any of them. Sound confusing? Welcome to the boundary-less consciousness of Pisces! After all the striving, testing, and trials in the previous signs, the 'self' is meant to be surrendered here at the final point of the constellations. Immediately following the focus on individuation in Aquarius, the intention becomes the transcendence of the personally developed self.

The totality that is Pisces gives it an association with consciousness itself – that which is invisible, yet lies behind and 'informs' all phenomenal existence. This association with consciousness is suggested with the image of Pisces as the cosmic ocean, implying that all life, all forms, and even consciousness itself emerge from these waters. This cosmic ocean, as the source of all things is the Alpha and the Omega. Everything comes from it and returns to it, thus it is also strongly suggestive of not only the individual but the collective unconscious. Jung defines this collective unconscious as the source of all the archetypes; a reservoir of the experiences of our species. All experience that ever has been, or potentially will be, is a part of the collective unconscious.

Of all the qualities of Pisces, many can be boiled down to a few central concepts; there is more to the conscious self than one is aware (the unconscious) and because of this, the egoic small self is at some point meant to be transcended, lost, sacrificed, or surrendered to gain a greater Self. The saying of the Piscean teacher, Jesus, epitomizes this surrender. "He who finds his life shall lose it; he who loses his life for my sake, shall find it". Surrender as a theme within Pisces relates to the spiritual intention of this sign: surrender, but not before its time! It can be easy and habitual to 'give ones self' away when the sense of self has not been highly developed. True surrender is a harder path that entails giving up a highly polished, often deeply cherished gem. One cannot give away what one does not fully possess. The main difference between true and premature surrender is a matter of the degree of conscious awareness that is present. When one consciously and willingly relinquishes each attachment, then the greater self is gained.

Dissociation is another condition of consciousness that is prevalent in the Pisces archetype. Psychic wounding is a term that can be applied to traumas that affect one's psychic structure. The psyche tends to dissociate parts of itself in the face of trauma. This is a natural reaction. It becomes problematic when it is chronic, and when the dissociated parts of the self do not return and reintegrate into the whole psyche. This is what shamans refer to as 'soul loss,' and bringing back the parts that have gone away is called 'soul retrieval', (discussed also in the Aquarius chapter). The act of dissociation happens to all of us. Numerous times during any given day our attention or awareness wanders, we do things on automatic pilot, we daydream. This is a minor dissociative state. In other ways, we are also dissociated from our true emotions and even our own bodies. We all have Pisces, Neptune and the twelfth house in our charts. When confronted with emotional, mental or physical pain, the same tendency to 'go away' protects a person in the moment, and can be seen as a merciful function of the psyche; yet for a variety of reasons that part rarely comes back fully on its own. In cases when trauma is repetitive, such as in cases of repeated abuse, torture etc., living in a chronic split and dissociative state is often the only way to survive.

Dissociation is commonly described by people as "I just go away". The feeling after such an event is that one never fully comes back and life can be experienced from that point on, as several clients have said, as "living in fog", "being in bubble", "feeling muted", or "being underwater". Others have said, "I feel like a part of me died", "I'm not fully here", or "I just disappear". These themes are repeated here in many of the Pisces cases, and this type of reaction in past lives is often behind a present life 'spacey' feeling.

In a case presented at the end of this chapter (Pisces SN in the ninth and three planets in Pisces), the woman laughingly said to me, "I feel like I've been out of my body all my life and didn't arrive until just about last week". This is the effect of chronic dissociation. When the source of this psychic wounding is in past lives, one is simply born not feeling all here. This is where soul retrieval work is essential, which happens in both present and past life regression and other forms of healing work. When dissociated parts are brought back, the effect in the current life has been described by clients as "feeling born again", "finally starting my life for the first time", or "I didn't know how much I wasn't here, until I was finally really here".

Dissociated parts of the self remain frozen in the state and time when they originally became separated. Identifying these parts, bringing them back and reintegrating them is a reflection of the promise of wholeness that the polarity point of Virgo offers. Virgo as the pregnant virgin is whole unto herself. While Pisces represents a different wholeness – 'all-that-is' – Virgo gives the boundary of the self and the body as the ground for wholeness. Virgo, with its Mercury rulership, allows first for the identification of the separated parts, and then through her earthiness the re-embodiment of them. In ancient Egypt, Virgo was associated with Isis, the one who 're-membered' the scattered pieces of Osiris, putting him back together. 'Remembering', then, can have different layers of meaning, including the bringing together of lost parts and the piecing together of the past.

Pisces in Past Life Experiences

The Pisces archetype is a part of the karmic axis when:

Pluto is in Pisces or the twelfth house or
The South Node is in Pisces or the twelfth house or
The ruler of the South Node is in Pisces or the twelfth house or
Neptune aspects Pluto, the nodal axis or rulers of the nodes.

The surrender and 'loss of self' tendency arises in many interesting ways in Piscean type past lives. There are five distinct archetypal personas that carry different imprints of this:

The Mystic who transcends the self in relationship to the divine,
The Martyr who sacrifices the self for a cause or another,
The Savior who forgets the self for the sake of another,
The Victim who loses the self at the mercy of another, or
The Madman whose conscious self is overcome by the contents of the subconscious.

These past life archetypal personas are not exclusive to Pisces, but each of these will show up in the past life stories in this chapter. Because of Pisces' association with consciousness itself, all states of consciousness become a part of the experience in this archetype. Following upon Capricorn, where reality is condensed and solidified, Aquarius and then Pisces traverse and include myriad states of alternate realities from altered states to unconscious states.

Amnesia and Addiction

One client with Neptune square an Aquarius SN had a past life experience of amnesia brought on by a trauma. The sudden fragmentation of the self (Aquarius/Uranus) occurred during an explosion of a bomb, leaving him trapped under debris. He was found several days later with no memory of who he was. He was a young man of about seventeen years of age when he was found and cared for by some nuns (Neptune, compassionate). He did survive and went on until he was in his thirties, living a minimal existence as a shop keeper's helper. His main imprint during the whole story, up through his death, was his constant questioning of "Who am I?" The past life imprint affected this man in his current life, leaving him feeling deep in his core that he had no sense of his real self or what he even wanted in this life. He felt he should know what to ask for in life, but when opportunities came he let them pass by. He simply wasn't present enough to respond to life. A vague sense of self is often associated with the Pisces archetype, and this story presents a very literal past life cause for this man's vagueness.

Following the theme of unconsciousness, addiction and escapism become a part of the way one either falls away from consciousness, or tries to avoid it altogether. Alcoholism or association with alcoholics is a common theme when Pisces is a part of the karmic axis. Alcohol as a substance tends to mute or dampen emotional awareness; the use of it in an addictive way can be an attempt to numb pain and a hyper-sensitive nature.

Chart A

A woman with a Pisces SN and Moon conjunct in the eighth house had this exact type of past life. She also has Neptune in Sagittarius square the nodal axis, further emphasizing the Pisces archetype. Her first memory in her past life was as a young boy of about five years old with his mother. He perceived his mother to be sweet and caring yet absent in some way (Pisces Moon). It was "like she's not all there". Regardless, he felt an immense amount of love for her. Unfortunately, with Moon in the eighth conjunct the SN in Pisces, life did not continue in this vein because his mother died only a year or so later. He was sent to an orphanage and was adopted by another couple.

He experienced his new 'mother' as nice but the 'father' was abusive and this abuse degenerated into sexual molestation (nodes are second/eighth house axis) additionally Pluto and Mars are in opposition. As a young boy he imprinted all of this as a loss of hope, feeling trapped and immersed in

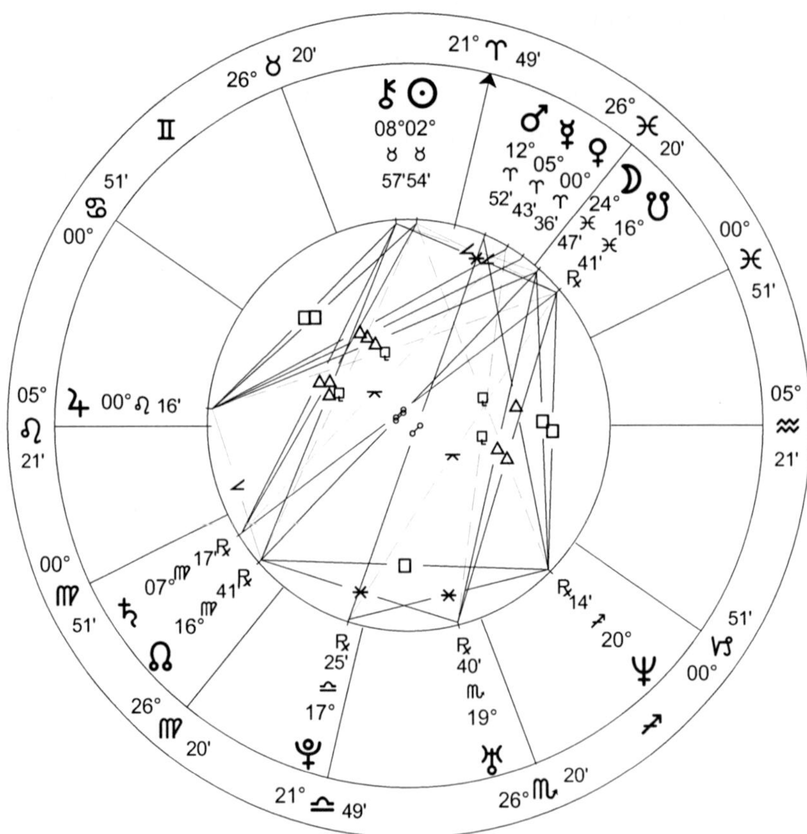

Chart A (Porphyry houses)

deep sadness. He longed nightly for his own mother and continued to grieve her loss.

The entrapment and loss of the eighth house combined with Pisces to create a bittersweet, melancholy longing. Eventually, by the time he was fourteen or so, he ran away (another Piscean way of escaping and also the Neptune in Sagittarius). At this point in the story it became clear that this lifetime was likely to have been the client's most recent past life, as the boy was hanging around in a fairly modern style airport (1950s-60s). The client was in her early twenties when this regression took place in 2004, so it is probable. The airport is a detail that I felt was symbolic to this young boy's life. The reason he was drawn to hang around in an airport, is that airports are places where people leave and reunite with each other. It is also a place where people escape their normal lives and go off on journeys, leaving the day to day routine behind (Neptune in Sagittarius and Mars in the ninth). The pain of his loss, and his longing to reunite with his mother to escape the conditions of his own life, made the airport a perfect external reflection of the state of his inner world. He shortly fell in with a group of other aimlessly wandering young people (Neptune in Sagittarius squaring the nodes). They begged, borrowed and stole their way through day-to-day life and he quickly descended into hard addiction to alcohol and any drugs they could get their hands on. This helped him numb the immense pain of his young short life. One night while stoned, he got into a fight and was killed violently by another youth who held him underwater, drowning him in a bathtub. Drowning lives are also common in Pisces/Neptune/twelfth house. The violence and premature death in a previous life are indicated in this chart by other factors of the karmic axis: Pluto opposes Mars in Aries (premature death).

In the after-death work, while healing the imprints from that life, spirit beings came in to help him clear the water from his throat (NN in the second). They urged him to hum and sing to start this process. At that moment he spontaneously went into an earlier memory from that life. He remembered that his mother and he sang together nightly and that she played the piano. He recalled that he did have dreams in that life of becoming a musician (Pisces). All of this was forgotten (Pisces) and sublimated behind the pain of losing her, with the addiction also serving to numb what was obviously his natural artistic and deeply sensitive nature (Pisces).

The main imprints the client felt that carried from the past life into her present life were aimlessness, escapism and a general feeling of dissociation, "As if I am living someone else's life and am always in a dream state". These were a past life reaction to the abuse, which also caused a deep fear of entrapment (eighth house). Beside these imprints, in her current life she felt she could never complete anything. Of course her NN in Virgo in the second house, with its ruler in Aries in the ninth, indicates that in her current life the lessons of focus, determination, and really going for her goals are at the forefront. Further, her NN is conjunct Saturn in the second, which challenges her to find comfort in boundary and form, within her own body and her general approach to life. All of these qualities of her evolutionary direction are perfectly suited to give her the means to bring that deeply sensitive and talented self out into the world. Clearing the residues of this past life aided her in 'waking up' and becoming more 'embodied' in her current life.

She said also that all her life she had an undefined deep sense of sadness (common with Pisces and also Capricorn). Interestingly, her present life experience with her mother was not that her mother was absent, but that she was too controlling and overprotective (Moon in the eighth). We did speculate afterwards, as it didn't come up during the session, that perhaps her current life mother may have been the past life mother that left her son, and this life she was coming back to make sure she was fully there for him/her (maybe even a little too much!) The astrological signatures indicate that this would be true.

'Showing up' is a theme for Pisces also. While Virgo can be front and center, totally involved in others' issues and crises, Pisces can have the tendency to simply 'check out', not being present for themselves or others. This can create a karma of omission where the present life becomes more about balancing what wasn't done in the past than what was. The stories of being lost, dissociation, and addiction all echo this theme, and many of the challenges that life throws at the Pisces type are designed to get the individual to 'show up' and be present.

Psychism

Before Neptune, Jupiter was considered the ruler of Pisces, and expansive states of consciousness are a part of Jupiter's influence here. These types of experiences fall into the category of altered states of consciousness. Not all of these experiences are fraught with difficulty, but when they are, it can result in a psychic wounding of another sort. Prophetic seers (especially when combined with Sagittarius) or natural born psychics, mediums and visionaries often are past life characters in the Pisces archetype.

A woman of the Neptune in Virgo generation had a Pisces SN in the third house, with Neptune conjunct her NN, therefore opposing the SN. She had a past life as a young child of about eight who had frequent otherworldly visitations. One of the most prominent was from the Virgin Mary (Virgo/Pisces), and like the children of Lourdes, she had messages that were meant to be shared with the people of her town. As she tried to communicate these (third house), she was laughed at and frowned upon by her family and the village. They took her to the church and she was scolded by the priests. Feeling humiliated (Virgo) and lacking any outward miracles to back her up, she started to deny and doubt (Neptune in Virgo) her visions and stopped communicating them all together (third house).

The emotional wounding from this treatment effectively repressed her visions and left her feeling bereft – something essential within her died when she did this. She lived the rest of her past life as an outwardly normal woman, marrying and having children, but inwardly felt as if a part of her had died long ago and she never recovered (Pisces SN – soul loss). She died with the imprints of this empty feeling and the sense of having been forced to give up this essential part of herself. This had left her with a current life imprint of fear and hopelessness around expressing her inner world and psychic abilities in her present life.

Another woman with a Libra SN conjuncted by Neptune and Mars in the first house, found herself in the first scene of a past life in what seemed to be a sarcophagus, small tomb or cave. As the story unfolded she was a young male Greek candidate for initiation (Libra SN and Mars/first house). She was expected, as part of her initiation (Mars/first house), to go into this sealed tomb and survive, while in an altered state of consciousness (Neptune). This past life memory is in line with current day research of several ancient mystery school initiations that involve the candidate being able to leave the body and traverse the astral planes while being buried alive. There has been speculation about whether this was aided by drugs. In this past life it seemed as if he was in a state of suspended animation. Because of the nebulous Piscean nature of the situation, it was hard to know if this state was drug induced or not. He was floating in a cosmic sense of bliss which, despite being 'entombed' was not unpleasant to him. The client reported feeling surges of energy through her body and that it was quite powerful yet indescribable.

As if this is not Piscean enough, it continued. The past life character was unable to distinguish for quite some time if he was actually in his body or not, or even if he was dead or alive. Eventually it became clearer that he did indeed die during this initiation attempt (this type of event is also described in the Aries chapter under failed initiations) and his spirit body simply stayed in this floating, blissful state, still earthbound and in the tomb. The healing from this story was a classic piece of soul-retrieval, as the young man part of her soul needed to first realize he was dead, and then, that he didn't have to stay in that tomb anymore. It was not an easy piece of work because he was quite blissed out floating in the cosmic sea and didn't feel compelled to be disturbed from this state! One might say that part of her soul was in a 'mock' blissful after-life state, not having actually left the earth plane to go into the light, yet feeling like it had. This points also to illusions and the illusory state that are aspects of the Pisces archetype, described more fully in following paragraphs.

Mysticism

Both of these previous stories of the young girl visionary and the initiate have elements of the mystic within them. The direct personal experience of otherworldly states of consciousness is part of the mystical experience. Other past life characters that embody the mystic in search of the divine are monks, who are quite common in the Pisces (and Sagittarian) archetypes. In Sagittarius, monks/priests and preachers represent the archetype's association with dogma and religion. In Pisces they represent the transcendent, mystical search for the divine and also Pisces' association with closed-off places, away from society. A monastic life in past times, with its focus on negation of the here and now in exchange for a transcendent reality, can bring complications in the current life. Not all past life monks were particularly saintly, but frequently their lives were spent seeking and often finding deep communion with the divine through pure intent, meditation or prayer. But the asceticism of past life monks is no less fraught with difficulty than for today's monks, priests and gurus. This following story relates all the themes just mentioned.

Chart B

This client has a Sagittarian SN in the twelfth house. He was a monk in medieval times. He lived a typical monastic existence with much sincerity but with the exception that he became enamored with a young woman in the village (Pluto is in Leo in the seventh house). Eventually he gave in to his romantic feelings and slept with her, causing her to become pregnant. The father of this young woman did not take the news so calmly and gathered a posse to teach this monk a lesson. They attacked him and castrated him (Mars inconjunct the SN, Mars square ruler of SN). He was torn with his own guilt (sixth /twelfth house nodal axis) and used his religious propensity to 'spiritualize' reality, so during the moments of the attack the monk had an epiphany (Pluto sextile Neptune/SN twelfth house). He described these

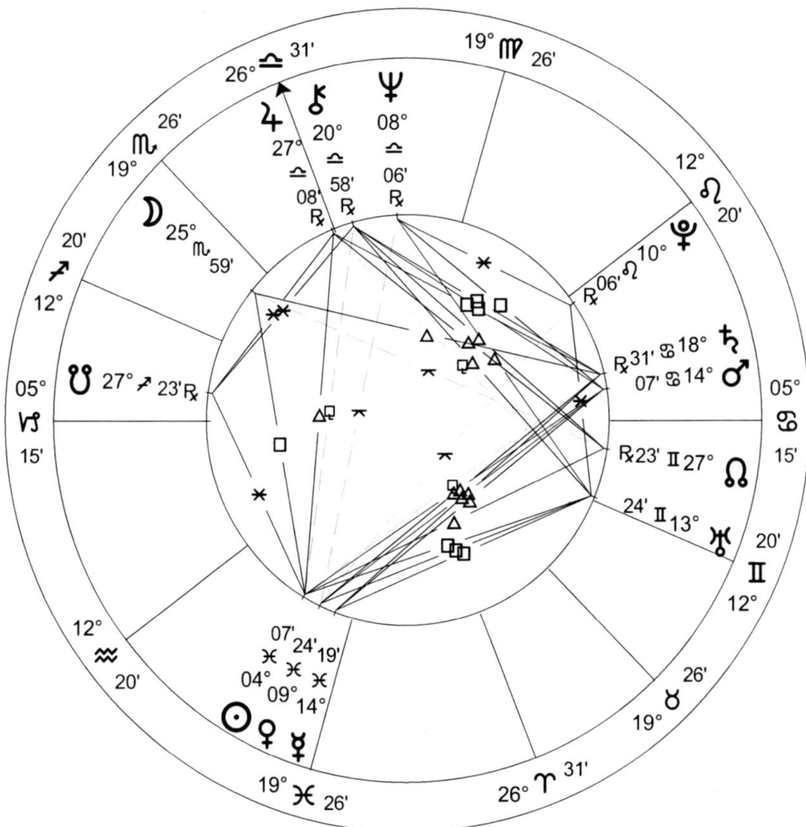

Chart B (Porphyry houses)

moments as entering a state of complete surrender and becoming one with Christ-like consciousness. He felt he deserved the punishment and willingly surrendered to the castration without a fight. He felt completely reconciled with it even before it happened, as it was a sacrifice that needed to occur because he had broken his vow. Somehow he survived this and went on living, but in a completely different state of consciousness.

His suffering became a way to transcend his guilt – a gift that kept him open to unity with the divine. He lived the rest of his life in what he described as a state of profound oneness (twelfth house). Some qualities from that past life carried forward into his current life as a mystical spirituality that he always had. But he was aware it was ungrounded. He said he realized that in this life he is trying to heal his personal split between body and spirit (sixth/twelfth house axis), caused by his religious beliefs (Sagittarius SN) in that past life and by the religious conditioning that came up in several other past lives. He felt the state of awareness achieved by his monk self in the past stayed with him, but in his own words he has "needed to try to bring this more down to earth into his lower charkas". Certainly the lessons of a twelfth house SN evolving towards the sixth house would involve being able to embody the numinous qualities of Pisces in a practical Virgo way.

Monks, mystics and meditators need at some point to come down from the mountains and out of the monasteries and apply their spiritual attainment in day-to-day affairs. As in the case of the castrated monk, this was a primary karmic lesson; the divine is found also in day-to-day life. Virgo as a Mercury-ruled earth sign is very much about body/mind, while Neptune/Pisces is spirit.

Another way to look at the healthy synthesis of the axis is the natural interplay of body/mind/spirit. Negation of one over the other, results in imbalance and the need to reintegrate that which has been overlooked. Peaks and valleys are both a part of the spiritual path, and the higher states need to be grounded in reality. Virgo provides that reality check and when integrated provides for a practical spirituality that is humble, divinely inspired and service oriented. When integrated, Pisces gains from Virgo the ability to do while maintaining the experience of being. This allows for a flow during the act of doing that can be divinely inspired. While Virgo alone may lose itself in doing, Pisces teaches Virgo to let go a little to transcend and surrender the outcome of personal actions.

The Pisces state of innocence and trust can feel threatened by Virgo's critical nature. The Piscean consciousness may struggle to hold on to innocence too long for fear of being exposed to harsh reality that may offend its idyllic world. But eventually a soul that holds out in this childlike state for too long will cause circumstances for itself that force it to come of age. All the water signs are opposed by earth, and for each there is a necessary growing up, coming of age, or giving of form and solidity. For Pisces these circumstances can involve experiencing the loss of innocence, disillusionment and confusion to reach Virgo's clarity. The art of moving through disillusionment without enacting the shadow side of Virgo as a critical cynic is a skilful blend of Pisces/Virgo working in synthesis.

Disillusionment and Discernment

A prominent lesson for those born with sixth/twelfth house or Virgo/Pisces as part of their karmic axis is that of discernment. This shows up in the present life in scenarios such as finding out that someone or something is not what was believed.

Pisces is often associated with purity which extends to pure intent. The impact of suddenly being exposed to others with less than pure motives, or in a believed reality that crashes down into a less than idyllic state, can leave the imprint of disillusionment. It is a difficult wound to heal, as it is as nebulous as the Piscean archetype it is associated with, but there is a higher intention behind this wound. It provides the fuel for one to come to clarity. Having placed one's faith, or trust, in something that was not real or was an illusion it only stands to reason that for real growth to occur, disillusionment must occur. As philosopher and poet George Santayana said, "Wisdom come by disillusionment", which also reminds us of Jupiter's (wisdom) influence as the old ruler of Pisces.

Quite often after a disillusioning experience, when the fog clears, one reports a sense of psychological sobriety, where the state of being caught in illusion is likened, in retrospect, to being intoxicated or drunk. This next story shows the impact of wounds caused by illusions and disillusionment in very literal terms.

Chart C

The main signatures in this chart that illustrate the past life dynamics are Pluto/Uranus in Virgo in the eighth house opposed by Saturn conjunct Chiron in Pisces in the second. Saturn in Pisces also squares the nodes. Transiting Uranus was also directly conjunct natal Saturn in Pisces and within orb of natal Chiron when the regressions took place. Often when transiting planets aspect the karmic axis, they indicate a time for release of karma. In this case, transiting Uranus reflected the energy of liberation from past life Piscean themes and brought the Pisces archetype into the forefront of this session.

This client found himself in one of his past lives as a middle-aged man living in a desert culture. He was a trader (Gemini/Sagittarius nodes) and made occasional long distance travels (SN in Sagittarius) across the desert with his wares. On one of these longer journeys he was ambushed and robbed of his goods. This was bad, but even worse, the supplies he needed

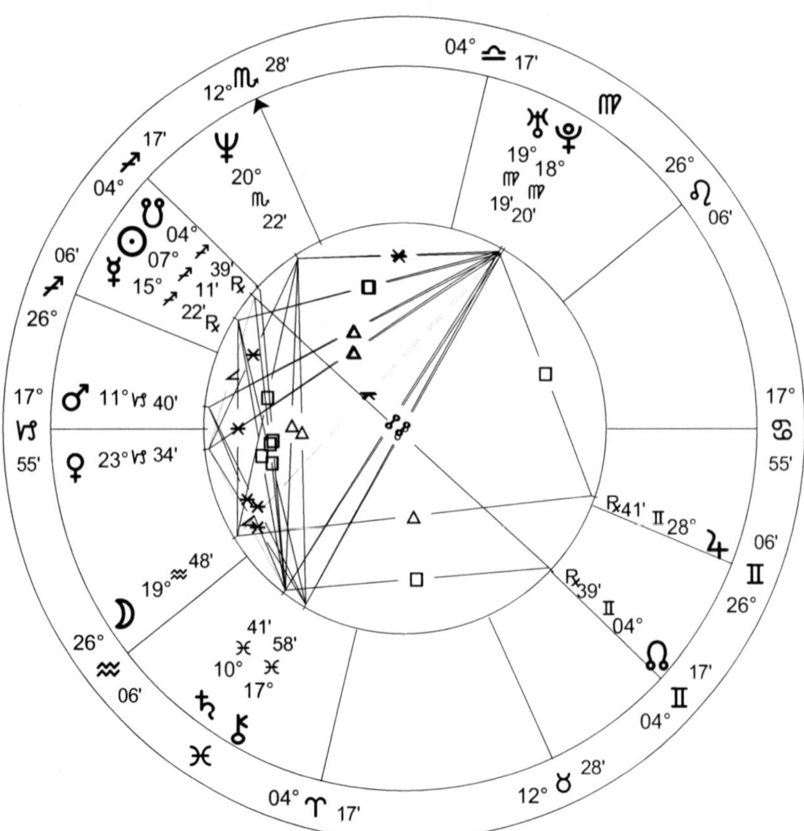

Chart C (Porphyry houses)

for survival were also stolen (second/eighth house axis). His first reaction was absolute panic, followed by determination to survive. During some of his panicked moments his deepest fears were revealed to be dying exposed (eighth house) and going mad (Saturn conjunct Chiron in Pisces – reality breaking down, also SN in the eleventh). As time passed he dehydrated, which did set into motion a psychological breakdown. One mirage and illusion after another arose. He believed each one, only to be crushed to find it was not true (Saturn in Pisces).

He had the typical mirages of water, but also saw people coming to help him, imagined he had made it back to his people etc. Slowly his determination to survive eroded (Pisces planets in the second house). After suffering through many of these disappointments, slipping into madness became his survival strategy. To stop himself from suffering the further pain of disillusionment, he started to fully believe that he had made it back to his family, and he went on for some time during the regression, clearly in a state of past life madness, with an imaginary life back in his village. It was a hallucination and he died in this state of insanity, no longer able to distinguish what was real and what was not. Upon his death he was in an absolute state of confusion, and each part of his soul that had felt crushed by disillusionment seemed to have become lost in the desert and had to be retrieved. It was as if the whole psychic structure of that past life character had been disintegrated and needed to be reassembled. (Saturn/Chiron – Pisces opposed by Uranus fragmentation/ SN and planets conjunct also in the eleventh house)

It was clear to him how this past life character had been active in his current life because he had been an addict and alcoholic who was using this as a way to avoid the reality of a painful childhood. As he said, "Parts of me are just like this past life character, still not able to face reality or to even know what that is". Working with this past life helped unravel the Pluto opposition from Saturn and Chiron. The opposition falling across the second/eighth house axis supplied the past life imprint of grasping at illusions with a life or death gravity, so in his current life, escaping into illusion through addiction was a way to enact a subconscious death wish. The life and death position of Pluto in the eighth house and the loss of the resources he needed to survive in that lifetime reflect current life lessons. He now needs to find these resources within himself (second house). Also as mentioned earlier, the clearing of the state of disillusionment is likened to psychological sobriety. For him, working with this past life story brought further strength to continue his sobriety both physically and psychologically.

Being Lost

In the often surreal realm of Pisces, it is not difficult to imagine how one can easily lose direction. From loss of the sense of self, an even more literal expression of this is to actually get lost. I have seen many cases in which getting lost is a prominent feature in a past life story. These cases generally involve the twelfth house/Neptune/Pisces with the karmic axis.

Chart D

This 'lost' story illustrates the more phantasmagoric aspects of Pisces through a Pisces SN squared by Neptune in Sagittarius and Mars in Gemini in the eleventh. Also in this chart, Saturn conjuncts the Virgo NN, so it is opposed to the SN and is also squared by Neptune along with the nodes.

This story started on a ship that had been out at sea for some time. The time period was around the sixteenth or seventeenth century, and this young man was a simple sailor on a large vessel with masts. One night, when they were sailing on a calm sea, a blinding flash of light occurred and a sudden fog descended. He described the fog as unusual – there was a static or electric type of energy to it (Mars square from the eleventh), but he found he couldn't explain what he was experiencing. The crew was stunned and some of them seemed to fall dead instantly after the flash. Panic broke out as they thought they had been struck by lightning, or were under attack. There was mass confusion onboard, and out of the fog they started to see shapes of other vessels. As the shapes became clearer, my client, reliving this as the past life character, was in stunned silence, trying to make sense of the situation. He required some time to describe what was going on.

A lack of clarity is characteristic of the Pisces archetype in relation to the Virgo polarity – the feeling of trying to make sense of, or bring some order to chaos. Some of the vessels were unlike anything they had ever seen, but some of them were familiar sailing ships of the twentieth century. In his present day consciousness, the client explained there were ships of many different time periods, with no one aboard. It became clearer that they had sailed into an inter-dimensional space that seemed to be very much like how the Bermuda Triangle has been described. Saturn (Kronos) squared by Neptune in this case creates a literal (second house) time warp.

The men on the ship started to have differing reactions. Absolute chaos broke out. Some were jumping off the ship; some had fallen onto their knees and were praying, others just fell limp on the deck, either dead or unconscious. After his stunned reaction, my client fell into the latter category and simply passed out or died instantly after he fell on the deck. He saw his body lying there but was in a state of utter confusion as to what had happened. He found that as much as he tried, he was unable to get back into his body. It took some effort to discern what had happened (like the case of the Greek initiate) but it became clearer to him that he was in shock/dead,

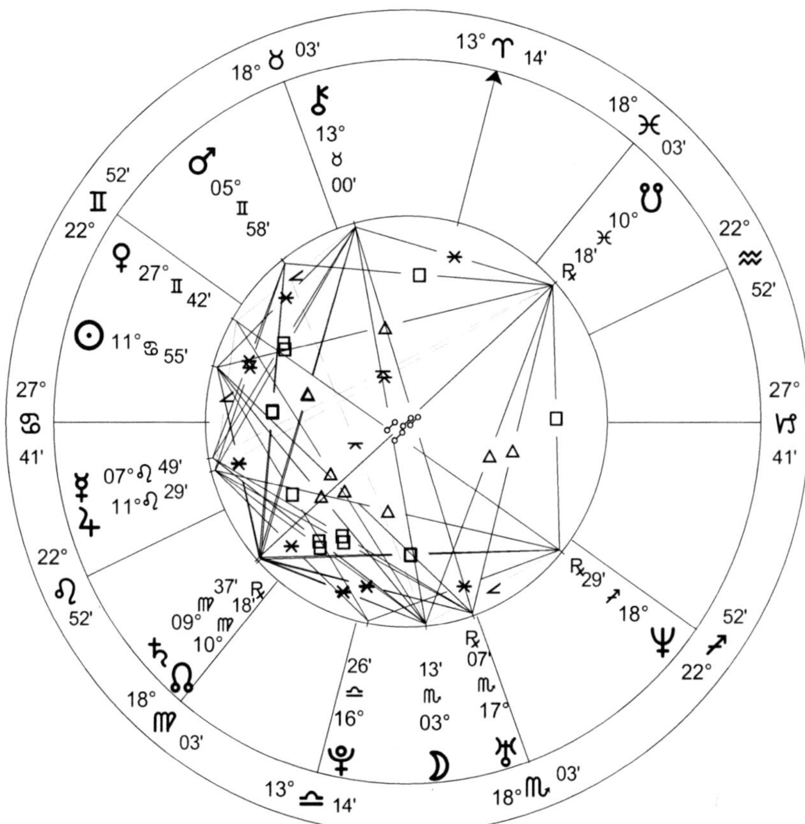

Chart D (Porphyry houses)

but was unaware of it. This part of his psyche had remained trapped in the inter-dimensional space for all these centuries.

It had affected his psyche in interesting ways, in that he said he was always fascinated with different dimensions and wanted to experience them. He was an active member of the church of Daime, a South American church whose sacrament is Ayahuasca (a tea produced from an Amazonian rainforest vine that has psychotropic properties that induce altered states of consciousness with the intent of merging with the divine). Interestingly, he said his ayahuasca journeys were emotionally but not visually profound, and he had felt blocked psychically (Saturn opposite Pisces SN). This past life character's state of fear and shock of being trapped inter-dimensionally at death, especially not being able to process what it was he was 'seeing', had not only fueled his interest in these areas but also blocked him from the very experiences he was seeking.

Chart E

This final case for the Pisces archetype has two stories that carry the themes of the entire karmic axis. In this chart the SN is in Pisces in the ninth house and the ruler, Neptune, is in Scorpio in the fourth. Pluto is in Virgo in the second. The nodes are also squared by Saturn in Capricorn in the sixth. This chart also has an intrinsic paradox; the SN is in Pisces moving towards Virgo and Pluto in Virgo has Pisces as its direction for growth and evolution. How this works out will become clearer through the following analysis.

This first story carries common Piscean imprints of losing the self (dissociation because of overwhelming circumstances), being the savior, forgetting, and feeling a deep loss of faith. This story started to surface for this client in the week before her actual session, as she found herself startling right before falling asleep. This state between waking and sleeping is also associated with the pineal gland, as is the dream state which is ruled by Pisces/Neptune. Quite frequently in this inbetween state all sorts of subconscious material releases into waking consciousness. She became aware that this jolt was associated with the hearing of gunshots.

When she went into her first regression she found herself in a concentration camp as a woman in her thirties just as rumors of freedom and liberating forces were starting to circulate. The promise of freedom is represented by her SN in the ninth; unfortunately she had been in the camp so long that all hope and desire to continue living had gone. She was deep in the Piscean imprint of 'giving up' and the progressive harsh reality of the camps (Capricorn) had eroded her to a point of deep dissociation. At this point in her past life she didn't care anymore and just wanted to die. She was herded into the gas chamber and was about to die as she heard gun shots outside (this was the psychic bleed through). She went through the moments of death and her last recollection before dying was that she had children, and was deeply grieved that she had forgotten them. Forgetting is also part of the Pisces archetype. She was crying saying, "I can't believe I forgot them", (the ruler of the SN, Neptune, is in Scorpio in the fourth house of mothering and children). This theme is also repeated by the signature in her karmic axis of Pluto in Virgo opposed by the Moon in Pisces in the eighth.

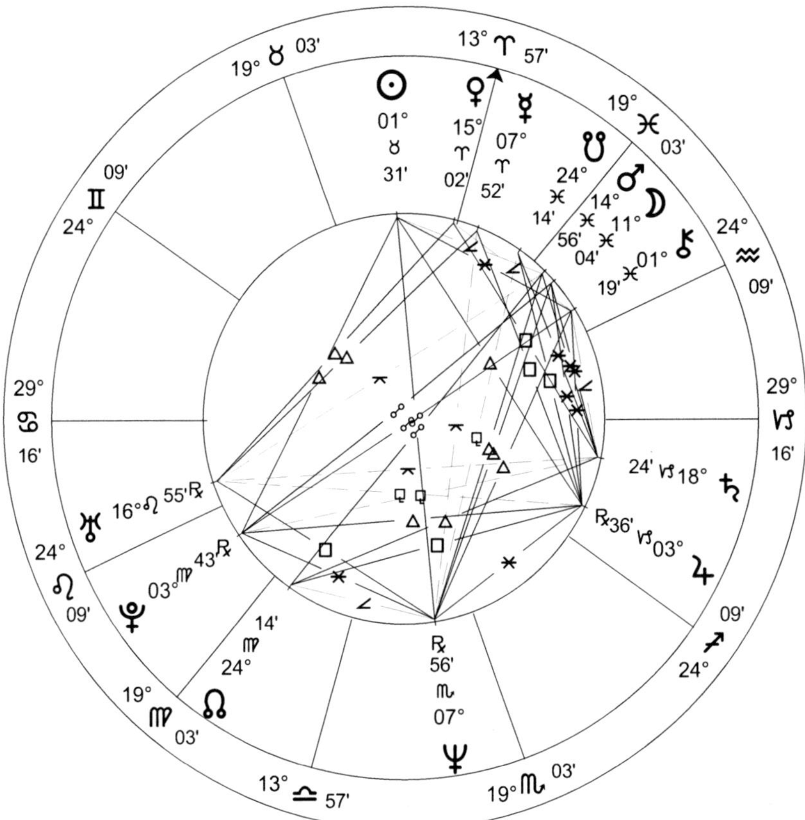

Chart E (Porphyry houses)

In this moment of death, the fog of dissociation that had been her life for the last several years, was temporarily pierced by the reality of imminent death. She suddenly became aware of what was happening to her, and her memory returned along with the grief at how 'lost' she had become, forgetting herself and her own children. As we moved back and forth in the story it was revealed that she lost a small infant to illness just before she was rounded up with another young son and sent to the camps. Early during the time in the camps her young son was forcibly taken from her and she went through this very painful moment clutching him and collapsing in hopelessness after he was taken. "I can't let him go. I've got to keep holding on". This is a twist on the theme of surrendering and letting go. She said it felt as if a large part of her just "went away" (dissociated) at the moment when they finally wrenched her son from her.

After this she still had to go on and she worked very hard in the camps to make sure everyone else was okay. She recalled being a light of enthusiasm, faith and inspiration to others (Pisces SN in the ninth and Pluto in Virgo). Being of service to others was the only thing that kept her going day to day, but over time it wore on her and she became quite Piscean – burnt out. Also in very self-sacrificial Piscean fashion, she found after her death that she had the spirits of others in the camp still attached to her, looking to her as a source of hope and help (Pisces/ninth house – savior). Much of the afterlife work she did on this story had to do with helping those spirits move on, in fact her spirit was still quite prone to forget about herself and the healing she needed (martyr) until she could help the others, including her own children.

The other imprint that was quite strong at death was the feeling that God had failed her (Pisces/ninth house also Jupiter in Capricorn square the nodes). She died bereft and feeling forsaken. By the time she died she had lost all hope and faith when ironically she had earlier been a beacon of that to others. This was also worked with in the afterlife. She said that this story was behind a prominent current life tendency of giving herself over to others as a counselor and helper (Pisces SN and Pluto in Virgo) and just letting them drain her (self-sacrifice). She said she is in the process of learning how to not just give herself away (healthy boundaries – Pisces/Virgo) or give up in this lifetime, and that it was clear to her it was a deep karmic pattern that she was meant to heal.

She also did a current life regression back to the womb which revealed similar imprints. Through this experience she felt at the moment before birth that her mother stopped pushing, she felt trapped, abandoned and that her mother gave up on her (Moon in Pisces in the eighth house). She felt a wide range of emotions fluctuating between giving up and fighting to survive; wanting to live and not feeling worthy to even try (Pluto in the second house – survival, opposed by the Pisces planets). She was aware that she had to actively participate in her own birth as a yet unborn infant, and felt the panic of trying to get herself out of the womb despite her feelings of absolute powerlessness and helplessness. She corroborated this memory with her mother, who confirmed that she was drugged during her delivery, and may have even passed out as she had no memory of how she gave birth.

Womb memories and past life memories often overlap with the same resonance of imprints (see the Cancer chapter). It is as if the soul re-imprints all of its past karmas relevant to the current life, in the womb. They are symbolically played out during the entire in uterus experience and during the different stages of the birth process. The mother's state, the surrounding environment while in the womb, and the events that happen during the birth are all a part of this re-imprinting process. In this case, it was the current life reminder (imprinted again subconsciously) of several of her past life patterns. Her mother during the birth process, was the mirror of some of her own past life tendencies to give up because of hopelessness, and also reflected her guilt at forgetting her own children and not feeling "there for them". Because as a fetus she felt she had to make an effort to be born, even in the womb she had started to counteract some of her own past life patterns!

She also said that the healing of her relationship with the divine has been of utmost importance in this life as she felt a simultaneous faith and doubt. Her faith had always been tinged with grief and hopelessness that she could not clearly identify. She said she always had a vague yet strong background fear, of either not having faith or of losing it. The ruler of her SN, Neptune, is in Scorpio, feeling abandoned (Scorpio/eighth house) by God and a loss of one's faith (Pisces and the ninth) is a clear expression of the combination of those archetypes.

The Pisces/Virgo axis is very often seen in the charts of current life healers who draw either consciously or subconsciously from experience in past life healing lineages. In this next story from the same client we see other aspects of Pisces and the ninth house combined with Scorpio and the eighth house.

She was a young woman living in the British Isles in the Middle Ages. She lived a simple life, close to the land and nature (Pluto in the second house/ SN in the ninth) and was born into a family of pagan healers. She was close to both her parents but especially her father who was her main teacher and mentor. She described their life as communal and that their service within the community extended beyond healing work, as they were also counselors and officiated over group ritual (second/eighth house axis, also ruler of the SN is in Scorpio – rituals and magic).

At one point a young man from another village entered their lives and she fell in love with him. She and her family welcomed him, and after some time her father started to mentor and teach him also. The young man was very interested in having a role within the community in the same capacity as her father. It was not immediately obvious the depth of manipulation and evil lengths (Scorpio) this young man would go to get what he wanted, but it was revealed as the story went on.

She married him, and they moved out of her father's house. Both her parents started to fall ill and she was consumed with tending to them and worked tirelessly to help them heal. As a healer she was uncertain what had stricken them, and frantically she tried to find the correct herbs and remedies to help. While this was going on, the young man saw his opportunity and maneuvered himself deeper into the community, meeting some of the responsibilities that would normally be her father's under the guise of helping them all.

A short time went by and after she had been out attending to others and her usual responsibilities, she went to her parents' house and found them both dead. In this moment a flash of intuition hit her (SN in the ninth), she was aware that they had been poisoned and that her husband was responsible. She was shocked, sickened and full of self recrimination for not having seen it earlier (Virgo/Pisces – guilt and naiveté). She was also angry at herself, because now in retrospect she saw that there had been inner nudges and feelings before that she simply hadn't trusted or listened to and had rationalized away. Her intuition had tried to reveal the truth to her (Pisces SN in the ninth and Pluto in Virgo – intuition-meets-doubt, also Jupiter in Capricorn in the sixth square the nodes). She realized also in those moments the depth of seduction she had succumbed to, and felt deeply shamed (Pluto Virgo). She did try to confront him about this, but found herself strangely with no strength or power in the moment to do so. This left her feeling "It's hopeless. I'm to blame; it is really my fault", (Virgo/Pisces/Capricorn). Shortly after this, she committed suicide by poisoning herself; dying again, as she did in the holocaust life, in a state of hopelessness (Capricorn/Pisces). In the afterlife work that we did, after reunion and reconciliation with her parents, she was able to let go of much of her doubt and guilt.

It took some effort to unravel all the layers of mind control and manipulation that were still with her from this man (Scorpio), but through working with it, she had a profound realization that he actually had no real power of his own, which is why he had to steal it from others. Once the illusions started to fall away she could see that her family, her people and her lineage, were truly the empowered ones, as they were aligned with nature and its truths. This is the higher octave and strength of her Pisces SN in the ninth that needed to be remembered and restored within her.

This was a theme that was present in other lives, which are not detailed here; of having been aligned with something natural, pure, numinous and innocent that became defiled, corrupted and taken over by evil (Neptune in Scorpio). This is a reflection of a combination of Pisces, the ninth house and Scorpio archetypes. The need to have discernment (Virgo/Pisces) was underscored in this story by the power of the seductive spell that she fell under, and it became clearer that he had been using drugs on her to aid him in his manipulations (Pisces/Scorpio). She also needed to realize that she did have intuition and inner knowing, but it was clouded by Virgo doubts and rationalizations. Her intuition, spirit guides and psychism did speak to her, but because she did not give it the sufficient power herself, it became overpowered. This was another version of her feeling that God had failed her, but now she was seeing that it was herself that got in the way.

The paradox of this chart is that Pluto is in Virgo, meaning that moving towards Pisces represents evolution, and the SN is in Pisces which means Virgo is the point of evolution. Put into her past life and present life circumstances, the resolution of this becomes clearer. Pluto's position in this chart is in Virgo in the second house opposed by the Pisces planets. It points to evolution occurring for this person beyond valuing herself only as in service to others. She needed to find a deeper sense of self worth. The Pisces archetype contained within the eighth house opposed by Pluto brings the themes of the second/eighth house into focus. The actuality of being of service has been tinged with life or death situations for this person. Such an imprint can leave this soul needing to first tone down the intensity of the meaning of service (it is not life or death this time) and then to release (second house – possessive attachment) to the act and outcome of serving others.

This soul has needed to recover from the loss of innocence, faith and sense of one's own truth and inner knowing implied by the Pisces SN in the ninth, to remember the strengths of the self, contained in Pluto in the second, before reaching out to others. The intimacy needs of the eighth house are very real, but cannot be pursued from the perspective of unequal relationships, such as forming relations with others only through serving them, or losing herself in being the savior (Pisces SN/ninth). The north node potential then becomes the ability to be open to many viewpoints, many different sorts of people (third house), with the ability to discern the boundaries of her helpfulness. Learning different approaches and techniques also provides a boundary for her and a framework to interact with others without losing herself in them and their problems (Virgo).

With the ruler of the NN in Aries in the ninth house, there is further emphasis that she must first look to herself from an identity that is rooted in her own truth, if she is not to continue to lose herself. This lesson has been reflected in her current life by a propensity to draw overly needy people and those with very damaged or weak boundaries into her life where she finds herself in a position of serving them. As her own lack of clear boundaries coming from past life imprints started to heal, she was able to begin to discern appropriate forms of serving, which had more to do with the self empowerment of others rather than her doing all the work for them. Just as she was learning to gather herself back into one cohesive being she was able to turn and offer that to others while holding them in compassion, yet allowing them the ability to stumble when they needed, to learn their own inner power and sense of being.

Her tendency to see the potential in others and focus only on that, and not the reality of how they were manifesting it, is a result of blurriness cause by the combination of the Virgo/Pisces and Sagittarius karmic signatures. Again, as her own boundaries became clearer it was possible for her to see others for where they really were. In her own words she said, "My counseling practice has changed; I have more clients now that are really showing up for their process and want to do the work". She also said that her ability to say "no" has changed radically, which has given her the exact boundary she needed. The more she continues to be present with herself, the more the outer world will reflect this back to her.

13

The Left Brain Approach to Reading Past Lives in the Chart

Now that you have some understanding of how the archetypes are expressed in a variety of past life scenarios, you can begin to look at a chart through a karmic lens. There are two main ways to perceive this; by looking at the karmic patterns in general, or by discerning specific past lives in relation to the general themes. Both approaches demand an acquired ability to synthesize information, and a healthy dose of intuition doesn't hurt either. Synthesizing all the elements of the karmic axis can seem overwhelming but in the following chart analysis you can see how a thorough understanding of the generalized karmic themes, without specific past life stories, can provide deep insight, and a map for evolution and soul purpose.

Chart For Analysis

This man is 59 years old. He is an astrologer and a carpenter. He is in a long term marriage. He has studied esoteric philosophy and New Age thought. He describes his childhood as being raised by a narcissistic alcoholic mother who put herself and her addiction in front of raising her children. This upbringing stripped him of self-confidence and made him fearful of life and the subsequent opportunities it brought to him. He feels one of his greatest accomplishments in life has been to raise a healthy and very successful child, who is not only confident but self-actualized. He is proud of his ability to do this despite the way he was raised, as he did not perpetuate the abuse of his childhood. He wants to support himself through his innate psychic talents and gifts but has been unable to do so. He said that the biggest challenges in his life have been:

- Gaining back self-esteem and confidence.
- Breaking free of need to accommodate others needs and being able to manifest own individuality.

- Learning to not be judgmental and to be open to others realities and points of view.
- Getting used to having a sense of 'entitlement' and needing to find personal and natural humility.
- Learning to relax, so as to be of better service to others.
- Trying to manifest more of the inner self (spiritual side) as a means of financial support, and living a dharmic path.
- Relationship challenges – has needed to learn to not put people on pedestals or give them all his personal power. Having healthy boundaries.

With this information, already one can see the karmic signatures jumping out from the chart.

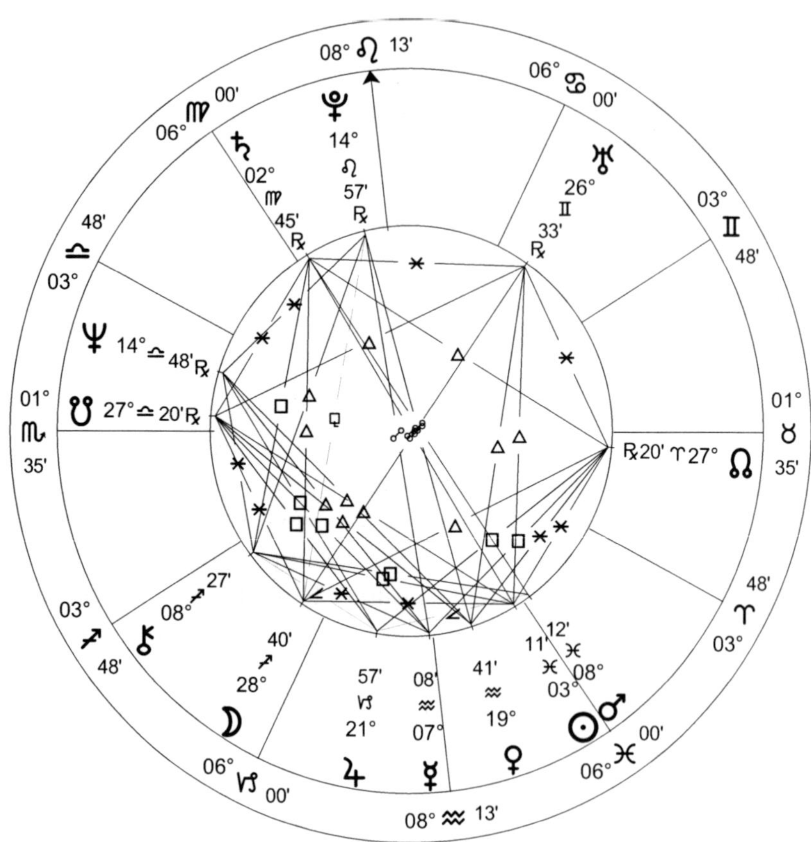

Pluto

Look at Pluto, by house and sign, to understand the 'why.' You can imagine that you are seeking answers to these questions:

> What are this soul's objectives? The natal position of Pluto will show you the qualities the soul has been seeking to integrate in a variety of ways.
>
> What has it been trying to achieve through its past lives?
>
> What wounds has it brought into this life, that it is still seeking resolution and healing for?

The basic psychology will be represented by the sign, which is also generational. The house position will show some of the past life circumstances the soul has encountered in meeting its objectives. In this chart Pluto is in Leo in the tenth house. To start with you can look at some of the keywords and diagrams at the end of this section for both the Leo and Capricorn archetypes. Let's isolate some of the important themes:

Capricorn
Conditioning
Authority
Responsibility
Father
Outer World

Leo
Creative self-actualization
Solar inner Child
Talents/Gifts
Personal Power

So just starting with this information, and also having listened to him and his challenges and concerns, we can start to see that this soul has had a desire to self-actualize (Leo), to find creative power within itself and the ways to express that in the outer world (tenth house). This soul has wanted to find and express its own authority, gifts and talents and be recognized for that. Pluto in the tenth also indicates that there is an accumulated karma of conditioning by society, parents, authorities, systems etc. The tenth house overlays the Leo impulse, indicating past suppression and oppression of this desire; or that he was repeatedly thwarted. He is meant to de-condition from such experiences, and this is further reiterated by the fact that Pluto is retrograde.

The retrograde function is meant to individualize the planet's expression even further, so one is meant to 'do that planet' in their own way. Pluto retrograde further internalizes the consciousness, causing a natural tendency to questions one's personal motives to bring deeper awareness about how and why one acts the way they do – or desires the things they do. Since both the tenth house and Leo can be about personal power, there must be a necessary examination of how this individual uses power in his current life. In essence he may not be allowed to 'slip under the radar' in this area. We know from his childhood that expression of his personal power was forbidden; this was the re-imprinting of the basic meanings of Pluto in Leo in the tenth house: creative self-actualization that meets with oppressive external authority. On the other side of such victimization, in his soul's search for self-empowerment (Leo); he may also have been a brutalizer and oppressor, or ruthless in his own search for power. The fact that he may have swung between such extremes is indicated by the SN in Libra (finding balance through extremity), but this is jumping ahead of ourselves.

From the past life perspective, neither the Leo or Capricorn archetypes have been fully experienced and integrated in a healthy way, which is why Pluto is still working to transform and heal these imprints. He needs to heal issues around authority, conformity, self-expression, responsibility, creativity, self-imposed or external limitations, depression or joyless-ness. Already we have a fairly good picture of some of his karmic themes.

Oppositions to Pluto

There are two main hard aspects to Pluto: the opposition by Venus and Mercury bringing in other archetypes to be examined. Since Venus and Mercury both have dual rulerships this means the archetypes of Libra/Taurus and Gemini/Virgo along with the house placements add to the karmic soup. This is not a heavily aspected Pluto, but any planets that are affected by Pluto come under increased evolutionary pressure. They represent elements in the person's psyche that are not only tied into past life experiences but need to be focused on in the current life in a transformative way. Venus represents our ability to relate, to others and our selves. Mercury is the ability to communicate, think rationally, and also represents splitting/duality.

With Venus opposed to Pluto there is an evolutionary emphasis on transforming the way he relates to himself and others. Venus contacts to Pluto also indicate the reliving of key karmic relationships in order to transform and heal them. Venus is the ruler of the SN and in this light, being placed in the fourth house in Aquarius shows that shocks to his emotional body, causing a wounded ability to have his own needs met, need to be healed and reformulated in this life. It also shows karmic connections with his mother and karma around the issues of the lunar inner child (nurturing) and mothering in general. From the basic information he told us about his mother we can see that not only are he and she most likely stuck in a karmic replay, but she also served to re-imprint much of his own personal karma.

The fourth and tenth house axis is emphasized by this opposition which brings in the polarities of Mother/Father, Anima/Animus, and Inner world/ Outer world and the need to find balance in these areas. As the polarity point to Pluto this opposition also points to a self-reliance (Venus) that needs to be birthed (fourth house) based on his own emotional security (fourth house), that is not dependent upon approval from the external world (Leo/tenth house). As he said already, one of his main challenges has been the need to re-develop self-confidence and self-esteem. The Leo/Aquarius opposition also indicates a karmic challenge in bringing his own gifts out into the world to be of use for humanity. The Aquarius archetype, because it opposes Pluto, also represents some of the past life development of his own individuality (Individuation). He has within himself the ability to not only rebel but also to objectify. He has worked already in the past with understanding himself as an individual, but may still struggle with issues of alienation from past Aquarian-type lives. Venus occupying the polarity point to Pluto points a way to evolution for him, to find comfort with like-minded others (Aquarius), who can mirror (fourth house) for him the ability to belong (empowered Leo), and share their gifts and talents equally.

Mercury opposing Pluto also shows that learning and communication can be karmic issues. In his case the spoken word and the karmic power of vows is a theme. Pluto opposing Mercury is the power to transform these vows and the way he communicates to others. Writing as a creative expression can be healing for him as he may feel inferior or deficient in this regard. Mercury in relation to Venus by Pluto aspecting both, can mean he requires to find his own voice and ability to express what he needs, clearly and without projected expectation. Duality/splitting is also a part of Mercury's domain and becomes a major part of a karmic quandary for him, not only by Mercury's involvement in the karmic axis but also because the nodes are squared by Jupiter in the third house.

The Nodes

The SN in Libra in the twelfth house shows a tendency to lose oneself in others (self-sacrifice). Past issues of co-dependency make development of the boundary of self crucial, as the Aries NN indicates.

You can look to the keywords for both Libra and Pisces to start to formulate an idea of what some of these lives have been like. The nodes are squared, making Aries and the sixth house part of the past life experiences. So you can also look to Aries and Virgo to understand more of his past lives.

The fluctuation between Libra/Aries can be boiled down to the simple understanding of others versus the self. This can play out in many scenarios like being overly involved in others (co-dependent) and in other lifetimes being totally alone. His soul has yet to find the balance between how to be in relationship yet still maintain individuality and freedom. It also can show a fluctuation between being in involved in war or peace. In some lifetimes he may have been totally immersed in interpersonal dynamics, and in other lives detached from these and in 'warrior' mode.

The Aries side of the opposition can indicate that he has expressed his will in the past; he has attempted to strike out as an individual (also emphasized by Aquarius). With that node in the sixth house he may feel doubt and guilt about the way he did express that in the past and may have a nagging need to atone. Further he may have been made to feel guilty in other lives, either by persecution or similar situations about expressing his will.

This is also reflected in his early childhood in this life, but again that can be looked at as a replay of his own internal conflict. The ruler Mars is in Pisces in the fifth house; passive aggressive action may be a learned karmic strategy of self-expression. Being lost in others' needs, and being swallowed up by their desires, has meant that direct action was probably not a successful strategy and maybe the times that he did try he went 'too far too fast' (Aries) and then regretted it. In order to access the NN he needs to reclaim the parts of himself that he gives over to others (Libra SN/ twelfth house) and get to the root causes of why he does that. But part of the conflict is that this cannot be done without addressing the underlying self-erosive guilt that is either actually based on past misdeeds or falsely internalized. Most likely it is this guilt (both Virgo and Capricorn), that causes his difficulty with owning his own power. The sixth/twelfth house axis is challenging him to develop discernment about these issues. He needs to ask himself "What belongs to me and what doesn't?" "What is real and what is not?"

Now we can look at the square to the nodes. The combined archetypes of Sagittarius, Gemini and Capricorn are represented here. Capricorn is a repeated theme as Pluto is in the tenth house. Jupiter and Capricorn both carry the energy of honor and integrity but specific to Jupiter is authenticity. Relative to what we know of the Libra SN and Pluto it would seem that it is essential for him in this life to find and integrate his own authentic self thus enabling him to express honor and integrity in a healthy way. The third house placements, square the nodes and also relative to the basic meaning of the Libra SN, shows that there is an essential truth he needs to reclaim and affirm within himself that he lost in the past.

The nature of revolving beliefs (Gemini), being too open to what others believe, is also a part of his history, as is the nature of judgmental (Capricorn) belief (his own and others'). Because his tendency has been to lose himself, the duality of Gemini is emphasized, as is the psychological splitting of Libra. When we try to conform too much to others' expectations, we split from our own authentic selves and truth. He has to regain his ability to hold, integrate and communicate his own truth (Jupiter/Mercury), while respecting and honoring the relativity (Gemini) of the truth of others. He needs to learn to do this in a balanced way (Libra) without losing himself, or (Aries/Capricorn) running others over.

Tying this understanding back into Pluto's basic intentions we can see that there is a need to transform past oppressive and limiting conditioning, be it societal or familial. The sixth/twelfth house axis points to a long soul history of victim, martyr, and savior type of karma; Jupiter square the nodes also indicates this. Since Pluto in Leo can be about roles and role-playing, this is another meaning of the de-conditioning that needs to happen.

Relative to the SN in Libra that conditioning extends to the way he relates to himself (self-worth) and others (relatedness). Pluto in the tenth opposing Venus (which is the ruler of the SN too) is also indicating that 'de-conditioning' from past learned ways of relating would lead him to learn to form equal relationships as part of his path of evolution: being neither greater or lesser than another, but in equal partnership. Finding a like-minded group is also a way for him to empower himself and enjoy the ability to share, in a free-flowing exchange of ideas. The NN and its ruler as part of the past life experience shows a confusion or blurriness (Pisces) around the expression of will, instinct and identity (Aries), and personal power (Leo/Aries).

The Aries NN in the sixth, with its ruler in Pisces, is also showing that even if he has misused power it is time to find a boundary (Virgo) around how much he needs to continue to punish (Capricorn) himself, and for him to find forgiveness (Pisces) for personal misdeeds and those of others towards him. Doing this can restore his Leonian personal power with joy and without strings attached, clarifying his ability to act. Finding the power of unconditional love (Leo/Pisces) in himself and the Divine Source, is a path of personal spiritual empowerment. Alignment and surrender to higher will also can alleviate his soul of natural or false guilt, allowing him to find comfort with others on equal terms with humility and grace.

Now maybe you want to know some of his specific past life stories? Several are shared in this book and you can find them in the Gemini (Chart A) and Capricorn (Chart A) chapters. Further to these stories there a few other scenarios to share:

In one very painful past life he was a young boy who was sexually molested by his father. This caused deep psychological splitting (Libra/Gemini) as he was unable to express his rage openly. Eventually it did come out when he got into his teens, and he killed his father with a knife. He became literally 'possessed' and taken over (Libra/Pisces) by the violence of this act, which caused him to go on a blood thirsty rampage (Aries). He became a serial killer who preyed upon the old and weak. He was eventually caught and hung, and died with deep remorse for what had happened.

He had a life as a conquistador who was consumed with only the desire to do his duty and conquer others (Capricorn/Aries).

These two lives, combined with other warrior/soldier experiences set into motion his deep feelings of guilt and the need to atone. He had many 'victim' lives as a result of his guilt, being kept captive or as a slave. Lives of complete humiliation and orphan lives.

A pivotal life for him came when he was a colonel in the army, slaying Native Americans. He was eventually caught by a tribe and brought before a counsel. Knowing who he was, they killed him, slowly and tortuously, but as he died the shaman from that tribe travelled to meet him in the spirit world and gave him a critical evolutionary opportunity…

> "Now you have a choice. You may choose to vow, to make an oath, to never again use your warrior powers to harm another human being". To which he replied, "I am so grateful for the opportunity to be able to make this choice, absolutely, positively, without hesitation and with complete commitment. I do so vow".

Since his Pluto is in the cardinal tenth house and his nodes are also cardinal, they indicate that he did set into motion a new evolutionary cycle in recent past lives. He knew in his soul, in his current life that his killing and warrior days were over. He was challenged by this when he was in high school and was on the verge of being drafted into the Vietnam War. He said

> "I ultimately reconciled with myself what the best route I could take would be. I decided I would, as early in the process as possible, sign up to be a medic, because something deep inside me cried out, 'You cannot try to kill your fellow man in the name of war!'"

He described his deepest intention for this new evolutionary cycle saying

> "So I hope and pray for the strength and courage and discipline of the warrior within me, to be manifest only for the growth and evolution of a progressive and constructive life on earth, spent on trying to achieve harmony and spreading some joy".

Reflecting upon all the work he has done in self-exploration and past life therapy, speaking from his now more empowered Pluto and NN he said

> "I realize now how important it is to remember our past so we need not be condemned to repeat it. The memory of my past mistakes makes me so mindful of how important it is, to make every action as honest, kind, humble, grateful, gentle and strong as I can".

This chart is an excellent example of how important it is to look at the total karmic axis. If we attempted to interpret this chart from just the classical perspective of the SN in Libra in the twelfth house, we would think this person was solely caught up in relationship, addiction, co-dependency, confusion etc., in all his past lives. Even if we added the dimension of meanings of the ruler of the SN, Venus in Aquarius in the fourth, we would see more but not the full picture. Without the understanding of Pluto, the square to the nodes and the NN as part of the past life experience, we would not truly understand his soul's inner workings.

Imagery, Storytelling and Astrology

> "The psyche consists essentially of images. It is a series of images in the truest sense, not an accidental juxtaposition or sequence, but a structure that is throughout full of meaning and purpose".
>
> Carl Jung[1]

This thought from Jung is rich with information and food for thought. If the psyche or soul consists essentially of images why do many of our modern forms of psychology that propose to work with the psyche discount or minimize this imaging expression of human nature as 'just imagination'? Standard therapy today (not including the more self-experiential forms) consists mostly of prescribing medications and controlling the contents of the psyche by talking 'about' it and its issues, but not delving into it on its own terms.

For example, a woman going into a clinician to try to get the bottom of a depression issue may start to talk about all the limitations in her life as the cause of depression. The clinician may nod in agreement as she goes on to describe how she feels like a slave to her job and her family. Here would be a unique opportunity to work with that metaphor, to let it take form as an inner character, with a life of its own. This is a powerful image that her own psyche has expressed, an inner part of her that is living the existence of the slave. Unfortunately, she will most likely walk out of that session with a prescription for Prozac and a schedule of therapy for the next six months. The very language of her soul was not listened to.

The potential for healing was in that simple statement, "I feel like a slave". The possibility exists for her to be guided to go into the experience of being the slave, help this part of her inner world have expression and closure, then set the slave free. Without even embracing the possibility of past lives (in this example case it is highly probable that this feeling of being

1. 'Spirit and Life' in *Collected Works*, VIII:325f. (p.52)

a slave was unfinished business from actual past life experiences), this image can be worked with and healing can happen if only the imagination, or dare I say, soul is engaged in the healing process.

You can also do this work with your clients.

An example of working with images that are not of a past life origin comes to mind of a woman who called to schedule a healing session. She was currently struggling with breast cancer. Shortly into the phone conversation I had an image of a goat precariously balanced on the very tip of a mountain top. All four feet held tightly together under it struggling to keep their tiny bit of foothold. After getting her chart information, I was not surprised to find a prominent Capricorn archetype emphasized. Her Moon was in Capricorn in the seventh, with an almost exact transiting Chiron conjunction. When she came for her session, I shared the image of the goat with her. She said, "Well that is exactly how I feel".

The illness had not only been a long hard struggle, but she felt isolated because of it and felt she had no one to support her. With those conditions it was a good sign that she even sought out a healing session for herself. I guided her to just start to become this goat on the mountain top and tell me what she was experiencing. She started to say (as the goat), "I am terrified; There is nowhere to go; I can't go up or down; I'm just stuck here, hanging on for life".

After spending time further identifying with this 'inner goat' I suggested that she imagine a broad plank being laid against the mountain top she was stuck on. She did this, and it brought up further fears, that it was unstable, she couldn't trust putting her foot (or hoof) on it. This plank symbolized to me, help that might be available to her that she was unable to reach for. She started to cry with this realization, that it was true; at a deep level she really didn't trust others to be there for her. She started to realize that it was she, who isolated herself. Her Moon in Capricorn role had always been the responsible one, the caretaker; now that she was helpless she was at a loss as to how to reach out. Because she had never really tried in her life, she had no blueprint or model for this. With Moon in Capricorn her tendency to suppress her own needs for nurturing had manifested physically. Her breast cancer was the part of her that was seeking attention, healing and nurturing, and needed to learn that she could have that also.

I worked with her to build her confidence to step out onto the plank and this took some time for her, but when she gingerly did so, she found it not only supported her but the descent down the mountain was quite easy. She arrived in a meadow and found there were other goats there. She said it was very peaceful in the meadow and she just wanted to be with the others, and lie down and rest. One can feel the exhaustion of that Capricorn Moon, after a lifetime of shouldering responsibility and the need for some real rest and relaxation. We left this inner journey with that image of her 'inner goat' lying and resting peacefully with others of its own kind, and went on to do other, related healing work. In the coming weeks she found a support group of cancer patients near her by 'coincidence'. She was happy to report that this was not only easy for her to do but that she had very much enjoyed her first few meetings. This sort of approach is described in Gestalt therapy as one of the basic principles of working with a client; the experience of something is greater than the description or explanation of it.

Why has our modern world seemingly lost its connection with soul? In our society it is often the material world that we give credence and validity to, and not the intangible psyche. All of our sciences follow this model; if we can dissect it, analyze it, categorize it, map it or medicate it, then it is real; if not it is just imagination. Lewis Mehl-Madrona M.D, Ph.D, a Native American psychiatrist who works with traditional storytelling and modern practices to bring about healing, summed this up quite eloquently saying, "Cutting up your dog will not tell me why he likes to play Frisbee".[2] He further concludes, "People, the subject of Psychology, cannot be adequately analyzed in natural scientific terms. The language of the natural sciences is mathematics… However, the story about human beings is incomplete with only a mathematical description. The story about human beings requires us to listen to their stories…"

Science has yet to be able to cut open a heart and find love, yet it is clear that love exists. PET or Functional MRI imaging of the brain of an individual looking at a picture of a loved one and showing certain blood flow or active areas in the brain, does not prove love resides in the neurological or chemical reactions of the body. A simple metaphor for this is a radio picking up a signal. If you look in the radio will you see a tiny band in there playing music? If you use functional imaging technology to map the areas of the brain that respond when an experience happens, is that experience

---

2. *Coyote Wisdom* by Lewis Mehl-Madrona, Bear & Company, Rochester, VT, Copyright © 2005 Inner Traditions www.InnerTraditions.com. Reproduced by kind permission.

contained within the brain? This is a trap of the intellect, and unfortunately it is devoid of soul. Our mind is not in our brain. This is also an argument that has been used to discount astrology; because there is no measurable natural known force, such as gravity or radiation, that reaches earth and us from some planets, it is impossible or 'imaginal' that they have any effect on us. What exists behind the world of appearances is a realm of meaning, of interconnectedness; in our attempts to understand it we have only just begun to scratch the surface.

Astrology in an attempt to be recognized as a valid science can try to straddle both worlds, but risks selling its depth and soul in exchange for materialist validation. Such thinking squeezes the life force out of archetypes causing dictums such as: because a certain symbol in a chart means one thing, it must apply that way to all individuals. Or because we have been able to categorize qualities of human experience by astrological archetype we have a system that has it all figured out. Astrology also has to be careful to not fall into dogmatic and reductionist thinking, lest we forget that at the heart of each chart is an individual unique psyche. The archetypes of astrology are not a standardized list of qualities that are static, they are alive and they are multi-dimensional. Barbara Schermer's work with Astrodrama points in this direction. Utilizing the basic principles of Psychodrama individuals stand in as actors for planets on a person's chart, and enact or role play what is arising in them as an expression of that planet.

The individuals start to become these planets; thoughts, feelings and body postures/movements express themselves through them. I have also facilitated Astrodrama sessions and it is striking, not only how the individuals standing in for the planets seem to get overshadowed by the qualities of the archetype, but also how individual details come through that are particular to the chart they are enacting, without any knowledge of that individual's life. This type of experience shows that opening the gates of imagination allows one to connect with this living world of meaning behind outer reality, and by so doing to tap into a deep reservoir of knowledge and wisdom beyond conscious rationalization.

What does this mean to you as an astrological counselor? For one thing you can start to listen to the energy behind the problems and issues your clients bring to you. Start to hear another layer of the archetypes, the layer that may contain metaphoric images or inner past life characters. Any problem, issue or complex, can have at its root an 'imaginal' story. Looking at current life issues through the lens of past life experiences adds a dimension to our understanding of how they may have come to be so problematic in the present life.

Many modern studies have shown that storytelling or listening to stories activates both hemispheres of the brain simultaneously thus enhancing memory retention as well as having other positive effects. This isn't telling us anything that earlier cultures and tribal cultures didn't seem to already know, as storytelling was an integral part of their society. To them stories were used to pass on knowledge, build community and act as a tool to facilitate healing. What lies at the heart of the power of storytelling (or listening to stories) is the ability to convey information to the left brain and engage the right brain by creating associated imagery (Imagination) at the same time.

Unfortunately in modern times imagination has been marginalized in favor of the rational intellect. It has long been proposed that through imagination, and the creative non-linear mind, the soul expresses itself most clearly. Metaphor, symbolism, parable, myth, allegory are all vehicles of expression of soul and in turn the use of them speaks directly to our souls. Lewis Mehl-Madrona talks about the healing power of storytelling in saying, "A miracle of stories is their ability to convey knowledge that we don't know we need, in a manner that we can easily incorporate, without ever knowing what we are learning, or even that we are learning. Stories teach us how to do things that are otherwise impossible to learn".[3]

The beauty of storytelling is that it can touch us in deep ways, in the same way our dreams do, bringing not only issues to the forefront, but also creative ways to transform them.

---

3. ibid

14

The Right Brain Approach to Reading Past Lives in the Chart

To begin to see specific past lives in the chart is a matter of opening the gates of imagination. The left brain analysis can happen first and can also lead to specific past life imagery.

When I first started working with charts even before I was doing regression therapy, I was very interested in these past life stories. I used to look at the symbols of the chart for about one minute and then close my eyes and let images start to flow. This is a simple form of meditation often called 'reverie' or 'waking dreaming'. Jung called this 'active imagination'. This state of mind is like letting one's eyes fall into soft focus; the attention of the mind is softened, like a daydreaming state. It is decidedly a completely right brain intuitive approach to chart reading, but you can also experiment with looking at charts that way.

Since synthesizing the information from the chart is a process that involves both right and left brain, I encourage you to use the following list in the same way to start the process. Look at the symbols of the chart you are working with. Start simply with the SN, its house and sign and ruler. Read through the list of possible expressions of the archetypes you are dealing with. This gives your conscious mind a focus and food for thought; it implants the range of possibilities. Once you have that information in your consciousness, close your eyes, let go of what you have just read and see what kind of story forms. Allow yourself to daydream the story, allowing it to arise spontaneously. I call this 'dreaming into a chart'. Sometimes you will only get glimpses with your inner vision, but the information may come in other forms also; words, feelings or simply just knowing.

Quite often, prior to doing any inner work with clients, I let the person know inner vision or clairvoyance is only one of the inner senses. Most people are not clairvoyant, but are clairsentient or claircognizant, which means information is felt as impressions without it being received in a linear form, such as through the senses or mental deduction. Most people call this simply intuition, but it is helpful to know that what you might discount as a fleeting feeling or knowing, if given the attention and space to reveal itself may be full of many layers of information. So when approaching a chart in this way, trust and treat all impressions that come as messengers full of knowledge waiting to be revealed to you. Practice it with people you know or even your own chart. Sometimes when you are looking over the possible expression of the archetypes, one will jump out at you more than the others; this is also a way of inner knowing that should be trusted. Just as sometimes when you are working with a chart one aspect in the chart seems to jump out, you may come to find out in that session with your client that it is exactly this aspect that is most important to them at the moment.

Following in the Appendix is a partial list of qualities of each archetype. In the first column is an aspect of the archetype in its natural empowered form or a quality of that archetype. The second column shows possible ways it may have been wounded in past lives or carries over into the current life as a wounded imprint from the past. This list is by no means comprehensive, but is a short compilation of the many ways I have seen the archetypes expressed in past life stories. For example one client had a Cancer SN in the sixth house. To begin to understand one of her past life stories would be to synthesize the Cancer and Virgo archetypes. If you glance over the list you will see that neglect as a child is a possible Cancer past life wound. With the extra emphasis of possible Virgo wounds, this makes that a distinct possibility. In fact this client had a past life, which she relived through regression, where she was treated as less than human (Virgo – not good enough), tormented by her mother (Cancer) and died at the age of five from neglect.

Keep in mind the wounded aspects I have outlined are generalized, in that the actual experience could have been either as the one who made the action or the one who experienced it. For example the Invader is a shadow aspect of the same Pioneer/Explorer energy of Aries. In any person's chart they could have been either the invader or at the mercy of invaders. To discern which, takes an ability to synthesize the overall themes in the chart and to understand what might be a predominate aspect that the soul is working on evolving. In many cases, it is possible in a soul's total history that they were the invader at one point and the invaded at another. It appears to me that the longer, or more in-depth, a soul has experimented with any particular theme, it will have experienced more layers of the archetypes it is seeking to integrate and would have more varied experiences with them, such as reversals within the same archetype.

In practicing with understanding the past life scenarios, trust your intuition and add in further layers of understanding, such as Pluto – what is this soul's bottom line intention? How would that color past life experiences? The understanding of Pluto and its placement and aspects will give you an overall underlying 'attitude' that is present through all the past life themes, the 'why' of having had a particular experience and how it facilities the ongoing evolution.

If you apply this to actual clients you have to listen to them first. Listen for the story behind the energy of what they are saying. Hear what the repeated patterns are and see if the karmic axis archetypes give clues to the types of past life experiences they might have had. I would suggest practicing with friends or others who would be open to let you experiment. What is most important is what the client needs to know at that moment in their life. By listening to them, it becomes apparent what themes are surfacing for them at the time or have been prevalent in their life. These would be the issues to explore deeper. Then you have the general feeling of which aspect is being expressed and might be helpful to illuminate for them in the context of a story. I also feel that it is not advisable to give graphic details of past lives you might perceive, when they are particularly tortuous or violent ones. While the cases that I have given from regression are graphic, that is appropriate, because this is what arose from the person's own psyche in the moment. These traumas also arose in a therapeutic context, where the container was present to work them through and not just stimulate the traumatic memories. I always preface my sharing of any images or stories that come to me when working with someone as that they can be literal or just metaphors for something I perceive the soul is expressing. I also include the possibility that any story or impression I perceive can be totally wrong! What gives a story its healing potential is how it resonates with the individual. If there is no inner response it most likely is either not the time for the story or the story is not theirs.

After sharing stories with clients it is important to involve the polarity point as the path to resolution. For example take a client with a Virgo SN in the tenth house who, not surprisingly, felt burdened by responsibility. You might perceive a past life as a servant, who worked her fingers to the bone and had no possibility of any other options. Her family was poor and she worked from the time she was six. You can tell that client, “Imagine you are that servant, you worked all your life and died young of disease. What would that servant want to do now?”

Looking at the potentials of the Pisces NN in the fourth house that client might respond, “I just want to relax, let go a little and have some fun”. Maybe that is not a bad prescription for such a karmic history. She never got to have a childhood in that past life, so have her imagine what relaxing and having fun means to that inner servant. Have her imagine what kind of childhood that servant would have wanted to have. This might involve the Cancerian nurturing she never got, or the Piscean dreams she never was able to have. Encourage her to do them now, in her imagination. You and your clients will be amazed at the creative potential that is released, when the images of the soul are invited to flow into consciousness.

APPENDIX

ARIES/1st House/Mars

Explorer/Pioneer	Pain of aloneness/Invader/Invasion
Willpower	Willfulness/Using will over others/Mission oriented/Wounds to expression of will/ Repressed or thwarted will
Anger	Rage/Violence/Vengeance
Self/Identity	Narcissism – false identity/Separation from others/My way is the only way/Over or under developed self image/Identity crisis
Primal	Clash with 'civilized society'/Hardships of primitive lives/The hunter and the prey
Sex	Sexual Violence/Using sex as a weapon/Over identified with self as sexual, or singled out or targeted because of sexuality
Warrior	Combatative/Rampage/Destroyer/Over emphasized 'fight or flight' response (unhealed battle traumas)/Paranoia/Kill or be killed/ Violent death
Initiative	Over enthusiasm/Stuck in high gear/Failed initiations/Lack or fear of
Spontaneity	Consequences of rushing into action/Wounds incurred by risky actions, impulsiveness/ Excessive fear of limitation
Instinct	Wounds to instinctual nature
Vitality/Youth	Life cut short/Premature death/Perpetual race against time/Anxiety

TAURUS/2nd House/Venus

Survival	Poverty/Inability to provide for self/Loss of resources/Hardships of surviving/Long prolonged past life deaths/Stubborn refusal,"I won't give in"
Self Reliance	Relying only on self/Survivor mentality, "It's okay, I can do it alone"/Self as only resource (prostitute)/Being used by others
Feelings	Delayed emotional response/Shut down of feelings for survival
Values	Damaged self-worth/Feeling invaluable/Being devalued
Possessions	Greed/Hoarding/"I am what I own"/Loss of possessions or land
Simplicity	Simple lives (farmer, shepherd) can result in current life inability to 'do better for oneself' or use one's abilities.
Solidity	Stagnation/Shut down
Material world	Materialism/Over emphasis on external resources
Security	Isolation/Self withdrawal
Fertility	Infertile/Over fertile/Complications in conception

GEMINI/3rd House/Mercury

Inquisitive/Curious	'Opening Pandora's box', consequences of over curiosity/Inquisitor/Inquisition/Nosey
Communication	Being the Messenger (death, persecution because of it)/Wounds to ability to communicate (mute, suppression etc)/People not listening/Inability to deliver the message
Intellect	Limitations in knowledge or learning/Needing to know it all/Interrogation/Over emphasized head at the expense of heart
Opinions	Revolving viewpoints/Everyone's opinion/ Over saturation/Cynical/Opinionated
Facts/information	Inability to synthesize/Doubt of intuition/ Withheld information
Changeability	Instability/Neurosis/Nervous disorder/ Scattered/Over flexible
Siblings	Twins (past life) causing current feeling of someone or something is missing/Loss of siblings
Immediacy	Reactiveness/Goal-less ness/Drifter
Duality	Many identities/Living a double life/ Psychological splitting/Compartmentalization
Trickster/Cleverness	Liar/Lies/Thievery
Ideas	Living in thoughts only/Inability to manifest/ Persecuted because of

CANCER/4th House/Moon

Ego/Self Image	Wounds to early development and ego formation /Low self esteem
Womb	Death in childbirth/Loss of child/Imprints in the womb from mother and environment
Childhood/ Inner Child	Wounded child/Neglect/Abandoned/Orphan/ Over attachment to shaping parent/ Childlikeness/Unconscious emotional expectations
Nurturing	Lack of, fear of, or excess of/Demanding need for
Emotions	Overly Emotional/Suppressed/Stunted/ Dependency/Childlike emotions/Displaced emotions
Inner World	Fear of or inability to cope in outer world/ Isolation/Cocooning
Ancestors/Family	Trapped in/Over responsible for/Overwhelmed by their needs/Conditioning/Imprinting
Anima/Animus	Limitations of gender roles/Discomfort or complications because of gender
Sensitivity	Wounds to vulnerability/Over sensitivity
Needs	Neediness/Dependency/Inability to fulfill needs (for self and/or others)/Helpless/Needs not met

LEO/5th House/Sun

Arts/Drama	Starving artist syndrome/'Van Gogh' type past lives (creative mania)/Dramatic past lives/ Tragedy
Actor/Actress	Playing a role/'Drama Queen' or caught in others dramas/Not knowing authentic self/Insecure without audience/Living just for entertaining
Self-Actualization	Wounds to/Inability to actualize
Talented	Singled out as special/Child prodigy/Over attachment to talents/Multitalented, unable to choose just one so none get expressed fully
Child self/Inner Child	Authentic self not validated/Need for approval/ Wounded ability to have fun or play/Avoiding adulthood
Joy/Love	Wounds to receiving and giving love/Wounded heart
Fame	Desire for/Had it and lost it/Need for applause and approval/Not being noticed
Ruler	King/Queen/Misuse of power/Subject to power plays/Subjugation of others
Creativity	Fear of or blocks to creating/Mania/ Self absorption/Offspring (illegitimate/affairs)

VIRGO/6th House/Mercury

Service	Servant/Slave/Inequality/Self -Sacrifice
Humility	Inferiority/Humiliation Shame
Self-Improvement	Perfectionism/Masochism/Guilt/Fear of mistakes/ Anxiety/"I'm not good enough"/Impossible standards
Apprenticeship	Inadequacy/Not ready yet/Lack of confidence in skills/Limitations of technique/Past life wounds to being in one's own power
Orderly	Crisis oriented/Addicted to Crisis/Panic/Details/ Overburdened/Mundane
Discriminating	Being critical or criticized/Persecuted
Health – Mind/Body	Psychosomatic/Neurosis/Nervous compulsions
Medicine/Healing	Persecuted because of/Burnout/Overwhelm
Purity/Purification	Atonement/Masochism/Guilt/Depravation/Nun
Analysis	What is missing/Lack/Void/Fear of action

LIBRA/7th House/Venus

Relationship	Co-dependency/Inequality/Polarized relationships/Knows self only through others/ Satellite to others/Love triangles (being the mistress/lover)/Wounds of relationship/ Arranged marriages/Karmic bonds
Comparison	Falsity/being compared to, or self to others/ Deferment to others/Being de-valued
Society	Societal role/Aristocratic/Pleasantries
Pleasing	Denial/Mask/False self/Psychological splitting
Social Grace	Flirt/Casanova/Public shame/Disgrace/ Philanderer/Being charmed by others
Trusting	Damaged Trust/Wounds to heart/Fear of relating/ Acquiescent/Conditional love
Needs	Not aware of own/Projected expectations/Other needs projected onto self
Harmony	Denial/Disharmony/Imbalance/Extremity/ Fantasy/ Romanticism
Beauty	Valued or value others only for physical beauty/ Surface/ Vanity

SCORPIO/8th House/Pluto

Intimacy	Fear of/Wounds to/Protection of vulnerability/ Being exposed/ Marriages of convenience – mutual misuse
Power	Powerlessness/Misuse of power/Corruption/ Manipulation/Magic – Curses/Fear of power
Intensity	Compulsion/Obsession/Trauma of intense experiences/Addiction to intensity/Fascination (object of or to others)/Vengeance
Resources	Loss of/Fighting over/Manipulating for/ Clinging to
Merging/ Deep bonding	Betrayal/Loss of/Fear of/Abandonment/ Consuming/Entrapment/Enslavement/ Karmic bonds
Transformation	Destruction/Annihilation
Mystery	Taboo/Secrets/Secrecy/Covert action/Macabre/ Suspicion/Paranoia/Hiding/Interrogation/Spy/ Being found out
Sex	Sex for power/Sexual abuse and trauma/ Prostitution/Sadist
Psychology	Mind games/Psychological torture/Svengali

SAGITTARIUS/9th House/Jupiter

Adaptability	Compensation
Travel	Trauma of displacement or immigration/ Nomadic/Homeless/Running away
Wisdom	Inability or fear of communicating knowledge
Philosophy	Out of touch with reality/Living in ideas/Over abstraction
Beliefs	Dogma/Dogmatic/Missionary/'Bible thumping'/ Conversion/Persecution because of
Inspiration	Deluded/Charmer/Silver-tongued devil
Truth	Untruths/Half-Truths
Higher Learning	Misuse of knowledge/Withheld knowledge, denied learning/Gullibility with teachers or gurus
Enthusiasm	Over-enthusiasm/Exaggeration
Trust	Wounds to trust/Naiveté
Freedom	Lack of/Over attachment to/Experienced limitations of

CAPRICORN/10th House/Saturn

Social Order	Conformity/Conditioning/Over attachment to or lack of or loss of social position/Social privilege
Politics	Politics/Totalitarianism/Nationalism/Dictator
Control	Repression/Suppression/Oppression/Rigidity/Fear
Maturity	Wounds of helplessness in old age/Old before one's time
Structure/ Boundaries	Conformity/Conditioning/Isolation/Immobility/Paralysis/External limitations/Depression
Discipline	Punishment/Self Defeat/Saboteur
Authority	Wounds to/Oppression by/Fear of/Misuse of/Doubt of
Responsibility	"It's all my fault"/Over responsible/Burdened/Futility/Guilt
Leadership	Loneliness because of/Failed leader/Misuse of
Accomplishment	Failure/Loss of Acclaim/Fall from Grace/Guilt
Tradition	Limitations because of/Conformity to/Trapped or forced by
Ancestors/Family	Trapped in/Forced by/Over responsible for/Conditioning

AQUARIUS/11th House/Uranus

Individuality	Anarchist/Persecution because of/Being singled out/ Fear and suppression of/ Wounds to individuation process
Unique	Bizarre/Loner/Alienation/Being different/Not wanting to be different
Community/	Limitations because of/Ostracized from/Tribes Betrayal by/Fringe of/Responsibility for/ Anti-social/Conformity
Revolutionary	Aloneness/Persecution because of/ Rebellion/Confrontations
Electric	Shocking/Shock/Trauma/Psychological fragmentation and splitting/ Hyperactivity/Insanity
Group Consciousness	No identity within/Group hysteria/Mass trauma
Brotherhood/ Sisterhood	Secret Societies/Fringe societies/Elitism/ Aristocracy
Ideals/Hopes	Loss of Hope/Impracticality/Inability or thwarted in manifesting
The Future	Fear of/Living in/Ahead of one's time

PISCES/12th House/Neptune

Trusting	Naiveté/Wounds to/Misplaced trust
Mystic	Loneliness/Escapism/Alcohol, drugs, addiction/ Insanity (madman)/Non-reality (shock caused by exposure to reality)/Inability to 'be in the world'
Psychism	Misuse of/Misused because of gifts/Delusions/ Astral glamour/Past drug initiations including death by/Confusion caused by/Persecution because of
Surrender	Helplessness/Damaged, weak boundaries/ Aimlessness/Suffering/Suicide/Fear of/Giving up/ Hopelessness/Soul Loss/Feeling like or being a coward
Innocence	Loss of/Wounds to/Folly/Foolishness
Helpful	Helpless/Victim/Martyr/Savior/Persecuted
Transcendence	Avoidance/Dissociation and traumas causing chronic dissociation/Erosion of sense of self
Imagination	Fantasy/Dreamer/Disbelief/Denial/Confused mental states/Fogginess/Disillusionment/Illusions
Subconscious	Taken over by/Victim to/Lost in (insanity)
The Collective	Lost or lack of identity/"Who am I?"/Mirroring others/Being projected onto/Chaos (creation of, victim of)

Bibliography

Achterberg, Jeanne *Imagery in Healing; Shamanism and Modern Medicine*, Shamballa, Boston MA, 1985.

Ackerman, Diane *A Natural History of the Senses*, Vintage, NY, 1992.

Assagioli, Roberto *Psychosynthesis: A Collection of Basic Writings*, Viking, New York, 1965.

Bailey, Alice *Esoteric Astrology*, Lucis Publishing, NY, 1982.

______ *Esoteric Psychology, Vol. 2*, Lucis Publishing, NY, 1942.

Bass, Ellen and Davis, Laura *The Courage to Heal*, Harper, NY, 1989.

Berne, Eric *Games People Play*, Grove Press, NY, 1959.

Bowman, Carol *Children's Past Lives*, Ballantine, NY, 1997.

Branden, Nathaniel *The Disowned Self*, Bantam, NY, 1978.

Bradshaw, John *Healing The Shame That Binds You*, Health Communications, FL, 1988.

Bray Haddock, Deborah *Dissociative Identity Disorder*, McGraw-Hill, NY, 2001.

Campbell, Joseph *The Hero With a Thousand Faces*, Princeton University Press, 1968.

Dalai Lama (The) and Cutler, Howard *The Art of Happiness: A Handbook for Living*, Riverhead-Penguin, NY, 1998.

Detlefsen, Thorwald *The Healing Power of Illness*, Element, London, 1990.

Dossey, Larry *Recovering the Soul*, Bantam, NY, 1989.

Durckheim, K. Graf von *The Way of Transformation*, Allen and Unwin, Australia, 1971.

Eliade, Mircea *Shamanism: Archaic Techniques of Ecstasy*, Princeton/Bollingen, NJ, 1972.

Evans-Wentz, W.Y. *The Tibetan Book of the Dead*, Oxford University Press, UK, 1960.

Fagan, Joel and Shepherd I.A. *Gestalt Therapy Now*, Harper, NY, 1970.

Fiore, Edith *The Unquiet Dead: A Psychologist Treats Spirit Possession*, Doubleday, NY, 1988.

Fisher, Joe *The Case for Reincarnation*, Bantam, NY, 1984.

Freedom-Long, Max *The Secret Science Behind Miracles* (Huna Tradition), DeVorss and Co., Marina del Rey, CA, 1997.

Gallegos, Stephen Eligio *The Personal Totem Pole: Animal Imagery, the Chakras and Psychotherapy*, Moon Bear Press, Santa Fe, 1987.

Gerber, Richard *Vibrational Medicine*, Bear and Co., Santa Fe, 1988.

Gershom, Rabbi Yonassan *Beyond the Ashes*, A.R.E. Press, Virginia, 1992.

Goodman, Felicitas D. *How About Demons?* Indiana University Press, Bloomington, Indiana, 1988.

Green, Jeffrey (Wolf) *Pluto: The Evolutionary Journey of the Soul*, Llewellyn, MN, 1998.

Green, Jeffrey (Wolf) and Forrest, Steven *Measuring the Night*, Volumes 1 and 2, Seven Paws/Daemon Press, Boulder, CO, 2000/2001.

Greene, Liz *Saturn: A New Look at an Old Devil*, Weiser, ME, 1993.

Grof, Christina and Stanislav *The Stormy Search for the Self*, Tarcher, NY, 1990.

Grof, Stanislav *Beyond the Brain*, SUNY Press, Albany, NY, 1985.

——— *The Adventure of Self Discovery*, SUNY Press, Albany, NY, 1988.

——— *The Holotropic Mind: The Three Levels of Human Consciousness and How They Shape Our Lives*, HarperOne, San Francisco, CA, 1993.

Hall, Judy *Patterns of the Past*, The Wessex Astrologer, UK, 2000.

Harner, Michael *The Way of the Shaman*, Bantam, New York, 1972.

Harpur, Patrick *Daimonic Reality*, Viking, NY and UK, 1994.

Hawkins, David *Power vs. Force: The Hidden Determinates in Human Behavior*, Hay House, Carlsbad, CA, 2002.

Hedges, Chris *War Is a Force that Gives Us Meaning*, Anchor, NY, 2003.

Herman, Judith Lewis *Trauma and Recovery*, BasicBooks, NY, 1992.

Hillman, James *A Terrible Love of War*, Penguin, NY, 2005.

Hoffman, Enid Huna: *A Beginner's Guide*, Whitford Press, West Chester, PA, 1976.

Ingerman, Sandra *Soul Retrieval: Mending the Fragmented Self*, Harper, San Francisco, 1991.

Initiates, The Three *The Kybalion: A Study of the Hermetic Philosophy of Ancient Egypt and Greece*, Stone Guild Publishing, Plano, TX.

Ireland-Frey, Louise, MD *Freeing the Captives*, Hampton Roads, Newburyport, MA, 1999.

Jung, C.G. *Analytical Psychology: Its Theory and Practice*, Vintage, UK, 1970.

——— *Memories, Dreams, Reflections*, (ed. Jaffe), New York, Pantheon, 1963.

——— *The Portable Jung*, Penguin, NY, sixteenth printing, 1976.

Kahlweit, Holger *Dreamtime and Inner Space*, Shambala, Boston, MA, 1993.

Kingsley, Peter *In the Dark Places of Wisdom*, Golden Sufi Center Publishing, California, 1999.

Kunz, Dora *Spiritual Healing*, Quest Books, Wheaton, IL, 1995.

Leo, Alan *Esoteric Astrology*, Destiny Books, Rochester, VT, 1983.

Levine, Peter *Waking the Tiger – Healing Trauma*, North Atlantic books, Berkeley, CA, 1997.

Lomas, Christopher *Turning the Hiram Key*, Fair Winds Press, MA, 2005.

Lorimer, David *Whole in One: The Near Death Experience*, Arkana, London, 1990.

Lowen, Alexander, MD. *Narcissism: Denial of the True Self*, Touchstone, NY, 1997.

Lucas, Winafred (ed.) *Regression Therapy: A Handbook for Therapists*, 2 Vols, Deep Forest Press, CA, 1993.

Mann, John and Short, Lar *The Body of Light*, Charles E. Tuttle Co., Rutland, VT and Tokyo, 1990.

Markides, Kyriacos C. *The Magus of Strovolos*, Arkana, London, 1985.

Mehl-Madrona, Lewis MD. PhD. *Coyote Wisdom: Healing Power in Native American Stories*, Bear and Co., Rochester, VT, 2005.

Miller, Alice *The Drama of the Gifted Child*, NY, Basic Books, 1983.

Miller, Sukie *After Death, How People Around the World Map the Journey After Life*, Touchstone, NY, 1997.

Mindell, Arnold *The Shaman's Body*, Harper Collins, San Francisco, 1993.

______ *Working with the Dreaming Body*, Arkana, London, 1988.

Moss, Robert *Dreamways of the Iroquois*, Destiny Books, Rochester, VT, 2005.

Netherton, Morris and Shiffren, Nancy *Past Lives Therapy*, Morrow, NY, 1978.

Ninh, Bao *The Sorrows of War*, Vintage, London, 1998.

Novak, Peter *The Division of Consciousness: The Secret Afterlife of the Human Psyche*, Hampton Roads, VA, 1997.

Peck, Scott M, MD. *People of the Lie; The Hope for Healing Human Evil*, Touchstone, NY, 1983.

Pierrakos, John *Core Energetics, Life Rhythm*, Mendocino, CA, 1987.

Radin, Paul *The Trickster: A Study in American Indian Mythology*, Schoken, 1987.

Reinhart, Melanie *Chiron and the Healing Journey*, Arkana, Penguin, 1989.

Roberts, Jane *Seth Speaks*, Amber-Allen Pub., New World Library, Novato, CA, 1994.

Rossi, Ernest Lawrence *The Psychobiology of Mind-Body Healing*, Norton, NY and London, 1986.

Rowan, John *Subpersonalities: The People Inside Us*, Routlege, London, 1990.

______ *The Reality Game: A Guide to Humanistic Counselling and Therapy*, Routlege, London, 1983.

Rudhyar, Dane *The Astrology of Personality*, Doubleday, NY, 1970.

Sannella, Lee *The Kundalini Experience*, Integral Publishing, CA, 1987.

Shealy, C. Norman and Myss, Caroline M. *The Creation of Health*, Stillpoint Publishing, Walpole, NH, 1988.

Sogyal Rinpoche *The Tibetan Book of Living and Dying*, Harper Collins, 1992.

Staunton, Tree (ed.) *Body Psychotherapy*, Routlege, London, 2002.

Steiner, Rudolf *Knowledge of the Higher Worlds and its Attainment*, The Anthroposophic Press, Great Barrington, MA, 1947.

Steinpach, Richard 'How is it that we Live after Death and What is the Meaning of Life?' (lecture), Grail Foundation of America, Binghamton, NY.

Stevenson, Ian Dr. *Children Who Remember Previous Lives*, University Press of Virginia, Charlottesville, 1987.

Stone, Hal and Winkelman, Sandra *Embracing Our Selves*, De Vorss, CA, 1985.

Stone, Merlin *When God Was a Woman*, Barnes and Noble Books, NY, 1976.

Storr, Anthony (ed.) *The Essential Jung*, Princeton, New Jersey, 1983.

Talbot, Michael *The Holographic Universe*, Harper Perennial, NY, 1991.

Taylor, Cathryn, MA. *The Inner Child Workbook*, Tarcher, Los Angeles, CA, 1991.

TenDam, Hans *Deep Healing*, Tasso Publishing, Holland, 1993.

Thurman, Robert (trans.) *The Tibetan Book of the Dead*, Bantam, NY, 1994.

Van Dusen, Wilson *The Presence of Other Worlds: the Findings of Emmanual Swedenborg*, Harper, New York, 1974.

Verney, Thomas and Kelly, John *The Secret Life of the Unborn Child*, Delta Books, NY, 1981.

Walsh, Roger *The Spirit of Shamanism*, Tarcher, NY, 1990.

Walsh, Roger and Vaughan, F. *Beyond Ego: Transpersonal Dimensions in Psychology*, St. Martins Press, NY, 1980.

Woodman, Marion *Addiction to Perfection*, Toronto, Inner City Books, 1982.

Woolger, Jennifer and Roger J. Ph.D. *The Goddess Within*, Ballantine, NY, 1989.

Woolger, Roger J. PhD. *Other Lives, Other Selves*, Bantam, NY, 1988.

Yeats, W.B. *A Vision*, MacMillan, New York, 1937.

Zukav, Gary *The Seat of the Soul*, Simon and Schuster, NY, 1989.

Zweig, Connie and Abrams J. (eds) *Meeting the Shadow: The Hidden Power of the Dark Side of Human Nature*, Tarcher, Los Angeles, 1991.

Other Books by The Wessex Astrologer

The Essentials of Vedic Astrology
Lunar Nodes - Crisis and Redemption
Personal Panchanga and the Five Sources of Light
Komilla Sutton

Astrolocality Astrology
From Here to There
Martin Davis

The Consultation Chart
Introduction to Medical Astrology
Wanda Sellar

The Betz Placidus Table of Houses
Martha Betz

Astrology and Meditation-
The Fearless Contemplation of Change
Greg Bogart

Patterns of the Past
Karmic Connections
Good Vibrations
The Soulmate Myth: A Dream Come True or Your Worst Nightmare?
Judy Hall

The Book of World Horoscopes
Nicholas Campion

The Moment of Astrology
Geoffrey Cornelius

Life After Grief - An Astrological Guide to Dealing with Loss
AstroGraphology - The Hidden link between your Horoscope and your Handwriting
Darrelyn Gunzburg

The Houses: Temples of the Sky
Deborah Houlding

Through the Looking Glass
The Magic Thread
Richard Idemon

Temperament: Astrology's Forgotten Key
Dorian Geiseler Greenbaum

Astrology, A Place in Chaos
Star and Planet Combinations
Bernadette Brady

Astrology and the Causes of War
Jamie Macphail

Flirting with the Zodiac
Kim Farnell

The Gods of Change
Howard Sasportas

Astrological Roots:
The Hellenistic Legacy
Joseph Crane

The Art of Forecasting using Solar Returns
Anthony Louis

Horary Astrology Re-Examined
Barbara Dunn

Living Lilith - Four Dimensions of the Cosmic Feminine
M. Kelley Hunter

Your Horoscope in Your Hands
Lorna Green

Primary Directions
Martin Gansten

Classical Medical Astrology
Oscar Hofman

The Door Unlocked:
An Astrological Insight into Initiation
Dolores Ashcroft Nowicki and Stephanie V. Norris

www.wessexastrologer.com

Lightning Source UK Ltd.
Milton Keynes UK
11 December 2009

147417UK00001B/4/P

9 781902 40543